50 Politics Classics

Freedom, Equality, Power

Mind-changing ideas, world-changing books

Tom Butler-Bowdon

NICHOLAS BREALEY
PUBLISHING

London • Boston

First published by
Nicholas Brealey Publishing in 2015

3–5 Spafield Street
Clerkenwell, London
EC1R 4QB, UK
Tel: +44 (0)20 7239 0360
Fax: +44 (0)20 7239 0370

20 Park Plaza
Boston
MA 02116, USA
Tel: (888) BREALEY
Fax: (617) 523 3708

www.nicholasbrealey.com
www.butler-bowdon.com

ISBN: 978-1-85788-629-0
eISBN: 978-1-85788-952-9

British Library Cataloguing in Publication Data
A catalogue record for this book is available from the British Library.

Praise for the

50 Classics Series

"...tler-Bowdon writes with infectious enthusiasm ... he is a true scholar of this type of literature."
USA Today

"...liant synthesis. The author makes complex ideas accessible and practical, without dumbing down the material."
Douglas Stone, Harvard Law School

"...mplex views on a range of important and enduring issues are made accessible ... Enjoyable and instructive."
CL Ten, National University of Singapore

...n Butler-Bowdon is an expert on the "literature of possibility," ...ering self-help, motivation, spirituality, prosperity, psychology ...d philosophy. *USA Today* described him as "a true scholar of ...type of literature." His first book, *50 Self-Help Classics*, won the ...njamin Franklin Award and was a *Foreword* magazine Book of ...ear. The 50 Classics series has sold over 300,000 copies and has ...published in 23 languages. A graduate of the London School of Economics and the University of Sydney, Tom lives in Oxford, UK, and Australia.
Visit his website at www.butler-bowdon.com

Contents

CONTENTS

Introduction

What kind of society offers the most freedom, the greatest chance for equality between its members, and yet possesses the most power to protect these values? Which understanding of the state is best? These questions are as important to us now as they were in ancient Greece, and in this book I look at some of the most notable answers, old and new, via commentaries that aim to give a sense of the key writings and the context in which they were written.

50 Politics Classics provides insights into the books, pamphlets, and speeches of major leaders, from Abraham Lincoln and Winston Churchill to Margaret Thatcher, and texts from Hobbes' *Leviathan* to Fukuyama's *The End of History and the Last Man* that have changed minds and changed the world. In politics the written word matters, because it has frequently driven real-world change: Rousseau's *The Social Contract* and *Discourse on Inequality* helped inspire the French Revolution; *The Federalist Papers* of Hamilton, Madison, and Jay gave crucial gravitas to those calling for a new American constitution; Marx and Engels' *The Communist Manifesto* galvanized oppressed workers but led to a divided world for almost a century; Solzhenitsyn's *The Gulag Archipelago* and Arendt's *The Origins of Totalitarianism* exposed the evil at the heart of the totalitarian regimes of Stalin and Hitler; and Hayek's *Road to Serfdom* and Orwell's *Animal Farm* damned collectivist "central planning" as the means to a just society. Sun Yat-sen's *Three Principles of the People* was essential in building the case for a Chinese republic free of centuries of dynastic rule or colonial powers, and Thoreau's *Civil Disobedience* inspired Gandhi, Nelson Mandela, and Martin Luther King in their campaigns for justice. Carson's *Silent Spring* was the catalyst for the modern environmental movement, and Klein's *No Logo* crystallized the feelings of anti-globalization protesters. A more recent example of the relevance of political classics is the popularity of Voltaire's *Treatise on Tolerance*, an attack on religious fanaticism that climbed the French bestseller lists following the Charlie Hebdo killings.

"The ideas of economists and political philosophers are more powerful than is commonly understood," John Maynard Keynes said. "Indeed, the world is ruled by little else. Practical men, who believe themselves quite exempt from intellectual influence, are usually slaves of some defunct economist." In this book I focus on political philosophy, although it does include some political economy titles such as Hayek's *The Road to Serfdom* and Acemoglu and

1

Robinson's *Why Nations Fail*. Obviously the two domains overlap, and as economics deserves a volume of its own, I plan to follow this book with *50 Economics Classics*.

50 Politics Classics spans 2,500 years, left and right, thinkers and doers, and covers economists (Mancur Olson), activists (Saul Alinsky), war strategists (Clausewitz), visionary leaders (Sun Yat-sen), philosophers of freedom (Lord Acton, Isaiah Berlin, Robert Nozick), agitators on the Left (Jean-Jacques Rousseau, Emma Goldman, Mary Wollstonecraft), and conservatives (Edmund Burke). It also considers liberalism, a political philosophy that emphasizes personal freedom as the highest value along with open societies and market economies.

Whether you consider yourself to be conservative, liberal, socialist, or Marxist, this book may give you more insight into the development of philosophies you oppose and the individuals behind them. I try to give a sense of the real people behind legends of political leadership such as Lincoln, Churchill, Gandhi, King, and Mandela, whose achievements demonstrate that the "power of One" is remarkably important in the great reform movements and fights for justice, and in government itself. Decisions by individual presidents and prime ministers still count, not only in policy matters but in guiding national consciousness.

✔ *"Man is by nature a political animal." Aristotle,* Politics

What is politics exactly? *Politikos* in ancient Greek meant the affairs of the city-state of Athens, and the *polis* was the body of citizens that ran the city. From the beginning, "politics" was something owned by the people. Government by a despot or tyrant was not so much about politics, but about rule.

In time, the word politics has come to mean the art and science of government, or the social relations involving authority and power. Most people today think of politics as the conflict between parties and ideas on the national stage, or the relations between states on the global scene. At a more basic social and cultural level, when we say that something is political, we are saying that it is contested, seen in completely different ways thanks to opposing, deeper philosophies of life and interpretations of what is "good."

These different ways of seeing come partly from our families, partly from societal conditioning and the times in which we live, and perhaps from some innate sense of justice.

Aristotle's famous statement seems rather obvious 2,300 years on. Nearly all of us live in a political community, usually a state, and abide by its rules. Whether our current nation is open or authoritarian, if we leave we are likely to find ourselves in another country with its own, possibly different rules. Even if we did find a corner of the world where states and laws did not exist, chances are it would not be a place worth living in. We come together for the sake of community and live under laws for good reason, and our lives are shaped by the polity in which we live. Aristotle believed that the state was a "creation of nature" that came *before* the individual. After all, people when isolated are not self-sufficient and will seek to become part of a larger whole. To him, individuals who decided to stay on their own would remain "either a beast or a god." The state was in every sense greater than the individual, and being part of it was a privilege. Humans existed for the glory of the state, not vice versa.

The story of Socrates further reveals this classical reverence for the state. Having been given a death sentence for exposing hypocrisy and corruption in the Athenian government, Socrates' friends wanted him to bribe the jailers and escape. Why not continue damning its rulers from exile? Surely that would be the most useful (not to mention satisfying) thing to do. Yet Socrates did exactly the opposite. Fully accepting his fate on the grounds that his sentence had been handed down in an Athenian court, he chose to die. The act would demonstrate that the state and its rules were more important than any one person, even one who felt that the laws were wrong.

For the ancient Greeks, what made us really different from other animals, apart from our power of speech, was our ability to discern what is just or unjust, good or evil, so it followed that the purpose of the state was also fundamentally moral. Though they differed in the details of how they thought societies should be run, Aristotle and Plato understood that when human beings enter society they are raised up and civilized, because they are made to live according to a higher principle: justice.

This way of seeing the relationship between state and citizen did not last, of course. While Christian thinkers such as Augustine and Aquinas maintained the moral dimension of politics by calling for the building of a "City of God" on earth, later political theorists such as Machiavelli and Hobbes developed a more sanguine view of the state. Machiavelli was in favor of republics, but believed that they could only stay afloat via a strong, centralized state, and even then the purpose of the state was not justice per se nor the elevation of the citizenry, but maintaining law and order. Hobbes' view of government was even more clear-cut. Prior to civilization, he noted, people lived in a state of continual fear of violent death and war. There was no sense of a "greater good," only people pursuing their own desire for power or pleasure or luxury. In this state of nature, Hobbes famously wrote, "the life of man, is solitary, poor, nasty, brutish, and short." The human condition would only be bettered within a state whose single, powerful monarch had an authority so great that war and strife would not be tolerated. In return for obeisance, people could pursue their lives in peace.

This more minimalist view of the social contract between person and state would find expression in philosophers such as John Stuart Mill, who noted that any increase in the state's powers, even if very well intentioned, meant a corresponding reduction in personal liberties. In the twentieth century, Isaiah Berlin, Friedrich Hayek, and Robert Nozick saw reason to criticize the bloody egalitarianism of the French Revolution inspired by Rousseau, the dead end of Marx's communism, and, to a lesser extreme, the contemporary welfare state for which Beatrice and Sidney Webb called. According to the ultra-liberal view, seeking to promote social justice and ensure citizens' well-being could actually be a dangerous conceit. People might be better off paying for a small, simple state that gave protection from violence, enforced contracts, provided basic education, and, at a stretch, built some infrastructure to keep things moving.

This is only a sketch of the perennial divide between those who believe that government is there actively to improve people's lives, and those who believe that its main purpose is to ensure liberty. Although this may seem like a subtle philosophical difference, in fact it can produce radically varying results.

A brief tour of the literature will serve as an entrée to the book itself.

PHILOSOPHY OF FREEDOM
Liberty as an end in itself   ✓

> *"Power tends to corrupt, and absolute power corrupts absolutely."*
> *Lord Acton*

✳ Lord Acton *Essays on Freedom and Power* (1948)
Hannah Arendt *The Origins of Totalitarianism* (1951)
Isaiah Berlin *Two Concepts of Liberty* (1958)
F.A. Hayek *The Road to Serfdom* (1944)
Robert Nozick *Anarchy, State, and Utopia* (1974)
Karl Popper *The Open Society and Its Enemies* (1945)

Lord Acton saw history as one long movement toward greater freedom, with Providence working behind events to ensure that good eventually triumphed over evil. Yet knowing that political liberty means freedom of action, he had no illusions of ever achieving a perfect society. The moment that a ruler or a state tries to achieve a certain perfection, or "one view" of how things should be, is when things start to go bad. For Acton, liberty was "the delicate fruit of a mature civilization." It takes a long time for freedom to become rooted in institutions, and even then it is prey to subversion and corruption.

Hannah Arendt noted that totalitarian movements get their power from a claim to be expressions of "inevitable" forces of Nature or History. Compared to these forces the individual life and its freedoms mean little, and so people become dispensable. Isaiah Berlin asked the question that we all need to ask when calling for greater equality or rights: Is the kind of freedom we are seeking in order to allow people to be as they are, or to give them the chance to live up to *our* vision of humanity and society? Our intentions may be good, and yet true freedom, Berlin suggests, is about Kant's affirmation that "Nobody may compel me to be happy in his own way." The perfection of humankind is a dangerous myth that, however well meaning, inevitably leads to illiberal and nasty outcomes.

Looking at European history from the medieval Italian city states to industrial Britain, Friedrich Hayek argued that it was economic liberty leading to more political freedom that had fueled the West's power and wealth. Yet the wish to "do something," to have the state step in and fix matters, inevitably lessened the principle of free agency and potential, and led to the rise of "planned" economies. The problem in such economies is that not only are governments not good at allocating resources efficiently, the life choices of individuals are progressively narrowed according to state-defined goals. John Stuart Mill articulated this problem in the nineteenth century with his essay *On Liberty*, noting that "The only purpose for which power can be rightfully exercised over any member of a civilized community, against his will, is to prevent harm to others." Such a philosophy of freedom logically leads to a position in which only a minimal state is justified. "Individuals have rights," Robert Nozick said, "and there are things no person or group may do to them (without violating their rights). So strong and far-reaching are these rights that they raise the question of what, if anything, the state and its officials may do." Nozick took aim at the term "distributive justice." Before we start talking about "what the state should do" to redress wrongs, we must go to the core: the fact that *someone* owns what is to be distributed. How could a redistributive state be just?

Finally, Karl Popper's "open society" was not about the creation of a Utopia, a City of God, a great Republic, or a Worker's Paradise, but rather a more modest desire to find solutions to specific problems, and otherwise to preserve individual freedom and responsibility. "Our greatest troubles," Popper said, come from "our impatience to better the lot of our fellows." Well-meaning schemes get all the attention and noise, while the voice of genuine freedom strains to be heard.

RECOGNITION AND RIGHTS
The striving for equality through the ages

"The moral arc of the universe is long, but it bends towards justice."
Martin Luther King

Mohandas K. Gandhi *An Autobiography* (1927–29)
Martin Luther King *The Autobiography of Martin Luther King, Jr.* (1998)
Nelson Mandela *Long Walk to Freedom* (1995)
Karl Marx & Friedrich Engels *The Communist Manifesto* (1848)
John Stuart Mill *The Subjection of Women* (1869)
George Orwell *Animal Farm* (1945)
Jean-Jacques Rousseau *Discourse on Inequality* (1755)
Richard Wilkinson & Kate Pickett *The Spirit Level* (2009)
Mary Wollstonecraft *A Vindication of the Rights of Woman* (1792)

History can also be seen as one long struggle for recognition and rights.

Karl Marx stood up for the class of people who once toiled in the fields for a local lord but now, thanks to industrialization, found themselves factory fodder. Having been forced into towns and cities, this suppressed majority could become conscious that they were a class with political power, not profitable commodities to benefit plutocrats and the bourgeoisie. Marx and Engels' *The Communist Manifesto* achieved its goal of sparking this new consciousness.

Mary Wollstonecraft's *A Vindication of the Rights of Woman* called for a reappraisal of the roles and abilities of women, particularly regarding the scandal of women's education, or lack of it. This thinking was so ahead of its time that 75 years later John Stuart Mill was still having to push the same barrow, and Britain's women would have to wait another 25 years before they could vote even in local elections. Although such resistance to change seems incomprehensible now, the long struggle gives a sense of what reformers and activists are up against.

Martin Luther King thought that he could defeat segregation through the power of Christian love, but soon found that other tactics were required. Only after he had borrowed Gandhi's non-violent resistance philosophy and began applying Thoreau's civil disobedience principles did King's work for black rights begin to bear fruit. Having initially flirted with terrorism, Nelson Mandela also came to the view that shaming the oppressor was more powerful than rising up in arms. The struggles of King, Mandela, and Gandhi cannot be seen as an affront to the freedom of others. Indeed, civil rights and the liberation from apartheid or colonial regimes are elemental to human dignity, and the victories of freedom fighters are eventually seen as wins for all of humanity.

To Jean-Jacques Rousseau, the good society is one that replaces the natural physical and mental inequality between people with an equality based on law, "so that however unequal in strength and intelligence, men become equal by covenant and by right." A society should not exist simply to keep order or protect property, but must have some moral purpose such as fairness or social justice. Otherwise, the longer a society exists, the more prizes and benefits fall to those who have simply inherited them. In *The Spirit Level*, epidemiologists Richard Wilkinson and Kate Pickett lay out research showing that a large number of physical and mental illnesses seem to be strongly related to income and class. Inequality tends to promote prejudice, reduces societal harmony, and erodes communities; it is not bad only for the poor, but for everyone in the population. Freedom matters little if we do not have access to low-cost healthcare, or have roads to drive on, or feel that we are the equal of anyone else in society. If, as some commentators suggest, we are currently seeing a shift in wealth in advanced economies from wages to capital, the inequality debate will continue to rage, and perhaps even see fresh attention to Marxist analysis and the rights of workers.

George Orwell had considered himself a democratic socialist, but his horror of Stalin prompted him to write his great satire of the Bolshevik revolution and the corruption of power in Soviet Russia. *Animal Farm* showed the naivety of those who still thought that Stalinist Russia was a noble experiment. The book is a chilling warning of how the idea of equality can become twisted by power. When the animals take over the farm, they begin with the principle that all animals are equal. By the end, the pigs in charge have taken a paintbrush to the commandment on the side of the barn, which now reads: *All animals are equal, but some animals are more equal than others.*

ACT NOW
The role of political activism

"There can be no darker or more devastating tragedy than the death of man's faith in himself and in his power to direct his future."
Saul Alinsky

Saul Alinsky *Rules for Radicals* (1971)
Rachel Carson *Silent Spring* (1962)
Emma Goldman *Anarchism and Other Essays* (1910)
Naomi Klein *No Logo* (1999)
Thomas Paine *Common Sense* (1776)
Upton Sinclair *The Jungle* (1906)
Henry David Thoreau *Civil Disobedience* (1849)

INTRODUCTION

As Saul Alinsky noted in the manual that inspired Barack Obama, among others, radicals need to understand the nature of power itself if they are ever to see their aims materialize. Just as Machiavelli's *The Prince* became a tool to help those in power to hold on to it, so Alinsky wanted to provide a handbook for the "have-nots" so that they could take back what they lacked. "The significant changes in history have been made by revolutions," he asserted, but in their haste for change, radicals rarely understand its mechanics.

Although a native of England, Thomas Paine was one of America's early activists. It is easy to forget that the idea of overthrowing British rule was a radical one, even if the colonial master was largely despised. Understanding this ambivalence, in his pamphlet *Common Sense* Paine attacked Britain's much vaunted constitution, portraying it as the handiwork of a privileged upper class who legislated to protect their interests. He was able to create a sense of historical inevitability, saying that America's cause was simply the latest version in humankind's long quest for greater liberty and equality. It was on the right side of history. Yet 75 years later, essayist Henry Thoreau was unhappy with what he felt the American republic had become, an aggressor whose annexation of Mexican territories in the name of "manifest destiny" and westward expansion was morally wrong. Without power or armies himself, Thoreau felt that the best way to protest was through refusing to pay his taxes since they would be used to fund war. Although it cost Thoreau little (he spent one night in prison), the idea of non-violent resistance would have a huge impact on political activism, from Gandhi's Salt March to King's bus boycotts to Mandela's township labor strikes.

American radicals Upton Sinclair and Emma Goldman largely failed to bring socialist values to a deeply capitalist country, but their thinking did have a legacy. Sinclair's famous exposé of the American meatpacking industry aimed to show the dehumanizing effects and corruption of raw capitalism, but people were more shocked by the low food hygiene standards he revealed, and within a few months stricter laws were brought in. Goldman's anarchism resulted in various attempts to silence her, including imprisonment and exile to Russia, which in her view only proved that corporate interests ran the show; democracy was a sham because it did nothing to change the position of women or the working class. The heirs to this radical tradition include Noam Chomsky (see *50 Philosophy Classics*) and Naomi Klein. In her exploration of the dark side of global capitalism, she drew attention to workers in Asia making electronic goods or expensive branded clothing for a pittance. Her refutation of the cheery "neoliberal consensus" that globalization was improving everyone's lot chimed with the rhetoric of anti-capitalist protests around the world.

The most salient point about political activism is that it only needs one person to begin a groundswell of change. When Rachel Carson's *Silent Spring* told the American public about food chain contamination, the wiping out of familiar birds and animals, and evidence that crop spraying could be causing cancer, what we now call environmentalism was suddenly a mainstream political issue. John F. Kennedy's scientists validated the book, and by 1972 America had banned DDT for agricultural use. Carson's story demonstrates that change only happens when people are not cowed by the status quo, but their success in turn depends on the guarantee of free speech. It is a strong nation indeed that can not only let people speak their mind, but remain open to ideas that bring political renewal.

GEOPOLITICS
Power never stays still

> *"Whatever the ultimate aims of international politics, power is always the immediate aim. Statesmen and peoples may ultimately seek freedom, security, prosperity… But whenever they strive to realize their goal by means of international politics, they do so by striving for power."*
> *Hans Morgenthau*

Norman Angell *The Great Illusion* (1910)
Carl von Clausewitz *On War* (1832)
Samuel P. Huntington *The Clash of Civilizations and the Remaking of World Order* (1996)
Paul Kennedy *The Rise and Fall of the Great Powers* (1987)
Hans Morgenthau *Politics Among Nations* (1948)
Joseph S. Nye *The Future of Power* (2011)
Fareed Zakaria *The Post-American World* (2008)

The motive for political action is always one of three basic types, Hans Morgenthau said: to keep power; to increase power; or to demonstrate power. We can try to make world affairs seem scientific or rational by using the term "international relations," but in reality we are always talking about *interests* rather than abstract ideas of equality or justice. Even when nations are trying to achieve some higher aim such as peace or justice, they can only do so if they are seen to be powerful or influential in some way. Morgenthau was an arch Cold War "realist" at a time when nuclear weapons seemed to threaten the world, but it is still hard to refute his claims about the nature of power at the international level. Even Joseph Nye's now-famous concept of "soft power," which he describes as the ability to influence others without using force, tends to be a choice made by nation-states that already have some degree of hard military power. Nye notes that nearly all states wish to be seen as peaceful and to be recognized for contributing to supranational bodies like the UN, yet at the same time not many are spending less on defense than they used to; big military budgets are seen as an expensive insurance policy that no sensible state can do without. Increasingly, power also means the ability to withstand cyber attacks. Such defenses might cost a fraction of the expenditure on a navy or army, but without them a nation is vulnerable.

Surely the world is so economically linked and interdependent now that war between major powers makes no sense? This was precisely Normal Angell's argument, but only four years later these same powers were at war, and would come back for another serving 25 years later. In both cases German feelings of national inferiority were compensated for by a lust for territory and power, which was hardly rational; yet Morgenthau observed that politics always comes down to human nature, or the "bio-psychological drives" to live, propagate, and dominate. Indeed, Clausewitz even claimed that only war is capable of instilling boldness in a people, and of counteracting the "softness and the desire for ease which debase the people in times of growing prosperity and increasing trade." He also assumed that military strength is the basis of national wealth, yet the nineteenth century was a time of relative peace, and the great battles he describes were small fry compared to the conflagrations of the twentieth century.

On the connection between military and economic might, in the 1980s historian Paul Kennedy observed that all great powers and empires are faced with huge costs for protecting their boundaries and interests, yet these costs are often at their greatest after economic growth has peaked. The "imperial overstretch" argument was easily applied to the decline of the British Empire, but Kennedy caused consternation by suggesting that the United States was headed the same way; the question was how it would manage its relative decline. In the 1990s, Samuel Huntington argued that not only America but the West itself was undergoing a slow eclipse in power. The western hemisphere's political trademarks, including the separation of church and state, social pluralism, and representative or democratic bodies, were all being rejected to various degrees by non-western countries. This process would only speed up as those countries became richer and more powerful. The world had always been divided into civilizations, and now the Cold War was over the major sources of conflict in the twenty-first century would again be cultural and religious, not economic. The events of 9/11 only seemed to support this thesis, and Huntington (who died in 2008) would not have been at all surprised at the killing of journalists by Islamist extremists in France, or anti-immigration marches in Germany.

Huntington's ideas remain politically incorrect, and contemporary pundits still tend to focus on how economics is driving world power dynamics. For Fareed Zakaria, the twenty-first century will be about "the rise of the rest" (China, India, Brazil, and so on), yet he argues that even in a world of fast-rising nations, America has the potential to remain politically dominant because, unlike previous hegemons, its power is backed by economic might. Its universities are the best, its innovation and technology outstrip everyone else's, and its openness allows it to keep attracting the world's talent. Such features outweigh the political deadlock, debt, and deficits that make the news, and guarantee that America's future will be bright no matter what other countries do. It will be decades, if at all, before China's military capability even approaches that of the US. For the foreseeable future, the United States is unassailable, militarily, economically—and politically.

POLITICAL LEADERSHIP
Vision and implementation

"The fourteen people involved were very significant—bright, able, dedicated people, of all whom had the greatest affection for the U.S.... If six of them had been President of the U.S., I think that the world might have been blown up."
Robert Kennedy

Graham T. Allison & Philip Zelikow *Essence of Decision* (1971/1999)
Edward Bernays *Propaganda* (1928)
Carl Bernstein & Bob Woodward *All the President's Men* (1974)
Winston Churchill *The Gathering Storm* (1948)
Abraham Lincoln *The Gettysburg Address* (1863)
Sun Yat-sen *Three Principles of the People* (1924)
Margaret Thatcher *The Autobiography* (2013)

Robert Kennedy's comment about his brother's decision-making abilities during the Cuban Missile Crisis is a reminder of what leadership is and can be. Allison and Zelikow's analysis of US and Soviet inner circles reveals that the biases and capabilities of each country's navy and intelligence apparatuses were crucial in the way the crisis unfolded, along with purely political factors (after the Bay of Pigs fiasco, John F. Kennedy had to redeem himself and appear strong against Republican criticism). Yet the path that the president took—a naval blockade of Soviet ships backed by force, allowing Khrushchev to save some face—proved to be exactly the right one to defuse the situation and save the world from nuclear conflagration. Kennedy's success also derived from his capacity to see Cuban events within a larger context (the Soviet desire to regain Berlin), instead of as an isolated incident. His finest hour is in contrast to the tawdriness of the Nixon White House, as revealed by Carl Bernstein and Bob Woodward. At the time of Watergate Nixon was electorally in a commanding position and had no need for a dirty tricks campaign, but the temptation to "do in" his opponents, rather than focus on the bigger issues, would in the end be fatal to his presidency.

Although the moral leadership of a Martin Luther King, Gandhi, or Mandela can be hugely significant in making the case for change, it is something else altogether to be sitting in the president's or prime minister's chair and making decisions that will affect millions. Churchill's prowess as a wartime leader came partly from his skill as a historian; he was able to see Hitler's rise as simply another example of pan-European aggression, and as the only one in his war cabinet to have seen service in the Great War, he had unusual clarity about Germany's true designs. What Britain should be doing, he felt, was as clear as day. The question was how it could properly put the fight to Hitler when the time inevitably came, and he spent his ten "wilderness years" up to 1939 immersing himself in the minutiae of the British navy's capabilities and technology. Churchill's brilliance lay in being absolutely correct on the policy side (where Chamberlain and many others failed), combined with an extraordinary grasp of detail. Clausewitz's statement that "Amateurs focus on strategy, experts on logistics" could not have been more apt.

Margaret Thatcher also had a deep sense of Britain's place in the world, and, although more realistic than Churchill about the eclipse of its empire, was still horrified at the way postwar Britain only seemed to stay afloat through government borrowing and the caprice of unions. Profiles of substantial leaders tend to bear out the truth of Australian Prime Minister Paul Keating's remark that "Good policy is good politics." The electorate will not necessarily like a politician for bringing in radical change, but people know the difference between policies that aim for long-term good and those devised to win the next election. Thatcher succeeded where few expected her to precisely because she was radical. Her program of deregulation and privatization would be copied around the world, and her small-state philosophy, shared with Ronald Reagan, shook up the cozy postwar consensus. Her unflinchingly hard line on the Soviet Union would prove to be correct, both morally and politically.

The word "propaganda" is much maligned, but as Edward Bernays pointed out, it simply refers to a concerted effort to get people behind a cause. By this definition Abraham Lincoln was one of its greatest exponents. Lincoln delivered his first big anti-slavery speech in 1854, and thereafter drew on his considerable powers in speech, language, and reasoning to convince the American public that he was right. The timeless Gettysburg Address rightly cast the slavery issue as part of a larger need for national integrity. Another great propagandist, Sun Yat-sen, despaired at China's vulnerability to Japanese aggression and colonial exploitation by the western powers. Sun ran a long campaign, mostly from exile, for China to rid itself of centuries of dynastic rule and foreign influence and stand on its own feet. His *Three Principles of the People*, in calling for a new Chinese nationalism that would restore its greatness, helped to awaken national consciousness. Self-determination is always hard to argue against in moral terms, but it takes leadership to turn it into reality. Sun is now revered as the "father" of the Chinese republic.

GOVERNMENTS AND STATES
The good, the bad, and the ugly

"To deprive man of freedom is to relegate him to the status of a thing, rather than elevate him to the status of a person. Man must never be treated as a means to the end of the state, but always as an end within himself."
Martin Luther King

"For all countries and provinces which enjoy complete freedom, make, as I have said, most rapid progress."
Niccolò Machiavelli

Aristotle *Politics* (4th century BCE)
Edmund Burke *Reflections on the Revolution in France* (1790)
Alexander Hamilton, John Jay, & James Madison *The Federalist Papers* (1788)
Thomas Hobbes *Leviathan* (1651)
John Locke *Two Treatises of Government* (1689)
Niccolò Machiavelli *Discourses on Livy* (1531)
Mencius *The Mencius* (3rd century BCE)
Plato *Crito* (4th century BCE)
Alexandr Solzhenitsyn *The Gulag Archipelago, 1918–56* (1974)
Alexis de Tocqueville *Democracy in America* (1835)

What makes for good government? What form of state delivers the most benefits to the greatest number? Humanity's search for answers has gone down many paths, some well lit and leading to a good place, others treacherous and ending in black pits.

In Aristotle's mind, the purpose of political science was not to alight on the "perfect" system, as Plato tried to do with his *Republic*, but simply to find the one with the most advantages and the least disadvantages. After considering tyranny, oligarchy, and democracy, Aristotle argued that a form of the latter was best, not because he saw all people as equal, but because democracy was inherently more stable than rule by a tyrant or oligarchy. "The many are more incorruptible than the few," he said, "they are like the greater quantity of water which is less easily corrupted than a little." The successful society or polity is built on a large property-owning class of citizens who have a direct say in the administration of the state. They provide the stability that oligarchies and tyrannies lack. Edmund Burke made much the same argument in his polemical reaction to the French Revolution. Because the French state had been taken over by unpropertied upstarts who had nothing to lose, they happily trashed all Ancien Régime institutions, even if they had done much good and formed France's social fabric. Like Aristotle, Burke argued that the state was not simply an administrative body to regulate the economy and keep law and order, but was to be revered as "a partnership not only between those who are living, but between those who are living, those who are dead, and those who are to be born."

So blinded by power are some monarchs that they cannot see that even they must govern with some degree of consent. Confucius's great interpreter Mencius put this well: "The people are of supreme importance; the altars of the gods of earth and grain come next; last comes the ruler." Like Burke, Mencius was a conservative who sought to keep many of the ancient customs and traditions of Chinese life, but at the same time build on this foundation with more enlightened government. The strength and longevity of empires, he noted, rest on benevolence and good relations between people and state, not on vainglorious conquest or expansion.

John Locke's emphasis on the rights of the people over the power of monarchs provided the perfect antidote to the absolutism and patriarchal philosophy of Thomas Hobbes, and though his philosophy of government by popular consent may now be taken for granted, it was very risky to voice such ideas in the seventeenth century. Lockean political philosophy was blamed for the subsequent French and American Revolutions, the secularization of western society (Locke supported religious toleration and the separation of church and state), and his notion that "Every man has a Property in his own Person which no Body has any Right to but himself" influenced the anti-slavery movement.

Also ahead of his time was Niccolò Machiavelli. Although *The Prince* is his most famous work, this manual of power was most likely written to ingratiate himself with the Medicis, who had come back to rule after usurping Florence's republic. Machiavelli's true philosophy is found in the much longer *Discourses*, which provides the rationale for a stable republic. He believed that only a society in which conflict was allowed, was indeed part of the system, would be robust, and moreover that such states in time tend to overshadow more controlled and homogeneous nations. In saying this, Machiavelli provided a model for the sprawling, pluralist, democratic republics that have been the most successful form of political organization in the modern era. Similarly, de Tocqueville's famous portrait of nineteenth-century America compared the "tranquility" of authoritarian or aristocratic government to the tumult of democracy, but he noted that it was largely an illusion, for the longer a people are oppressed by the rule of a few who probably do not govern in their interests, the more fragile a regime becomes, and the more ripe for revolution. De Tocqueville concluded that what more equal and democratic societies lack in noble refinement, they make up for in being more just.

The brilliance of America's new constitution recognized that because people are self-interested and will push for their own values to be upheld over others ("If men were angels, no government would be necessary," wrote Founding Father James Madison), it was better to have a system that allowed for a multiplicity of interests to flourish, yet in their very number they would serve to check each other's power. The large, pluralistic republic envisioned by Hamilton, Madison, and Jay in *The Federalist Papers*, with its machinery of government built on checks and balances, turned out to be exactly what the new nation needed to flourish. Strong central government would not mean a European-style tyranny, but simply allow for protection from violence, the preservation of property rights, and the provision of uniform regulations for commerce across the states. The leaders of today's breakaway movements might profit from reading *The Federalist Papers*; they might be reminded of the many benefits of a strong union, and the costs of independence.

So much for good government. Orwell's portrayal of Stalinism in *Animal Farm* was borne out by the accounts of dissidents such as Aleksandr Solzhenitsyn, whose harrowing *The Gulag Archipelago*, smuggled out of the country and published in America, helped to shatter the myth of the USSR as a great social experiment in equality. The book reminds us that, despite the best of intentions, most revolutions simply substitute one ruling class for another. States that claim to be "servants of the people" often turn out to be the most brutal.

AND THE FUTURE GOES TO...

"Countries that can establish 'good government' will stand a fair chance of providing their citizens with a decent standard of life. Countries that cannot will be condemned to decline and dysfunction."
John Micklethwait & Adrian Wooldridge

"The growth of liberal democracy, together with its companion, economic liberalism, has been the most remarkable macropolitical phenomenon of the last four hundred years."
Francis Fukuyama

Daron Acemoglu & James A. Robinson *Why Nations Fail* (2012)
Francis Fukuyama *The End of History and the Last Man* (1992)
John Micklethwait & Adrian Wooldridge *The Fourth Revolution* (2014)
Mancur Olson *The Rise and Decline of Nations* (1982)

Does national prosperity provide for political stability, or is it the other way around? According to economists Acemoglu and Robinson, the poorest countries in the world have something in common: failed political institutions. Without the stability and transparency that good government brings, the incentive to create wealth disappears. The key difference between rich and poor countries, they argue in *Why Nations Fail*, is that their economic institutions provide different incentives for individuals and businesses, which in turn rest on *political* laws and rules. Long-term stability and prosperity require a country to get the political aspects right first. The argument of the book is not necessarily new (de Tocqueville wrote: "I have no doubt that the democratic institutions of the United States... are the cause of the prodigious commercial activity of the inhabitants"), but the evidence the authors amass seems incontrovertible.

This argument is qualified by Mancur Olson, who observed that the longer a society exists, the more likely it is that its policy and laws become driven by special-interest coalitions (industry organizations, cartels, unions, farmers' lobbies, and the like) that seek to benefit their members at the expense of society as a whole. Pressure groups may be viewed as a healthy part of a democracy, but in reality, all groups are not equal. The ones with an advantage (in funding, organization, or influence) tend to see that advantage increase over time, which has a corrupting effect on a supposedly democratic polity. The result is political polarization, the growing power of lavishly funded lobby groups, and a widening gap in incomes as a small portion of society manages to win tax relief and gain most of the benefits of growth. When the state becomes captured in this way, grievances and instability grow. Only revolution or war can reset the society to its former social mobility and economic dynamism.

Micklethwait and Wooldridge argue that the West's economic and political dominance in the last couple of centuries, particularly of America and Britain, has been down to openness to new ideas on government and willingness to implement them, from the liberalism of John Stuart Mill's minimal state, to the Founding Fathers' technocratic checks and balances on the American constitution. Yet the natural tendency is for the state to grow, grow, and grow. "Government used to be an occasional partner in life," these authors note. "Today it is an omnipresent nanny." At the risk of stating the obvious, the increasing size of the state has not been matched by more effectiveness. In the 1960s, 70 percent of Americans said that they had confidence in the federal government. Today, with congressional gridlock, deficits, and increasing inequality, that proportion has dropped to 17 percent. If the West has lost confidence in the way it is governed, demography is not helping. Europe's aging population means that spending will increasingly go on welfare and defense, leaving less for education, investment, or anything else. Micklethwait and Wooldridge's "fourth revolution" in government is partly driven by the need to make more of fewer resources, partly by competition between nations, and partly by the sheer availability of new ideas and technologies that can help government work better. If western nations can stop government bloat and make democracy more truly democratic, there is still a chance that they can fulfill their promise.

Indeed, it was Francis Fukuyama's argument that, because it is free of the inherent "defects and irrationalities" of authoritarian and collectivist forms of government, liberal democracy would prove itself to be the only sustainable form of state. Liberal democracies have their problems, he admitted in *The End of History and the Last Man*, but they are problems only of "the incomplete implementation of the twin principles of liberty and equality." One could not better a system "which aimed to deliver prosperity yet at the same time largely preserved the freedom of its members." Today, the obvious objection to Fukuyama is the authoritarian capitalist model in places like China and Singapore. Time will tell whether their success has made his thesis obsolete, particularly when liberal democracies have had a bad few years in the Great Recession. As people become richer they tend to demand more rights, and to resent the inequality that comes with crony capitalism. Singapore's dedication to the rule of law is protection against corruption, but nothing is certain with China, Russia, or the Middle Eastern oil kingdoms. In contrast, although democracy is messy and inefficient, it tends to have more stability than either oligarchy or tyranny, as Aristotle knew.

However, attacks on the West or rejection of Western values seem to be in the ascendant, and it could be argued that radical Islam provides an alternative to liberal democracy, particularly as it transcends nation or ethnicity. On the other hand, because the Muslim world lacks political unity, there is no concerted effort to overthrow the Western model of government, and indeed there is some chance that liberal ideas will take root. There is a backlash already underway against Islamist government in Egypt and Tunisia, and time may well show that the separation of church and state is not a Western principle, but basic to good government the world over. Radical Islam, of course, gains much of its power from the idea that the West is "decadent" and immoral, yet political visions that develop only out of the perception of an enemy, and do not offer a complete alternative philosophy for the long-term flourishing of society, tend to falter.

No one can predict the political future, but we can say with some confidence that ideas that can deliver prosperity, peace, and a measure of freedom for the individual are likely to endure, no matter what other ideas arise. Government needs to reflect the realities of human nature, to see that people are not just consumers. A person will be grateful to a state that makes them well-off and provides physical security, but somewhere along the line they will also seek recognition òf their dignity as a free human being. Plato and Aristotle argued that a city or a state had a purpose beyond being merely a good municipal manager; it had to represent something higher, seek to increase the virtue of its citizens. Yet achieving this while not destroying personal liberties is difficult. Helping to elevate people, but at the same time recognizing that they are free, may be the greatest challenge of politics in our time.

The List: Why This 50?

50 Politics Classics is necessarily subjective. With more space I could cover 100 titles, but failing that you will find a supplementary list of 50 More Politics Classics at the back of the book. A few other points to note:

- Some titles that may have been natural choices for inclusion, such as Simone de Beauvoir's *The Second Sex*, Confucius's *Analects*, Machiavelli's *The Prince*, John Stuart Mill's *On Liberty*, John Rawls' *A Theory of Justice*, Jean-Jacques Rousseau's *The Social Contract*, and Plato's *The Republic*, I have already written about in *50 Philosophy Classics*. Instead of going over the same ground, I include different books by some of these authors here.
- Political ideas are subject to constant change, so to keep the list relevant and fresh it includes a handful of more recent works. *Why Nations Fail*, *The Future of Power*, *The Spirit Level*, *The Fourth Revolution*, and *The Post-American World* may not yet be "classics" in the conventional sense, but each has added something new to contemporary politics and political economy.
- This book makes no claim to be an exhaustive, country-by-country survey of politics, but instead focuses on the books and ideas that have made an impact. If so many are from the West, that reflects the fact that political innovation over the last few centuries has mostly sprung from Europe and America.
- A separate biography box is not included for those chapters where there is sufficient biographical information in the commentary itself.
- Although important in the rise of modern democracy, the thirteenth-century Magna Carta was a legal document rather than a political text, and for that reason is not included here.
- Finally, if you were wondering why Hitler's *Mein Kampf* is not on the list, or for that matter Mao Tse-tung's *Little Red Book*, I take the view that "classic" refers to a book that has enduring positive value. This excludes documents of racism or propaganda that should now only be read for their historical value.

Bonus

Please email me at tombutlerbowdon@gmail.com with "Politics" in the title bar and I will send you a bonus bundle of politics commentaries featuring Frantz Fanon's *The Wretched of the Earth*, Frederick Douglass' *Narrative of the Life of Frederick Douglass*, and Moisés Naím's *The End of Power*. I can also inform you when *50 Economics Classics* is released. I hope you enjoy these, and indeed the book itself.   TBB

Essays on Freedom and Power

"History is not a web woven with innocent hands. Among
all the causes which degrade and demoralize men,
power is the most constant and the most active."

"The most certain test by which we judge whether a country is
really free is the amount of security enjoyed by minorities."

"Liberty is not a means to a higher political end.
It is itself the highest political end."

In a nutshell

Politics must rest on a moral foundation that accords
freedom to people for the sake of it.

In a similar vein

Isaiah Berlin *Two Concepts of Liberty* (p 60)
Francis Fukuyama *The End of History and the Last Man* (p 104)
Alexis de Tocqueville *Democracy in America* (p 292)

CHAPTER 1

Lord Acton

You may not have heard of Lord Acton, but you will certainly have heard some of his words. In 1877 Mandell Creighton published his *History of the Popes*, and in a private letter Acton, a well-known campaigner against "papal infallibility," tells Creighton that he could have been a lot harder on papal power grabs and rampant Vatican corruption, not to mention the siring of illegitimate children. He writes:

> *"I cannot accept your canon that we are to judge Pope and King unlike other men, with a favourable presumption that they did no wrong. If there is any presumption it is the other way, against the holders of power, increasing as the power increases. Power tends to corrupt and absolute power corrupts absolutely."*

He continues:

> *"Great men are almost always bad men, even when they exercise influence not authority: still more when you add the tendency or the certainty of corruption by authority. There is no worse heresy than that the office sanctifies the holder of it."*

Thus, the famous "power corrupts" line must be seen within the context of papal infallibility, which Acton vigorously opposed at the First Vatican Council in 1870. As a staunch Catholic, he believed that the moral laws of the Church were perfect, but that human beings certainly were not. To stay in power a good person may need to become bad, and their potential for badness grows in line with the extent of their power.

Though he published no books in his lifetime, Acton worked for years on a history of liberty that would trace the slow emergence of freedom from classical times through to the modern world. He never completed it, and his collected essays were published only after his death. Indeed, Acton's view of history as a morality tale in which liberty and truth unfold over time was unfashionable during his lifetime; according to biographer Gertrude Himmelfarb, it was only during the Second World War that his unyielding moral outlook came into its own and was seen as a prophetic warning against totalitarianism.

The history of freedom

As a historian, Acton is distinguished by three factors: a cosmopolitan view (we must range across countries and cultures to extract universal truths instead of sticking to national histories); a trust in empirical research (he was a keen visitor to European archives); and the judgment of history according to timeless moral standards, preferably Christian ones ("The short triumph of Athenian liberty, and its quick decline," he writes, "belong to an age which possessed no fixed standard of right and wrong.")

Acton follows a Liberal/Whig approach, viewing history as the progress of increasing freedom. There is a "constancy of progress... in the direction of organised and assured freedom," he writes; moreover, this is "the characteristic fact of modern history." Like de Tocqueville, he believes that Providence works through history, slowly ensuring that the good triumphs over ignorance and evil. This, he admits, goes against the modern view of historians such as Ranke and Carlyle that there is no pattern or direction to events.

Still, Acton qualifies this approach by saying that "the wisdom of divine rule appears not in the perfection but in the improvement of the world." He has no illusions about the virtual impossibility of achieving a perfect society, knowing that political liberty means freedom of action. The moment a ruler or state tries to achieve perfection, or "one view" of how things should be, is when things start to go bad. Instead, he describes liberty as "the delicate fruit of a mature civilization," and notes that "at all times sincere friends of freedom have been rare." It takes a long time for freedom to become rooted in institutions, and even then it is prey to subversion and corruption.

Yet if freedom is always fragile, Acton notes, it is also true that absolutism and tyranny never last. No power group can ever attain implicit obedience for long. Power continually has to justify itself, and often it has a hard time doing so. In direct contrast, societies where "there has been long and arduous experience, a rampart of tried conviction and accumulated knowledge, where there is a fair level of general morality, education, courage, and self-restraint" do after a time have a certain strength and resilience. It is the absolutist regimes, so powerful looking, that are as fragile as an egg.

Liberty and absolutism

Acton defines liberty as "the assurance that every man shall be protected in doing what he believes his duty against the influence of authority and majorities, custom and opinion." Freer societies, he says, can be distinguished by universal representation, the absence of slavery, the sway of public opinion, and also, crucially, "the security of the weaker groups and the liberty of conscience, which, effectually secured, secures the rest." Despite being wealthy and well connected, Acton was also part of a minority group that had long been discriminated against: he was a Catholic in largely Protestant England, and as a young man was rejected from Cambridge University because of his faith. Unsurprisingly, for Acton freedom of worship is the foundation of political freedom. And on freedom he is clear, giving us another of his famous statements: "Liberty is not a means to a higher political end. It is itself the highest political end."

The history of liberty, Acton says, is the history of "the deliverance of man… from the power of man." He is pleased to admit that much of the progress had happened in England, which had always been relatively tolerant and less lustful of power than other nations. Yet no nation should ever rest on its political or institutional laurels, and we only need think of Greece and Rome to be reminded of that. Indeed, the history of liberty is far from finished; it is high maintenance and its growth is never certain.

Liberty and democracy

Acton characterizes medieval Europe as a fight between an emerging democratic outlook and an entrenched aristocracy determined to hold on to its social and economic power. States were not as strong as they are now; their authority was restricted by powerful classes and associations. Over time, though, church and state combined in power to balance the aristocracy, and this came with its own corruption and abuses. It took someone of the fiber of Martin Luther to challenge the paradigm, and a kind of consensus developed on the right blend between liberty and good governance. Rudimentary democracy with limited suffrage became established, along with the principle of no taxation without representation or consent; and although serfdom remained, slavery itself disappeared.

In an essay on Erskine May's *Democracy in Europe*, Acton spells out his view on the difference between liberty and democracy. We should not forget, he says, that democracies have allowed the slave trade to flourish, and many of the most religiously intolerant societies have been democracies. Moreover, a tyranny of the majority could be as bad as a tyranny of one: "democracy, like monarchy, is salutary within limits and fatal in excess." We saw this in the Terror that followed the French Revolution, and it happened centuries before in Athens, where the voting populace believed that nothing could stop the mighty city-state and it grew drunk on power. By the time it saw the error of its ways, Acton says, it was too late to save the Republic.

The framers of the American constitution, Acton notes, combined the French revolutionary insistence on popular sovereignty with some of the caution of the English parliament. The final result was a system of wise checks and balances that ranged from an independent judiciary to an empowered executive, from a clear separation of church and state to a Second Chamber – and underlying it all the federalism that would ensure a central government that was strong enough to get things done, but whose power would be balanced by the states. "It was democracy in its highest perfection," Acton writes, "armed and vigilant, less against aristocracy and monarchy than against its own weakness and excess."

In contrast to the fierce hatred of the Ancien Régime that brought on the events in Paris in 1789, the defining aspects of American independence were moderation and people's simple desire to get on in life. Property ownership and monetary wealth became the new arbiters of social standing. What mattered was equality of opportunity rather than actual equality, in contrast to the French revolutionaries' lust for wealth distribution, an equality "drenched in blood," as Acton puts it. One of his most important points is that there are no obvious links between liberty, democracy, and equality. There are tradeoffs to be made, and his conviction was that liberty was the most crucial of the three. What was a democracy worth if it did not enshrine and protect personal liberties? And how could one justify redistribution if it meant violence and theft from the rich?

Final comments

Acton scholar Josef Altholz opined in a lengthy entry in the *Oxford National Dictionary of Biography* that Acton's life "was largely a failure." Acton was indeed a failed politician, a poor manager of his inherited estates (he had to go into debt to service them, and sold his library under duress), and, despite his legendary learning, completed no books. His insistence that successful societies must have a moral, Christian backbone would seem to reduce his relevance to the twenty-first century even further.

Yet Acton's bigger ideas on freedom, democracy, and power can still inspire and guide. One of his great insights is that democracies end up having to choose between the sovereignty of the people (which can simply become the "rule of the mob") and the rule of law. The latter, he felt, always provides a much stronger framework of liberties. It is too easy to put liberty and democracy together as if they are simply the same, but Acton reminds us that individual liberties can easily be trampled on by the force of an apparent "popular will." A democracy with full suffrage is not worth much if individuals are not protected by a solid constitution and laws that vouch for their individual freedom to believe what they want and associate with whom they wish.

Acton's final message is that we who live in democratic systems should never be complacent. Democracy is desirable to the extent that it enhances and preserves liberty. If it does not achieve this, casting a vote in a ballot box is a hollow act.

Lord Acton

John Emerich Edward Dalberg-Acton was born in 1834 in Naples, a former sovereign state of which his grandfather had been prime minister. He was the only child of Sir Ferdinand Acton and Marie Louise Pelline de Dalberg, of a German noble family. After his father died, his mother took him to live in England where she married Liberal politician Lord Leveson, second Earl Granville, who became foreign secretary under William Gladstone.

Cosmopolitan from birth, as a boy Acton could speak Italian, German, French, and English fluently. (Himmelfarb notes that as an adult, "he chatted in English with his children, in German with his Bavarian-born wife... in French with his sister-in-law, and in Italian with his mother-in-law.") After being schooled in Paris and at the Catholic Oscott College in England, he tried unsuccessfully to gain entry to Cambridge. The renowned Catholic historian Ignaz von Döllinger then became his tutor, and instilled in him an aversion to any kind of religious or state absolutism.

In his late teens and early 20s Acton met eminent people across Europe and the US, including Pope Pius IX, and attended the coronation of Tsar Alexander II of Russia. In 1857 he settled at the Acton family seat in Aldenham in Shropshire, where he built up his great library. He began to enter the political arena, but was only partially successful. However, he would later become an adviser and confidant to Gladstone. Acton became influential through his editorship of The Rambler, *an organ of English liberal Catholicism, which became the* Home and Foreign Review. *Under pressure from Rome Acton folded the* Review *and turned to historical research into religious persecution.*

In 1865 Acton married his cousin, the Countess Maria Anna Ludomilla Euphrosina. In 1869 he was created Baron Acton on Gladstone's recommendation, becoming one of the first Catholic peers. In 1872 he received an honorary doctorate of philosophy from Munich University, followed by honorary degrees from Cambridge (1889) and Oxford (1891). In 1892 he was made regius professor of modern history at Trinity College, Cambridge, giving popular lectures on the French Revolution and other areas. He was appointed editor of the Cambridge Modern History, *but he had a paralyzing stroke in 1901. After being moved to his wife's family home in Tegernsee, Bavaria, Acton died the following year.*

Why Nations Fail

"While economic institutions are critical for determining whether a country is poor or prosperous, it is politics and political institutions that determine what economic institutions a country has."

"Inclusive economic institutions that enforce property rights, create a level playing field, and encourage investments in new technologies and skills are more conducive to economic growth than extractive economic institutions that are structured to extract resources from the many by the few and that fail to protect property rights or provide incentives for economic activity."

"Chinese growth, as it has unfolded so far, is just another form of growth under extractive political institutions, unlikely to translate into sustained economic development."

In a nutshell

The poorest countries in the world have something in common: failed political institutions. Without the stability and transparency that good government brings, the incentive to create wealth disappears.

In similar vein

CHAPTER 2

Daron Acemoglu & James A. Robinson

What do people in poor countries desire most? *Why Nations Fail: The Origins of Power, Prosperity, and Poverty* begins with quotes from some of the young protesters who helped bring down the Mubarak regime in Egypt, with the aim of trying to untangle what they were after. For instance, software engineer and blogger Wael Khalil, one of the movement's leaders, made a list of 12 things that he wanted to change. Rather than issues such as higher wages and lower prices, all his demands were political. Egypt's economic malaise was a direct result of an elite's monopolization of politics and political institutions. If this did not change, nothing else would—including the economy.

Putting politics first might seem obvious, note Acemoglu (economics, MIT) and Robinson (political science, Harvard), but professors and pundits usually put forward other explanations for a country's failure. In Egypt's case these would include geography—its lack of water and arable land has inevitably held it back, compared to more verdant places; culture—Egyptians are seen as lacking the work ethic to succeed, and the people's Islamic beliefs are inimical to economic success; and bad decision-making by its leaders—if the country had been better managed and ruled, it would be much better off by now.

The protesters have it right, Acemoglu and Robinson argue, and the experts are wrong. Whether it is Egypt, Sierra Leone, Zimbabwe, or North Korea, the poorest countries have much in common. They have elites who have seized political power and looted nearly all the wealth, drying up opportunities for advancement and prosperity for the mass of people. By contrast, successful, rich countries tend to have political rights that are broadly distributed, governments accountable to citizens, and economic opportunities open to all. The key difference between rich and poor countries, *Why Nations Fail* argues, is that their institutions offer different incentives for individuals and businesses. These incentives are provided by economic institutions, but they rest on *political* laws and rules.

History is important. The reason that nations like Britain, France, and the US are wealthy today is because a long time ago each of them overthrew the groups that had monopolized power and wealth. Of course, many "revolutions" simply turn out to be one group replacing another as the elite (Egypt was ruled by the Ottomans, then colonial Britain, then a monarchy, then a secular autocracy), with no real transformation in political rights and, consequently, no increase in popular wealth. Yet occasionally (such as 1688 in England or 1789 in France) lasting political change happens, and it breaks open the coffers of national wealth for all.

Power and wealth: To share or not to share

Transparent property rights, the freedom to exchange, a legal system to enforce contracts, the building of roads to assist commerce—all of these can only really be achieved by the state. And when they are organized so that everyone can partake in and benefit from them, they are called inclusive institutions. However, when the legal system and economic institutions are set up to benefit one portion of the community (the Spanish in colonial Latin America, the plantation owners in Barbados, the ruling elite in North Korea, for instance), these extractive institutions give no incentive and no ability for the mass of people to try to advance and work for the good things in life. When this happens, an economy will stagnate.

It is not only public amenities such as clean water, a constant electricity supply, good roads, and healthcare that mark the difference between wealthier and poor countries, better law and order and transparency of criminal law also generally feature. In a developed country, one does not expect to be dragged from one's home in the middle of the night for no apparent reason, and the government cannot simply take your home or your business away from you. Perhaps even more important is the gulf in opportunity. People do not try to cross the Rio Grande or get on an overcrowded boat to cross the Mediterranean simply to obtain running water in their homes, but to have the chances they will never get at home because they are not part of an elite. They want to partake in a labor market in which they can choose the area to work in that best fits their talents and thus where they will have the greatest productivity.

Yet if it has been proven time and again that inclusive economic institutions make a country rich, Acemoglu and Robinson ask, why doesn't every state want to establish them, even authoritarian regimes?

Elites in any country usually resist setting up more pluralistic and open economic institutions because these would threaten their extractive power, and power is hard to give up. Most dictators (the authors' example is former dictator Joseph Mobutu, who controlled Congo from 1965 to 1997) believe that they would be better off looting their country and spending lavishly on planes and houses for themselves, compared to being merely the leader of a wealthier country. Unfortunately, Mobutu and those like him are correct. In places like Congo, one group or another will always be seizing and holding on to power, whether it is corrupt kings, colonizing powers, socialist revolutionaries, or usurping militias. In contrast, inclusive institutions distribute wealth and power in a way that makes it hard to amass illegal spoils and get away with it. If that does happen, whoever is in power will just be voted out.

The huge nineteenth-century monopolies in America such as that possessed by Standard Oil tell us that markets alone do not bring inclusive institutions. Indeed, a market monopoly can be used to amass power and wealth, crowding out opportunities for others. "Trust busting" remains one of the most important roles of government. Muckraking journalists such as Ida Tarbell highlighted the shady practices of "robber barons" including Vanderbilt and Rockefeller, putting pressure on politicians to act, even if some of them were in the pockets of the barons themselves. A free press continues to be vital as a check on extractive tendencies. Indeed, control of the media is perhaps the most important plank in extractive regimes, whether it is television, newspapers, or social media.

Distribution of power: The shadow of history

World inequality not only persists, but even strengthens over time, because a country's institutions (which are often "deeply rooted in the past," Acemoglu and Robinson note) push it one way or another. The way a country has organized itself originally sets in motion a way of seeing and acting that is hard to change. If lack of opportunity for all is not addressed in the first place, it tends to become entrenched. And if the present set of arrangements suits a certain group or class, there will be no incentive for them to change to benefit a larger proportion of the population. Thus what shapes society is not a rational assessment of the institutions and policies that would ensure more benefit for more people, but the policies put in place by the powerful to protect their interests. One group that feels disenfranchised—say, a leftist political party—may overthrow the government, only to empower its group at the expense of the rest, and so a pattern of instability is perpetuated. Sociologist Robert Michels calls this the "iron law of oligarchy," and it has proved hard to overturn.

Only systems that ensure a wide distribution of power create genuinely successful nations in which all have the chance to prosper and participate. Often, the reason a nation moves in the direction of distributed power seems to be down to chance or a "critical juncture." The North American colonies were originally intended to replicate European feudal conditions, with rich landowners extracting wealth through cheap or slave labor. While this certainly occurred in the Southern plantation economy, in the Northern colonies the lack of available labor (both white and native) meant that the settlers had more bargaining power, and the land itself was better suited to small freeholdings that could be farmed by a single family. These realities forged a self-reliant outlook, and the English authorities realized that the new land would only be developed if people had the incentive of enriching themselves.

Why growth is not all it seems

Not all countries with extractive institutions fare poorly, at least in the short term. Between the 1930s and the 1970s the Soviet Union rapidly expanded economically as it shifted resources from agriculture to industry, assisted by the power of the state. However, it all ran out of steam in the 1980s.

Sometimes an extractive government can make an economy grow fast if it monopolizes production in something that the world wants (e.g., Barbados and sugar production) or transfers resources from less valuable (agriculture) to more valuable (factory production), which is what Stalin did when he collectivized the farms and transferred the income into building up Russian industry. Even if the process is inefficient compared to a market economy, the technology is lagging, and it is achieved by coercion, growth can still happen. Between 1928 and 1960 the Soviet economy grew by 6 percent, and this fooled many people into thinking that this was sustainable, and that it would even overtake the US economy. In fact, by the 1970s "lack of innovation and poor economic incentives prevented any further progress," Acemoglu and Robinson note, and growth came to a halt.

Chinese growth of the last 10 years is very similar, these authors say, to the burst of growth in the Soviet Union. They admit that the contemporary Chinese economy is much more diversified than the Soviet one was, and there are also millions of Chinese entrepreneurs. Yet the same principles apply. "As long as political institutions remain extractive," they comment, "growth will be inherently limited, as it has been in all other similar cases." Sustained growth will only happen in China if "creative destruction" is allowed within the economy—and how likely is that when the government owns or controls a large chunk of the big state companies? Moreover, creative destruction can only come about through inclusive political institutions, and there is no sign of these emerging.

Final comments

It is easy for people in rich democratic societies to tut-tut at the inability of some countries to get their political and constitutional houses in order, but

Acemoglu and Robinson repeatedly make the point that institutions like parliamentary democracy, a free press, an independent judiciary, and property rights take decades, if not centuries, to bed down. They usually emerge not through high-minded motivation but because they guarantee the best economic outcome for the most number of groups in the polity; paradoxically, ensuring that people's selfish motives can be satisfied provides for a more equitable outcome for all. Yet the authors reject the idea that their theory is deterministic. It was not historical necessity that the United States or Britain or France became rich and dominant players in modern history, or that it had to be Europe that colonized other parts of the world. One just cannot predict when countries will make a permanent transition, after many false starts, from extractive institutions to inclusive ones; there is a fair amount of contingency or luck involved, and even if the conditions seem right, one should never underestimate the iron law of oligarchy.

Why Nations Fail will open your eyes to the deadening and weakening effects of colonization on host countries, just how prevalent a force slavery has been throughout history, and the extent to which, given any opportunity, humans choose domination over others rather than the distribution of power, even if that distribution will lead to the prospering of the nation as a whole. You may become angry as you read how various regimes did whatever it took to prevent the advance and enrichment of their people, only because of a threat to their control. Yet the book may also make you want to glory in the small and infrequent decisions in favor of freedom and openness that would, in time, have big results.

Daron Acemoglu & James A. Robinson

Daron Acemoglu was born in 1967 in Istanbul, the son of a lawyer and a teacher. After a degree at York University he took an MSc in Econometrics and Mathematical Economics at the London School of Economics, and there also obtained his PhD. He joined the staff at MIT in 1993, became a professor in 2000, and is currently its James Killian Professor of Economics. He is an editor or co-editor of several economics journals, and a Fellow of the American Academy of Arts and Sciences. Other books include Introduction to Modern Economic Growth *(2008).*

James Arthur Robinson has degrees in economics from the London School of Economics and Warwick University and gained his PhD from Yale University. He taught at the University of Melbourne, the University of Southern California, and the University of California, Berkeley, before taking up his current position as David Florence Professor of Government at Harvard. Robinson and Acemoglu are also the authors of Economic Origins of Dictatorship and Democracy *(2005).*

Rules for Radicals

"There can be no darker or more devastating tragedy than the death of man's faith in himself and in his power to direct his future."

"It is impossible to conceive of a world devoid of power; the only choice of concepts is between organized and unorganized power."

"The Prince was written by Machiavelli for the Haves to hold on to power. Rules for Radicals is written for the Have-Nots on how to take it away."

In a nutshell

Radicals need to understand the nature of power if they are ever to see their aims materialize.

In a similar vein

Mohandas K. Gandhi *Autobiography* (p 110)
Emma Goldman *Anarchism and Other Essays* (p 114)
Naomi Klein *No Logo* (p 156)
Nelson Mandela *Long Walk to Freedom* (p 180)
Henry David Thoreau *Civil Disobedience* (p 286)

CHAPTER 3

Saul Alinsky

The McCarthy era and its witch hunt for communists decimated the ranks of American radicals, yet it did not stop the disillusionment that America's young felt in the 1960s about politicians and institutions, and the materialistic lives their parents seemed to lead. To the young, the world as it was ordered made no sense and was full of injustice. Yet when Saul Alinsky heard people saying they wanted a better world, this pioneering community organizer felt like asking: Exactly what kind of world, and how would you achieve it? He wrote *Rules for Radicals: A Pragmatic Primer for Realistic Radicals* for people who were committed to real change, not merely to talking about a world of peace and love.

Equality, justice, peace, cooperation, opportunities for education, meaningful employment, and health are all worth fighting for, but they are not achieved easily: "The significant changes in history have been made by revolutions," Alinsky asserts, but in their haste for change, radicals rarely understand the mechanics of mass movements and revolutionary change. It was this gap that *Rules for Radicals* aimed to fill. "There are certain central concepts of action in human politics that operate regardless of the scene or the time," Alinsky writes. "To know these is basic to a pragmatic attack on the system." Among many other people, *Rules for Radicals* is said to have inspired a young Barack Obama in his days as an organizer on Chicago's South Side.

The making of an organizer
Alinsky ran courses in grassroots community organizing, training everyone from middle-class female activists to Catholic priests, from Black Panther black nationalists to radical philosophers. An activist or organizer's life is not easy, he warns; the activity is around the clock and often seems fruitless.

Alinsky draws a contrast between a leader and an activist. Whereas a leader's work tends ultimately to benefit him- or herself, the aim of the activist is to empower others. The one trait an organizer must possess is the ability to communicate and inspire people. One part of this is the deployment of humor, which so few of the rebellious generation knew how to use. Real radicals will even cut off their long hair, Alinsky says, if they want to get through to conservatives; the public is often so turned off by rabble rousers and their shouting that they never bother to learn what the protesters are after. Alinsky also condemns those who in the 1960s burned the American flag as part of their protests. Such an act could only alienate; the focus should rather have been on individual politicians who had failed to live up to American ideals.

Organizers should be willing to use their imagination to put themselves in the enemy's shoes, if only to get a better result. "Compromise" is not a dirty word; in fact, it is what makes for a free and open society. A society without compromise is a totalitarian one. Moreover, Alinsky says, "If you start with nothing, demand 100 percent, then compromise for 30 percent, you're 30 percent ahead."

Yet it is important that organizers see their issue in black and white. To get things done, you have to believe—or make others believe—that your cause is 100 percent just, and that the other side is totally immoral. For example, the Founding Fathers knew that to turn a skeptical collection of states and colonies into a united nation, they needed to instill a sense of moral superiority. The Declaration of Independence omitted mention of any good the British had done, pointing only to the bad.

Therefore, organizers must divide themselves in two: believe that they are totally on the side of right, and yet in actual negotiations be willing to compromise to get things done.

Activists *act*

Alinsky does not shrink from the question of whether ends justify means. For him, the only question is whether particular ends justify particular means. Life naturally involves continual tradeoffs to get what we want, and there is no one alive who has not corrupted themselves in some way. "He who fears corruption fears life," he writes. When we act, it is better to do so thinking of what is best for humankind over whether it suits our individual conscience. If we choose the latter, it means that we don't care enough for people to be corrupted for their sake. When we see injustice, the most unethical kind of behavior is not taking any action at all.

Alinsky observes a rule of ethics: The less a person is directly involved in an issue, the more moralistic they are about it. The more they are involved, the fewer qualms they have about moral niceties and the greater the focus on getting something done.

The privilege of protest

"As an organizer I start from where the world is, as it is, not as I would like it to be," Alinsky says. We have to work in "the system" in order to change it, not just drop out of society to "do our own thing." And one only gets a revolution that lasts if the people themselves have decided that they want things to change. A revolution without this just becomes a tyranny, as seen in Soviet Russia and Maoist China. Being actively engaged on a regular basis in the issues that matter to you is a responsibility as much as a right. If you don't act as a citizen, Alinsky argues, you lose your identity as a person.

Final comments

The American literature on social change was pretty thin when Alinsky sat down to write this book. The radical writing that did exist tended to be communist, or at the other extreme to sing the praises of the status quo. His intention was to provide something that was neither capitalist nor communist, but simply for all the "have nots" to be able to effect change. Today, this would arguably include the Tea Party movement of the right as much as the Occupy movement of the left, and indeed Tea Party activists have adapted Alinsky's teachings in a handbook titled *Rules for Patriots*.

Rules for Radicals seems timeless because it does not present any specific ideologies, only that of change. Alinsky deplores dogma as "the enemy of human freedom," and warns that its growth is something to be very careful about in any kind of revolutionary movement. Any kind of cruelty or injustice can be justified in the name of someone's version of the truth. The book's larger message is about power itself: We need to become a close student of power to achieve anything, but if not handled properly it will corrupt or destroy the ideals we fought for.

Saul Alinsky

Saul Alinsky was born in 1909 in Chicago, to Russian-Jewish immigrant parents. He studied archaeology at the University of Chicago, then worked for a time as a criminologist with the State of Illinois. After working for the Congress of Industrial Organizations (CIO), he shifted from the labor movement to community organizing.

He worked on behalf of poor areas of Chicago, notably the Back of the Yards meatpacking area (the setting for Upton Sinclair's The Jungle; see page 260), and his success led to invitations to help communities across America. In 1950 he returned to Chicago to work in its black ghettos, then in San Francisco. The Industrial Areas Foundation that he established has trained scores of community organizers.

Alinsky died from a heart attack in 1972, the year after Rules for Radicals *was published. He has been the subject of a number of documentaries and three biographies, including Nicholas von Hoffman's* Radical: A Portrait of Saul Alinsky *(2010).*

Essence of Decision

"The essence of ultimate decision remains impenetrable to the observer—often, indeed, to the decider himself... There will always be the dark and tangled stretches in the decision-making process—mysterious even to those who may be most intimately involved."
John F. Kennedy

"The fourteen people involved were very significant—bright, able, dedicated people, of all whom had the greatest affection for the U.S.... If six of them had been President of the U.S., I think that the world might have been blown up."
Robert Kennedy

In a nutshell

Political action is shaped by a range of actors and interests, but it still takes a superior leader to choose the best path among them.

In a similar vein

Carl Bernstein & Bob Woodward *All the President's Men* (p 72)
Hans Morgenthau *Politics Among Nations* (p 208)

CHAPTER 4

Graham T. Allison & Philip Zelikow

How did a small, poor country in the Caribbean become the most dangerous flashpoint of the Cold War, and the scene of the near annihilation of the human race? Allison and Zelikow outline in *Essence of Decision: Explaining the Cuban Missile Crisis* that, as the only communist country in the western hemisphere, Cuba was extremely important to the Soviets, and its close proximity to the United States made it an affront to capitalist America. In 1961, President Kennedy and the CIA had launched the disastrous Bay of Pigs invasion of Cuba, hoping that contingents of Cuban exiles would foment a revolution to overthrow President Castro. The failure of the operation was not merely a humiliation for Kennedy, but instilled paranoia in Castro and Soviet leader Nikita Khrushchev.

In summer 1962, the Soviet Union began sending arms and some troops to Cuba to help thwart a possible US attack. The world went on high alert, and Kennedy warned that if any of the weapons were "offensive" (that is, nuclear warheads capable of reaching American cities), the US would find it unacceptable and would act. Until this point, the official and unofficial communication between the two sides had followed normal rules of diplomatic deterrence; though worrying, the situation seemed under control. Furthermore, an internal CIA report, which considered matters from the Soviet side, said it was far too risky for the USSR to place offensive weapons in Cuba.

All this changed on 15–16 October, when US intelligence discovered there were indeed Soviet ballistic missiles on Cuban soil. Kennedy was shocked, yet had an idea that this was as much about Berlin as Havana. The Soviets saw democratic, capitalist West Berlin as a big threat and a "rotten tooth" that had to be pulled. Khrushchev had delivered an ultimatum in 1961 for western troops to leave the city by the end of the year. Kennedy's predicament, Allison and Zelikow suggest, was either to go to war over Cuba or over Berlin. But Khrushchev was also facing significant pressure domestically from failing programs, and had seen no result from his Berlin ultimatums. Cuba seemed a way to restore his and Soviet pride.

Allison and Zelikow describe the Cuban missile crisis as "the defining event of the nuclear age and the most dangerous moment in recorded history." Yet he did not intend *Essence of Decision* to be simply a blow-by-blow account of what happened, but a case study in crisis management and decision-making. What was the best way to look at the crisis? Was it simply a psychological battle between two of the great Cold War personalities, or a conflict played out between the military-intelligence bureaucracies of the US and the USSR? Was it about people or institutions?

The original book, published in 1971 with Allison as sole author, was a bestseller, but a resurgence of academic interest in the crisis, the surfacing of new information, and the publication of secret White House audio tapes made during the crisis prompted a substantial revision of the original in the late 1990s with the help of Philip Zelikow, a diplomat and scholar who set up WhiteHouseTapes.org.

Three ways of looking at it

Allison was known for his "rational actor" model of analyzing politics, which challenges the assumption that governments or states act like rational, self-maximizing individuals. The reality, he felt, is more complicated, with many parties, interests, and dynamics involved in the position that a state ultimately takes. Given this, it is better to have a selection of models or lenses through which to view events, each asking different questions.

The first model should look at a state's or nation's goals: How does it hope to achieve them? The second must consider what organizations are involved in key decisions: How do their standard operating procedures constrain or assist their performance? The third considers the people making the important decisions: What are the political and personal factors influencing them and the processes they follow to reach their decisions?

Model 1: Rational actor

The study of international relations, Allison and Zelikow argue, has become too infused by ideas from economics, specifically the "rational expectations" philosophy, which says that when faced with a range of options, people (and governments) always act according to their own best interests. In fact, Herbert Simon demonstrated that all rationality is limited by knowledge and the ability to process information, and there are plenty of examples from history where states and governments made moves that on any objective basis were irrational. For instance, why did Saddam Hussein invade Kuwait when he knew that his forces could easily be wiped out by US firepower? The invasion was not, as some pundits thought, simply to gain access to oil supplies so he could fix Iraq's poor finances (the rational view); rather, it would fit Saddam's view of himself as a historic leader of the Arab world (an idiosyncratic, irrational desire).

Kennedy and most of his advisers were shocked when they received the intelligence that Khrushchev had located missiles on Cuba, only because they themselves did not think it a rational move. Would he really risk a nuclear war over it? But to the idiosyncratic Soviet leader it "sent a message" to America while also providing a bargaining chip to regain control of Berlin. It was as much about Soviet pride as a clearly thought-out military act.

Model 2: Organizational behavior

According to a model 2 analyst, decisions are not the result of a single leader, cabinet, or government acting rationally and deliberately, but rather, the behavior of a state is the output of a wide array of loosely connected organizations, all of which have particular interests and tasks.

What impact did organizational factors have on the Cuban missile crisis? Allison and Zelikow note that the Navy and the CIA had their own view of the situation, as did the Kennedy administration. While the world waited, it took many meetings over several days to sort through these competing views and get to some kind of consensus about what to do.

On the Soviet side, Khrushchev's decision to send some nuclear missiles to Cuba as a tactical step was pushed further by the Soviet military, which deployed all manner of missiles and warheads to the country. As a result, the US was shocked by the extent of the armory. Yet the discovery of the missiles was itself an organizational achievement, the result of a powerful and long-standing US intelligence-gathering system.

At one point an American U2 pilot in Alaska strayed into Soviet air space. It was not ordered, was the result of an electronic issue, and had nothing to do with the ongoing crisis, but nevertheless this "routine" action of a US serviceman could have brought on a Third World War. The incident showed how normal institutional activity can intrude on a leader's apparently sovereign decision-making.

Model 3: Governmental politics

Historians tend to look only at the course of action that was taken, not the options that were on the table and the competing views. One forgets that decisions might come down to the dynamics of the people in the room, forcefulness of personality, "court politics," and politics between nations.

Cuba was the "Achilles' heel" of the Kennedy administration. The Bay of Pigs invasion had been a military and political disaster. Kennedy called it his "heaviest political cross" and it made him determined to appear decisive in the Cuban missile crisis, which notably occurred in the lead-up to Congressional elections. The Republican Party stood to make much mileage out of it if anything went wrong. To do nothing, Attorney-General Robert Kennedy remarked to his brother, would have probably brought impeachment.

Maxwell Taylor, new head of the Joint Chiefs of Staff, wanted a blitz attack on all Soviet missiles and planes on Cuba, taking them "right out with one hard crack." Secretary of Defense Robert McNamara, on the other hand, did not believe that the missiles greatly altered the overall nuclear balance. The deployment was a political rather than a military problem, therefore he resisted an invasion; he was more in favor of a blockade. George Ball, Undersecretary of State, raised the moral objection that an invasion would involve many deaths, and compared it to Pearl Harbor. Robert Kennedy agreed. President Kennedy reasoned that an invasion would give the Soviets reason to invade West Berlin, which would leave the US little option except nuclear retaliation. Therefore, he said, "the question really is what action we take which lessens the chances of a nuclear exchange, which obviously is the prime failure—that's obvious to us." Yet as the President moved toward the blockade option and diplomacy, the Joint Chiefs of Staff now believed that an attack was the only possible move. Whatever JFK decided, inevitably some actors and their organizations would feel pushed aside.

The outcome

A National Security Council meeting decided on two options: a blockade of Soviet ships heading to Cuba, combined with negotiation about US bases in Turkey and Italy (a thorn in the Soviet side) and Guantanamo Bay; and a blockade backed up by an ultimatum, by which the US would launch an air strike on Cuba if Soviet military shipments to Cuba did not cease.

Kennedy decided on the second option, noting that willingness to trade military bases with Khrushchev would signal that the US was in a panic, and that it would do anything to resolve the situation. The blockade and ultimatum sent a clearer, tougher message and provided an opportunity to weaken the Russian sphere of influence permanently in the Americas if it worked. However, he did not give a time limit for removal of the missile sites, possibly because it would unnecessarily increase tension and the possibility of war. That gave Khrushchev some wiggle room and a chance to save face. It worked. Khrushchev dispatched a letter to Kennedy saying: "Give us a pledge not to invade Cuba, and we will remove the missiles." Kennedy was happy to oblige, and the crisis was largely over.

Allison and Zelikow relate that Khrushchev's final decision to stop shipments was influenced by an intelligence report provided by a Soviet spy working as a barman at the National Press Club in Washington, who had been told by a *Herald Tribune* reporter than an attack was "prepared to the last detail" and "could begin at any moment." On such obscure details, history spins.

Final comments

Despite representing two opposing halves of humanity, Allison and Zelikow note, Kennedy and Khrushchev had much in common. Each had to chart the best course through a large array of advice, interests, and information, and each was potentially the "final arbiter" of the lives of billions of people. This fact seemed to have belatedly prodded Khrushchev's conscience (he told his colleagues in the Presidium, "In order to save the world, we must retreat"), while Kennedy's ardent desire to avoid nuclear confrontation was strengthened by a need to act steadfastly to preserve confidence in him as Commander-in-Chief.

Despite the attention to the impact of organizational politics and imperatives, what comes across in the book is Kennedy's leadership intelligence; unlike Khrushchev, he was never impulsive and kept weighing the different arguments and options until a best path emerged. Beyond the leadership lessons, it would be a mistake to look on the events of 1962 merely as a fascinating episode of the Cold War, because it could conceivably all happen again. As Allison and Zelikow put it, "No event demonstrates more clearly than the missile crisis that with respect to nuclear war there is an awesome crack between *unlikelihood* and *impossibility*."

Graham Allison & Philip Zelikow

Born in 1940, Graham Allison obtained his first degree from Harvard in 1962 and after a two-year stint at Oxford returned to Harvard to earned his PhD in political science. He has been in teaching roles there since 1968. From 1977 to 1989 he was dean of the John F. Kennedy School of Government, and is currently Douglas Dillon Professor of Government; he is also Director of the Belfer Center for Science and International Affairs. Allison is a long time adviser to the Pentagon and Secretaries of Defense, and was recognized by President Clinton for his work shaping US policy on the ex-Soviet Union states, particularly efforts to reduce the former Soviet nuclear arsenal.

Philip Zelikow, born in 1954, has a PhD in international relations from the Fletcher School of Law and Diplomacy at Tufts University. He was an adviser on electoral reform and terrorism in the administration of George W. Bush, and was Executive Director of the 9/11 Commission. He is a professor of history at the University of Virginia, and sits on President Obama's Intelligence Advisory Board.

The Great Illusion

"The commerce and industry of a people no longer depend upon the expansion of its political frontiers … military power is socially and economically futile, and can have no relation to the prosperity of the people exercising it… it is impossible for one nation to seize by force the wealth or trade of another—to enrich itself by subjugating, or imposing its will by force on another; that, in short, war, even when victorious, can no longer achieve those aims for which peoples strive."

In a nutshell

War between advanced nations makes no sense
in an age of economic integration.

In a similar vein

Daron Acemoglu & James A. Robinson *Why Nations Fail* (p 26)
Winston Churchill *The Gathering Storm* (p 90)
Carl von Clausewitz *On War* (p 98)
Hans Morgenthau *Politics Among Nations* (p 208)

CHAPTER 5

Norman Angell

"Every great Power must employ its efforts towards exercising the largest influence possible, not only in European but in world politics, and this mainly because economic power depends in the last resort on political power, and because the largest participation possible in the trade of the world is a vital question for every nation."

German statesmen Baron Karl von Stengel's remark typified the accepted wisdom in Europe prior to 1914. Germany was jealous of Britain's colonies, dominions, trading prowess, and wealth, and believed that these had only come about through the possession of superior naval power. With its growing population, Germany wanted what Britain had, and began a large military buildup to achieve it, sowing the seeds for the First World War.

In a long pamphlet published in 1909 at his own cost, "Europe's Optical Illusion," young English intellectual Norman Angell took a different view. Since Europe's last major conflict (the Franco-Prussian War of 1870–71), he wrote, economic integration had increased between states to such an extent that it would be in no one's interests to go to war again. In this new age, large-scale conflict was the greatest folly.

Only five years later, Germany invaded Belgium, and the ensuing bloodbath claimed 16 million people. Twenty years later, it would happen again at a cost of 50 million lives.

Clearly, Angell and many smart people like him had been deluded. Economic integration may have helped to keep Europe at peace, but it was clearly no barrier against the human irrationality (fear, greed, pride) that was the usual cause of war. It had always been thus, and always would be.

Angell's pamphlet stirred up such controversy (even Churchill responded to it) that in 1910 it was enlarged and published as a book, *The Great Illusion: A Study of the Relation of Military Power to National Advantage.* His later editions (including one published in 1933 to warn against the threat of another war) responded to criticism and added fresh material to buttress his argument.

But what does Angell actually say, and are we too quick to dismiss him today?

Where the power is

Angell begins by noting the assumption of his time that "a nation, in order to find outlets for expanding population and increasing industry, or simply to ensure the best conditions possible for its people, is necessarily pushed to territorial expansion and the exercise of political force against others." For example, the buildup of Germany's naval power was an expression of its growing population and wish to gain Britain's colonies and trading wealth through conquest. Put more simply, this is the idea that national prosperity rests on political power. Yes, nations may compete peacefully to win business or trade, but in the stiff competition between them, the country that is best backed by military force will win the day. In the Darwinian geopolitical struggle, weaker nations will also be poorer nations.

Angell sees this outlook as a relic. To him, national wealth does not depend on territorial expansion; a country can become wealthy and influential without being backed by a large military, because in modern times it is wealth rather than raw power that matters. War itself is futile, Angell says, because even if a country takes over and subjugates another, it will not achieve anything valuable. Yes, it will have more territory, but what does that translate into? "For a modern nation to add to its territory," he writes, "no more adds to the wealth of the people of such nation than it would add to the wealth of Londoners if the City of London were to annex the county of Hertford."

In a complex and interconnected global system, not only does war make no sense, Angell argues, those nations who go to war are actually the "less fit" in a Darwinian sense. That is, they seek conquest of other countries because there is something lacking at home. The fittest nations are those who are doing so well economically and politically that there is no reason for them to try to appropriate another country's resources illegally. "The warlike nations do not inherit the earth," Angell says, "they represent the decaying human element." He was farsighted in seeing that, in a technologically connected age in which ideas spread quickly, states that attempt to exploit or deny their populations certain rights are vulnerable to uprising. It is only weak states that will wage offensive war, perhaps to buttress the regime's power and disguise inherent domestic disunity and weakness.

Where the wealth is

Angell describes as a "superstition" the idea that national wealth emerges from military power, and as a myth that the size of a country's military is a guarantee of its prosperity. Many smaller countries of Europe, including Switzerland, Belgium, Holland, Denmark, and Sweden, he says, are on a per person basis every bit as wealthy as the bigger states such as Germany, Russia,

France, and Austria; in some cases more so. He notes the big difference in the worth of financial securities of small trading nations with no military to back them, such as Belgium and Norway, compared to the less valuable securities of highly militarized Russia and Germany. The market therefore knows where value lies—it is not in military strength, but in the smarts and abilities of a nation's entrepreneurs and traders. Financiers knew that Holland was richer than Germany and would remain so whether or not it fell under Germany's sway. This is because by invading a country you do not suddenly gain the wealth of that country, which after all is generated by individuals. Wealth lies in relationships, and when war or invasion occurs these relationships are often broken.

Angell also seeks to expose the idea that Britain was only rich thanks to its colonies, which were begotten through naval power. Britain had never "owned" its colonies; rather, they were relatively independent nations that were simply part of a trading network, and they never paid cash tributes to the mother country. Therefore, any country seizing these colonies would no more be able to exact tribute than Britain had done.

Philosophy of force

In a chapter called "The psychological case for war," Angell addresses what may be the chief objection to his theory: that although there may be no logical case for war among economically linked countries, this ceases to matter up against the greater power of human beings' irrational nature.

War, he says, may result from "vanity, rivalry, pride of place, the desire to be first, to occupy a great situation in the world, to have power or prestige; from quick resentment of insult or injury [or] from the 'inherent hostility' that exists between rival nations." If war were simply a matter of economics it would happen much less often. Rather, nations go to war "when their blood is up," or for some moral reason that has nothing to do with material conditions.

Angell outlines what he calls the "philosophy of force." He notes that bellicose Germans saw war as both a way to increase Germany's living space, and an idealistic right. War was also portrayed as a means that God used to weigh up the virtue of nations, since loyalty, tenacity, heroism, inventiveness, economy, and physical health were all qualities that would be exposed in war. Writers in Britain and America also gave their pro-war views a scientific sheen by invoking the law of evolution. It was obvious, they said, that the nations that emerge on top through warfare are the fittest. War is not a human perversity, but the playing out of universal law. Yet when warring is simply accepted as a part of what nations do, Angell notes, it tends to preclude the value of patience, which is as much needed in global politics as in personal life.

Philosophy of peace

Pacifists in Angell's time had been criticized as "unduly idealistic, sentimental, oblivious to the hard necessities of men in a hard world of struggle, and disposed to ask too much of human nature." But there had been a shift in this attitude. Those seeking peace were now seen as materialistic, denying the moral or idealistic reasons for war and instead opting for the comforts bought by trade and industry.

However, to Angell this accusation missed a more fundamental change at work. In the past, governments and states even in democratic countries would wage war for the slightest ideological or power-gaining reasons, but he rightly predicts that countries would now only go to war if the general public in a particular country had a stomach for it. They had to consider whether it would increase their wellbeing if they engaged in war. Sure enough, today's opinion polling determines the decisions of prime ministers and presidents on war issues as much as geopolitical strategy. For those who ignore it, such as George W. Bush and Tony Blair, waging war without public support comes at a significant cost, and the instigators can even be branded war criminals.

Angell went to some length to refute the Darwinian "struggle for life" analogy that in his time was a major intellectual support for war-making. Britain became prosperous and peaceful not through Wessex trying to take over Northumbria, he says, but through the various parts of the country uniting as one. People could see that the sum was greater than the parts. Looking globally, the "best adapted" nation will employ cooperation to achieve the best outcomes for all, not just itself. After all, the human environment is not merely the borders of a nation, but the whole planet. As this awareness grows, so does collective responsibility. Angell is farsighted in noting that the real conflicts in the modern world are between different ways of seeing the world: democratic vs. autocratic; socialism vs. individualism; reaction vs. progress.

Final comments

On the eve of the centenary of the First World War, *The Economist* ("Look back with angst," December 2013) noted the eerie parallels between today's ever-closer economic interdependence and the period prior to 1914. Perhaps we had taken on too much of an Angellian mindset, it suggested, and were being too complacent. It was a prophetic thought, as only a couple of months later Vladimir Putin's Russian army seized Crimea in sovereign Ukraine in a land grab reminiscent of Hitler or Stalin. The cheery consensus had been that no contemporary leader would be mad enough to risk his country's economy, credit rating, and international standing for the sake of some new territory, but none of these things stopped Putin. Emotion had trumped economics and rationality, and once again Angell's thesis that there is a "diminishing rôle of physical force in all spheres of human activity" seemed disproven.

Yet one could also argue that over the long term, Angell's view that "much of the present motive to aggression will cease to be operative" has proved correct. Despite the two world wars of the twentieth century and multiple genocides, the average person has a much lower chance of violent death through war than at any time in history, as books such as Steven Pinker's *The Better Angels of Our Nature* have pointed out.

Angell's work is not, as many critics have said, the delusion of a pacifist. Yes, he admitted, he had too much faith that economic interdependence would preclude war, but he stood by his argument that conflict paid no dividends. In fact, he never said that war could no longer happen, only that it would be futile.

•

Norman Angell

Born in 1872 in Holbeach, Lincolnshire, Ralph Norman Angell Lane was one of six children. His father was a well-off merchant. He attended schools in England and France, and as a young man spent time at a business school in London and at the University of Geneva. Despairing of Europe's problems, he went to live in California, working as a manual laborer, prospector, and reporter in San Francisco. In his mid-20s Angell moved to Paris and wrote for newspapers, including American papers reporting on the Dreyfus Affair. He had a book published, Patriotism under Three Flags: A Plea For Rationalism in Politics, *and in 1905 became editor of the Paris edition of the London* Daily Mail. *During his seven years in this post he published "Europe's Optical Illusion." The fame of the work, which was published in 24 languages and sold over 2 million copies, led him to resign his post and focus on writing and speaking full time. Other books include* America and the New World-State *(1912),* Why Freedom Matters *(1917), and* Foreign Policy and Human Nature *(1925). The* Great Illusion—1933 *(1933) and* The Great Illusion—Now *(1938) continued to sound the warning of his best-known work. His autobiography,* After All, *was published in 1951.*

Angell edited Foreign Affairs *from 1928 to 1931, and from 1929 to 1931 was a Labour Member of Parliament for Bradford North, but lost his seat along with the Labour government. He continued to give lectures on peace and international issues, touring the world every year until he was 90. He won the Nobel Peace Prize in 1933. Angell never married and died in London, in 1967, aged 94.*

The Origins of Totalitarianism

"Terror as the execution of a law of movement whose ultimate goal is not the welfare of men or the interest of one man but the fabrication of mankind, eliminates individuals for the sake of the species, sacrifices 'the parts' for the sake of 'the whole'. The suprahuman force of Nature or History has its own beginning and its own end."

"The ideal subject of totalitarian rule is not the convinced Nazi or the convinced communist, but people for whom the distinction between fact and fiction and the distinction between true and false no longer exist."

In a nutshell

Totalitarian movements get their power from a claim to be the expressions of "inevitable" forces of Nature or History. Compared to these forces the individual life means little, and so is dispensable.

In a similar vein

Winston Churchill *The Gathering Storm* (p 90)
F.A. Hayek *The Road to Serfdom* (p 126)
George Orwell *Animal Farm* (p 232)
Alexandr Solzhenitsyn *The Gulag Archipelago* (p 266)

CHAPTER 6

Hannah Arendt

I n the aftermath of the atrocities of the Second World War, Hannah Arendt was desperate to know, along with millions of others, how it had happened. As the Nazi party had risen to influence and power, this German-Jewish intellectual had been prevented from teaching in German universities and was arrested by the Gestapo. She fled first to France, where she and her husband escaped from a German camp, and then to America, where in 1951 she became a citizen. *The Origins of Totalitarianism*, which she took five years to write in her New York apartment, brought her to prominence. She followed it a decade later with *Eichmann in Jerusalem*, a study of the Nazi war criminal that included her concept of "the banality of evil."

For Arendt, the totalitarian regimes of Hitler and Stalin were quite different to the tyrannies and dictatorships of the past, which merely sought to control populations. The most striking aspect of totalitarianism is that "it is let loose when all organized opposition has died down and the totalitarian ruler knows that he no longer need be afraid." Stalin began his great purges, for instance, only in 1934 when all potential opposition had been executed or sent to the Gulag. The totalitarian leader is not content simply to control the population; he seeks to control hearts and minds, so that the leader, the state, and the people are as one. This not only requires great organization on a mass scale, but brings with it new levels of evil, since the individual means nothing and every kind of state crime can be justified.

Totalitarian movements can take many forms. In Germany Nazism was based on race ("the laws of life and nature"), while Bolshevism was focused on class ("dialectics and economics"). Arendt's great insight was that Hitler and Stalin were two sides of the same totalitarian coin, and morally the same. This was a bold assertion in the early 1950s, when the true horrors of Stalin's regime had not been revealed, and when many western intellectuals still thought of Soviet Russia as a well-intentioned socialist experiment. Arendt was vindicated when dissident accounts such as Solzhenitsyn's began appearing.

In the first two parts of her book Arendt focuses on Germany in the decades before Hitler, when anti-Semitism and imperialism, she argues, were the parents of the totalitarian beast.

Anti-Semitism

The conventional explanation is that the Nazis simply used anti-Semitism as "a pretext for winning over the masses" and a good rallying call for creating nationalist fervor, Arendt notes. Yet the Nazi philosophy always went much further than simple German nationalism, just as Bolshevism was about more than Russia.

Anti-Semitism remained on the political fringes as long as there was rising prosperity, she argues. Indeed, as the twentieth century dawned the "Jewish issue" was on the back burner in Germany, but it returned with a vengeance after the destruction of the First World War and postwar economic misery. Rich Jews had played the role of financier to governments in Germany, Austria, France, and England in the seventeenth and eighteenth centuries, but by the war Jews had become a symbol of "useless wealth," contributing little to capitalistic enterprise and industry, and no longer having a political function. They were to be eliminated as a vestige of an old, conflicted order.

The Austro-Hungarian Empire, with its patchwork of nationalities, came to seem weak and dissolute compared to the vision of a pan-German state based on "Aryan blood" uniting Germany and Austria. Jews, still identified as the servants of imperial monarchs and princes and representing a sort of pan-Europeanism, had no place within this vision. All this seemed obvious to a young man living in Vienna by the name of Adolf Hitler, who was to make the cleansing of Jews from Europe his priority. Anti-Semitism would not merely be an opinion shared by some Nazis, but the heart of Nazism.

Imperialism, nationalism, and race

The 1880s scramble for Africa gave a new lease on life to European nation-states, which had been under threat from internal social and political forces. Imperialism "spirited away all troubles and produced that deceptive feeling of security," Arendt writes. It was supported by the middle classes, as they had a lot to lose if the political status quo changed. Expanding a domestic economy to embrace the markets of overseas territories would even out the business cycle and the various crashes and recessions. Thus imperialism seemed a hope for the future, benefiting all strata of society. Capitalists warned that unless workers played a role in imperialist conquest they would lose out to those of other countries, and so what emerged was an alliance between "mob" (that is, Europe's working classes) and capital. The world began to be divided up not according to rich and poor, but according to imperial propaganda between "master" and "slave" races, black and white, and "higher" and "lower" breeds of humanity. Colonies and their wealth became the birthright of white working people. Such arguments won the day because they nullified the problem of class and inequality. As Arendt incisively notes, in a time when all Russians have become "Slavs," when all Englishmen have become "White Men," and all Germans "Aryan," you can draw the curtains on the idea of western man.

Arendt argues that the idea of the state was hijacked by "the Nation" as an idea. This meant that any nation-state could align itself with its dominant population and brush aside any ethnic minorities. Hitler did not consider Jews to be German, so paving the way for their rightful elimination. The legal elements of the state, such as an independent judiciary, also had to serve the Nation rather than protect all citizens of the state. To Arendt, this was "the supremacy of the will of the nation over all legal and 'abstract' institutions." At a psychological level, she says, race thinking is more powerful than allegiance to nation-states, which tend to support the idea of equality. It allowed for the rise of Hitler not simply as Germany's new national leader, but as the head of a *race* destined to show its superiority. That Germany had failed to defeat the arch-imperial nation and ruler of the seas, Britain, was a great shame for Hitler. He was determined to avenge this loss, but doing so would require the ruthless purification of the German nation.

Totalitarianism in practice

Although Europe had seen plenty of tyrannies that had sought to equalize and flatten social hierarchies to make countries more governable, these were not able to destroy the non-political bonds of community and family. Stalin and Hitler both saw the danger of leaving some spheres of life non-political, and made sure that every aspect of life and relationship was carried out in the name of party and country. With this demand for absolute loyalty, their regimes also required the elimination of any kind of rationale for why they should exist. While Lenin, naturally, saw all government policy in terms of whether it fitted Marxist theory, under Stalin policy itself no longer mattered, only control and power. Soviet Russia became a government of whatever Stalin had decided the night before.

Whereas fascist governments are content to establish an elite in power strong enough to rule over all elements of the society, totalitarian ones, Arendt says, "discovered a means of dominating and terrorizing human beings from within." The gap between the state and the people is eliminated; they are one. Hitler acknowledged this when he said in a speech to the SA: "All that you are, you are through me; all that I am, I am through you alone." The real aim of Hitler, Stalin, and any totalitarian leader is not specific domestic or foreign achievements, but rather encompassing the whole population within the government's way of thinking. This aim is unlimited, and is therefore much more sinister than a simple tyranny that seeks to hobble the aristocracy or successfully invade a neighboring country. For the totalitarian, the territory to be taken is the *mind*. In achieving this, objective truth becomes irrelevant and propaganda reigns. A state can say that unemployment no longer exists, for example, simply by abolishing unemployment benefits.

Totalitarianism aims to translate the core of the propaganda message—a conspiracy of the Jews or of Trotskyites—and turn it into a functioning *organization*. Elimination of opponents is achieved by extreme loyalty of the organized ranks, and as these ranks are built and fortified, no one is allowed to escape. Indeed, the only means of surviving or moving ahead is by being more extreme in one's loyalty and outlook than the next person. Just as the good Nazi progressed by seeming to be more concerned for the elimination of the Jews than his colleague, in Stalinist Russia it was no longer enough simply to be committed to the emancipation of the proletariat or the international class struggle, one had to be brutal in one's prosecution of one's security or military role.

Totalitarian governments are hard to read, Arendt says. Other states make the mistake of thinking that they are dealing with a normal state, whether it be a bureaucracy or a dictatorship, without realizing that the totalitarian leader sees their country as "only the temporary headquarters of the international movement on the road to world conquest." The SS were not only fighting to expand Germany into other parts of Europe, but saw themselves as the seed for the domination of the world by the master race. Many a movement can sustain a big lie, but it takes much more effort to carry out and maintain the lie in government. A totalitarian leader does not exist for his country, Arendt notes, but for his grand idea or illusion of it, and the well-being of the people is the least of his concerns.

Final comments

Without totalitarianism, Arendt writes in her Preface, "we might never have known the truly radical nature of Evil." Hitler and Stalin were not aberrations to be swept under the carpet, but central to the new way we must see humanity. The most striking weapon these regimes wielded was their ideologies, which were so successful because they could claim to be "scientific." Arendt recalls what Engels said at Marx's funeral: "Just as Darwin discovered the law of development of organic life, so Marx discovered the law of development of human history." Unfortunately, such "laws" take time to be evaluated, and by then it is usually too late.

One saving grace that Arendt notes is that totalitarian regimes tend to be short-lived. They seem to come from nowhere, are supreme while they exist, but can quickly collapse and leave little trace. This happens, she says, because there is a fateful paradox at work as soon as a movement transforms itself into a nation. On one hand the totalitarian leader must "establish the fictitious world of the movement as a tangible working reality of everyday life," yet on the other he cannot let it become too stable, as the fire of the movement would burn out and it would lose its lust for world domination and become just one nation in a diverse community of nations. Eventually, reality and inconvenient facts creep in from the outside world and the fictitious world begins to crumble. It is therefore quite logical and inevitable that concentration camps are set up to maintain total domination of thinking, even when the police alone would have been sufficient to quell any internal dissent. For the regime to last, it must become ever more total in its rule, and eliminate "private" life so that all people are the same in relation to the state.

Why, with Hitler and Stalin long gone, is this book still relevant? Arendt notes that every form of government, from the republic to the dictatorship, has stayed around despite temporary defeats. There is no reason to believe that totalitarianism will not continue to reappear. Thanks to forensic dissections of it such as her book, at least we know the true nature of the beast.

Hannah Arendt

Born in Hanover in 1906, Johanna Arendt grew up in Königsberg in a Jewish family. Her father died when she was 7, but she was close to her mother, an active German Social Democrat. Following high school Arendt studied theology at the University of Marburg, where one of her lecturers was Martin Heidegger. She had an affair with him before leaving for the University of Heidelberg. There, under her mentor philosopher Karl Jaspers, she wrote a PhD thesis on the concept of love in St Augustine's thought. She married in 1930, and as the Nazi party rose in influence she was prevented from teaching in German universities; she became involved in Zionist politics, from 1933 working for the German Zionist Organization. The Gestapo arrested her but she fled to Paris, and there worked for another Jewish organization trying to rescue children from Austria and Czechoslovakia.

Having divorced her first husband, in 1940 Arendt married Heinrich Blücher, but only a few months later the couple were interned in German camps in southern France. They escaped and found passage to the US. During the 1950s she moved in New York's intellectual circles and worked as an editor. Her The Human Condition *(see commentary in 50 Philosophy Classics) was published in 1958. She was the first female professor of politics at Princeton University, and also taught at the University of Chicago, Wesleyan University, and the New School for Social Research. She died in 1975.*

Politics

"Man is by nature a political animal."

"And it is a characteristic of man that he alone has any sense of good and evil, of just and unjust, and the like, and the association of living beings who have this sense makes a family and a state."

"The proof that the state is a creation of nature and prior to the individual is that the individual, when isolated, is not self-sufficing; and therefore he is like a part in relation to the whole. But he who is unable to live in society, or who has no need because he is sufficient for himself, must be either a beast or a god: he is no part of a state."

"Property should be in a certain sense common, but, as a general rule, private; for, when everyone has a distinct interest, men will not complain of one another, and they will make more progress, because every one will be attending to his own business."

In a nutshell

The purpose of the state is to achieve the happiness and elevation of its citizens.

In a similar vein

Plato *Crito* (p 244)

CHAPTER 7

Aristotle

Human beings are political animals, Aristotle writes in the first paragraphs of *Politics*, and are lost if they do not live with others as part of some purposeful grouping. Until this point they are either "a beast or a god," existing only according to urges like lust and gluttony. It is only when they enter society that they are raised up and civilized, because they are made to live according to higher principles.

To the ancient Greeks things were defined according to their purpose or use, and Aristotle's view of the state is teleological—it exists for some definite purpose or end. Apart from our power of speech, what makes us really different from other animals, he believed, is our moral sense, or the ability to discern what is just or unjust, good or evil. Thus, the purpose of the state is fundamentally moral: It exists not only to ensure that we can flourish in a social or economic sense, but so that we will live justly.

The state itself "is a creation of nature and prior to the individual," Aristotle boldly asserts. While it may seem that the city-state exists for the protection of citizens, its real purpose is to enable its citizens to reach a higher spiritual and philosophical level as well as having greater material abundance. Aristotle's ideal state is not simply a watchtower to prevent violence against persons, its aim is expressly their development and well-being. In saying this, Aristotle has been a big influence on state-builders ever since, giving them the excuse to trim some personal liberties in order to create laws and policies that actively seek to bring about these positive ends.

Aristotle and his teacher Plato were roughly in agreement on the purpose of the state, but diverged on the means of its achievement. Plato believed that the quality of the state was only as good as the quality of its citizens, therefore social engineering was required. In his schema censorship, common property, and rule by an enlightened elite were necessary to achieve society's goals; his *Republic* explained how this would work. Aristotle had more faith in people, and thought that family units (or at least households, including slaves) and private property were the bedrock of a stable society. Both philosophers were skeptical that democracy, in all its messiness, could achieve the "right" ends of society, but Aristotle's keener appreciation of human nature meant his politics was more realistic, and as a result more influential on states and governments through the ages.

The purpose of the household

The state is fundamentally made up of households, Aristotle notes, therefore it is worth looking at their components. His analysis includes the question of whether owning slaves is unjust. If things are defined by their purpose, he asks, could there really be anyone intended by nature to be a slave? Yes. Some people are born to rule, others to be ruled, not merely for the sake of it but because it is necessary for things to work. As such a duality is witnessed everywhere in the universe, why should it not exist in society? The bare fact is that some people are born superior to others; some are suited to a life of politics, while others are best used in physical work to support a household. They are rational enough to do various jobs, but their minds cannot extend to abstractions. Yet the slave/master relationship only works if both recognize and accept their station; then they will serve or support each other in good heart. When the relationship only occurs through force and law, Aristotle says, it will be bad for both.

The problem with Aristotle's defense of slavery is that it is not taken to its logical conclusion. If, for instance, a slave is smart enough to run a household, if he were given the opportunity of an education it would be hard to argue there would be some invisible bar that would stop him thinking, acting, and speaking at the level of a freeman. But Aristotle knew that the whole Greek city-state system rested on slavery, and he could not agree to this support being removed.

Aristotle's conclusion is that the government of a household and that of a state are not the same. While a household must be a monarchy, recognizing the fundamental inequality between members, a state should be composed of freemen and equals and ruled according to a constitution.

The purpose of the state

In *Nicomachean Ethics* (see commentary in *50 Philosophy Classics*), Aristotle argues that the primary purpose in life is happiness, and that happiness can only come from living according to virtue. Consistent with this, in *Politics* he argues that the purpose of the state should be similar:

"A state is an association of similar persons whose aim is the best life possible. What is best is happiness, and to be happy is an active exercise of virtue and a complete employment of it."

He starts by considering how a state should be best organized. Should everything be in common? It does not work for relationships and children to be made common, along Spartan lines, but what about property? While it is a nice idea for property to be shared equally, it goes against human nature. People love to possess things and attempt to enrich themselves through their efforts, and society will be more stable and have less enmity if they are left to pursue their own interests without coercive sharing. People should be encouraged to share as much as possible, and the greatest kindnesses to a neighbor can only happen when a person has private property.

Plato believed that the state would only be strong if fully unified, and social and cultural life strictly controlled, whereas Aristotle maintains just the opposite: A state becomes strong thanks to its plurality of voices and ideas. While Plato condemned what today we call capitalism and the accumulation of property, Aristotle considers both to be in harmony with human nature, although within limits. It is the state's role to create laws on the accumulation of wealth and property that will benefit all.

Aristotle was much more of a democrat than Plato, who believed that the state should be run by a tier of "philosopher kings." Aristotle had a more grass-roots view, saying that as long as one is a citizen then one should take part in the affairs of the *polis* (the Greek city-states were not the representative democracies of today, but allowed citizens a direct role in governance, even though citizenship excluded women, slaves, and foreigners). He also advocated a system of state education on the grounds that education was too important to be left up to families. This is one belief he shared with Plato, although Aristotle's vision of state education was more a system of public schools than one of mass indoctrination in the way that Plato envisioned.

The best form of government

For Aristotle, political science is really the comparison between types of constitution so as to arrive at the right one. The purpose is not to alight on the "perfect" system in Plato's sense, just the one that is the best fit for the city or state concerned, with the most advantages and the least disadvantages. Aristotle discusses at length the pros and cons of monarchies, oligarchies and democracies, and gives examples from Crete, Carthage, Sparta, and other places.

His novel schema divides government according to the number of rulers (One, Few, Many) and then suggests a "correct" and "deviant" form of each. For single rule, for instance, Kingship is the correct form, and Tyranny is its deviant. For rule by a few, Aristocracy is the correct form compared to its deviant Oligarchy. With rule by many, the Polity (outlined below) is preferable to Democracy.

Aristotle was not in favor of untrammeled democracy, but felt that it was more stable than oligarchy. "The many are more incorruptible than the few," he writes, "they are like the greater quantity of water which is less easily corrupted than a little." The successful society or polity is built on a large middle class of citizens with modest property ownership and direct political involvement in the administration of the state. For a polity to be just, he says, "no one should do more ruling than being ruled, but all should have their turn." This works because it is not inherently unbalanced, as are systems where there is only rule by the rich (oligarchy) or rule by the poor (democracy). The former has too much to protect, and the latter too little to lose, both of which can create the justification for violence and upheaval. The interests of a large middle class, in contrast, form a stable mass between them.

Aristotle warns that if society becomes too unequal economically, there will be a transition from democracy to oligarchy: "When the rich grow numerous or properties increase, the form of government changes into an oligarchy or a government of families." Within the context of today's debates about "the 1 per cent" and suggestions of rising inequality made in Wilkinson & Pickett's *The Spirit Level* (see page 298), it is fascinating to read Aristotle's 2,300-year-old warning.

The weakness of tyranny

Aristotle notes that "no forms of government are so short-lived as oligarchy and tyranny." As has been noted in our time, for example by Hannah Arendt in *The Origins of Totalitarianism* (see page 48), tyrannies can seem to come out of nowhere with great force, but are equally susceptible to sudden collapse. This is logical, since any form of government that is so fully based on coercion builds up pressures and enmities that can suddenly burst out in revolution. In contrast, a moderate or democratic system may rise or decline, but is likely to do so over a long period. Aristotle observes that "whereas sickly constitutions and rotten ill-manned ships are ruined by the very least mistake, so do the worst forms of government require the greatest care." Large and populous democracies generally stay that way because in their plurality there is an inherent stability; in oligarchies and tyrannies huge resources must go into maintaining order. Aristotle would not have been at all surprised to see today's authoritarian regimes restricting internet usage, banning demonstrations and the right of association, or controlling judges, in order to keep a lid on the population. Neither would he have been shocked at the fragility of these regimes.

Final comments

In asking what the best form of government is, any polity must first ask: What is the kind of life we are trying to achieve for people living here? How do we define the good life? While external goods are important to the good life, Aristotle notes that they are generally achieved through "virtues of the soul": honesty, temperance, and so on. And whereas external things eventually have a limit, or in too great an amount tend to corrupt the owner, personal virtues are unlimited and can have unlimited positive effects. Virtue and right action do not come about by chance, and yet without them a good state and society cannot be built.

If the best life for an individual is in pursuit of virtue, as Aristotle sees it, then a state must be ordered so that it moves in the direction of virtue. It should not be set up simply to regulate markets, or to support contracts, or for defense. To prosper and move forward the state must have higher aims.

Aristotle

Born in the Macedonian city of Stagira (now northern Greece) in 384 BCE, Aristotle was the son of a doctor to the king of Macedonia. At 17 he began his study at Plato's academy in Athens and remained at the school until his teacher's death in 347 BCE. He then traveled to Turkey and the Greek island of Lesbos, doing research into what we now call marine biology, botany, zoology, geography, and geology. Aristotle married Pythias, one of his fellow students at Plato's Academy, but his son Nicomachus was born to his mistress, the slave Herpyllis.

During Aristotle's lifetime the Macedonian kingdom under Philip and his son Alexander (the Great) was a conquering power, taking over Greek cities and the Kingdom of Persia. Aristotle enjoyed the patronage of Alexander the Great and was his close adviser until the last years of the emperor's reign, before he fell out of favor because of his Macedonian origins. He died on the island of Euboea, aged 62.

Two-thirds of Aristotle's work is lost, but his corpus covers a vast array of subjects. Notable works include Metaphysica, On Interpretation, De Anima *or* "On the Soul," Ars Rhetorica, *and* Magna Moralia *or "Great Ethics." The quotes in this commentary are from Benjamin Jowett's translation of* Politics.

Two Concepts of Liberty

"Humanity is the raw material upon which I impose my creative will; even though men suffer and die in the process, they are lifted by it to a height to which they could never have risen without my coercive—but creative—violation of their lives. This is the argument used by every dictator, inquisitor and bully who seeks some moral, or even aesthetic, justification for his conduct. I must do for men (or with them) what they cannot do for themselves, and I cannot ask their permission or consent, because they are in no condition to know what is best for them."

"There has, perhaps, been no time in modern history when so large a number of human beings, in both the East and the West, have had their notions, and indeed their lives, so deeply altered, and in some cases violently upset, by fanatically held social and political doctrines."

In a nutshell

What kind of freedom do we seek: to allow people to be as they are, or to give them the chance to live up to our vision of humanity and society?

In a similar vein

Lord Acton *Essays on Freedom and Power* (p 20)
F.A. Hayek *The Road to Serfdom* (p 126)
George Orwell *Animal Farm* (p 232)

CHAPTER 8

Isaiah Berlin

S ir Isaiah Berlin was both a political philosopher and a historian of ideas, one of the great intellectuals of the twentieth century. "Two Concepts of Liberty," his famous essay, was originally given as a lecture at Oxford University in October 1958. A decade later it was included in his book *Four Essays on Liberty* (1969) and was published again as part of *Liberty* (2002), an edited collection of his writings.

The essay was groundbreaking because in the 1950s the dominant view was that the various forms of socialism and communism had served to "liberate" oppressed peoples. Berlin, whose well-off timber merchant father had pulled his family out of Russia just after the Bolshevik Revolution and fled to England, had no such illusions. He wondered why leftists in the US and Britain hailed the new socialist states of the Soviet Union and in the East while turning a blind eye to the destruction of personal freedom that was a part of those regimes.

In the opening paragraphs of the essay Berlin refers to an "open war" between two opposing views on "what has long been the central question of politics." That question is: Should we be free to act as we wish and, if not, to what extent should we obey, and whom should we obey? As the question concerns billions of people, Berlin thought it worth examining more closely, specifically what we actually *mean* by "freedom."

The two concepts

There are two concepts or ways of understanding freedom and liberty, Berlin says. *Negative liberty* is the extent to which we are free from interference; that is, the area or realm that a person or a group can enjoy without being coerced by another person, group, or government. Hobbes summed up negative liberty in *Leviathan*: "A free man is he that... is not hindered to do what he has a will to."

Positive liberty is the freedom to be something or someone, "to be conscious of myself as a thinking, willing, active being, bearing responsibility for my choices and able to explain them by reference to my own ideas and purposes." We are free "to the degree that I believe this to be true, and enslaved to the degree that I am made to realise that it is not," says Berlin.

Positive liberty seems very laudable, but Berlin takes it to its logical conclusions. The idea of it, he says, gave rise to the "self-mastery" ethic, wanting to become my "true" or "higher" self so that my potential is fully realized. And if I wish to do this, and I can see its benefits, there may be situations where I believe it is justified to coerce others to take steps that will lead to greater public health, or education, or justice. After all, my reasoning would likely run, if people were slightly more enlightened, they would voluntarily take these actions anyway, so I am just acting for their own good.

The problem, Berlin argues, is that once you take this view about people you give yourself license to "bully, oppress, torture them in the name, and on behalf, of their 'real' selves." After all, if they were slightly more enlightened they would be choosing the same path as you have set out for them, and they are free only to the extent that they can be liberated from their ignorant selves.

Berlin accepts that there are occasions when coercion may be justified for the sake of a person's own good (we make children go to school because we know it will benefit them later, for instance), but it is something else altogether to pretend that because it is for their own good they are not being coerced, that it is what they really want. "The ideal of true freedom is the maximum of power for all members of human society alike to make the best of themselves," said T.H. Green in 1881. But although Green was a liberal, Berlin notes, "many a tyrant could use this formula to justify his worst acts of oppression." A regime can defend any kind of action along the lines of: "We are making you be like this or do this, even if you don't like it or it restricts your freedom, because it is for your own development and for the progress of society. If you refuse to go along, you are clearly an enemy of the people."

True freedom, in total contrast, revolves around the belief that "Nobody may compel me to be happy in his own way," as Kant put it. While positive liberty is invoked to create a certain kind of person, supporters of negative liberty know that the perfection of humanity is a dangerous myth; however well-meaning, it inevitably leads to illiberal and usually nasty outcomes.

For the good of all

Spinoza, Hegel, and Marx all assumed that in a rational society the human lust for power and domination would fade away. If you create a truly rational society, then everyone will naturally want to pursue their aims in accord with the greater good, and there will be no need for coercion. Engels expressed the view well when he wrote about "replacing the government of persons by the administration of things."

In place of naked power, a rational society has laws, which, although they may impede and restrict at an individual level, benefit the whole. Locke said that "Where there is no law there is no freedom." Montesquieu, Kant, and Burke said the same: political liberty is not permission to do what we want, but the power and means to "do what we ought to" within a rational social structure. Behind the declarations of the rights of man made in the eighteenth century was the idea that liberation and law are the same, because rational laws have the authority of God, nature, or history behind them; they are "self-evident." In short, we need the state and its laws to shape us toward timeless values and productive ends and away from our irrational and base desires and instincts. For Berlin, Fichte summed up the outlook perfectly: "No one has rights... against reason."

Yet however good the intention, the desire for a rational society that encourages "doing what we ought" inevitably comes at the cost of liberty. After all, Comte pointed out, if we do not allow free thinking in chemistry and biology (that is, if the sciences are built on reason and not fancy), why should we allow it in politics and social matters? Indeed, Berlin notes that if one follows the rational view to its end, "There can be only one correct way of life." Wise people follow this way naturally, but the rest of society has to be shoe-horned into it for their own good. This was the rationale behind Plato's enlightened class of philosopher-rulers ("Guardians") described in *The Republic*, who could justifiably ask: "Why should demonstrable error be suffered to survive and breed?"

The problem, Berlin comments, is that this view only makes sense when it is presumed that we are rational, and that those who do not agree with us are not. And if they are obviously irrational, all kinds of restriction of freedom and punishment of them become OK. We have a clear path from the "obvious" truth of reason to despotism.

Berlin lists the basic assumptions of the rational model:

1. All people have one true purpose: rational self-direction.
2. The ends of all rational beings must of necessity fit into a single universal, harmonious pattern, which some men may be able to discern more clearly than others.
3. All conflict, and consequently all tragedy, is due solely to the clash of reason with the irrational or the insufficiently rational (the immature and undeveloped elements in life, whether individual or communal) and such clashes are, in principle, avoidable, and for wholly rational beings impossible.
4. When all people have been made rational, they will obey the rational laws of their own natures, which are one and the same in them all, and so be at once wholly law-abiding and wholly free.

Yet, he asks, are any of the above either true or demonstrable? Not only are they not, he argues, but if you follow the assumptions to their end you can arrive at a chilling conclusion: If I can see and appreciate what is true, then I have the authority to shape and control your life.

The French Revolution is said to have liberated France. However, this "sovereignty of the people," Berlin notes, did not mean more freedom for individuals. Rule by the "popular will" as Rousseau had imagined it meant "rule of each by the rest" in practice. Mill wrote of the "tyranny of the majority" as being little different from any other kind of tyranny. For French political philosopher Benjamin Constant, the real question was not *who* was in power but *how much* power any government should have. Constant could not bear Rousseau's statement that "In giving myself to all [i.e., the democratic body politic], I give myself to none." The fact is that in this kind of republic the individual can be oppressed just as easily as in a tyranny. Hobbes never tried to pretend that monarchs did not oppress or enslave, but at least, Berlin remarks, he did not call such slavery "freedom" as Rousseau did. If one kind of slavery was voluntary, it still amounted to the same reduction of personal liberty.

Ideas matter, politics matter

An idea dreamed up by a professor in the quiet of his study, Berlin notes, can uproot a civilization. He mentions German poet Heine, who warned the French about the power of ideas, seeing the works of Rousseau, for instance, as "the blood-stained weapon which, in the hands of Robespierre, had destroyed the old regime."

Contemporary philosophers, Berlin observes, so pleased with their abstract reasonings, look down on politics. It is unlikely to yield glorious new discoveries, and it is so messy. Philosophers have gone out of their way to separate the two realms, yet the reality is that politics is "indissolubly intertwined" with every kind of philosophizing. In putting abstract philosophy above the level of politics, danger creeps in. If we do not appreciate the power of political belief, some of these beliefs will inevitably go uncriticized and unnoticed—until it is too late.

Final comments

Berlin was careful to note that he was not against all social and political movements that seek to improve the lot of humankind. In fact, he applauded them. What he was against was "the belief that some single formula can in principle be found whereby all the diverse ends of men can be harmoniously realized." The "single formula" has been the justification for terrible regimes and paternalistic states that all thought they were in accord with nature or history, or simply believed that they were doing what was best for the people under their sway.

Yet as Kant told us, there is no value higher than that of the individual, and it can never work when people are treated as a means toward an end. As Berlin puts it: "to manipulate men, to propel them towards goals which you— the social reformer—see, but they may not, is to deny their human essence, to treat them as objects without wills of their own, and therefore to degrade them... to behave as if their ends are less ultimate and sacred than my own."

Just as Lord Acton said, freedom is an end in itself. This means that millions of "experiments in living" (as John Stuart Mill put it) will take place, many of which will fail, but at least those who fail will learn their own lessons. The problem with grand unifying visions of humanity or absolute theories is that they do not take account of people as they actually are (in their endless diversity) rather than how we might like them to be. It seems natural to admonish people to live up to some higher universal standard, and yet social and political life is surely one realm where problems are best approached obliquely. We are on safer ground when freedom is made the highest value. This may be incomprehensible to those whose mission is to "raise up" the world through changing people, but the pluralist ethic of our time is preferable to the wish for absolutes, which Berlin believed was a sign of moral and political immaturity. His essay is reminiscent of the parable of the Grand Inquisitor in Dostoyevsky's *The Brothers Karamazov*, who chillingly proclaimed: "We shall triumph and shall be Caesars, and then we shall plan the universal happiness of man."

Isaiah Berlin

Born in Latvia in 1909, Isaiah Berlin and his parents, who were Russian-speaking Jews, moved to London when he was in his teens. He won a place at Oxford, and was considered so brilliant that he was made a Fellow of All Souls College by his mid-20s. He wrote an acclaimed biography of Marx (1939), and during and just after the war served as a British diplomat in Washington and Moscow. He was made Oxford's Chichele Professor of Social and Political Theory, and was president of Wolfson College from 1966 to 1975.

Other works include Historical Inevitability *(1954),* The Age of Enlightenment *(1956),* Vico and Herder *(1976), and many notable essays, including* "The Hedgehog and the Fox" *(1953). He was also a translator of Turgenev. See Michael Ignatieff's* Isaiah Berlin: A Life, *published a year after Berlin's death in 1997.*

Propaganda

"The conscious and intelligent manipulation of the organized habits and opinions of the masses is an important element in democratic society. Those who manipulate this unseen mechanism of society constitute an invisible government which is the true ruling power of our country."

"Propaganda will never die out. Intelligent men must realize that propaganda is the modern instrument by which they can fight for productive ends and help bring order out of chaos."

In a nutshell

Propaganda is a neutral tool that can be used for good or ill, but in order to have power in modern society once must know its techniques.

In a similar vein

CHAPTER 9

Edward Bernays

For a very long time, since its origination with the Congregatio de propaganda fide, or "office for the propagation of the faith" at the Vatican in 1622, propaganda simply meant the concerted effort to promote a particular philosophy, or set of ideas or practices. It was only in the twentieth century, when governments increasingly began to use it to inspire and justify war to the masses, that the term gained its negative tone. As the First World War broke out, British and US propagandists demonized Germans as "the Hun" and Germany as the seat of "Prussian barbarism," while painting themselves as noble bastions of democracy and freedom. This effort, in which the young Edward Bernays played a key role within the Woodrow Wilson administration, was such a success that he parlayed what he had learned into creating a new field of "public relations."

Bernays portrayed PR as an intelligent step up from the hucksterism of mere advertising and publicity, and he became recognized as the master of this new "manufacture of consent," as political commentator Walter Lippmann famously described it. Lippmann took a low view of the ability of average voters to make rational judgments, distracted as they were by so many concerns and stimuli; democracy could only work if there were a class of disinterested administrators to sift the data and make intelligent decisions. Propaganda simply meant explaining a preferred course of action and making sure that people were behind it.

Bernays added to this intellectual armory his uncle Sigmund Freud's ideas on the basic irrationality of man, plus the new thinking on "crowd psychology," whose best known exponents were Wilfred Trotter (for a time Freud's personal physician) and Gustave Le Bon. Is it possible, Bernays wonders, to get a population to do things as if by flicking a switch? In reality it is not that simple, he ruefully notes. Propaganda will always be an inexact science because it deals with human beings, who although they may be led to some extent, are not so easily read.

Propaganda in a democracy

In a democracy, Bernays says, everyone can vote for whom they please, but the US constitution never imagined the importance of political parties as filtering bodies that could set the public agenda and narrow down the choices to only a couple of candidates. In theory everyone will examine the issues and data themselves, but in reality they leave it up to politicians to highlight the main issues. In the same way, individuals do not construct their own moral code from scratch, but are guided by religion or culture; in obtaining the things we need, we do not have to make exhaustive searches of products and prices, but can rely on the shorthand of brands to guide our shopping decisions.

Thus in a pluralist democracy we are subject to a great competition of ideas and voices promoting policies, ideas, and products, and these efforts are undertaken largely by professionals. For efficiency's sake, we have allowed this to become the normal state of affairs, even if it means that sometimes the news is manipulated, personalities are inflated, and products are hyped. It is technology that has increasingly allowed the means "by which opinion may be regimented." Even in Bernays' time, the vast distances in America were made small by the advent of radio, telegraphy, and the daily newspaper. He discusses the great campaigns against tuberculosis, cancer, and Southern racism—campaigns that required knowledge of how the public mind works and mass psychology as much as campaigns to sell cars or toilet paper.

Bernays lists some of the thousands of interest groups and civic organizations in America that all have a voice of some kind and strive to get their message across. Individuals are always banding together to highlight an issue or cause, and can use propaganda techniques to be seen and heard, just as governments do. Indeed, he says, "Only through the active energy of the intelligent few can the public at large become aware of and act upon new ideas."

Shaping the news

Bernays defines modern propaganda as "a consistent, enduring effort to create or shape events to influence the relations of public to an enterprise, idea or group." From building a cathedral to endowing a university, from marketing a new film to floating a new bond issue—none of these things happens without a concerted attempt on the part of professionals to engineer a certain view of the event in the public's eye. Charities and public bodies "have to work on public opinion just as though they had tubes of toothpaste to sell," Bernays writes. Most news stories are not "accounts of spontaneous happenings" but come from a particular institution or body that has produced a report or created a policy that it wants to get over to the public to shape opinion. In every such report there is usually something that might be considered news.

"Everyone has the right to present his case in the best light," Bernays says, just as a lawyer does. Generally, the job of the PR professional, whether in business or government, is to provide enough information so that there is no misunderstanding on the part of the public. The work involves heading off potentially damaging rumors, replacing them with correct information; this task is surely all the more important in our age of social media. Misunderstanding creates costly friction, which burns up resources.

An organization being clear about its purpose and policies is not "spin," but a simple requirement to get out an unambiguous message. The PR professional or propagandist is not in the business of trying to hoodwink the public. After all, as soon as he were "found out" his effectiveness would be at an end. The term propaganda is warped, Bernays says, only when these efforts are consciously used to promote mistruths and lies, or when it is known that it will hurt the common good. Rather, the task is to let news editors see the original sources, and to be given the chance to judge for themselves whether something is worth reporting.

Propaganda and political leadership
It is ironic, Bernays says, that although politics was "the first big business in America," it failed to copy big business in its efficient mass distribution of ideas and products. Political campaigns involve a huge waste of time and effort as politicians crisscross the country speaking to thousands, when in reality it will only be a handful of voters in key seats who will decide the result. Politicians may know the public mind and have good policies, but they are not experts on the mass distribution and dissemination of ideas; this must be left to public relations experts. The platforms they employ must be honest and carefully worked out and scripted; if a politician kisses a baby, it should be linked to his or her policies on child care. Impromptu emotional rallies may make the politician and crowd feel good, but have little actual return. One has to work out what media and events have the most effect, and put all one's resources into them.

Bernays notes that voter apathy is the result of politicians not being able to provide a platform that is meaningful to the public. Yet he does not call for greater "personalities" to transform politics. Though such figures can be useful, more important in the longer term is the success of the *party* and its aims. The politician is successful if he or she carries the party to victory. Bernays notes that even Henry Ford "has become known through his product, and not for his product through him." Bernays refutes the notion that a top PR person or press agent can "puff up a nobody into a great man." For their ideas to fall on fertile ground, the public figure "has to have some vital seed to sow," leading and educating the public.

The politics of business
Smart businesses know that they are not merely in the business of creating products, but represent a certain ideal. They must always be trying to express their "true personality," conveying to the public what they stand for.

One of Bernays' examples is life insurer Metropolitan Life. It made every attempt to make itself known to the public, and to be of use to people, providing health surveys and advice to communities, and health creeds and advice to individuals. Even the location and design of its headquarters in Manhattan were chosen so that it would have an effect on the public mind. As the breadth and number of its contacts with society increased, so did the number of people wanting to have Metropolitan Life as their insurance provider.

Smart companies understand that their success is as much down to perceptions as product. Bernays approves of a corporation that realizes that its labor policy is causing ill feeling, and so introduces a more equitable policy just to increase public goodwill. If he were alive today, he would no doubt counsel global companies to pay their fair share of taxes to national governments, even if it is legal for them to shift profits offshore and thus pay less tax. For a company to prosper over the long term, the public have to feel that their interests and the company's are one and the same. For that to happen, the firm must engage in constant self-reflection and adjust its ways as need be.

Final comments

When the various falsehoods propagated by the Allies in the First World War came out in the press and in books like Arthur Ponsonby's *Falsehood in War-Time* (1928), propaganda became a dirty word. According to Bernays scholar Mark Crispin Miller, *Propaganda* was an attempt to rescue the term and burnish the author's own credentials as America's "Counsel on Public Relations," but he was often attacked and even portrayed by one journalist as "the Machiavelli of Our Time." This was, after all, the man who had been paid by the United Fruit Company to persuade the CIA and the Eisenhower administration to overthrow the democratically elected government of Jacobo Arbenz in Guatemala in 1954, after which a junta was put in place that retained the neocolonialist arrangement of cheap compliant labor and profits flowing back to America.

The difference between mere advertising types and propagandists, Bernays claimed, is that the latter must actually believe in what they are promoting, and he did seem to think that the Arbenz government was a communist plot. In another example, when he learned the true effects of smoking on health, he stopped doing any work for tobacco companies (he had helped promote Lucky Strike cigarettes) and lobbied other public relations professionals not to do so either.

What Bernays could not have foreseen was the liberation and multiplication of voices through social media, blogging, and so on, which can, in a second, poke holes in a policy, destroy a company's reputation, or bring down a politician. Is this sweet revenge against the wealthy or skilled propagandists using the mainstream media? Perhaps, except that big business and government now devote a great deal of resources to defending their policies and positions in the same social media.

If every group in society started employing propaganda, Bernays wondered, would it not become obvious to the public, and would they not just switch off? No, he says, because people still welcome anyone who can make life simpler for them on an intellectual level, limiting their choice of ideas, wishes, and opinions. This is the surprising aspect of propaganda, he notes: not only can anyone engage in it themselves, it has a clear social function. The word propaganda may retain its Orwellian aura and stigma, but the activity behind it remains a part of modern life.

Edward Bernays

Edward Bernays' parents emigrated to New York City from Vienna in 1892, the year after he was born. His mother was Sigmund Freud's sister, and Freud's wife Martha was the sister of his father Ely. After high school Bernays studied agriculture at Cornell University, before working as a press agent promoting theater and the ballet; for a time he promoted the singer Caruso. While still in his 20s he was a member (with Walter Lippmann) of Woodrow Wilson's Committee for Public Information. In 1919 Bernays opened his own public relations business, and in 1923 he ran the first ever course in PR, at New York University.

In the 1920s it was not socially acceptable for women to smoke in public, so when Bernays was engaged by the company making Lucky Strike cigarettes, he got some models at New York's Easter Parade to light up cigarettes, which were called "torches of freedom." The event made the news and helped increase women's cigarette smoking, while proving Bernays' idea that news was more effective than advertising in promotion. In 1929 he organized a huge celebration of Thomas Edison's invention of the light bulb in many American cities, which was actually a propaganda exercise for General Electric and the National Electric Light Association, a vehicle for GE to keep ownership of utilities out of private hands. Bernays was also an adviser to Calvin Coolidge, and during the Depression worked on Roosevelt's Emergency Committee on Employment. In addition to his work for companies including Alcoa, CBS, and Procter & Gamble, he raised the profile of non-profit organizations including the National Association for the Advancement of Colored People, the New York Infirmary for Women and Children, and the Multiple Sclerosis Society.

Bernays' writings include Crystallizing Public Opinion *(1923), said to have been used by Joseph Goebbels in Nazi propaganda,* Public Relations *(1945), and* "The Engineering of Consent" *(1947), an influential article. He died in 1995, at the age of 103. For more background see Larry Tye's* The Father of Spin: Edward L. Bernays and the Birth of Public Relations *(1998).*

All the President's Men

*"It was 9.30 pm, just an hour from deadline for the
second edition. Woodward began typing:*
A $25,000 cashier's check, apparently earmarked for the
campaign chest of President Nixon, was deposited in April
in the bank account of Bernard L. Barker, one of the five
men arrested in the break-in and alleged bugging attempt at
Democratic National Committee Headquarters here June 17.
*The last page of copy was passed to Sussman just at the deadline.
Sussman set his pen and pipe down on his desk and turned to
Woodward. 'We've never had a story like this,' he said. 'Just never.'"*

*"Despite the deletions, the story—headlined 'Key Nixon Aide
Named as "Sabotage" Contact'—broke new ground. Almost four
months after the break-in at Democratic headquarters, the spreading
stain of Watergate had finally seeped into the White House."*

In a nutshell

Beyond laws and institutions, the best-known means of
preventing corruption in government is a free press.

In a similar vein

Graham T. Allison & Philip Zelikow *Essence of Decision* (p 36)
Edward Bernays *Propaganda* (p 66)
Alexander Hamilton, John Jay, & James Madison *The Federalist Papers* (p 120)
Abraham Lincoln *The Gettysburg Address* (p 162)

CHAPTER 10

Carl Bernstein & Bob Woodward

On the night of June 16, 1972, five men were arrested for burglary at the Watergate building in Washington, DC. Wearing business suits, they were carrying rolls of film, cameras, lock picks, and bugging devices. Though four of the men were Cuban Americans from Miami, the fifth was James McCord, then working as the security manager for Nixon's Committee for the Re-election of the President (CRP or CREEP). An address book on the person of another of the burglars contained contacts for Howard Hunt, a White House consultant connected to Charles Colson, special counsel to the President.

The fact that common burglars did not usually have connections to the White House made the incident fishy from the start. Yet White House press secretary Ronald Ziegler described it as a "third-rate burglary attempt" not worthy of comment. Indeed, it made no sense that the White House would be going to such extremes to get information that might discredit their Democratic opponents. President Nixon was way ahead of all Democratic contenders in the polls, and there was talk of the Republicans dominating US politics for a generation. The fact that the burglary was profoundly unnecessary is one of the quirks of the Watergate story, but also points to the reason it happened in the first place.

It is easy now to forget that Nixon inspired fierce loyalty among Republican troops, and yet his vaulting ambition, attachment to power, and hatred of the Democrats (particularly the Kennedys) made him attract people of similar mind. Watergate turned out to be the tip of an iceberg of unethical or illegal activity that had gone on before Nixon was elected President, and continued into his administration.

Reading *All the President's Men* today (or watching the excellent Alan Pakula film starring Dustin Hoffman as Bernstein and Robert Redford as Woodward), one is taken back to a cellphone-free era of typewriters and telex machines, when most people bought physical newspapers and it really mattered what appeared on the front page. News and investigative journalism may have found other channels, but a free press remains as important as ever to the claim of being an open society—and this is why Watergate still matters.

The story unfolds

Bob Woodward had only been at the *Washington Post* for nine months and was used to writing stories on local police corruption or unsanitary restaurants. So when the city editor called one Saturday morning asking him to investigate a burglary at the local Democratic Party headquarters, he wasn't particularly excited—until he discovered that it was not the local Democratic office that had been broken into, but the HQ of the Democratic National Committee in the fancy Watergate office-apartment-hotel complex.

Woodward was not pleased that another reporter, Carl Bernstein, had started working on the story too; Bernstein had a reputation for muscling in on good stories and claiming them as his own. At 28, he had been a reporter since he was 19 and was a long-haired college dropout, while the 29-year-old Woodward was a Yale graduate whose father was a judge. Nevertheless, Woodward admitted that Bernstein was a better writer, and as they began working together their trust in each other grew; most of the stories relating to Watergate appeared under a joint byline. Woodward was divorced, Bernstein was separated, and neither had children, so they could work into the night at the *Post* newsroom or go knocking on doors in the evenings, and jet off to Los Angeles or Mexico in a hurry if the story required it. Barry Sussman was their immediate editor, but they were ultimately answerable to flamboyant *Post* executive editor Benjamin Bradlee, who had been a close friend of President Kennedy, and *Post* publisher Katharine Graham, who had taken over at the helm of her family-controlled paper after her husband committed suicide.

Bernstein called a former official of the Nixon administration and asked whether the White House could have been involved in the Watergate raid. Instead of dismissing the suggestion out of hand, as he expected, the aide said that Nixon liked to have direct access to political intelligence and gossip. Bernstein learned that White House Chief of Staff H.R. Haldeman was obsessed with the idea of Teddy Kennedy running for President, and had ordered research that could be used to discredit him. He was also surprised by the way a Republican party official spoke of the men around the President: "They couldn't care less about the Republican party. Given the chance, they would wreck it."

One of the reporters' important sources was Hugh Sloan, who had resigned as treasurer of CRP because he did not like what was going on. He confirmed that there had been a secret White House/CRP slush fund amounting to hundreds of thousands of dollars, used to pay for "ratfucking" or "black ops"— political sabotage against Democratic candidates, including bugging; following members of candidates' families; creating fake letters on Democratic letter-head; messing up Democratic rallies (e.g., getting 200 pizzas ordered to the premises, cash on delivery); stealing documents; false press leaks; and planting spies in enemy groups or organizations. Sloan noted that since Watergate the President had tried to make out that CRP was like a private company set up by supporters, when in reality it "was the White House, wholly its creation, staffed by the White House, reporting only to the White House."

Meanwhile, Woodward began receiving information from an important source in the government whom he would meet late at night in a car park. The source was given the moniker "Deep Throat," the title of an early porn movie. Deep Throat noted that there were 50 people in the White House and CRP focused on intelligence gathering and dirty tricks. He talked of their "switch-blade mentality," that they were always willing to play dirty to win at all costs.

Getting closer

Ironically, the fact that the Watergate burglary was bungled may have fore-stalled exposure of the White House's involvement. After all, the "President's men" were seen as a controlled and efficient team, and it was hard to believe that the White House could have helped organize such an effort. Yet the reporters were getting closer to confirming that one of the five people who controlled the secret fund was none other than Haldeman, who was known for his ruthlessness in promoting and protecting the President; he described himself as "the President's son-of-a-bitch." Haldeman had gone to some lengths to ensure that nothing could be pinned on him; yet as the proxy for the President, he could not have done what he did without the knowledge or at least tacit approval of the Commander-in-Chief.

In October the *Post* published a story about Haldeman's probable involve-ment in Watergate, but the White House flatly denied it, suggested that the paper was in league with George McGovern, the Democratic presidential candidate.

Nixon's reelection on November 7, 1972, with a large majority, seemed to put the newspaper on the wrong side of public opinion. What if, the report-ers wondered, they were indeed damaging the institution of the Presidency by making false allegations? Challenges were made regarding the newspaper's ownership of two Florida television stations by a "citizen's group," which was actually people linked to the President. *Post* stock dropped by nearly 50 percent.

Strange justice

A federal grand jury investigation had been underway for some time, with hun-dreds of confidential interviews recorded, including with all key White House personnel. Unfortunately for the press, they were not made public, and the investigation was deeply flawed. From the start it focused on the burglary itself, and seemed uninterested or unwilling to look into the question of who had ordered it and why. As White House staffers and other sources told Woodward and Bernstein, it was asking plenty of questions, but not the right ones.

Only the Watergate burglars themselves were indicted, and in the trial it emerged that the accused had been told they would be "looked after" once out of jail, and even be paid $1,000 for each week they were behind bars. Yet McCord testified that he had feared for his life in revealing the truth, and that the operation had been approved by John Mitchell when Attorney-General.

Meantime, Senator Ervin set up a Senate Select Committee to investigate Republican campaign funding. At first, Nixon refused to allow his aides to testify, pleading executive privilege. This had the effect of turning public opinion away from the President. Nixon relented, and held a press conference to state that no position in his administration would be immune to prosecution. Bernstein noticed that the President's hands were shaking as he gave his statement. Then under oath, White House aide Jeb Magruder said that Mitchell and presidential counsel John Dean had been behind both the Watergate operation and the cover-up. The dam of the story seemed about to burst.

Woodward asked for an interview with the President, still believing Nixon had somehow stayed above it all. Yet the White House was rapidly descending into chaos, with mutual accusations and loyalty going out the window. One of Dean's associates told the reporters the President was willing to buy Dean's silence for $1 million. In the end, Haldeman and presidential assistant Ehrlichman resigned, without admitting they had done anything criminal, and Dean was fired. Woodward and Bernstein felt vindicated, and Ziegler even apologized to them and the *Washington Post*.

Nixon might have stayed President were it not for the secret taping system he had set up in the White House, known only to a few associates and Secret Service agents. Judge Sirica ordered the tapes to be surrendered, but one had an 18-minute erasure, which Nixon's secretary Rose Mary Woods claimed she had made by accident (despite advances in technology this part of the tape has never been restored). Nixon refused to surrender the tapes, citing executive privilege, until a decision from the Supreme Court had them handed over.

The fallout

The tapes revealed that although Nixon may not have know the details of the Watergate break-in, he had condoned most of what CRP was doing, and was prepared to cover up what had happened. But it was a conversation recorded on June 23, 1972 that conclusively harmed the President. In a meeting with his Chief of Staff, Nixon agreed with Haldeman's suggestion to ask the CIA to stop the FBI's investigations into Watergate on the grounds of "national security." This amounted to an obstruction of justice, according to prosecutors, as did a conversation on August 1, 1972 in which Haldeman raised the matter of paying off the Watergate defendants to keep them quiet. Nixon responded, "Well… they have to be paid. That's all there is to that. They have to be paid."

In the wake of the tapes, most Republicans in the House of Representatives who had backed Nixon now advocated impeachment. Lacking support in the Senate too, Nixon gave a press conference on August 8, 1974, stating he would resign the Presidency "effective noon tomorrow."

It emerged that in the summer of 1973 Secretary of State Henry Kissinger had attempted to get the President to come clean about Watergate and accept some responsibility, but press secretary Ziegler had angrily rejected the idea, saying "Contrition is bullshit."

Final comments

Bernstein and Woodward describe Watergate as a "many-headed monster," of which the break-in itself was only the most obvious facet. The suffix "-gate" is now, of course, used for any kind of scandal, and although shocking to a US public used to venerating the President, the affair should be put in some context. The activities of the CRP had long been a part of politics, and today theft, spying, electoral corruption, and character assassination are the order of the day in many countries. What left a bad taste was that it could happen in an apparently enlightened democracy. Watergate proved one thing conclusively: that a free press is a foundation of liberal democratic society, as important as the right to vote, the separation of church and state, and an independent judiciary.

Carl Bernstein & Bob Woodward

Born in Washington, DC in 1944, Carl Bernstein started his journalism career as a copyboy for the Washington Star, *then earned a reputation as an investigative reporter for New Jersey's* Elizabeth Daily Journal. *He joined the* Washington Post *in 1966 to cover local news. In the 1970s he was married to screenwriter and novelist Nora Ephron. Between 1980 and 1985 he was Washington bureau chief for ABC News.*

Bob Woodward was born in 1943 in Illinois. He studied at Yale before service in the US Navy, and his first journalism job was at Maryland's Montgomery County Sentinel. *He moved to the* Post *in 1971, and has remained an editor and writer there ever since.*

The pair won the 1973 Pulitzer Prize for their reporting, and followed All the President's Men *with* The Final Days *(1976), a gripping account of the last months of the Nixon presidency.*

Reflections on the Revolution in France

"So this legislative assembly of a free nation sits, not for the security, but for the destruction of property, and not of property only, but of every rule and maxim which can give it stability…"

"The state ought not to be considered as nothing better than a partnership agreement in a trade of pepper and coffee, calico or tobacco, or some other such low concern, to be taken up for a little temporary interest, and to be dissolved by the fancy of the parties. It is to be looked on with other reverence… it becomes a partnership not only between those who are living, but between those who are living, those who are dead, and those who are to be born. Each contract of each particular state is but a clause in the great primaeval contract of eternal society."

In a nutshell

Revolutions always claim to be new beginnings for "the people," but the price of destroying old institutions is instability and vulnerability to despots.

In a similar vein

Aristotle *Politics* (p 54)
Isaiah Berlin *Two Concepts of Liberty* (p 60)
Thomas Paine *Common Sense* (p 238)
Mary Wollstonecraft *A Vindication of the Rights of Woman* (p 304)

CHAPTER 11

Edmund Burke

When revolution broke out in France, fascination and much goodwill were expressed around the world. Organizations such as the London Revolutionary Society were in correspondence with the French National Assembly, and in the British parliament even leading figures such Charles James Fox and William Pitt offered support for the new government.

Edmund Burke, philosopher and man of letters, was not overly worried to begin with, but when people began to talk of the "applicability" of the Revolution to England he realized it was a spreading infection that must be halted. In a few months he wrote *Reflections on the Revolution in France*, the first "anti-revolutionary" text; a bestseller in England, it quickly went through 10 printings in France. The book provoked a backlash in the form of Thomas Paine's *Rights of Man* and Mary Wollstonecraft's *A Vindication of the Rights of Men*, and Burke, who had hitherto been seen as a progressive, was denounced as reactionary.

However, many in the liberal intelligentsia (including William Wordsworth and Samuel Taylor Coleridge) would in time revise their opinion and view Burke as a seer, for not only did he predict the Terror that followed the revolution, but also the rise of a military strongman. Nine years later, Napoleon would bring on a major war with European powers.

Though writing about a particular historical event, Burke's interpretation of what happened in France in 1789 and after turned out to be a perfect statement of modern conservatism and a warning against the overpowering of any country by godless rationalists. He was the first to say that the excitement of revolution inevitably gives way to abuses of person and property. Liberty and equality sound good, but if they are taken suddenly and by force, what is the cost?

Evolution, not revolution

Reflections on the Revolution in France is in fact a long letter to Burke's Parisian friend Chames-Jean-François de Pont, who had just become a member of the new French National Assembly. The epistolary format conveniently allowed Burke to explain the features of the English political system to an outsider, while at the same time providing an excuse to be informal and opinionated. What actually sparked his wrath, though, is a sermon by popular dissenting clergyman Richard Price, asserting that the people of England should, in the style of the French Revolution, be able to create their own government irrespective of the monarchy. Price and the London Revolution Society (set up to commemorate the Glorious Revolution of 1688) put the uprising in France in the same basket as the American Revolution, and argued that Britain should be moving a similar way.

A furious Burke was keen to nip such "historical inevitability" in the bud, pointing out that Britain and France had very different political evolutions. He notes that the Glorious Revolution did indeed end the arbitrary power of English monarchs and establish the concept of parliamentary sovereignty. However, in the "Declaration of Right" statute to which new king William of Orange had assented, there was no suggestion that the public could *choose* the monarch, only that the system of succession be made clearer "for the peace, quiet and security of the realm." For England to follow France would mean suddenly throwing out principles that had been established for 100 years, and had resulted in a successful constitutional monarchy. He hails the English constitution as a great structure that grew organically over a long period, slowly increasing liberties and retaining the monarchy as a stabilizing influence, while ending arbitrary monarchical power. England's pedigree of liberty went back to Magna Carta, and its citizens' political rights were an inheritance, not some abstract "rights of man" in the Paine sense, but specifically the rights of English*men*.

Burke was not a blind conservative, though, and notes that the principle of inheritance does not at all preclude the principle of improvement. What is inherited is simply a base, which cannot be withdrawn, and more freedoms can be added to it. He contrasts this with what had just happened in France, a violent grab for rights that required destruction of the established order, writing to his French friend: "You began ill, because you began by despising every thing that belonged to you. You set up your trade without a capital."

Property and stability

As Burke scholar and statesman Conor Cruise O'Brien noted, the French Revolution was merely a forerunner of what Marxist philosophy would produce in the twentieth century, but on a greater scale: the total overthrow and uprooting of the established order, always characterized as rotten to the core; the seizure and nationalization of property; the end of all rights built up over generations; and the crushing of the nobility and church, disregarding the family as the cementing institution of society.

Burke could see that "a clean slate" involved a certain anti-human philosophy that would inevitably have a violent conclusion. This is indeed what happened with the Revolutionary Tribunal's bloody zeal in seeking to finish off all who were perceived as enemies of the state. The correctness of his analysis was also borne out by the way various communist revolutions from Stalinism to Maoism ended in a brutal fashion.

Burke's problem with France's new rulers was that many of them were smart operators but they owned no property: it was therefore in their interests to destroy and delegitimize the established order so that people like themselves, without anything at stake, would benefit from the new "equality." They did not see society as a contract between people and state built up over many generations, but as something to be replaced when it was not to their liking.

Burke admits that the British system is not based on full equality of democratic right, and for good reason. More weight is given to those with property, particularly in relation to the House of Lords, where it was a requirement to have some wealth based on inherited property. This was a kind of assurance that only people of substance could weigh in on national matters, people who would not be making decisions for their own financial benefit, since they did not need to. It was a link to the classical Roman principle that substantial property ownership was one of the requirements for serving in the Senate. For Burke, property is "the ballast in the vessel of the commonwealth." By perpetuating families, it perpetuates society, and therefore "some decent regulated pre-eminence, some preference given to birth, is neither unnatural, not unjust, nor impolitic."

Begin with equality, end with despotism

Burke is sickened by the fact that Englishmen who saw the procession of Louis XVI to his death describe it as a "triumph," when to Burke it is more like a line of savages preparing for blood sacrifice. He hates extremes, including the idea that monarchy is all bad. In reality, it is possible to have a monarchy whose power is balanced by laws and hereditary wealth. One should not have to be painted as a "friend of tyranny" just because one supports some aspects of monarchy and is not totally convinced by democracy. Burke talks of the "despotism of the multitude," and warns that the new France "affects to be a pure democracy, though I think it in a direct train of becoming shortly a mischievous and ignoble oligarchy." *Reflections on the Revolution in France* contains a prophetic passage about "some popular general, who understands the art of conciliating the soldiery" taking over the army, and with the army becoming "the master of your whole republic."

A better description of Napoleon Bonaparte could hardly be written, and his rise demonstrates perfectly how societies that sweep away the old often fill the vacuum (consciously or not) with some new figurehead to restore a sense of security or confidence. What revolutionaries fail to appreciate, Burke says, is that government is not merely a means for people to achieve their wants and needs, it is also a brake on their passions and a reminder of conventions. Whenever "the people" becomes the guiding principle, a country is open to exploitation by an oligarchy or a dictator offering a single great solution, and then it is individual, families, and civil and private institutions that suffer. These solutions are often "infinitely captivating," Burke notes, but in practice they tend to result in great boons for a few who can corrupt the system. In contrast, a constitution that has evolved organically, like Britain's, offers no simple or immediate answers, but over time it tends to deliver benefits for all.

Beware the lust for the new

In a famous passage Burke recalls the time, 16 years before, when he saw Marie Antoinette "just above the horizon, decorating and cheering the elevated sphere she just began to move in, glittering like the morning star, full of life, and splendor, and joy." Regretting that such a figure could be crushed by what was once a "gallant nation," he adds: "But such an age of chivalry is gone. That of sophisters, oeconomists, and calculators, has succeeded; and the glory of Europe is extinguished forever."

When a society is based only on logic and reason, it loses all sense of elegance, taste, and beauty. There needs to be a sort of irrational love and respect for things greater than one's self, and a royal family provides the charm and awe that may be absent from everyday life. In contrast, the "barbarous philosophy" of reason alone ends not in truth and beauty, Burke says, but in the hangman, an insight that would help to make him relevant again during the communist revolutions of the twentieth century.

The institutions of the nobility and the clergy, both of which the French revolutionaries sought to destroy, had provided continuity of learning, manners, and civilization through a stream of upheavals and wars. Thanks to them, society did not have to keep starting over. The essence of Burke's conservatism is a political ethos that above all respects the values and institutions that transcend time and person.

Final comments

Why did Burke, one of the eighteenth century's leading liberal figures and a great sympathizer with the American revolutionaries, come down so hard against the French Revolution? For O'Brien an answer is to be found in religion. Whereas the US Constitution went to some lengths to preserve religious liberties and freedom of conscience, the French Revolution involved systematic "dechristianization," with attacks on priests, seizure of the property of the dominant Catholic Church, and the creation of an atheistic Cult of Reason. But religion only partly accounts for Burke's vehemence. For several years he had been the greatest critic of Britain's imperial adventures in India, and headed the parliamentary prosecution of Warren Hastings, Governor-General of India and controller of the East India Company. Burke thought Hastings had, in his zeal for domination and profit, rid India of many of its worthwhile ways and traditions. Britain had failed in its moral responsibility to fill the gap with new institutions that would benefit the Indian people. His conscience toward the Indian population seems farsighted today, but it reveals a common thread: in both India and France traditions and institutions built up over centuries were being trashed for questionable motives. Beneath Britain's propaganda of "civilizing India" was a simple lust for enrichment, and in France the revolutionaries' high ideals were a perfect foil for the ambitious to grab power and property.

Burke admits the French nobility had become too lax in its morals, and France had in addition not allowed for social mobility in the same way as England had. Yet in Burke's mind none of this really justified the total upheaval of the Revolution. The Terror of 1793–94 saw around 25,000 people executed, including over 16,000 guillotined. France would need to go through two restorations of the monarchy and the Napoleonic era before the Third Republic began. Was it all really worth it?

Edmund Burke

Edmund Burke was born in Dublin in 1729. In his mid-teens he enrolled at Dublin's Trinity College, and after graduating in 1748 followed his solicitor father's wishes and entered the law. After a period at Middle Temple in London, he left to go traveling in Europe, resolving to make a living as a writer. His first two books, the satirical A Vindication of Natural Society *(1756) and the philosophical* Enquiry into the Origin of Our Ideas of the Sublime and the Beautiful *(1757), became well known. He created and was chief editor of the* Annual Register, *a popular current affairs journal.*

In his late 20s Burke became assistant to the British Chief Secretary for Ireland, then private secretary to Whig prime minister Charles Watson-Wentworth, who supported American independence. In 1865 he was elected a Member of Parliament, calling for more leniency and flexibility in Britain's American dominions, and strong political parties to balance the king's powers and create effective opposition to the government. He worked for a free market in corn and for free trade with Ireland, opposed capital punishment, and supported Catholic emancipation, an unpopular cause. In 1782, while Paymaster of the Forces, an Act he spearheaded abolished many royal sinecures and offices that had been funded at public expense.

He married Jane Nugent in 1757, had a son and an adopted son, and maintained (with some difficulty) a large estate, "Gregories" in Beaconsfield. Burke was good friends with writer Samuel Johnson, painter Joshua Reynolds, and actor David Garrick. He died in 1797.

1962

Silent Spring

"Then a strange blight crept over the area and everything began to change. Some evil spell had settled on the community; mysterious maladies swept the flocks of chickens; the cattle and sheep sickened and died. Everywhere was a shadow of death. The farmers spoke of much illness among their families."

"One part in a million sounds like a very small amount—and so it is. But such substances are so potent that a minute quantity can bring about vast changes in the body... Because these small amounts of pesticides are cumulatively stored and very slowly excreted, the threat of chronic poisoning and degenerative changes in the liver and other organs is very real."

In a nutshell

Because clean water and air and healthy soil are basic to life, the environment is arguably the most political issue.

In a similar vein

Naomi Klein *No Logo* (p 156)
Mancur Olson *The Rise and Decline of Nations* (p 226)
Upton Sinclair *The Jungle* (p 260)

CHAPTER 12

Rachel Carson

Most people have heard of Rachel Carson and *Silent Spring*, and some even know she was already a successful author by the time it was published. *The Sea Around Us*, for instance, won her the 1951 National Book Award. Few realize, though, what a courageous leap *Silent Spring* was in her career.

In the 1950s, Carson began investigating DDT (dichlorodiphenyltrichloroethane), a synthetic pesticide discovered in 1939 by Swiss chemist Paul Hermann Muller. DDT was first used to kill off lice among soldiers during the Second World War to prevent the transmission of typhus, but was then allowed for agricultural use as an insecticide. It became popular on farms and orchards across America, strongly supported by the US Department of Agriculture in its campaign against fire ants, but when Carson began pitching articles to major magazines on the pesticide's effects, she was rejected every time. It was one thing to produce lyrical titles on aquatic biology and be known as the lady naturalist, quite another to take on the mantle of investigative reporter and come up against government policy and the might of corporations.

She decided to pour her ideas into a book. It took four years to write, but a serialization in *The New Yorker* gave it the start she had hoped for, along with selection by Book-of-the-Month Club and her appearance on a CBS current affairs show. In the 1950s and 1960s nature conservation was a side issue; most people were on the side of farmers who were, after all, in a fight against nature to feed America. Chemicals were the future; if you were against them you were out of step with the times. But when, in the pages of Carson's book, people read about food chain contamination, wiping out of familiar birds and animals, and evidence that crop spraying could be causing cancer, what we now call environmentalism suddenly became a mainstream issue.

Silent Spring marked the point when the environment became a *political* matter. John F. Kennedy got the Science Advisory Committee to examine the evidence in the book, and its validation of the conclusions was one step toward America's 1972 ban on DDT for agricultural use. This only came after years of public relations efforts from agricultural and chemical companies, which continued to export DDT until the 1980s. Monsanto published a parody of *Silent*

Spring, "The Desolate Year," which imagined starvation in a world in which insecticides had been banned; and another manufacturer of DDT, Velsicol, tried to suggest that Carson was in the pay of Soviet Russia and was seeking to decimate America's productive potential.

Farm chemical use has long been superseded by environmental issues such as climate change, but as evidenced by the success of Al Gore's film *An Inconvenient Truth* (2006), it takes the power of storytelling to change people's minds. Six years before the world marveled at the Apollo 8 "Earthrise" image, and long before James Lovelock's *Gaia* (1979), Carson argued that Earth's environment is a complex, holistic system that needs to be revered and respected.

Overkill

Silent Spring begins with a two-page "Fable of Tomorrow." A scene is sketched of the US countryside at an undetermined time, when people live in accord with the land around them and its abundance of wildlife, diversity of plants, and purity of rivers. Then one day, animals begin dying for no apparent reason, and the fields grow silent for lack of birds. Apple trees still bloom, but there are no bees to be seen among the blossoms. In the gutters of farm buildings and houses collects a fine white powder that has fallen some weeks before. "No witchcraft, no enemy action had silenced the rebirth of new life in this stricken world," Carson tells the reader. "The people had done it themselves."

The period of time in which humans have actually shaped their environment, rather than being shaped by it, is tiny within the history of life on earth. Yet in the 25 years before Carson was writing, air, earth, rivers, and sea had all been contaminated to varying degrees with dangerous, sometimes lethal, man-made chemicals. Of course, radiation had always emanated from certain rocks, and the sun, but animal and plant life had adjusted to these dangers over millions of years. However, in the modern world many new chemicals were being created each year whose effects were unknown. In the year before *Silent Spring* was published, 200 chemicals had come to market for killing weeds, insects, rodents, and other "pests," and they were being used to blanket farms, killing whatever life existed on them indiscriminately. As insects evolved with immunity to chemicals, stronger insecticides had to be developed. Insects also exhibited "flareback," coming back in greater strength after fields had been sprayed. "Thus the chemical war is never won," Carson writes, "and all life is caught in its violent crossfire."

Along with the threat of nuclear war, chemical contamination is the great threat of the age, she argues. And if we are appalled by the thought of radiation, she asks, how "can we be indifferent to the same effect in chemicals that we disseminate widely in our environment?"

Consequences unknown

Nearly all of the earth's fresh water supply was once ground water, which moves beneath our feet. Because water moves, pollution of it in one place will pollute locations tens or hundreds of miles away. "Seldom if ever does nature operate in closed and separate compartments," Carson writes, "and she has not done so in distributing the earth's water supply."

In a famous case in Colorado in the 1950s, ponds containing chemicals at an industrial plant seeped into the ground water, and several years later began poisoning crops and making people sick in the countryside. It had taken that time for the water to move a few miles, but once the chemicals were in the ground water nothing could be done to treat it. The scarier fact is that when "harmless" chemicals mingle in the ground water, they can form lethal cocktails, combinations that no responsible scientist would dare to make.

Chemists in Carson's day somehow thought that insect pests could be destroyed without having any effect on the ecology of soils, including the countless organisms in them, including worms. What those effects were was only just emerging, and Carson maintains that scientific prudence should dictate the banning of insecticides until more is known about them. Agricultural chemicals could not simply be a private matter for the farmer, since the effects could be universal. The political aspects of this were obvious to Carson:

"If the Bill of rights contains no guarantee that a citizen shall be secure against lethal poisons distributed either by private individuals or by public officials, it is surely only because our forefathers, despite their considerable wisdom and foresight, could conceive of no such problem."

Another example of the unintended effects of insecticides is Clear Lake in Northern California. The lake was popular with anglers, but they could not stand the gnats it attracted, so the decision was taken to put tiny amounts of DDD (a close relative of DDT) into the water. After three such treatments the gnats seemed to disappear, but then Western Grebe birds began dying, down from 1,000 pairs to 30. When tested the water had no trace of DDD; what had happened was that the plankton had absorbed the chemical, they had been eaten by herbivorous fish, which had been eaten by carnivorous fish, which were eaten by the Grebes. With each link in the food chain, the presence of DDD was further concentrated, to become much higher than the original one fiftieth part per million by the time the birds consumed it. "The poison had not really left the lake," Carson writes, "it had merely gone into the fabric of the life the lake supports."

Fresh horrors

The twentieth century saw a rapid increase in the number of cancer-causing chemicals being used. Where once they might have been an occupational hazard, found in factories or mines, now "they have entered the environment of everyone—even as children yet unborn," Carson observes.

She reports on emerging research into how synthetic chemicals, specifically a number of pesticides, disturb human cells' vital processes, ranging from chromosome damage to gene mutation. Most of the evidence was circumstantial, as obviously farm chemicals and the like could not be tested on human beings. But four out of five chemicals tested on animals had already been found to be carcinogenic, and mosquitoes exposed to DDT over several generations "turned into strange creatures call gyandomorphs—part male and part female."

In 1930s America cancer among children was rare, but 25 years later, when pesticides had become widely used on farms and in domestic gardens, more US children were dying of cancer than any other disease (12 percent of all deaths between ages 1 and 14). Carson links carcinogens to babies being born with tumors, the result of carcinogenic exposure in the mother during pregnancy. In the 1950s, when DDT-type insecticides came into civilian use, there was also a marked increase in leukemia and related blood malignancies, from 12,290 cases in 1950 to 16,690 in 1960. While cancers often take years or decades to present after their original cause, leukemia has a much shorter latent period. The fact is, Carson writes:

"the public can be exposed to a known carcinogen for several years before the slowly moving legal processes can bring the situation under control... what the public is asked to accept as 'safe' today may turn out tomorrow to be extremely dangerous."

Final comments

Though many more safeguards have been instituted in relation to agricultural chemical use and food safety since the 1960s, even today reading *Silent Spring* will make you wonder where the food you are eating originated and under what conditions it was grown, as well as whether the chemicals you use around the house are safe.

Carson's impact was multiplied by the fact that she was a skilled, even beautiful, writer, able to absorb and convey information published in scientific journals that the public neither knew of or cared about, and from it produce a warning about threats to life and nature that had a huge emotional effect. By today's standards of science writing her evidence is selective, but

Silent Spring is a polemic; it carries the anger of the citizen in the same way as Ralph Nader's exposé of the car industry, *Unsafe at Any Speed* (1965), another book that led to regulatory change.

On the 50th anniversary of Carson's book's publication, Eliza Griswold argued in a *New York Times* article ("How 'Silent Spring' ignited the environmental movement," Sept 2012) that its success was followed by a new era of well-funded attacks on environmentalists' assertions. Websites such as rachelwaswrong.org even claim that Carson's campaign against DDT was a false alarm that deprived millions of an effective treatment for malaria. That this website is funded by lobby group the Competitive Enterprise Institute would not have surprised Carson, who felt that agencies such as the Department of Agriculture were in the pocket of industry, with no one to represent the safety of US citizens. The Clean Air and Water Acts were not passed until after her death, followed by the establishment of the Environmental Protection Agency. Carson helped to make the environment good politics.

Rachel Carson

Born in Springdale near Pittsburgh in 1907, Rachel Carson grew up on a small farm where she could smell a nearby factory that made glue from the body parts of old horses. She was an avid reader and nature lover.

After graduating from high school in 1925 at the top of her class, she attended Pennsylvania College for Women. She studied for a master's degree at Johns Hopkins University, intending to gain a doctorate, but had to support her family through the Depression. Carson obtained a temporary job with the US Bureau of Fisheries, writing material for a radio series on sea life, and then was hired as the Bureau's first female aquatic biologist. She wrote many of its brochures and publications, and began publishing articles in major magazines and newspapers. The success of The Sea Around Us *allowed her to leave the Bureau and write full time. For most of her working life, after the death of her father in her 20s, she was the breadwinner for her mother, sister, nieces, and a niece's orphaned son.*

In 1963 Carson gave evidence to a Senate subcommittee on pesticides, but was already ill from breast cancer and died the following year. Her childhood home and her home in Maryland where she wrote Silent Spring *are Historic Landmarks, and the book itself was made a National Historic Chemical Landmark by the American Chemical Society. A number of US schools and conservation parks are named after her.*

Carson's sea trilogy includes Under the Sea Wind *(1941),* The Sea Around Us *(1951), and* The Edge of the Sea *(1955). For more on her life see Linda Lear's biography,* Witness for Nature.

The Gathering Storm

"One day President Roosevelt told me that he was asking publicly for suggestions about what the war should be called. I said at once 'the Unnecessary War.' There never was a war more easy to stop than that which has just wrecked what was left of the world from the previous struggle."

"[Hitler] could not comprehend the mental and spiritual force of our island people, who, however much opposed to war or military preparation, had through the centuries come to regard victory as their birthright."

"At last I had the authority to give directions over the whole scene. I felt as if I were walking with destiny, and that all my past life had been but a preparation for this hour and for this trial. Ten years in the political wilderness had been so numerous, so detailed, and were now so terribly vindicated, that no one could gainsay me."

In a nutshell

The best political leaders are able to place current events within the context of history.

In a similar vein

Norman Angell *The Great Illusion* (p 42)
Hannah Arendt *The Origins of Totalitarianism* (p 48)
Carl von Clausewitz *On War* (p 98)
Margaret Thatcher *The Autobiography* (p 278)

CHAPTER 13

Winston Churchill

I n 1938–39, Winston Churchill was neck deep in the research and writing of his mammoth *History of the English Speaking Peoples*. He was under pressure from his publisher to deliver a manuscript, and the advance would keep paying the bills for Chartwell, his beloved home in the Kent countryside that he had bought in 1922. He was also earning money by writing articles for British and foreign newspapers, and though he held no office of state (he was simply MP for Epping), his strident warnings about impending war were increasingly noted, if an irritation to Neville Chamberlain's pacifist government.

As Jonathan Rose notes in *The Literary Churchill* (2014), the man's huge and important output as a writer were overshadowed by his fame as a leader. Yet Churchill would never have been as successful without his literary sweep of mind and skill with words. His speeches in the House of Commons were often compelling, as were his wartime radio broadcasts; it was he who coined the phrase "Iron Curtain" in a postwar speech.

The Gathering Storm is the first of his six-volume series *The Second World War*, which won him the Nobel Prize for Literature in 1953. Written between 1948 and 1954, the first part of the book covers the years 1919–39, and the second the first few months of the war from September 1939 to May 1940, when Churchill became prime minister. So the reader is not mistaken about the book's purpose, its subtitle is *How the English-Speaking Peoples through Their Unwisdom, Carelessness, and Good Nature Allowed the Wicked to Rearm*. The work is a wonderful insight into the lead-up to war and into the mind of its author, who notes that his inspiration came from Daniel Defoe's *Memoirs of a Cavalier* (1720), a chronicle of military and political events seen through the eyes of one who was part of them.

The axiom that the further you go back into history, the more you can see the future never found a more apt expression than in Churchill, who could put Hitler's terrifying rise into some context. He was steeped in Britain's past as a nation that had often stood up to apparently superior forces—and won. His multivolume life of John Churchill, Duke of Marlborough (1650–1722), for instance, describes his ancestor's unlikely victory against Louis xiv's forces at Blenheim. This time, it was Winston Churchill who would be at the center of the action.

A bad peace...

In his first chapter, "Follies of the victors," Churchill notes that after the horror of the First World War, almost everyone thought that nothing like it could happen again. There was a deep desire for peace. US President Woodrow Wilson nursed the League of Nations into existence, and Germany was so soundly defeated that the victorious powers had the chance to redraw the boundaries of Europe almost as they wished. The Treaty of Versailles was designed to ensure that Germany could never again become an aggressor, but France's Marshal Foch was overhead saying at the signing ceremony: "This is not Peace. It is an Armistice for twenty years." The terms of the treaty were considered harsh on Germany, and £1,000 million worth of German assets were appropriated by the winning powers, yet a few years later the United States was making huge loans to Germany to rebuild itself and pay its reparations, and many of the Versailles terms were never enforced. Germany was allowed to keep its borders intact, and nothing could be done about the fact that its population was a third greater than France's and continued to grow quickly.

The Locarno Treaties of 1925, agreed to while Churchill was Chancellor of the Exchequer, aimed to end the "thousand-year strife" between France and Germany. Britain agreed to join and support either country if it was a victim of aggression by the other, thus providing a balance of power in Europe. In addition, Germany was required to join the League of Nations. There was great hope after Locarno, and it was followed by three years of peace and growing prosperity in Europe. Yet even as the treaties were being signed, Germany was finding ways to rearm, hiding its efforts from the Allied Commission. New factories built with American loans were quickly converted to war production, and arsenals were not destroyed according to treaty obligations. Meantime Britain's leaders were assuming that no major war could be on the horizon; Churchill admits that even he was lulled into a false sense of security.

He argues that Britain, France, and the United States were too inwardly focused after the First World War, their politicians living from one election to the next, yet "the middle course adopted from desires for safety and a quiet life may be found to lead direct to the bull's-eye of disaster." In hindsight, preventing Germany's rearmament and building a strong League of Nations were simple tasks, but the leaders of the victorious powers failed at both—with terrible costs.

After the war Germany adopted a democratic constitution, but because the Weimar Republic was considered from the start to be enemy imposed, even with the revered Field Marshal Hindenburg at the helm it lacked the respect and stability that a constitutional monarchy might have provided. "It could not hold the loyalties or the imagination of the German people," Churchill writes. Into the void "there strode a maniac of ferocious genius, the repository and expression of the most virulent hatreds that have corroded the human breast—corporal Hitler."

...produces a bad man

As Hitler lay in a hospital bed in 1918 after being injured on the Western Front, "his personal failure seemed merged in the disaster of the whole German people," Churchill writes. Hitler contrasted his position and that of the German state with the prosperity of European Jewry, in his mind exploiters of the Nordic-Germanic peoples. Germany had been undermined by Jewish war profiteers, and the Russian Bolsheviks were a conspiracy of Jewish intellectuals.

Hitler came to dominate the German Workers' Party, in a year or two ousting its less charismatic leaders. His cause was assisted by the collapse of the mark and hyperinflation, which destroyed the middle class and made them ripe for any new party or figure who could channel their fury and patriotism. After a failed putsch Hitler wrote *Mein Kampf*, which called for the gathering together of all the scattered elements of the "German race," which of course did not include Jews.

Hitler's Storm Troopers or Brownshirts came up against German's traditional military caste, the Reichswehr. Both wanted Germany to rise again and avenge its defeat, but the Nazi party was more in tune with the mass of the people and the Reichswehr leaders could see this. Once an alliance was formed, nothing stood in Hitler's way. Anyone who had read *Mein Kampf* would have been in little doubt about what would happen if he became German leader, but bizarrely, at the 1932 Disarmament Conference at which Germany demanded the right to rearm, it had much support in the British press and intelligentsia on the grounds of "the equality of states." The result was a deal in which France would reduce its army from 500,000 men to 200,000 and Germany was allowed to increase its forces to the same amount. Churchill thought this was madness, and though pacifism was a Labour-Socialist movement, he lays a substantial part of the blame for allowing Germany to rearm on Stanley Baldwin, the Conservative PM who, along with Labour's Ramsay MacDonald, governed Britain in the 1920s and 1930s. Baldwin sought peace at all costs, was little interested in foreign policy, and disdained Britain's own rearmament.

Watching with alarm

The events of Hitler's 1934 "Night of the Long Knives," when 5,000-7,000 people were "liquidated," combined with vicious anti-Semitic pogroms, sent a chill through Churchill. He started agitating in parliament for Britain to bolster its air power, as Germany's air force seemed to be reaching parity (it would soon outsize the Royal Air Force). But at this time Churchill was a private MP with no power. "To be so entirely convinced and vindicated in a matter of life and death to one's country," he writes, "and not be able to make Parliament and the nation heed the warning… was an experience most painful."

Even when Baldwin subsequently admitted Britain had been misled about Germany's air force, the nation still seemed to be fixated on a new age of peace and disarmament under the League of Nations. Meanwhile, in 1935 Hitler was building 26,000-ton battle cruisers when Germany had previously agreed to build maximum 6,000-ton vessels; it would also have 57 U-boats by the late 1930s. In these years Churchill threw himself into increasing his technical military knowledge, notably the state of Britain's weapons systems. Through the Air Defence Research Committee he learned of the country's development of radar.

In 1935 Churchill hoped to be made First Lord of the Admiralty in the new government of which Baldwin was prime minister, but in a sop to the pacifists he was not given any post. Baldwin was still asserting that Britain must keep peace at any price, but in the same year, Mussolini invaded Ethiopia and joined up with Hitler, marking the end of the illusion of "collective security." Britain's diplomats were learning of the German hierarchy's contempt for Britain, portrayed in the German press as preferring a comfortable life over war glory. When Hitler's forces began occupying the Rhineland, which France had evacuated under treaty, it was the clearest sign yet of his real intentions. If Britain had teamed up with France the two countries might have finished off the German threat, perhaps for good. But the British PM reiterated that the country could not risk going to war. For Hitler domestically, the occupation was a public relations success.

In retrospect, Baldwin keeping Churchill out of the government was a blessing in disguise, as he would not be associated with its pacifist, appeasing outlook. And it allowed him, he notes, to keep writing his *History of the English-Speaking Peoples*. Ever the historian, he observes that for 400 years England's foreign policy was to "oppose the strongest, most aggressive, most dominating Power on the Continent, and particularly to prevent the Low Countries falling into the hands of such a Power." It had previously thwarted Philip ii of Spain, Louis xiv, and Napoleon. Now it would surely do for Hitler, too.

Dominos fall

Baldwin retired in 1937 and was replaced by Chamberlain, whom Churchill respected for his knowledge of foreign affairs. Yet when in 1938 Chamberlain foolishly rebuffed an offer from President Roosevelt for America to help, Churchill felt that Europe had seen its last chance to stop Germany. After Hitler annexed Austria, then invaded Czechoslovakia, Churchill issued a statement: "It is not Czechoslovakia alone which is menaced, but also the freedom and the democracy of all nations. The belief that security can be obtained by throwing a small state to the wolves is a fatal delusion."

Chamberlain met Hitler for the second time and took him at his word that Czechoslovakia was "the last territorial claim I have to make in Europe." As part of the Munich Agreement of 1938, France and Britain "allowed" Germany to annex part of Czechoslovakia that was mostly German speaking, to be named Sudetenland. Chamberlain had Hitler sign a declaration on Anglo-German relations, saying that the two countries would not go to war. He later waved this joint declaration from the windows of 10 Downing Street, saying: "I believe it is peace for our time." Churchill, however, saw right through the Munich Pact, seeing the annexation of Sudetenland as a crime, a "defeat without a war" that would only allow worse to follow. He argues that Britain and the allied countries would have been much wiser to help defend Czechoslovakia and try to nip the Nazi spread in the bud, when the German army was not fully mobilized on the Western Front. In the event, the Allies waited until the invasion of Poland to do anything, by which time Germany was stronger. Churchill's lesson for all time: If you are not willing to fight when you will win comparatively easily, you may be forced to fight later at great cost.

Until this point Russia had stood aloof from events. Then Maxim Litvinov, its Commissar for Foreign Affairs, made a formal offer of a Tripartite Alliance with France and Britain. But the British government hesitated and when Stalin lost faith in Litvinov, he was replaced by the ruthless Vyacheslav Molotov, who believed that Russia could not depend on the Western powers to fight Germany. Russia must look after itself, or come to an agreement with Hitler.

While he did not care for Stalin or the Soviet regime, Churchill believed that sometimes you must dance with a devil in order to destroy an even greater foe. After all, Soviet Russia was not, at this time, an aggressor, while Germany threatened all of Europe. Moreover, having Russia and Germany fighting on an Eastern Front would divert Germany's resources from the Western Front. For Churchill it all made sense, and he watched in dismay as the opportunity became bogged down in detail and negotiation.

Having had enough of Britain and France's prevarication, Stalin announced his intention to sign a non-aggression pact with Germany, which Churchill notes "broke upon the world like an explosion." Churchill understood that Russia was acting out of its own interests, even though it was unclear what they were. In a broadcast on 1 October 1939 he famously said: "I cannot forecast to you the action of Russia. It is a riddle wrapped in a mystery inside an enigma."

Twilight war

In summer 1939 there was a sea change in opinion in the British press and public. Thousands of hoardings urged "Churchill Must Come Back." Meanwhile, he was ensconced at Chartwell, working day and night to meet his book deadline.

When in May 1940 Churchill was finally made First Lord of the Admiralty, his knowledge of the Royal Navy was crucial. Indeed, he was the only member of the government who had held high office in the First World War. In a telling aside, Churchill relates that when the Great War ended he had ordered a large amount of heavy artillery to be safely stored in case it were ever needed again. Everyone seemed to have forgotten about these big guns, but he had them brought out and reconditioned for use. On entering the War Cabinet he also started up a statistical department of his own that could crunch all the data on the war effort. Echoing Clausewitz's famous remark about great leaders, Churchill was focused on logistics, not merely strategy.

The second half of *The Gathering Storm* is a detailed account of the early days of the war, variously called the "twilight war," the "pretend war," and the "phony war," when Britain's deployment was nearly all naval. Churchill was concerned with protecting shipping lanes and establishing the naval base of Scapa Flow in Scotland. All was strangely quiet on the Western Front. However, in April 1940 the twilight war came to a shocking end with Germany's seizure of Norway, which naively believed Hitler would respect its neutrality. The British War Cabinet approved measures to take back the ports of Narvik and Trondheim, and after much dillydallying on strategy, took back Narvik on 28 May. Though a very costly distraction to Britain in terms of lives lost and ships destroyed, the effort served to ruin Germany's navy. When Germany later attacked Britain, it had to do so only with air power.

The Norway episode further stirred up the British public into war mode, and Churchill's warnings about Germany over the years now made him seem a seer. As Chamberlain was relentlessly attacked in parliament, there were calls for a National Government to prosecute the war above party politics. Chamberlain invited Churchill to his office and noted that he had been unable to form such a government and would resign. After Lord Halifax, also present, ruled himself out, it became clear that the office would go to Churchill.

As Holland and Belgium fell to Hitler, Churchill now possessed, at 65, the chief office of state. "I felt as if I were walking with destiny," he writes, "and that all my past life had been but a preparation for this hour and for this trial."

Final comments

Churchill would be prime minister for five years and three months, before being unceremoniously dumped by the British public in the 1945 election. The electorate seemed to feel that Labour's more collectivist, socialist approach better suited hopes for a more equal Britain than the policies of an aging Tory. Though in his 70s, remarkably Churchill chose to fight on as Opposition Leader for the next six years.

It was during this period, in 1946, that he made his famous speech in Fulton, Missouri, saying: "From Stettin in the Baltic to Trieste in the Adriatic, an Iron Curtain has descended across the continent. Warsaw, Berlin, Prague, Vienna, Budapest, Belgrade, Bucharest and Sofia, all these famous cities and the populations around them lie in what I must call the Soviet sphere." Churchill clearly saw the "cold" nature of conflict in the decades ahead, and he viewed Britain's future not as part of Europe, but as a special partner to the United States in an "Anglosphere" marked by commitment to democracy, capitalism, limited government, and personal liberty. When, remarkably, he got a second tilt at the prime ministership in 1951, in his 70s, he set out to avert Britain's decline as a great power, but with little success. The second term is now little celebrated, but the state funeral for Churchill a decade later saw genuine outpourings of grief.

Winston Churchill

Winston Churchill was born in 1874 at Blenheim Palace, Oxfordshire, seat of the Dukes of Marlborough. His father Randolph was the third son of the 7th Duke and a Conservative politician, and his mother Jenny was the daughter of American financier Leonard Jerome, the "King of Wall Street."

Churchill was educated at Harrow, but was never academic and failed the entrance exams for Sandhurst Military Academy before finally being admitted. He joined a regiment of the Queen's Own Hussars in 1895 and served in campaigns in Cuba, the Punjab, and on the Nile. During the Boer War he earned fame as a newspaper correspondent, was captured, and then escaped. At 26 he became a Conservative MP, and served in the Liberal government as Colonial Under-Secretary, President of the Board of Trade, and then Home Secretary. He was First Lord of the Admiralty from 1910, Minister of Munitions from 1917, and Secretary of State for War and Air from 1919–21.

From 1924–29 Churchill was Chancellor of the Exchequer and oversaw Britain's return to the Gold Standard, which in making the pound stronger contributed to recession, deflation, and a miners' strike. He considered the decision his greatest mistake. Churchill suffered two strokes during his second term in office, and retired in 1955. After his death in 1965 the Queen gave him a state funeral. He was survived by wife Clementine and their three children.

On War

*"Policy is the guiding intelligence and war
only the instrument, not vice versa."*

*"The fact that slaughter is a horrifying spectacle must make
us take war more seriously, but not provide an excuse for
gradually blunting our swords in the name of humanity."*

*"One cannot explain the effects of a victory without taking
psychological reactions into account. Hence most of the matters
dealt with in this book are composed in equal parts of physical
and moral causes and effects. One might say that the physical
seem little more than the wooden hilt, while the moral factors are
the precious metal, the real weapon, the finely-honed blade."*

In a nutshell

With its psychological dimension war can never be a science,
and even as an extension of policy it is a blunt instrument.

In a similar vein

Norman Angell *The Great Illusion* (p 42)
Winston Churchill *The Gathering Storm* (p 90)
Hans Morgenthau *Politics Among Nations* (p 208)

CHAPTER 14

Carl von Clausewitz

Before Clausewitz, the literature on war consisted of dull handbooks on logistics, terrain, or troop maneuvers, or flowery accounts of great battles. With *Vom Kriege* ("On War"), this German general and military theorist sought to put the study of warfare onto a more scientific foundation. In the preface he writes: "I wanted at all costs to avoid every commonplace, everything obvious that has been stated a hundred times and is generally believed."

The 600-page work covers all the traditional ground of camps, marches, the order of battle, billeting troops, lines of communication, and the intricacies of battle tactics, yet what made *On War* stand out was its insights into the psychology of war and its political dimension. Lenin, Mao, and the American military intelligentsia were drawn to these aspects of the book, which is still required reading in military academies the world over. It is from Clausewitz that we have the expression "the fog of war"—"War is an area of uncertainty; three quarters of the things on which all action in War is based are lying in a fog of uncertainty to a greater or lesser extent"—and also the notion of war as policy, albeit in an extreme form.

What is noticeably missing from *On War* is the moral hand-wringing that is part of most war calculations today. Clausewitz's philosophy of force is simple expediency: If it is possible to overrun, invade, or take a territory, do it. Technology's transformation of warfare has of course dated large chunks of the book, but his thoughts on the psyche of warfare, its political context, and general strategy can still be read with profit.

What is war?

Defining it as "an act of force to compel our enemy to do our will," Clausewitz notes that war is "such a dangerous business that the mistakes which come from kindness are the very worst." If one side holds back, worrying about the loss of life, they will immediately lose the upper hand to the enemy. Bringing moderation to war, he says, is a "logical absurdity." War is by nature a matter of extremes.

Following the idealist thinkers of his time such as Kant and Hegel, Clausewitz starts from the standpoint of war as a single, pure idea, in which combatants seek an ideal, perfect outcome of total victory at minimal cost. Yet since humans themselves are far from perfect, such an outcome never happens. The full force of war is moderated by error on both sides, and by the natural caution not to expend all one's energy in a single, initial blow, but to keep some back for a second assault if the first is not successful.

Clausewitz argues that war is "never an isolated act." It does not happen spontaneously, and if we are surprised by its onset it suggests that we were seeing the potential enemy in terms of our own expectations, not reality. We can be sizing up a national leader in terms of what he should be doing according to international law, and meanwhile his tanks are invading a sovereign territory.

One of Clausewitz's headings is "In war the result is never final." Just as the commencement of war is a continuation of policy, so its ending may be, for the defeated, not really an ending. It may simply be a "transitory evil" on the road to attaining what one wants. Clausewitz's point is fascinating if considered in a larger historical and economic perspective. In the twentieth century, for instance, Germany's humiliation at the end of the First World War sowed the seeds for its resurgence under Hitler. When it was defeated once again in the Second World War, Germany's economic desolation and peaceful constitution ensured that it would direct all its energies to industrial success. The same happened in postwar Japan.

Policy turned violent

War is not simply a random act of violence brought on by emotion. Particularly when civilized nations go to war, it is always an act of *policy*. Moreover, war (as opposed to a random outbreak of violence) always lasts long enough for it to be directed, at least to some extent, by the intelligence of those conducting it. The military effort should continually come back to the policy from which it was initiated. "The political object is the goal… war is the means of reaching it," Clausewitz writes.

He follows this with a smart observation: When the motives to go to war are clear and strong, military activity will closely accord with the political objectives. But when the motives are less clear and less powerful, warfare is more likely to become protracted and its outcomes uncertain. If the nation is not united behind a war effort, the soldiers know it, and the military operations will be half-hearted.

In our time, this is arguably what happened with the war in Afghanistan and the second Iraq War, where uncertain political motives led to uncertain military outcomes. Contrast this with, for instance, the Allied fight against Hitler. So strong was the motive that all odds were overcome and all energies were focused on victory. Every war is driven by politics, but only some achieve the intended policy outcomes. This makes it all the more crucial that politicians and generals know exactly what they are going to war over, and think through whether war would achieve that.

The "total phenomenon" of war, Clausewitz says, comprises three elements, each of which involves a different actor:

- The trinity of "primordial violence, hatred and enmity"—which is the concern of the people.
- Probability and chance—a matter for the generals planning the moves.
- As an instrument of policy, subject to reason—the preserve of politicians.

Without full recognition of the power of each element, the act of going to war is flawed from the start. A successful theory must therefore look for a balance between the three, so that the motive and practice for war will be "like an object suspended between three magnets."

War is not really a science, nor is it an art. It is better seen as a part of the social dimension of human life. Like commerce, it is about a conflict of interests, and only differs in the way it is resolved. "Politics is the womb in which war develops," Clausewitz writes, "where its outlines already exist in their hidden rudimentary form, like the characteristics of living creatures in their embryos."

Strategy

Clausewitz's theory of war was based partly on his experience as a veteran of several conflicts, but also his contacts and discussion with distinguished soldiers. He believed that great soldiers and generals are born, not made, and that they make good decisions on instinct. Yet it is often necessary to persuade others or give reasons for one's actions, and this is where a "theory of major operations" (or strategy) becomes important.

Defense has much the greater power in war than offense, Clausewitz repeatedly asserts, and the strategy of wearing down the enemy by making the conflict more costly than it is worth is often used by a weak power against a strong one. Does it have the heart for it or the will for it? This is what a resistance or smaller army tries to test with a larger foe.

Yet the chief strategy of war will always be total destruction of the enemy's armed forces. Other strategies may suffice if the stakes are smaller, but destruction is the starting point. All strategy is ultimately about the basics of combat in the engagements that make up the war. All of a soldier's training and effort come down to being ready to fight at the right place and at the right time, and to be in a position to annihilate the enemy forces. This is true even if no fighting occurs, because it is more often than not judgments about the opposition's strengths that decide matters.

Psychology of war

The material considerations of war are simple enough for anyone to learn; more challenging is the intellectual aspect, which must take account of the complexity of an unlimited number of factors working in real time, and of course of human nature. Generals can take most inspiration from the "intangibles" of battle, Clausewitz says—the esprit de corp of an army that helps it overcome a much bigger foe, for instance—and will learn to become more effective not by reading critical studies of war, but through "broad impressions, and flashes of intuition."

War is thought to be a matter of prudent calculation, but in the end it is always a gamble because it revolves around human psychology. War, Clausewitz says, "deals with living and with moral forces," including courage, boldness, even foolhardiness. Though he hoped that his book would be the first scientific study of war, he does not claim that war itself can be scientifically prosecuted, because "no other human activity is so continuously or universally bound up with chance." Warfare can only be an exercise of assessing probabilities, guessing, and hoping that luck will be on your side. Success involves getting into the mind of the enemy—hardly an exact science, but it can make the difference between winning and losing.

It is easy enough to work out the objective in war and devise a strategy to serve it; what is more difficult is to stick to the aims and plan despite a thousand diversions. There is plenty of room for fear, apprehension, and doubt to creep in, and generals can also be swayed by vanity, ambition, and vindictiveness. All such things can leave the original strategy forgotten and the purpose of particular engagements unclear.

Clausewitz apologizes to the reader who expected to find a scientific treatise on war and instead is presented with truths about human nature. The reality is that "in war more than anywhere else things do not turn out as we expect." A general's trade is uncertainty. He is bombarded with reports all day long and must decide which are true and which false, which ones matter and which do not. He must put up with disobedience, ill will, laziness, and accidents that could not have been foreseen. Along with courage and strength he must have perseverance, keeping on the course he has set unless compelling reasons arise to change it.

A great commander is distinguished by his mastery of time and space. He will, as the saying goes, choose his battles wisely, determining the right conditions, time, and precise place where he will launch the full might of resources under his command. The good general will actively seek to reach a point where he has to concentrate all of his forces in a single blow. This is risky, yet it brings the greatest chance of victory.

Final comments

Where Clausewitz is problematic for the contemporary reader is in his assumption that war is good for the character of people and society. At the end of Chapter 6, for instance, he says that only war is capable of instilling boldness in a people, and in counteracting the "softness and the desire for ease which debase people in times of growing prosperity and increasing trade."

This belief in the "character-building" qualities of war and the assumption that military strength is the basis of national wealth are exactly what Angell tore apart in *The Great Illusion* (see commentary on p 42). Both led to the horrors of the First World War. That Germany thought only in terms of what was good for it, and that it was prepared to run roughshod over other nations to achieve its interests, was entirely in accord with Clausewitz's ethics-free zone. However, the nineteenth century in which he was writing was a time of relative peace, and the great battles he describes were small fry compared to the conflagrations of the twentieth century.

On the plus side, Clausewitz's "three elements" theory of war does illuminate many of the failings of contemporary warfare. Unless the people, the military, and the politicians are broadly united in the reason for going to war, the war effort itself is likely to be ineffectual (cue Vietnam and Afghanistan).

Carl von Clausewitz

Carl Philipp Gottfried von Clausewitz was born in 1780 in Burg bei Magdeburg, Prussia. At the age of 13 he became a cadet in the Prussian army, and the following year was already on the battlefield against France. He was promoted to lieutenant while still in his teens, and at 21 was admitted to the Kriegsakademie (national war academy) in Berlin. After graduating with the top ranking in his year, he became aide-de-camp to Prince August.

In 1806 Clausewitz was captured by the French and spent two years as a prisoner, but on release became assistant to General Gerhard von Scharnhorst in his reorganization of the Prussian army. In 1810 he became a professor at the war academy, and married Countess Marie von Brühl, but his tenure was interrupted by more war service including, in 1815, the Battle of Waterloo. In 1818 he was made a Major-General and named director of the Kriegsakademie, and for most of the following decade he was able to devote himself to research. However, in 1830 and 1831 he was back in charge of Prussian troops in Poland, and fell victim to a cholera outbreak. He died in Breslau in 1831. The publication of On War *was organized by his wife, whose preface appears in most editions.*

The End of History and the Last Man

"What is emerging victorious, in other words, is not so much liberal practice, as the liberal idea. That is to say, for a very large part of the world, there is now no ideology with pretensions to universality that is in a position to challenge liberal democracy, and no universal principle of legitimacy other than the sovereignty of the people."

"The growth of liberal democracy, together with its companion, economic liberalism, has been the most remarkable macropolitical phenomenon of the last four hundred years."

In a nutshell

Liberal democracy will prove to be the only viable form of political organization because it is based on the universal desire for freedom and recognition.

In a similar vein

Lord Acton *Essays on Freedom and Power* (p 20)
Daron Acemoglu & James A. Robinson *Why Nations Fail* (p 26)
F.A. Hayek *The Road to Serfdom* (p 126)
John Micklethwait & Adrian Wooldridge *The Fourth Revolution* (p 196)

CHAPTER 15

Francis Fukuyama

When in 1989 Francis Fukuyama wrote an article for the American political journal *National Interest*, "The end of history?," it provoked such interest that a mainstream publisher asked him to turn the idea into a book. Three years later *The End of History and the Last Man* made its author into a major public intellectual. Fukuyama's idea that history had ended, in the sense that the world had reached a point where liberal democracy had proven itself to be the only viable form of political organization, seemed believable at the time, not long after the fall of the Berlin Wall and the collapse of Soviet Bloc communism. But as the 1990s proceeded, major events such as Saddam Hussein's invasion of Kuwait and the massacre in Beijing's Tiananmen Square seemed to make a mockery of the idea.

Yet much of the criticism, Fukuyama said, came from a misunderstanding of his use of the term "history." He never said that big events would no longer occur, only that history as "a single, coherent, evolutionary process," in the way that Hegel and Marx saw it, had reached its end point. Humankind had progressed from cave-dwelling and tribal government, to slavery and feudalism, to theocracy and monarchy, to liberal society and laissez-faire capitalism, with each form of society attempting to solve major problems of equality and prosperity. Because it was free of the inherent "defects and irrationalities" of authoritarian and collectivist forms of government, Fukuyama argued, liberal democracy would prove itself to be, in the long term, the only truly sustainable form of government. Of course liberal democracies have plenty of problems, but they are problems only of "the incomplete implementation of the twin principles of liberty and equality," he writes. One cannot improve on a system that aims to deliver material well-being at the same time as largely preserving the freedom of its members.

Fukuyama admits that the very idea of history being part of a coherent, directional process is ridiculous to many people, particularly in light of Hitler, Stalin, and Pol Pot. But all of these horrors (today we might add Bin Laden) can mean that we miss the wood for the trees. Over the long term, he argues, the movement toward greater freedom and enfranchisement is unmistakable.

The liberal idea

The unexpected, irrational brutality of twentieth-century events stands in stark contrast to the relative rationality, peace, and optimism of the preceding hundred years, in which there was a belief that freedom and prosperity would naturally increase and spread around the world. Indeed, the 1910–11 *Encyclopaedia Britannica* wrote under the heading "Torture" that "the whole subject is one of only historical interest as far as Europe is concerned." Norman Angell famously predicted on the very eve of the First World War that free trade had made war between developed countries irrational and obsolete (see commentary on p 42).

Yet the Great War shattered the idea of "progress." What was the point of advanced civilization if it was put to the use of killing men of the same age who happened to be from a neighboring country? If this war did not end the illusion that there was a positive direction to history, the war that followed certainly did, with modern science employed to gas millions of people and eliminate whole cities in an instant. At the same time, totalitarian states of unparalleled brutality were created that could control the lives and even the thought of millions. In light of the prevalence of both fascism and communism, as well as apparently enlightened Europe's predilection for self-destruction, Fukuyama asks—playing devil's advocate—is it not mere ethnocentrism to believe that liberal democracy is the final type of political organization that the world is moving toward? Perhaps democracy would prove to be a fleeting phenomenon in the course of history.

While Secretary of State in the 1970s, Henry Kissinger considered it wishful thinking that communism would fade, and accepted that the United States would be in permanent Cold War with the Soviet Union. Virtually everyone (scholars, journalists, politicians on both left and right) believed in the stability, permanence, and even legitimacy of such regimes through the 1970s and 1980s. At the same time there was "a profound lack of confidence in democracy," Fukuyama notes; it might simply be a "Western thing," and communism might even be a better cultural fit for the Chinese, Russians, and Cubans, whose histories showed they were not interested in liberal democracy. Besides, if leftist regimes in poor countries were doing good things like improving health and education, was political freedom not a reasonable price to pay?

Fukuyama admits that if you look only at a 10- or even 20-year period there is little pattern to the prevalence of liberal democracy, but over the scope of history there is a very clear trend. It has been "the most remarkable macropolitical phenomenon of the last four hundred years," he says, taking root far beyond its traditional homes of Europe and North America, and cannot be seen as Western cultural imperialism. It has often lost ground to new forms of political organization such as fascism, communism, or authoritarian capitalism, only to see these implode over time. Liberty and equality are adopted or kept because they are seen to work best in delivering peace, stability, and prosperity over the long term.

Can you recognize me?

Hegel's "First Man" wanted to be recognized by other humans, and indeed could take action that went against his instinct for survival, risking his life in battles for glory, not only resources. Fukuyama's "Last Man," in contrast, is the modern person whose life is so good in a material sense that he or she is not prepared to risk anything. Yet humans are ultimately not driven by economics alone, Fukuyama argues, but by a non-rational drive that Hegel called the "struggle for recognition." That people are still prepared to die for the sake of freedom, from Tiananmen Square to Tahrir Square, is evidence of this. Fukuyama's critique of communism is not simply that it did not match up to capitalism in generating wealth, but that it did not give full recognition to the uniqueness of the individual. The struggle for rights and recognition may seem surprising in the contemporary world, which appears so consumerist, yet it continues to shape politics. Scotland's recent drive for independence had little economic basis; it was a wish to be recognized as culturally and socially different from Britain. The same is true of every region or ethnic grouping that has sought to secede from a larger political union.

Democracy, wealth, and stability

Fukuyama mostly agrees with Seymour Martin Lipset's theory that there is a strong empirical link between stable democracy and economic development, noting that the acceptance of technology and modern science invariably leads to industrialization, which in turn throws up a rising middle class and consumerism. Yet the evidence shows that such a process can lead *either* to greater political freedoms (that is, liberal democracy) or to a bureaucratic-authoritarian state that delivers a rising standard of living but still keeps a firm grip on the population. Fukuyama argues that if a country wants to put economic growth first, it is probably better off combining liberal economics with an authoritarian state (exactly as China has done since he wrote the book; historical examples include Meiji Japan, Imperial Germany, and Chile under Pinochet). Democracy alone is not a means to national wealth, because special interest groups are always seeking protection, which creates inefficiencies. The welfare state that voters demand leads to large public debt and deficits, and politicians are pressured to prop up declining industries. In contrast, a nation that has none of these limitations can "go for growth" in an extraordinary way, by a combination of social discipline and openness to new technology and innovation—that is, the best of both worlds.

Final comments

Intellectuals have tended to support pessimistic universal histories of human-kind, reviling any approach that suggests a positive direction to history. Fukuyama says that this pessimism is "something of a pose," suggesting pro-fundity and seriousness, and is taken on as lightly and groundlessly as the triumphal optimism of the nineteenth century. Yet we need not be blindly pessimistic *or* optimistic, we only have to look at the data on economic and political liberalism around the world. Despite a fall in the number of coun-tries classed as "free" in recent years (see FreedomHouse.org), graphs cov-ering the last 200 years show a steeply inclining freedom axis. Not only has democracy appeared where no one ever expected it to, but many apparently rock-like authoritarian regimes have crumbled. More than this, with the obvi-ous failures of absolute monarchy, communism, aristocracy, theocracy, and fascism, there is today "a complete absence of theoretical alternatives to liberal democracy," Fukuyama says. Even oppressive regimes pay at least lip service to liberal ideas, holding (sham) elections, putting on a show of a "parliament," and proclaiming "free" speech (media companies owned or controlled by the state). Writing in the *New York Times* in 2008 ("They can only go so far"), Fukuyama notes, "Most autocrats, including Putin and Chávez, still feel that they have to conform to the outward rituals of democracy even as they gut its substance."

An obvious fly in Fukuyama's ointment is the success of modern China, Singapore, and other countries flying the authoritarian capitalism flag. Have they not made his thesis obsolete, particularly when liberal democracies from the US to Europe have had a bad few years, either in economic terms or with political institutions turned to gridlock? State capitalism seems to be a clear and increasingly attractive alternative to liberal democracy. Yet time will tell. As people become richer they tend to demand more rights, and to resent the inequality that comes with crony capitalism. Singapore's dedication to the rule of law is a protection against revolution, but nothing is certain with China or the Middle Eastern oil kingdoms. Even Aristotle noted that democracy, although messy and inefficient, is more stable than either oligarchy or tyranny.

Some might say that Islam, with its universal appeal beyond nation or ethnicity, is an alternative to liberal democracy, and indeed, 20 years since Fukuyama was writing, the attempts of groups such as Islamic State to create a new world caliphate unite many extremist Muslims in their hatred of "deca-dent" liberal democracy. However, he argued then that such extremism would never take off given that the larger Muslim world was divided by sectarianism and nationality. Rather than Islam spreading beyond its current cultural territories, there was a much greater likelihood to him that liberal ideas would grow in Islamic countries. "Part of the reason for the current, fundamentalist revival," he said, "is the strength of the perceived threat from liberal, Western values to traditional Islamic societies." He was right. There is already a backlash against Islamist government in some Muslim countries, including Egypt and Tunisia, which have seen that it does not work. Time is likely to show that the separation of church and state is not merely a western concern, but basic to good government the world over.

There will be more big events and more regimes to come that will seem to prove Fukuyama's thesis wrong, but even these are likely to be a reaction against the compelling logic of liberal democracy, which, among all forms of government, takes the most account of human nature in terms of our deep desire for freedom and recognition. All the others may seem to work, but only for a while.

Francis Fukuyama

Born in 1952 in Chicago, Francis Fukuyama is a third-generation Japanese-American whose father Yoshio was a sociologist of religion. He grew up in New York City and Pennsylvania, and took his undergraduate degree at Cornell University, majoring in classics. After a period studying comparative literature at Yale, he began a political science degree at Harvard, where his teachers included Samuel Huntington, author of The Clash of Civilizations and the Remaking of World Order *(see commentary on p 136). After taking his PhD Fukuyama worked at the Rand Corporation, a policy think tank.*

From 1996 to 2000 he was Professor of Public Policy at George Mason University, then for a decade Professor of Political Economy at Johns Hopkins University. He is now Senior Fellow at the Center on Democracy, Development, and the Rule of Law at the Institute for International Studies at Stanford University. Other books include Trust: The Social Virtues and the Creation of Prosperity *(1996);* Our Posthuman Future *(2003), a fierce criticism of biotechnologies that challenges the basic idea of liberal democracy that all people are born equal;* America at the Crossroads *(2006), a history of American neoconservatism;* The Origins of Political Order *(2011), on what creates a stable state; and* Political Order and Political Decay: From the Industrial Revolution to the Globalization of Democracy *(2014). The last two books take account of events since* The End of History and the Last Man, *and emphasize the sheer time it takes for countries to develop stable liberal democratic institutions.*

An Autobiography: The Story of My Experiments with Truth

"Those who say that religion has nothing to do with politics do not know what religion means."

"It is quite proper to resist and attack a system, but to resist and attack its author is tantamount to resisting and attacking oneself. For we are all tarred with the same brush, and are children of one and the same Creator, and as such the divine powers within us are infinite."

"Remember that all through history, there have been tyrants and murderers, and for a time, they seem invincible. But in the end, they always fall. Always."

In a nutshell

Power can be built on an unassailable moral stance.

In a similar vein

CHAPTER 16

Mohandas K. Gandhi

At the start of his autobiography, Gandhi points out that it is no mere description of events, but the story of his inner life and influences. These include Sanskrit author Patanjali, Hindu philosopher Vivekananda, and the Bhagavad Gita, which he describes as a "dictionary of conduct" that led him to most of his principles. He also made a point of reading the Koran, and among secular authors found life-changing ideas in Leo Tolstoy's *The Kingdom of God Is within You* (1894) and John Ruskin's *Unto This Last* (1860), which inspired his setting up of a commune, Tolstoy Farm, in Transvaal, South Africa in 1910. Thoreau's *Civil Disobedience* (1849; see p 286), and Plato's *Apology*, recounting the trial of Socrates, were also influences.

Most of the autobiography is devoted to Gandhi's youth and the 21 years of his adult life that he spent living in South Africa, and it stops in 1921. By the time it was published he was well known for his civil disobedience campaigns and had spent time in jail, but events such as the Salt March and international notoriety and fame still lay in the future.

Martin Luther King was fascinated by Gandhi's story and his philosophy of non-violent resistance. The concept of *satyagraha*, the "truth force" (which Gandhi also called the "love force") allowed King once again to consider non-violence as a way to social reform; it chimed with Jesus' command to love one's enemies and "turn the other cheek" if necessary. King came to the view that "true pacifism is not unrealistic submission to evil power," rather "a courageous confrontation of evil by the power of love." It was better to be the recipient of violence than the one who inflicts it, because it creates a sense of shame in the opponent, which eventually causes a transformation in thinking. Here King sums up perfectly the power of Gandhi: how he was able to bring about the end of an empire, and a shift in our understanding of power itself.

Spiritual roots of political strategies

The first hint about the true nature of Gandhi's book is the odd wording of the title. A regular politician might have called it something like "An Autobiography: How I Saved India from British Rule," but instead the title is *An Autobiography: The Story of My Experiments with Truth*.

The first of his experiments was vegetarianism, which goes from a commitment to his family (his Bania caste was vegetarian) to a moral mission, and he develops the view that sexual and dietary restrictions are important in becoming free of animal drives and base concerns. The purifying exercise of "going without," Gandhi came to believe, provides a moral force and strength of purpose that can get the universe on one's side. He was in his mid-30s when, with his wife Kasturbai's agreement, Gandhi took the vow of *brahmacharya*, or celibacy.

The concept that led directly to his political force was *ahimsa*. In Hindi, *himsa* means the perpetual destruction and pain of normal existence—the way of the world. We can, however, adopt an outlook of compassion—*ahimsa*—which requires us to do all we can to avoid the recurrence of suffering and aggression. Gandhi believed that *ahimsa* had to be central to a quest for truth, because any effort would ultimately be self-defeating if it involved mental or physical injury to our fellow sentient beings. He had also discovered the principle of *satyagraha*—non-cooperation or non-violent struggle. Unlike normal conflict, in which we become inflamed by emotion, the action of *satyagraha* is based on a detached stubbornness that gains strength from the quality of its principles. Gandhi first practiced it in his various battles for the rights of Indians living in South Africa, and his success inspired a young African freedom fighter by the name of Nelson Mandela.

Gandhi's "simple living" philosophy was underpinned by the principle of *aparigraha*, non-possession. This incorporates the idea of trusteeship, or wisely utilizing goods for the benefit of all. Gandhi came to believe that possessions only create the illusion of security and certainty, which in reality cannot be provided by anything or anyone except God. Despite being quite well off in his barrister days, he made a point of cutting his own hair and doing his own laundry. When his ashram was established near Ahmedabad, he controversially made everyone get involved in cleaning the latrines. This was a time when only "untouchables" did this work, and the event was the genesis of the emancipation of the Dalit class.

Apart from the triumph of self-rule itself, Gandhi's campaigns on the rights of women, ending child marriage, the status of "untouchables," and poverty all left a strong mark on India. Less successful were his ideas about turning the country into a nation of cottage industries and sustainable village communities, which, although fashionable today, would have kept India in the economic dark ages.

Final comments

Politics is ultimately the battleground of deep inner beliefs about reality. Is power the fundamental fact in the world, or is it love? Which tends to win out in the end? Gandhi showed that a *satyagraha* approach is power when undertaken correctly. As the British found, it is almost impossible to defeat a political movement that uses it, since it seems to have all the time and resolve in the world. Yet as Joseph Lelyveld argues in *Great Soul* (2012), Gandhi's struggle was not just with the British, but with Hindu nationalists. Not for them a New Society based on compassion and toleration; they imagined India becoming a great independent power, and so the secession of a big chunk of the nation in 1947 seemed a great blow. So long under colonial domination, now it was all being thrown away, partly thanks to Gandhi's principle of religious harmony.

Today there is another stirring in Hindu nationalism, to which India's leader Narendra Modi is sympathetic, yet it is Gandhi's tolerant, secular vision of India that still holds sway. On the other hand, Gandhian principles often seem lost in India's burgeoning economy and growing political power. If he were alive today, the Mahatma (an appellation, meaning "great soul," that he never liked) might ask: What did we achieve our freedom for, to become a nation of consumers? Why do we need to mimic the West?

Gandhi's dislike of modernity and the profit motive arguably makes him a patron saint not only of peace movements, but of today's anti-capitalist and anti-corporatist crusades. Pankaj Mishra (in the *New Yorker*, May 2011) suggests that Gandhi failed in bringing about the kind of ecological, spiritual paradise of which he dreamed, and may have been disappointed that India became just another emerging economy with no claims to moral leadership. Yet Gandhi's ideas always transcended India itself—his gift to the world was a reminder of the power of cooperative action to end wrongs, wherever they are.

Mohandas K. Gandhi

Mohandas Karamchand Gandhi was born in 1869 in Porbandar on the northeastern coast of India. His father, Kaba, was a local politician. A bright student, he studied law in London and then worked in an Indian law firm in Natal, South Africa. After two decades there he returned to India in 1915 and threw himself into the Swaraj or home rule movement. He became leader of the Indian National Congress in 1920, and his non-violent campaigns against British rule landed him in prison in 1922 and 1924. The 200-mile Salt March to coastal Dandi in 1930 was a symbolic protest at the government's monopoly on the commodity. Three months after Britain had finally given India its independence in 1947, Gandhi was unable to prevent the Partition of India and Pakistan. One of his last acts was a hunger strike to protest the Indian government's reluctance to give Pakistan its fair share of resources. The funeral in New Delhi after his assassination in 1948 by a Hindu nationalist fanatic attracted two million people, and prime minister Jawaharlal Nehru lamented that "Bapu," or the father of the nation, would no longer be around to guide it.

Anarchism and Other Essays

"Anarchism stands for a social order based on the free grouping of individuals for the purpose of producing real social wealth; an order that will guarantee to every human being free access to the earth and full enjoyment of the necessities of life, according to individual desires, tastes, and inclinations."

"Only in freedom can man grow to his full stature. Only in freedom will he learn to think and move, and give the very best in him. Only in freedom will he realize the true force of the social bonds which knit men together, and which are the true foundation of a normal social life."

In a nutshell

People are capable of organizing themselves to live fruitful, meaningful lives. State, religion, and capitalism provide a moral veneer covering a framework of exploitation.

In a similar vein

CHAPTER 17

Emma Goldman

Radicals can often trace their awakening to a particular event. For Emma Goldman, a Lithuanian immigrant who had come to America for a better life, it was a rally of workers in Haymarket Square, Chicago in 1886, at which an explosion killed seven policemen. No evidence of who placed the bomb was ever found, but eight anarchists were arrested, only one of whom had actually been present. With the press and police baying for blood, the presiding Judge Gary said: "Not because you have caused the Haymarket bomb, but because you are Anarchists, you are on trial." All were sentenced to death, and the affair aroused passions around the world. A year later, four of the anarchists were hanged, one killed himself, and three were kept in prison. The Haymarket affair was marked by annual memorials for decades afterwards, and the "Chicago Eight" remain a symbol of state willingness to crush dissent even in a "free" society, and to put people on trial for their ideas.

Though on the surface Goldman's life was devoted to highlighting the dark side of the American Dream, in fact her political philosophy was universal, shaped by anarchist thinkers and activists including Pierre Joseph Proudhon (famous for the line "property is theft"), Mikhail Bakunin (a Russian revolutionary who believed that communism was simply a step on the path to anarchism), and Peter Kropotkin (who was imprisoned for five years in France for his anarchist beliefs). Goldman was also one of America's early feminists, challenging women to question the basic institutions of marriage and religion that she believed kept them captive, body and mind.

Anarchism in a nutshell

Goldman defines anarchism as "The philosophy of a new social order based on liberty unrestricted by man-made law; the theory that forms of government rest on violence, and are therefore wrong and harmful, as well as unnecessary." Later she describes it as "the philosophy of the sovereignty of the individual." This puts it in direct opposition to the state, and therefore only revolution can make the philosophy manifest.

Since time immemorial, she notes, people have been taught that if they want to progress, they must give up some power to society and state. But for the anarchist this is the wrong way around. People will only live together in a just way if the individual is given prominence, if before all else they have the chance to grow. The individual is "the heart of society," and society is the lungs that extend and support it.

To Goldman, anarchism is a great liberator from two forces that keep most people captive: religion, which makes them subservient to an imaginary God; and property, which corrupts individuals and divides societies. People's lust for more property, she says, is a lust for power, specifically the power to enslave and degrade others. People talk of the abstraction of "national wealth," but what use is it, she asks, if people can continue to live in squalor and filth while there is little concern for their dignity?

The modern state exists for the purpose of human bondage. It does not care for the individual, only that the system runs like clockwork, that laws are obeyed, and that the exchequer is full. "The State is the altar of political freedom and, like the religious altar, it is maintained for the purpose of human sacrifice," Goldman writes.

She runs through the usual counterarguments to anarchism. Rather than the state maintaining order, most "order" is maintained by terror and submission, with "the entire arsenal of government—laws, police, soldiers, the courts, legislatures, prisons… strenuously engaged in 'harmonizing' the most antagonistic elements in society." As to the argument that the state prevents crime, Goldman replies that all taxes are a form of stealing, and wars and capital punishment are the biggest of crimes. As long as people are made to do what they hate, they will look for other ways to earn their living. She compares the notion that it is natural for people to live in an organized structure to animals confined in a zoo. As it is the only life they know, they cannot imagine what it is like to live freely and powerfully in nature. In the same way, people cannot know what they are missing by living narrow, submissive lives.

Goldman shares Thoreau's distrust of voting and democracy, noting that the parliamentary process had done little to fix social wrongs and inequalities. Labor laws and child protection laws had rarely been followed, and exploitation was rife. Parliament is simply a stage, she contends, for the ambition of politicians to be played out, while the people gullibly go on thinking that their representatives are achieving something.

In her time, she notes, 50,000 Americans were being killed while at work every year, and 100,000 maimed or injured, all for the sake of excess profits. Moreover, modern methods of production meant that the worker was reduced to an automaton, with no room for initiative, easily replaceable, and paid at barely subsistence level. "Strange to say," she writes, "there are people who extol this deadening method of centralized production as the proudest achievement of our age. They fail utterly to realize that if we are to continue in machine subserviency, our slavery is more complete than was our bondage to the King." Anarchism would result in the end of such conditions because there would be no need for massive profits to be made. Instead, people would choose what sort of work they do and it would be a source of pride, an expression of their individuality.

Political violence

Unfortunately, Goldman observes, the masses are coerced and brainwashed into believing that their current condition is the best they can hope for. It is up to "intelligent minorities" to awaken them, and sometimes effective activism requires violent means. People who revolt do so not out of a wish for violence; quite the contrary, they feel so downtrodden and ignored, and they burn so deeply for justice, that this desire simply finds expression. Yet because anarchists seem to threaten every vested interest, the backlash against them is often terrible. At the very least, anarchists and socialists lose their jobs due to their opinions, but such is their threat to the system that many lose their lives.

"Compared with the wholesale violence of capital and government, political acts of violence are but a drop in the ocean," she maintains. "That so few resist is the strongest proof how terrible must be the conflict between their souls and unbearable social iniquities." She likens political violence to storms and lightning—destructive, but in some ways a necessity that brings relief.

Status of women

Goldman stood out from the Suffragette movement by insisting that votes for women would not greatly improve their lives. The more crucial question was whether society allowed women power over their own bodies: to decide whether they wanted to have children or not, and to be able to defy the strictures of religion and social convention. She lambasts America's puritan values, which either elevated women to the status of angels who had no sexual feelings, or saw them as "fallen" and therefore the subject of disdain and abuse.

Marriage, she says, is "primarily an economic arrangement, an insurance pact," differing only from a normal life insurance agreement in that it is more binding and exacting. With the "premium" being her husband, she pays dearly for it with "her name, her privacy, her self-respect, her very life… the marriage insurance condemns her to life-long dependency, to parasitism, to complete uselessness, individual as well as social." Goldman contrasts this state of bondage to love itself, which is life-affirming and free of social conventions.

"The most dangerous woman in America"

In the deep recession that began in 1893, hundreds of banks failed, thousands of businesses closed, and 3 million were unemployed out of a labor force of 15 million. There was no government relief or safety net, only soup kitchens. When Goldman gave a speech to a mass demonstration in New York, urging mothers to take food from stores without paying if they needed food, she was sent to prison for a year for "incitement to riot." While inside she devoured books by Emerson, Thoreau, Whitman, and Mill, and studied medical textbooks with a view to becoming a midwife. After release she went on a lecture tour of Britain and Europe, meeting Louise Michel, Peter Kropotkin, and other anarchists, and gained nursing qualifications in Vienna. Back in the United States she began working as a midwife along with more speaking, and then in 1899 returned to Paris and took a central role in the International Anarchist Congress.

In 1901 President McKinley was assassinated by Leon Czolgosz, an unemployed man who claimed to have been inspired by Goldman's speeches. Czolgosz had tried to become part of Goldman's anarchist set in Chicago, but they had rebuffed him, believing him to be a government spy. She was interrogated, and the press painted her as instrumental in the assassination, but no evidence was found linking her to Czolgosz, who was executed.

In 1906 she started *Mother Earth*, a national radical magazine, and fellow anarchist and lover Alexander Berkman, famous for his unsuccessful attempt to assassinate industrialist Henry Clay Frick in 1892, became its editor. Goldman crisscrossed America for years giving talks and getting support for the publication. After campaigning with Margaret Sanger for birth control, in 1916 she was imprisoned for two weeks for violating the Comstock Law, which forbade dissemination of "obscene, lewd, or lascivious articles." The following year she and Berkman were put on trial for campaigning against military conscription, but defended their right to free speech. During the trial Goldman asked how America could claim to be a beacon of democracy abroad while gagging people at home. The pair were sentenced to two years in prison, and were seen as such a threat to national security that during the Red Scare of 1919–20 they were deported to Russia with other radicals.

Initially Goldman and Berkman were enthusiastic about the Bolshevik Revolution, but as they traveled around, their reservations about the corruption and power of central governments of any stripe were borne out. Lenin, for instance, told them that freedom of speech had to be sacrificed in times of revolution. Despairing of Russia, they moved to Riga, then settled in Berlin.

Goldman moved to London in 1924, and after an initially big welcome by leftist thinkers including Bertrand Russell, Rebecca West, and H.G. Wells, she lost support because of her condemnation of the Soviet experiment. She was allowed to return to the United States for a lecture tour, but was forbidden to speak on current events. She set up home in Canada, and continued to write articles for American and international newspapers from Toronto.

Final comments

Given that America, more than any other nation, is identified with the capitalist spirit, the extent to which anarchist, socialist, and communist organizations flourished there between 1890 and the Second World War is surprising. This was partly due to the spread of ideas from Europe, the source of nearly all the new immigrants, and partly due to their disillusionment with a country that had promised so much but delivered so little. As a young factory worker, Goldman felt that both the Tsarists of Russia and the plutocrats of America were concerned to keep the proletariat in their place. Humanity would only reach its potential when individuals were allowed to flower, rather than being seen as means to some economic or political end.

Goldman believed that patriotism was, like religion, a fraud. The world is divided by arbitrary boundaries, and we are taught to want to fight for "our" country, while the state takes billions from the public in order to fund wars that have nothing to with us and our well-being, but protect and further the commercial interests of the ruling classes. She decried the millions of dollars spent by American cities to celebrate and honor the new US naval fleet, for instance, money that could have been spent on keeping people from starvation.

Goldman never gave prescriptions for how anarchism might work in practice. Her main target was the hypocrisy of a "free" America that paid lip service to free speech, allowed companies to treat workers as chattels, and threatened social stigma for any woman who dared to live differently.

Emma Goldman

Born in 1869 in Kaunas, Lithuania, from 7–13 Emma Goldman lived with her grandmother in Konigsberg, Prussia. The family then moved to St Petersburg, hoping to start a business and avoid anti-Semitism. In 1886 she emigrated to America with her older sister Helene, and found work as a seamstress with long hours and low pay. The following year she moved to New York City, throwing herself into the anarchist cause. She became a protégé of Johann Most, publisher of the anarchist newspaper Freiheit *("political freedom"), and later joined the activist group Autonomy. Goldman organized female workers in the cloakmakers' strike of 1889, and headed the anarchist contingent in the May Day demonstration for workers' rights of 1891.*

In her last years she supported the anarchists in the Spanish Civil War, and spent two years in a cottage in Saint-Tropez writing her autobiography, partly supported by Peggy Guggenheim. Living My Life *was published in 1931. Goldman died in Toronto in 1940 and was buried near the Haymarket martyrs in Chicago.*

The Federalist Papers

"The powers delegated by the proposed Constitution to the federal government are few and defined. Those which are to remain in the State governments are numerous and indefinite. The former will be exercised principally on external objects, as war, peace, negotiation and foreign commerce; with which the power of taxation will, for the most part, be connected. The powers reserved to the several states will extend to all the objects which, in the ordinary course of affairs, concern the lives, liberties, and properties of the people, and the internal order, improvement, and prosperity of the state."

In a nutshell

A unified republic with popular representation, strong executive powers and an independent judiciary is inherently more stable and prosperous than a loose confederation of states.

In a similar vein

Niccolò Machiavelli *Discourses on Livy* (p 174)
Thomas Paine *Common Sense* (p 238)
Alexis de Tocqueville *Democracy in America* (p 292)

CHAPTER 18

Alexander Hamilton, John Jay, & James Madison

G iven how revered the American Constitution is now, it is easy to overlook just how fragile its existence was at its birth. In 1776 Thomas Paine wrote: "If there is any true cause of fear respecting independence, it is because no plan is yet laid down. Men do not see their way out." Many Americans who wanted their country to be free of British rule were at the same time apprehensive about the *form* of government that would emerge, particularly whether a fledgling republic would quickly go the way of tyranny. The Constitution that emerged from the Convention of 1787 required ratification by each of the 13 states, but some, such as New York, were loathe to adopt it for fear that it would erode their self-determination and existing privileges. Framers of the Constitution Alexander Hamilton (1755–1804) and James Madison (1751–1836) felt that a public relations assault was necessary to promote it to the American public, and, together with prominent lawyer John Jay (1745–1829), began writing anonymous articles for New York newspapers under the name Publius. As the savior of the Roman republic and the wise steward who put lawgiver Solon's original laws into practice, Publius was a good *nom de plume*. In total 85 essays were published, of which Hamilton wrote 51. The quality and number of the essays within a short space of time make them a remarkable achievement.

Published in book form as *The Federalist* in 1788 (now known as *The Federalist Papers*), the first volume included essays advocating a strong federal structure with a clear center, so that there could be no split into Southern and Northern Confederacies, and also looked at defense and the protection of life and property. The second volume discussed the separation of powers and the accountability of government, its representatives and its officers.

Thomas Paine's polemics arguably had more of an impact on the average person than *The Federalist Papers*, and the fact that George Washington and

Benjamin Franklin supported the Constitution likely had more of an effect on the public than lengthy newspaper articles. Yet in their reasoned tones, appealing to the reader's logic and slowly building a watertight case for the Constitution and its powers, the *Papers* commanded respect. Their attention to detail allayed suspicion that the new republic was a power grab that would end up like a local version of the British monarchy, with a president instead of a king, or another imperial Rome in the making. The *Papers* became the first great American contribution to political theory and philosophy, and have been cited countless times by the US Supreme Court in cases where it is necessary to ascertain the real intentions of the makers of the Constitution.

Confederation vs. unified republic

One cannot understand the motivation for *The Federalist Papers* and the new Constitution without knowing something of the Articles of Confederation, effectively the first Constitution of the United States that was in place through most of the 1780s. The Articles were not so much the constitution of a sovereign republic but the legal basis of a "league of friendship" between the 13 independent and sovereign states. Operating through a Congress giving each state a single vote, the federation had the power to wage war, conduct diplomacy, create and borrow money, and run a postal service, but was severely lacking in other powers. It was not able to raise taxes, build up an army, or regulate commerce (domestic or foreign), and it provided for no federal executive or judiciary. Dependent on cooperation, and without a real center of gravity or executive power, it lacked strength and authority.

Confusingly, Hamilton and Madison stole the "Federalist" name early on, forcing the supporters of the Articles of Federation to call themselves the "anti-Federalists." In reality federalism was a matter of degree, and the anti-Federalists simply opposed the much stronger centralized federalism of the Constitution. They argued that the proposed arrangements for strong central government amounted to tyranny, and that they were fighting for "the rights of the people." Hamilton countered by noting that a zeal for popular rights is often merely a mask for the power hungry or avaricious to climb the ladders of power. In truth, he says, history has demonstrated that libertarian and weak government is a sure route to despotism. One may begin with demagogues defending the people, but the demagogues turn into tyrants. In practice, "the vigor of government is essential to the security of liberty."

One nation undivided

Writing together in paper 18, Madison and Hamilton draw an analogy with ancient Greece and the fundamental weakness of its federal system of government. Rather than being a true union, Greece was a loose confederacy of republics united under the Amphictyonic Council, with the more powerful republics taking turns to dominate each other. Might ruled, and the smaller states, although equal in theory, were in fact "satellites of the orbs of primary magnitude."

If the Greeks had been wiser, they would have seen that a closer and more genuinely equal union, in which all parties had equal rights and sheer power was not the arbiter of rule, would have prevented "the mutual jealousies, fears, hatreds, and injuries ending in the celebrated Peloponnesian war" that ruined its originator, Athens. The story of Greece provides the perfect warning of what could occur under a confederate system in America, in which whoever happened to be the strongest at the time could dominate the others. In contrast, a full and proper union would ensure that weaker states would have as many rights as stronger ones, and that the stronger ones knew their place within a clearly articulated Constitution that allowed only the Union itself to go to war.

The bigger, the better

In essay 9, Hamilton refers to the "new science of government," laying out an array of mechanisms and institutions that can safeguard republics. These include separation of government into executive, judiciary, and legislative bodies; checks and balances in the law-making process; and popular rather than direct representation.

In paper 10, Madison observes that societies are always vulnerable to being taken over by "faction," or the interests of a few, and this is particularly true of smaller republics. However, the advantage of a very large republic is that there are so many competing interests that it will be more difficult for a single group to gain power over the others. Here Madison makes his famous case for the sheer size of the American republic, to counter the view that it would be too big and unmanageable. He argues that size ensures there will be a good number of groups serving different interests, making it less likely that one can dominate or tyrannize the rest. In a single state or confederacy, in contrast, a religious sect or a particular political position, such as the forced redistribution of property, has a much greater chance of success, but across a vast nation such singular interests are never going to hold sway. Instead, the government will tend to reflect and promote the interests of the whole.

Power of taxation

In paper 23 Hamilton argues for an "energetic" central government whose purposes would be defense of the Union against external attack; achieving internal stability; regulating commerce within America and with foreign nations; and managing relations with other countries. To achieve these ends, the ability to raise armies and equip fleets should be unlimited. He reiterates the position in paper 30, asking how a country can remain stable, free, and prosperous if its government is not able do its job. It needs to be capable of raising money for its needs, not least defending itself properly. Hamilton notes that the Constitution does not add any new powers to Congress that were not already there under the Articles of Confederation (save for the regulation of commerce, to which few were opposed anyway). Rather, the Constitution simply aimed to "reinvigorate" existing powers. He tries to demonstrate that the central government's powers of taxation can exist equally with those of the states, which will have plenty of ability to raise funds for their needs.

Power of the president

Hamilton saw that a United States of America could only come about through the existence of strong executive power. There was a need for a "single chief magistrate" to be elected for four years at a time, making a break with the unaccountability of hereditary rulers. If a president acted wrongly he could be impeached, compared to a king's "sacred and inviolable" right to rule. He would be commander-in-chief of the military, compared to the English king's right to declare and wage war. His absence of power over commerce would be contrasted with the monarch's ability to create corporations, establish markets, and coin money. Finally, the American president would have no spiritual authority, in contrast to the king as the supreme defender of the faith.

Strong executive government was a crucial differentiator to a confederate government, and one of the three pillars of the new American republic. The others were a Congress and Senate with enough members to represent the American population adequately, and a national judiciary (the Supreme Court) independent of both the executive branch and the states.

Final comments

The brilliance of the Constitution was that it was not based on an idealistic view of humanity, but quite the opposite. People are self-interested and will push for their own values to be upheld over those of others, so it is better to have a system that allows for a multiplicity of interests to flourish, yet in their very number serving to check each other's power. Hamilton and Madison's vision of a sprawling, pluralistic republic guided by a few fundamental principles, with its machinery of government built on checks and balances, turned out to be exactly what the new nation needed to flourish. None of this was obvious, though, and the genius of *The Federalist Papers* was to make a great case for what were really counterintuitive ideas.

Yet the fight over the Constitution between Unionists and those pushing for a confederation of states put in place a fundamental divide in American politics, between the wish for local self-determination and strong central government. It was a split that would lead to the Civil War, and remains alive today with the libertarian and Tea Party movements resisting an overpowering, high-taxing, welfare statist Washington that involves the country in unnecessary foreign wars. Amid much hand wringing about America's future, pundits on all sides should periodically pick up the antique spectacles of Hamilton, Jay, and Madison and remember how they originally saw the nation's purpose. Yes, one had to guard against the state becoming too large and intrusive, but at the same time one should never forget the advantages of effective central government: protection from violence, preserving property rights, laws of contract, and uniform regulations for commerce across the states. Such things made America great as one nation and one people. The leaders of today's breakaway movements, from Scotland to Catalonia to Quebec, might profit from reading *The Federalist Papers*; they may be reminded of the many benefits of strong unions, and the costs of going it alone.

Alexander Hamilton, John Jay, & James Madison

Alexander Hamilton was born in 1757 in Nevis, West Indies. During the American Revolution he was a captain and, in 1777, was made Washington's aide-de-camp. After the war he became a distinguished lawyer and in 1782 was elected to the Continental Congress. Secretary of the Treasury in the first American government of 1789, he was killed in a duel with vice-president Aaron Burr in 1804.

John Jay was born in New York City in 1745. He served in the Continental Congress (1774–77) and wrote the 1777 constitution of New York State. His positions include Chief Justice of New York State, president of Congress (1778), Minister to Spain (1779), Secretary for Foreign Affairs (1784–89), and Chief Justice of the Supreme Court (1789–95). His last role was Governor of New York (1795–1801). Jay died in 1829.

James Madison was born in Virginia in 1751. He played important roles in the Virginian Convention (1776), the Continental Congress, and the Virginia legislature. At the 1787 Constitutional Convention he became known as the "master builder of the Constitution" thanks to his ability to get all parties on side. Secretary of State in the Jefferson administration, in 1809 he was elected President, serving two terms. Madison died in 1836.

The Road to Serfdom

*"Once you admit that the individual is merely a means to serve
the ends of the higher entity called society or the nation, most
of those features of totalitarian regimes which horrify us follow
of necessity. From the collectivist standpoint intolerance and
brutal suppression of dissent, the complete disregard of the life
and happiness of the individual, are essential and unavoidable
consequences of this basic premise, that his system is superior to
one in which the 'selfish' interests of the individual are allowed to
obstruct the full realisation of the ends the community pursues."*

*"The state ceases to be a piece of utilitarian machinery intended
to help individuals in the fullest development of their individual
personality and becomes a 'moral' institution… In this sense the Nazi
or any other collectivist state is 'moral', while the liberal state is not."*

In a nutshell

In a planned economy not only are resources allocated inefficiently,
the life choices of individuals are progressively narrowed.
A true democracy must be based on a free market economy.

In a similar vein

Lord Acton *Essays on Freedom and Power* (p 20)
Hannah Arendt *The Origins of Totalitarianism* (p 48)
Isaiah Berlin *Two Concepts of Liberty* (p 60)
Robert Nozick *Anarchy, State, and Utopia* (p 214)
Karl Popper *The Open Society and Its Enemies* (p 248)

CHAPTER 19

F.A. Hayek

B efore arriving in England in 1931 to take up a post at the London School of Economics, Friedrich von Hayek had spent most of his life in Vienna. A cousin of philosopher Ludwig Wittgenstein, after university he had worked for economist Ludwig von Mises. For all its faults, Hayek considered himself a child of the Austro-Hungarian empire, and watched aghast as Hitler rose to power in Germany and then, in 1938, annexed Austria.

As a newly minted British citizen, Hayek became increasingly dismayed at the "progressive" outlook of many intellectuals in England, who were not able to see the true nature of Hitler's National-Socialism and were taken in by the propaganda of Soviet Russia. Fearing that Britain would experiment with the same kinds of anti-freedom ideas that had led to such regimes, he resolved to expose the link between "planned" economies and political repression. The result, *The Road to Serfdom*, made the shocking assertion that countries including Britain and the United States could easily slide into totalitarianism, not by revolution but through good-intentioned steps toward greater organization of the economy.

The book was written between 1940 and 1943 while Hayek was pursuing a job in pure economic theory at the LSE. It was not published until 1944 due to wartime paper restrictions, but then had an immediate impact in Britain. It was also a surprise bestseller in America (the spread of its ideas greatly assisted by a condensation in the *Reader's Digest*), and attracted the ire of US radicals.

At only 260 pages, *The Road to Serfdom* was not meant to be a fully worked-out, scholarly position on freedom and the market system (this would come with *The Constitution of Liberty* in 1960), but its simplicity only increased the power of its message. Ronald Reagan, Margaret Thatcher, Milton Friedman, and the leaders of central Europe's post-Soviet revolutions were all deeply influenced by Hayek, who was the first free market economist to win the Nobel Prize for Economics (in 1974), along with, ironically, Swedish socialist economist Gunnar Myrdal.

The roots of oppression

Why does Hayek make an express link between planned economies and totalitarianism? If one looks at economic history from the medieval Italian city states to industrial Britain, he explains, it was the growth of commerce that allowed people to be freed of the hierarchical society in which birth alone determined position in life. Economic liberty begetting ever greater political freedom was the process that fueled the power and wealth of the West.

Yet the very success of liberalism, Hayek says, was the basis of its decline. Though it had lifted up most of Europe, greater prosperity created ever more ambition and desire, so it was easy to blame the existing system as a failure. In reality, to paraphrase Franklin Roosevelt, it was not that free enterprise had failed, but that it had not yet been properly tried (i.e., to its full extent). The wish to have the state step in and fix things inevitably entailed the diminution of the principle of free agency and potential. Attempting to provide more for those without brought with it less freedom for the whole, and thus a gradual erosion of the traditions of the individualist, liberal West.

Socialist ideas took root in Europe in the last part of the nineteenth century and the first 25 years of the twentieth. The major socialist parties in Germany and Austria began to frame individualism, liberalism, democracy, and capitalism as "English liberal values." Free trade was a British conspiracy to dominate the globe. The rise of Germany, in contrast, seemed to prove that the planned nature of its economy and its increasing anti-liberalism were the future.

The truth about planning

Hayek defines socialism as a species of collectivism in which "the entrepreneur working for profit is replaced by a central planning body." The attractions of planning are clear: If we consider ourselves rational people, we will want to plan instead of leaving everything up to fate. Yet problems arise with how we go about this. Socialists say that we need *central* direction and coordination to shape the future, while Liberals seek a system that allows the free forces of competition to achieve the same good ends, but with the least amount of coercion. In the main, societies flourish when people are free to make their own decisions based on available information, including prices.

Advocates of central planning often claim that it is "necessary" because an economy is so complex that it needs guidance by the state (by this logic Germany developed corporatist "monopoly capitalism"). Yet Hayek says that precisely the opposite is true: The greater the complexity, the more impossible it is to get an overview of what is happening. Development is best achieved through *de*centralization; that is, market forces responding to price signals.

The wish to organize all of society's resources for a definite social end sounds good, but in one stroke it ends personal freedom, and demonstrates a lack of faith in individuals' ability to achieve the "social ends" for which socialists call, even assuming we could agree what they are. Hayek notes that as early as 1928 the German government controlled almost half of national income. In practice, this meant that "scarcely an individual end… is not dependent for its achievement on the action of the state"—surely a worrying thought.

Socialism and the rule of law

Under the rule of law by which liberal societies operate, laws "are intended for such long periods that it is impossible to know whether they will assist particular people more than others," Hayek notes. In a planned society, it is not left up to future or unknown people to allocate resources; rather, certain priorities are decided to exist, which identify gainers and losers. This is the difference between providing the "rules of the road" in a Highway Code, Hayek says, and telling people where to travel.

The key point about the rule of law is that it safeguards equality. It assumes that no one is going to be treated better because of their status or connections. Hayek admits that the rule of law does nothing to protect against economic inequality, yet neither is it designed to benefit particular people in particular ways. Socialists detest the law and the independence of judges for this very reason. Yet as soon as laws are designed for "distributive justice," some people are put above others; even if this is done with good intentions, it inevitably leads to the destruction of the rule of law. Indeed, the rule of law does not mean simply that a society is run according to law, but that the powers of government itself are circumscribed by a constitution or laws set *well in advance* of its coming to power. When governments change the ground rules once they are in power (e.g., Stalinist Russia, Hitler's Germany), it is not the rule of law in operation, only a sham of it.

Planned economies and totalitarianism

The defenders of a planned economy say that planning "only" applies to the economy; if we give up control in this aspect, we will be provided for to pursue the higher things in life. However, economic striving is never a "secondary" aspect of our lives, Hayek observes, but rather our fundamental means to achieve heartfelt goals and live out certain values. The real question is not whether a planned economy will give us what we want or need, but whether it takes away our freedom to *decide* what is important or desirable. In a planned economy we may work for years to buy something, only to find that the state does not consider it worthy and bans it, or it is grossly overpriced thanks to price controls, or it is simply unavailable because of other production priorities. Thus, "mere" direction of the economy can end up shaping the sort of life we can live.

Those in charge of planned economies always maintain that there will be freedom to choose one's occupation, but the reality is that economic direction requires certain jobs, industries, and sectors to be more important than others, which means that access to other fields will be more difficult or restricted, or offer little opportunity. Instead, everyone will be judged according to their fitness for certain defined categories of work, just as they are in the military. One will no longer work to fulfill one's own interests or potential, but become merely a means toward achieving "the good of all."

Freedom vs. economic security

In a directed or planned economy, the biggest problem is incentives for people to do their best. If your position does not depend on your skills or imagination, but on the state's judgment of the job's importance, it will not really matter whether you work harder or smarter, since it yields no particular gain to you. Multiply this effect by millions, and you have a society whose productivity is well below what it could be. Moreover, when everyone is assured of a job under some national program of "economic security," what matters most is not the quality or need for those jobs, but the fact that everyone has some kind of occupation. In a competitive economy, where there is less economic security (you can be sacked, or your occupation becomes obsolete due to technological change), there is much more incentive for you to retrain or study to make yourself more employable. The result is that not only do you end up fulfilling your potential, society as a whole becomes more productive.

In a competitive economy, Hayek notes, failure can end with the bailiff (i.e., in bankruptcy), whereas in a planned economy it can end with the hangman. Although in theory everyone's job is secure in a socialist system, in reality anyone who bucks the will of superiors is committing a "crime against the community" and faces severe punishment. He includes a 1937 quote from Trotsky, critical of what had happened in Russia: "In a country where the sole employer is the State, opposition means death by slow starvation. The old principle: who does not work shall not eat, has been replaced by a new one: who does not obey shall not eat."

In a society in which economic security is considered more important than freedom, freedom itself becomes mocked, since it is worthless in providing "the good things of this earth." In these circumstances, people will happily sacrifice liberty for security.

Surprisingly, Hayek was not against some form of welfare state. Extreme privation should be protected against, he thought, but economic security should not trump freedom as society's basic value. The market system must not be undermined, or it creates distortions and unintended consequences.

Final comments

Faced with a choice of a reasonably liberal dictatorship or a democracy where the state is involved in every aspect of the economy and society, Hayek said he would choose the former. On this basis he had observed events in Chile, where the economically disastrous socialist experiment of Salvador Allende segued into a coup and Augusto Pinochet's authoritarian regime. Hayek admired the market liberalization reforms occurring under the latter, and visited Chile in 1977 and 1981. He may have been naïve about what was happening there in terms of human rights, but as Hayek scholars Bruce Caldwell and Leonidas Montes have noted in a 2014 working paper, Hayek was never an adviser to the regime, which he saw as transitional before a return to democracy.

Hayek's interest in Chile was tied to his insight that a democracy does not imply real personal and economic liberty. Indeed, the price controls and nationalization of private businesses that occurred under the elected Allende government were an assault on the basic freedoms of exchange and ownership. Economic freedom may seem less important than the right to vote, yet is fundamental in people's ability to chart their own destinies.

Once on the fringe of economics, Hayek's ideas have become mainstream alongside Friedman and other free marketers, even if politicians find it hard to put them fully into practice, such is the tendency of the state to grow. Hayek's warning about the link between overzealous economic planning and the erosion of personal freedoms may seem subtle, yet it is crucial if we are to preserve open societies as well as healthy economies.

F.A. Hayek

Born in 1899, Friedrich August von Hayek enlisted in the Austro-Hungarian army in the First World War, and spent time on the Italian front. He studied law, political science, economics, philosophy, and psychology at the University of Vienna, and was influenced by Austrian school economists Carl Menger and Friedrich von Weiser. Hayek worked under Ludwig von Mises for the Austrian government, and in 1923–24 was a research assistant to economist Jeremiah Jenks in New York.

In 1927 Hayek and von Mises founded what is today the Austrian Institute of Economic Research; their primary interest was in business cycles and prices. In 1931 Hayek was lured to the London School of Economics by Lionel Robbins, who was keen to provide a counterview to Keynes. In 1947, together with Karl Popper, Milton Friedman, and von Mises, he set up the Mont Pelerin Society to promote open societies based on the free market. In 1950 he took a professorship at the University of Chicago, followed by posts at the universities of Freiburg and Salzburg. Hayek was awarded the Presidential Medal of Freedom by George H.W. Bush, and made a member of the Order of the Companions of Honour by Elizabeth II. He died in 1992.

Leviathan

"In such condition, there is no place for Industry; because the fruit thereof is uncertain; and consequently no Culture of the Earth; no Navigation, nor use of the commodities that may be imported by Sea; no commodious Building; no Instruments of moving, and removing such things as require much force; no Knowledge of the face of the Earth; no account of Time; no Arts; no Letters; no Society; and which is worst of all, continuall feare, and danger of violent death; And the life of man, solitary, poore, nasty, brutish, and short."

"For as long as every man holdeth this Right, of doing any thing he liketh; so long are all men in the condition of Warre."

In a nutshell

Under authoritarian rule life may not be perfect, but in return for some loss of freedom come order and physical protection.

In a similar vein

Edmund Burke *Reflections on the Revolution in France* (p 78)
John Locke *Two Treatises of Government* (p 168)

CHAPTER 20

Thomas Hobbes

Though today his name is synonymous with politics, like many enlightened men of his time Thomas Hobbes took the whole of human knowledge as his domain. He wrote on philosophy, mathematics, ballistics, optics, and psychology, and thanks to his work advising British aristocrats and taking their sons on European "grand tours," he was able to meet European thinkers and scientists including Descartes, Marin Mersenne, Pierre Gassendi, and (it is said) Galileo. In England he knew Francis Bacon, dramatist Ben Jonson, and John Selden, the historian who opposed the divine right of kings. Hobbes was strongly influenced by the new "materialism," from Galileo's fresh understanding of the physical universe to William Harvey's exposition of the human body. At the age of 40 he discovered geometry and, inspired by its exactitude and certainty, wondered whether its rigor and certainty could be applied to the murky world of human affairs and politics.

The result (eventually) was *Leviathan, or the Matter, Forme and Power of a Common Wealth Ecclesiasticall and Civil*, which provided a rationale for the modern centralized nation-state. When he was writing, imperial China's cities were bigger and more powerful than any in Europe, and people were in awe of the Ottoman Empire. Yet Europe was on the rise, its traders circling the globe, its natural philosophers making new discoveries. Crucially, because no one state was able to dominate, this sparked technological and military competition. It also made the search for the perfect state more urgent, for if the people, the nobility, and the king all felt relatively secure, there was no limit to what a state could achieve.

The wisdom of submission

In the time before government, laws, and civilization, people lived in a state of continual fear of violent death and war. There was no sense of a "greater good" (*summum bonum*), only people pursuing their own desires for power or pleasure or luxury. In this "state of nature" before civilization, Hobbes famously says, "the life of man, is solitary, poore, nasty, brutish, and short."

If there is no government, there will be no law, and "where no Law, no Injustice," Hobbes says. Right and wrong mean nothing; indeed, dishonesty and aggression are "cardinall vertues" in a state of war. It is every man for himself, and every man has a natural right to go after whatever someone else has. Yet constant one-upmanship is matched by anxiety about the future, by the thought of suddenly losing all we have gained. This drives people to solutions that may reduce insecurity, including seeking protection from a ruler or state.

The only thing preventing conflict between individuals is the existence of authority, be it the leader of a family, a clan, a region, or a country, whose word is final, and which everyone accepts on pain of isolation, exile, or death. For Hobbes, the obvious and best form of authority is a single ruler, a monarch. He arrived at this belief not because of a supreme faith in monarchy (although he was on the Royalist side in the English Civil War), but ironically through giving due accord to the individual. People can only prosper if there is some unquestionably powerful umpire to bring justice to their dealings with others. If contracts, for instance, are to mean anything, there has to be an ultimate enforcer. Without such an absolute power, humans will quickly question the legitimacy of the state, and there will be strife and a return to a state of nature.

Order over freedom

Some commentators (among others Francis Fukuyama; see commentary on p 104) argue that in fact Hobbes' political philosophy was liberal (if not democratic), and was important in the development of England's liberal tradition, the model for the rest of Europe and later America. This is because, although he opts for monarchy as practically the best form of government, he breaks from the past in denying the divine right of kings to rule. Monarchs have no *natural* superiority, but will rule by tacit consent of the people, who will gain order and security in return for their recognition of the sovereign's power. Thus even if a government is absolutist, it can still be legitimate.

One must remember that *Leviathan* was written within the context of England's bitter civil wars (1642–51), when the choice was either a dominant king or a republic. In the face of Charles I's arbitrary actions such as imposing harsh new taxes and appropriating property, for Hobbes whether or not an individual or a group likes the king's behavior is irrelevant next to the fundamental fact that now there is order, where before there was only chaos and every man for himself. Democracy to Hobbes is simply a kind of formalized state of nature in which competing interests make for permanent instability. Much more important than the democratic impulse is the instinct of self-preservation. He casts his great state—or "Leviathan," named after the mythical creature who dominated the seas—as the great subduer of the pride and lust for glory that had since time immemorial led men into war. People could now exchange the culture of attack and revenge for peace and security under a powerful, unifying monarch.

Final comments

Today, "Leviathan" is a term that conveys a bloated state, the monster that spreads its tentacles into all parts of society; at its extreme, Hobbes' philosophy has been held responsible for fascism and totalitarianism. Yet his real point is that no polity can be maintained without due authority, and as contemporary writers have argued (see commentary on Acemoglu and Robinson, p 26), states fail primarily not because of poor economics but because they lack centralized power.

Of course, peace and material security are never enough on their own. Hobbes underestimated the passion for freedom of religion and speech, which is why his views now seem archaic. It was left to Locke to turn Hobbes' idea of tacit popular consent into a call for parliamentary government directly representing the people. Locke's claim for the natural rights of the people would in time be expressed in English law, but also in the US Constitution's right for people to "life, liberty and the pursuit of happiness." Despite the Founding Fathers' avowed dislike of monarchy, the American president, as not merely the nation's chief administrator but also its head of state and Commander-in-Chief, is an echo of Hobbes' all-powerful sovereign.

Thomas Hobbes

Thomas Hobbes was born in Malmesbury, Wiltshire, in 1588. His father, a vicar, deserted the family when Hobbes was still a boy; his uncle provided for him and his mother and ensured that he went to university. He spent several years at Oxford, and in 1608 began working for William Cavendish, later the 1st Earl of Devonshire. Over the next decades Hobbes would serve the Cavendish family as tutor and traveling companion, acting as political adviser and helping with business interests. He was 40 before he published his first book, a translation of Thucydides' The History of the Peloponnesian War.

After writing The Elements of Law Natural and Politic *(1640), Hobbes moved to France along with other English royalists in exile. In Paris he wrote a critique of Descartes, published a book on moral and civil philosophy,* De Cive *("On the Citizen," 1642), and became tutor to the Prince of Wales.*

In 1660 the monarchy was restored under Charles II, who gave Hobbes a pension and defended him against the clergy's accusation that Leviathan *was atheistic and heretical. Hobbes was banned from publishing and waited several years before releasing (through a Dutch publisher) his history of the English Civil War,* Behemoth *(written in 1668). He wrote into his 80s and 90s, including a book on physics,* Decameron Physiologicum *("Ten Dialogues of Natural Philosophy"), and verse translations of Homer. Hobbes spent his last years living between the two Cavendish estates, Chatsworth and Hardwick in Derbyshire, and died in 1679.*

The Clash of Civilizations and the Remaking of World Order

"In fundamental ways, the world is becoming more modern and less Western."

"Civilizations are the ultimate human tribes, and the clash of civilizations is tribal conflict on a global scale."

"The dangerous clashes of the future are likely to arise from the interaction of Western arrogance, Islamic intolerance, and Sinic assertiveness."

In a nutshell

The major sources of conflict in the twenty-first century will be cultural and religious, not economic.

In a similar vein

CHAPTER 21

Samuel P. Huntington

n 1993, America and the West were still digesting the fact that it had "won" the Cold War. With the Berlin Wall crumbling less than four years before, liberal democracy and Western values seemed triumphant.

Yet that summer, Harvard professor Samuel Huntington fired a missile at this self-satisfied version of events with an article in *Foreign Affairs*. In "The Clash of Civilizations?," which he later turned into a book, he argued that rather than a moment of victory, the end of the Cold War exposed just how transient had been the division of the world into East and West, communist and capitalist. In the absence of such arbitrary political divisions, much older cultural and religious fault lines were revealing themselves again. There was no better example than the bloody collapse of the former Yugoslavia and its reconfiguring according to religion (Christian, Orthodox, Muslim) and ethnicity.

Huntington had more uncomfortable things to say. The West was declining in influence and that of Asian civilizations was expanding, while Islam was undergoing a "demographic explosion" that would destabilize Muslim countries and their neighbors. The West's "universalist pretensions" were causing conflict with other civilizations, particularly Islamic countries and China; instead of trying to impose themselves on the world, Western countries should unite to affirm their unique identity and values against non-Western societies, including limits on immigration. Huntington also ventured that modernization was leading to "neither a universal civilization in any meaningful sense nor the Westernization of non-Western societies." Countries around the globe were happily accepting modernization, but rejecting Western values.

Huntington's often overlooked point was that this new multipolar, multi-civilizational world was not doomed to perpetual war. Rather, world peace rested on each civilization accepting the other's dominance in its own sphere, and cooperating so that those spheres were respected.

Two decades on, did *The Clash of Civilizations* foretell the future, or was it a sophisticated, fearmongering rant?

New world order

Nation states are still the main actors in world affairs, Huntington says, but they are shaped by the world's civilizations: Sinic (Chinese-Confucian), Japanese,

Hindu, Islamic, Orthodox, Western, Latin American, and African; Buddhism, Huntington says, although a major world religion, has never been the basis of a large civilization. The six powers that will dominate the twenty-first century—America, China, Europe, Japan, Russia, and India—belong to five different civilizations, and there are several Islamic states whose big populations, resource wealth, and strategic importance will make them influential. Africa's relative poverty and disunity will prevent it from being a major player in our time. The most significant conflicts, Huntington says, will not be between classes or rich and poor, but between people identifying themselves as part of different civilizations.

While countries united by culture will increasingly come together (think East and West Germany, South and North Korea), those united by historical circumstance or ideology alone, yet with significant cultural differences, will split or fall under intense strain. This happened with the Soviet Union, but Huntington claims we will also see it with Ukraine, Nigeria, Sudan, India, Sri Lanka, and elsewhere. Since the book was written, Sudan has indeed split in two, and Ukraine seems to be dividing into European and Russian spheres. Where the principal dividing line in the world was once the Iron Curtain, Huntington says, today it is the line separating Europe and the West from Orthodox and Muslim countries.

Huntington's view is almost the opposite of that put forward by Francis Fukuyama (see commentary on p 104), which posits that ideological battles are being replaced by liberal democracy. Yet Huntington observes that in the five years following the collapse of the Berlin Wall, "the word 'genocide' was heard far more often than in any five years of the Cold War," and there was a rise in neo-fascist movements. This is hardly evidence of a "post-historical" age, but rather a new world order hinging once again on culture, race, and religion.

The fading West vs. the rising rest

The West is characterized by the separation of church and state, the rule of law, social pluralism, representative or democratic bodies, and individualism, all of which non-Western countries have rejected to various degrees. Many have been very willing to accept modernization, but that is not the same as Westernization. The big discord of the twenty-first century will be the West's desire to promote what it sees as universal values, and its lessening ability to do so. When the Cold War finished the West thought it had won the argument over the best form of government (liberal democracy combined with free markets), but "what is universalism to the West is imperialism to the rest," Huntington notes.

Indeed, he argues that "the West's victory in the Cold War... produced not triumph but exhaustion." Western states are now beset with their own problems including slower economic growth, stagnating populations, big government debt, and low savings rates, at exactly the same time as economic power is rapidly heading to Asia. In 1900, Western nations ruled half the world's population; today they rule only themselves. They can no longer be seen as the healthy, wealthy minority, as non-Westerners become healthier, better educated, and more urban. And while the West's military power will continue to dominate, the trend is for rising military expenditure by China, Russia, and India compared to the traditional big spenders. As non-Western countries become richer and more powerful, they will have little need to adopt or even admire Western institutions, values, and ideas.

Many countries that adopted Western political institutions during the Cold War are going through "indigenization," Huntington claims, going back to their Confucian, Islamic, or Buddhist roots. Politicians in non-Western countries win elections by appealing to an ethnic, nationalist, or religious sense of identity. In Muslim countries that have experienced upheavals and changes of fortune and rulers, Islam provides a continuous sense of identity, just as the Orthodox church does in Russia, a stable presence going back 1,000 years. The worldwide religious revival is counter to the consumerism, secularism, and relativism that characterize modernity, which in many non-Western minds is synonymous with the "degenerate" West.

Rise of China

The great story of our times has been Asia's, particularly China's, economic rise. As Singapore's first prime minister Lee Kuan Yew said: "It's not possible to pretend that this is just another big player. This is the biggest player in the history of man." Huntington suggests that the greatest potential flashpoint in Asia will be if America challenges China's attempt to dominate in this part of the world.

Outside of Japan and Korea, Huntington says, the economy of Asia is basically Chinese. From Thailand to Malaysia to Singapore and Indonesia, the local economic elites are Chinese, and the "bamboo network" between mainland Chinese and those in other East Asian countries gives them extra advantages in commerce. Huntington sees war between China and Taiwan as unlikely because there is too much cultural kinship. Conflict is more likely in Asia between other states over borders and territorial disputes. Asia may well start to look like Europe once did—lots of states and lots of potential for conflict. While the West tends to thing of "Asia" as one bloc, the fact is that it takes in half a dozen civilizations. Even so, Huntington sees China becoming the hegemon of Asia, and all (including Japan) eventually bowing to it instead of America.

Conflict and the Muslim world

In the twenty-first century relations between civilizations will range "from distant to violent," Huntington says. Boris Yeltsin used the term "cold peace" to describe future relations between Russia and the West. Those between Islam and the West are likely to be worse.

Western politicians like to say that the West does not have an issue with Islam, only Islamist extremism, but they are not telling the truth, writes Huntington. The conflict between liberal democracy and Marxism in the twentieth century was a mere blip in a much longer and deeper animosity between Christianity and Islam. There is a fundamental divide between the Western idea of separation of religion and state, and the Islamic idea that everything (including government) must be ordered in the name of Allah. Although Muslims see the West as amoral, they also know its attractiveness, so the only way to defend against it is to make the West more of an enemy, and their own societies more purely Islamic. What they cannot abide is not so much Christianity, but the secularism and religion-free nature of the West.

In a paragraph prophetic of the terrorist attacks on 9/11, Huntington writes:

"Somewhere in the Middle East a half-dozen young men could well be dressed in jeans, drinking Coke, listening to rap, and, between their bows to Mecca, putting together a bomb to blow up an American airliner… Only naïve arrogance can lead Westerners to assume that non-Westerners will become 'Westernized' by acquiring Western goods."

He argues—even before the war in Afghanistan, the toppling of Saddam Hussein, and drone attacks on fundamentalists—that the West and Islam are in a "quasi war." Actual fighting is only the most overt manifestation of a long-term battle of civilizations. The few Muslim states that remain friends with the West are those who depend on it militarily (Saudi Arabia, Kuwait), and even those who have been supported by it economically (Egypt) resent that dependency.

Huntington believes that Islam is a destabilizing force primarily because it has no core state. Whether it is Indonesia, Egypt, Iran, Pakistan, Saudi Arabia, or Turkey, there is no Muslim state strong enough to referee or resolve conflicts within the Islamic world, and none strong enough to represent the Muslim world against the non-Muslim world. The other big source of instability is Muslim demography. The Islamic population surge has produced millions of angry young men, often unemployed, who can be egged into action against non-Muslims. Yet looking on the bright side, Huntington notes that this Muslim demographic boom will not last for ever, and if it occurs alongside economic development then the source of instability may wane.

Natural affinities, long-standing animosities

Huntington uses the terms "cleft" and "torn" to describe countries. Cleft nations are those that physically bestride the fault lines between civilizations. They tend to have grave problems of maintaining national unity. Sudan has already been mentioned, split along Muslim and Christian lines. Nigeria and Kenya are also destabilized by Christian–Muslim animosity; Tanzania has its Christian mainland and Muslim Zanzibar; and then there is the split that occurred in 1993 between Christian Ethiopia and Muslim Eritrea. India, despite the 1948 partition, still has regular conflicts between Muslims and Hindus; and in the Philippines the division is between Christians and Muslims.

Huntington's "torn" countries are those where the populace belongs to one civilization but its leaders want to make it part of another. For instance, Turkey is fundamentally part of Muslim civilization, but from President Ataturk onwards its leaders saw it as part of the modern West. Because Turkey has not succeeded in becoming part of the EU, it has forged closer links with the Turkic-speaking former Soviet republics, including Uzbekistan, Turkmenistan, Kazakhstan, and Kyrgyzstan, and funded Islamic schools and institutions to placate internal Islamists. Huntington notes that Turkey's leaders often like to describe their country as "a bridge between East and West," but in doing so, "they euphemistically confirm that it is torn."

Australia is an excellent example of politicians' weakness in the face of civilizational realities. In the 1990s its politicians (notably Paul Keating) talked of the country being part of Asia, even though it was clearly a Western nation. The public would have none of it. The attempt to make Australia a republic without the Queen as the head of state failed, as have attempts to create a new Australian flag without the Union Jack. Asian states, in turn, have been reluctant to accept Australia as an "Asian" country, seeing it as culturally still very much a Western nation. Australia's attachment to liberal Western values, including human rights and press freedom, jars with many East Asian states. Even the indirect and non-confrontational Asian way of doing things is opposite to Australian candor and openness.

Core states and civilizations

In the new world order, Huntington asserts, *no* country has "global security interests," including the United States. "The world will be ordered on the basis of civilizations or not at all," he says; peace will only exist if the core states representing different civilizations can respect the others' sphere of influence. What happens is that civilizational spheres of influence in which there is a core state, such as China, the US, or Russia, that state (with consent) dominates those within the sphere. Yet these spheres only work if there is a cultural affinity with the core state. Pakistan, Sri Lanka, and Bangladesh will not accept India as their core state and order provider, for instance, and similarly no country sees Japan in this role because culturally it stands on its own.

"Europe" is demarcated by a line running from Finland down to the Mediterranean, dividing Christian Europe to the West from the Orthodox and Islamic states and regions to the East. The Iron Curtain obscured this natural line for a few decades, but it has reasserted itself. "With the Cold War over," Huntington presciently writes, "NATO has one central and compelling purpose: to insure that it [prevents] the reimposition of Russian political and military control in Central Europe." He correctly predicted that Greece's membership of the EU would become problematic, as culturally it is an Orthodox country and never held itself to the standards of the EU.

Final comments

Criticism of *The Clash of Civilizations and the Remaking of World Order* has included the following points:

- Dividing the globe into civilizations is too simplistic, as the world is more complex than that.
- In pointing to the power of civilizations, Huntington underestimates the power of states to shape the world and their own destinies.
- The deep splits within the Muslim world (e.g., Sunni vs. Shi'ite) preclude a single Muslim identity, so the idea of Islam vs. the West is too simple. In addition, the split is exaggerated. For long stretches of history the two religions have lived peacefully alongside each other.
- Huntington's focus on "culture" as the driver of politics is simply not shared by most political scientists and economists. For example, Acemoglu and Robinson's *Why Nations Fail* says that East Asian economic success cannot be explained by "Confucian values" alone. In his book *Trust*, Fukuyama argues that rather than causing conflict, civilizations rubbing up against each other produce cross-stimulation and creative change.
- Huntington's "Realpolitik," rightwing analysis provided an intellectual basis for the misguided Bush/Blair invasions of Iraq and Afghanistan.
- His thesis borders on racism. His work as an adviser to the Botha regime in South Africa would suggest he has a personal interest in the separation of races and cultures. Edward Said commented that Huntington's views justified old-fashioned Muslim-bashing by the West.

These points may all be valid, and yet much of what Huntington predicted in the mid-1990s has come true, including the divisions of countries along cultural or religious lines (e.g., Sudan, Ukraine), the rise of the Chinasphere and Russia's rejection of Europe and the West, the attempted Islamization of secular Muslim countries (Turkey, Egypt), and the impact of Islamic fundamentalism. The success of rightwing anti-immigration parties in Europe, from Marine Le Pen's National Front to Nigel Farage's UKIP to Geert Wilders' Party for Freedom, are a sign that electorates in the West see their values and institutions and once homogeneous populations as under threat from "foreign" cultures and religions.

The idea that globalization and modernization will naturally erode the differences between people was for Huntington pure idealism. World trade did not bring about world peace, but simply provides more opportunities for clashes between competing value systems. Huntington's "first rule" for living in a multicivilizational world is that the core states of each civilization respect the domain of the others, and do not engage in fault line wars by proxy. If it is to ward off decline, to Huntington the West will need to become less arrogant, less missionary, and more concerned with preserving its unique values and institutions within its natural boundaries. His final message is that an appreciation of humanity as one can only occur by first having taken account of its deep differences. Only if that happens will we be able to see what is shared, and use the term "civilization" in the singular; that is, a single world community.

Samuel P. Huntington

Samuel Phillips Huntington was born in 1927 in New York City. His mother was a short-story writer and his father a publisher. After graduating from Yale, Huntington spent time in the US Army before getting a master's degree from the University of Chicago. He did his PhD at Harvard, and taught in its department of government until 1959, then took up a post at Columbia University. In 1963 he gained tenure at Harvard and stayed there for the rest of his career.

In 1970 Huntington co-founded Foreign Policy *magazine and remained its co-editor until 1977. A lifelong Democrat, he advised Hubert Humphrey in his 1968 presidential campaign, and in 1977–78 worked on security issues in the Carter administration. At Harvard he was a mentor to Francis Fukuyama (*The End of History and the Last Man, *see p 104), and while a consultant to the US State Department influenced Fareed Zakaria (*The Post-American World, *see p 310). Huntington died in 2008.*

Other books include The Soldier and the State *(1957);* Political Order in Changing Societies *(1968), which argues that modernization does not necessarily lead to democracy;* The Third Wave: Democratization in the Late Twentieth Century *(1991);* Culture Matters: How Values Shape Human Progress *(2000); and* Who Are We? The Challenges to America's National Identity *(2004).*

1987

The Rise and Fall of the Great Powers

"It sounds crudely mercantilistic to express it this way, but wealth is usually needed to underpin military power, and military power is usually needed to acquire and protect wealth. If, however, a large portion of the state's resources is diverted from wealth creation and allocated instead to military purposes, then that is likely to lead to a weakening of national power over the longer term."

"The difficulties experienced by contemporary societies which are militarily top-heavy merely repeat those which, in their time, affected Philip II's Spain, Nicholas II's Russia, and Hitler's Germany. A large military establishment may, like a great monument, look imposing to the impressionable observer; but if it is not resting upon a firm foundation (in this case, a productive national economy), it runs the risk of a future collapse."

In a nutshell

Economic superpowers tend to become militarily dominant too, which creates a vicious circle of high defense spending and low civil investment, and hence a decline of power.

In a similar vein

Hans Morgenthau *Politics Among Nations* (p 208)
Joseph S. Nye *The Future of Power* (p 220)
Fareed Zakaria *The Post-American World* (p 310)

CHAPTER 22

Paul Kennedy

The link between wealth and power in world affairs may be obvious, but we often need reminding of it. Because the might and reach of hegemons are so plain to see, it is easy to think that their dominance will last forever, yet history is full of great powers whose military and geopolitical ambitions and commitments could not be sustained; at a certain point, they simply could no longer afford what the Romans called *Imperium*.

The Rise and Fall of the Great Powers would have remained a brilliant work of history had its discussion stopped with 1987, the year of publication. What brought it fame was that the author dared to make predictions on the likely fate of world powers, including America, at the end of the twentieth century. The book shocked Americans because Kennedy, a British-born Yale historian, dared to suggest that the United States might be simply another example of an age-old pattern of "imperial overstretch." Its decline relative to other powers was clear, and the task of policy-makers was simply to manage it well.

There always seems to be a time lag between a nation becoming wealthy and the point at which its political and military influence increases. Many nations have wealth as their focus at the beginning, and only later do they realize that their prosperity (including overseas investments) needs to be protected, particularly in relation to other growing powers. They then have to spend more on this protection just as their growth rate is slowing. Britain's defense spending was much bigger in 1910, for instance, than it was at the height of its imperial expansion in the 1860s when its economy was booming. What happens, Kennedy says, is that "Great Powers in relative decline instinctively respond by spending more on 'security' and thereby divert potential resources from 'investment' and compound their long-term dilemma."

A pattern emerges
The bulk of the book is an exhaustive survey of all the main powers in the modern (that is, post-Renaissance) era, from Spain to the Netherlands to France to the British Empire, and finally the United States and the Soviet Union. Kennedy is able to demonstrate a clear correlation over the long term between national wealth and military power.

Around 1500 there were several power centers around the world: Ming China, the Ottoman Empire, the Mogul Empire in India, Muscovy, Tokugawa Japan, and the cluster of states in central-western Europe. Why did these European states grow massively in power while the others declined?

The problem with all the non-European powers, Kennedy says, is that they were illiberal. Not only did they require uniformity in religious belief, commerce and weapons development only happened with the consent of the ruler. In contrast, Europe had no overarching ruler, and the constant warring between kingdoms and city-states only encouraged the development of military technology, which spilled over into other technological developments. Competition also encouraged an entrepreneurial culture that helped to create wealth. European societies thus began "a constantly upward spiral" of economic growth and enhanced military effectiveness that saw them move ahead.

Kennedy relates that the Spanish and Austrian Habsburgs went all out to achieve the domination of Europe, but in doing so they spent way too much on arms and war relative to their economic base, and their power gradually faded. Other nations and empires were not as powerful, but kept more within their means. After Napoleon's bid to dominate Europe came to an end in 1815, the rest of the century was characterized by relative stability and peace. While America and Russia were focused on domestic instability and developing their huge landmasses, Britain was able to achieve naval domination and extend its commercial and colonial interests while achieving industrial power at home. In the second half of the nineteenth century, other nations found their feet and started to industrialize, but as the twentieth century began there was great inequality of wealth and power in Europe. Because some nations had not modernized their military and did not develop the industrial infrastructure to support it, to compensate there was a scramble to gain new colonial territories in Africa, Asia, and the Pacific.

These adventures, however, would mean little compared to the cataclysm of the First World War, which once and for all changed global power structures. Austria-Hungary was finished, Germany was defeated, and Britain and France had to spend huge amounts just to maintain their place. The US emerged as the world's strongest power, but turned isolationist, as did Russia under the Bolshevik regime, although both nations were becoming unsurpassable in industrial strength. The Second World War, despite some spectacular advances by Germany and Britain's ultimate victory, only seemed to confirm the decline of Britain, Germany, and France relative to the growing power of the US and Russia, which now had far greater industrial resources to draw on, larger landmasses, and much bigger populations. "By 1943," Kennedy writes, "the bipolar world forecast decades earlier had finally arrived, and the military balance had once again caught up with the global distribution of resources."

Can you afford it?

While stating that there is "a dynamic of world power, essentially driven by technological and economic change," Kennedy does not claim that economics alone drives world events. Geography, national morale, alliances, and other factors can all affect the relative power of nations within the state system. However, in the long term victory tends to go to "he who has the last escudo," as Spanish captains would say; or in modern terms, to the coalition or country that has "the most flourishing productive base." Looking across 500 years of history, he sees a strong correlation between the winners of major conflicts and the extent of their resources. A lengthy conflict "turns into a test of the relative capacities of each coalition," and as the struggle goes on the possession of "more of it" proves vital.

Even in 1987 Kennedy wondered how the USSR could maintain its superpower status. The failure of many of its wheat harvests meant that it had become a huge importer of grain, and its steel industry was very wasteful. Its commitment to modernization was severely compromised by its need for control. If even making photocopies was forbidden (allowing this could spread dissent), it was hard to see how the country would adopt productivity-enhancing computers, email, and so on without ending censorship and the police control of information. Demographically, its decreasing birth rate and life expectancy and increasing infant mortality rate did not help either. He could not see how it could continue this way—and indeed it did not.

Kennedy could not have been surprised that America "won" the Cold War thanks partly to its ramping up of military technology through the Strategic Defense Initiative. The Soviet Union knew that it would never be able to compete with "Star Wars" unless it diverted more and more national resources into military research and development, which it could ill afford to do. The longer the Cold War went on, the more glaring would have been America's military superiority.

Yet this superiority could be its own curse. In the last speculative chapter of the book on the possible fates of the five great power blocs—China, Japan, the EEC, the Soviet Union, and the US—Kennedy focuses on the costs of America's dominance: the deficits needed to sustain it, and the unlikelihood that it could continue. The need to divert investment away from "butter" toward "guns," he says, leads any great power to "the downward spiral of slower growth, heavier taxes, deepening domestic splits over spending priorities, and weakening capacity to bear the burdens of defense."

Kennedy sees America in the late 1980s as being similar to Britain in 1914: an apparently unassailable great power about to have an uncomfortable reckoning. He warns of a "multipolar" world in which US and Soviet dominance is giving way to a rapidly developing Eastern sphere (Japan's economic might at the time seemed a great threat to America, even if it was about to enter two decades of recession) and an industrializing Third World.

Although Kennedy did not foresee how quickly the USSR would collapse, his broad point was right: that the cost of maintaining superpower status is so substantial that, even if this power is retained, it is an obstacle to continued economic dominance compared to other rising powers. This has certainly been borne out by China's rise since he wrote the book. Unconstrained by the need for huge military spending, it has been able to focus on commercial enrichment, which has now set it up to become a major military power if it wishes to.

Final comments

The ability to defend a nation is usually a short-term need, whereas economic growth is a long-term requirement of national power, and it can be hard to balance both. The heart of Kennedy's argument is that there is a tension between strategic security (having the latest weapons systems, a large standing army, a naval fleet, an air force), which requires significant diversion of the nation's resources, and economic security, which depends on growth and high demand, both of which can be eroded by the higher taxation needed for substantial defense spending. He notes that a lag of only 1 percent of economic growth compared to other countries can turn a world power into a small one in less than a century, as happened with Britain.

Is America going the same way, and will China replace it as the world's great superpower? Kennedy's former student Fareed Zakaria (see the commentary on p 310) has argued that US defense spending is quite affordable given that the country is still way ahead of China in terms of technology and education, and that America cannot be seen as a top-heavy military power with a weakening economic base—the classic profile of empire-fallers according to Kennedy. Moreover, recent research by Lant Pritchett and Larry Summers at Harvard University ("Asiaphoria meets regression to the mean," National Bureau of Economic Research) suggests that, given the drop in its growth rate from 10 percent per year to around 7 percent, China will not match America in economic output for another 20 years. Chinese economic power is already held back by authoritarian rule and corruption, but even if the country were to become increasingly liberal, history suggests that democratic transitions are accompanied by falling growth rates. The combination of American economic resilience and Chinese political fragility may well prove Kennedy's thesis about American decline to have been wrong.

Paul Kennedy

Born in 1945 in Wallsend, Northumberland, Paul Kennedy went to school in Newcastle upon Tyne and studied history at Newcastle University. His doctorate was from St Antony's College, Oxford.

From 1970 to 1983 Kennedy taught history at the University of East Anglia, and in 1983 he became a professor of British history at Yale University. He is presently its Director of International Security Studies. In 2007–08 he was the Philippe Roman Professor of History and International Affairs at the London School of Economics. Kennedy is a Fellow of the Royal Historical Society and the British Academy, and in 2014 was made the Hattendorf Prize Laureate by the US Naval War College.

The Rise and Fall of the Great Powers *won the Wolfson History Prize. Kennedy's other books include* The Rise and Fall of British Naval Mastery *(1976);* The Rise of Anglo-German Antagonism 1860–1914 *(1980);* Preparing for the Twenty-First Century *(1993);* The Parliament of Man: The Past, Present, and Future of the United Nations *(2006); and* Engineers of Victory: The Problem Solvers Who Turned the Tide in the Second World War *(2013).*

1998

The Autobiography of Martin Luther King, Jr.

"Along the way of life, someone must have the sense enough and morality enough to cut off the chain of hate and evil. The greatest way to do that is through love."

"The reality of segregation, like slavery, has always had to confront the ideals of democracy and Christianity. Indeed, segregation and discrimination are strange paradoxes in a nation founded on the principle that all men are created equal."

"To deprive man of freedom is to relegate him to the status of a thing, rather than elevate him to the status of a person. Man must never be treated as a means to the end of the state, but always as an end within himself."

In a nutshell

Revolutions need leaders, and the best ones change the minds of the oppressors as well as liberating the oppressed.

In a similar vein

Saul Alinsky *Rules for Radicals* (p 32)
Mohandas K. Gandhi *An Autobiography* (p 110)
Nelson Mandela *Long Walk to Freedom* (p 180)
Henry David Thoreau *Civil Disobedience* (p 286)

CHAPTER 23

Martin Luther King

K ing's "I have a dream" speech at the March on Washington in August, 1963 is one of history's great orations, and he was perhaps the greatest twentieth-century civil rights activist, but how much do we really know about King and what drove him?

The Autobiography is an edited collection of King's own words drawn from his books, journals, and speeches, edited by Clayborne Carson, a close aide of King's who became a Stanford University history professor, and who now directs the Martin Luther King, Jr., Research and Education Institute.

The book tracks the evolution of King's political and religious philosophy from his college days, to his leadership roles in the Southern Christian Leadership Conference, to his winning of the Nobel Peace Prize in 1964. Like no one before him in America, King was able to thrust issues confronting the black community into the public consciousness. As the focus of many high-profile protests such as the Montgomery bus boycott and the sit-ins in Birmingham, Alabama, he forced the American public and its political leaders, including several US presidents, to deal with and respond to his agenda.

King's influence on black Americans is far-reaching and led to what he refers to as the "new Negro," who was free of the stereotypes of the black male. Figures as diverse as film director Spike Lee, musician James Brown, boxer Muhammad Ali, and of course President Barack Obama have been inspired by his outlook and rhetoric. King's use of metaphor and conduplicatio (repetitive phrases in successive sentences), combined with powerful skills in oratory, made his words resonate, and the civil rights movement opened the door to similar movements of Native Americans, Latinos, women, the lesbian, gay, bisexual and transgender community, and disabled people. Martin Luther King, Jr. Day is an American public holiday.

Influences

Born in 1929, the son of a Baptist pastor, King had a relatively comfortable upbringing. Growing up he felt drawn to the ministry himself, yet had from the start a questioning mind and so would not accept anything uncritically. His assertiveness came partly from his father. King, Sr. once walked out of a shoe shop after poor service from a racist shopkeeper, and on another occasion was slapped by a white woman who told him: "You are that nigger that stepped on my foot." The rage his son felt at such treatment would soon be balanced by an idea about refusing to cooperate with a system in which segregation and racism were normal, indeed written into legislation. A defining moment for King, Jr. was winning an oratory competition with a speech entitled "The Negro and the Constitution." The triumph was short-lived when, on the bus journey home, he was made to move out of his seat to make way for a white person.

While a student at Morehouse College and then Crozer Theological Seminary, King read widely. He devoured the works of Marx, Hobbes, Mill, Rousseau, and Nietzsche, but did not find intellectual and moral satisfaction in them. Though attracted to Marxism, he felt that the materialism of Marx's view of history left no room for God, and he did not believe that totalitarianism was ever justified. He was interested in Reinhold Niebuhr's critique of the pacifist position, but decided that it confused pacifism with passive non-resistance; they were not the same. Gandhi's non-violent struggle on a massive scale against the British colonialists, however, had a huge impact on King. Later he would travel to India and draw parallels between the circumstances of the "untouchables" in that country and African Americans in his.

King had learned from a young age the dangers of retaliation in the face of oppression, and so was attracted to Gandhi's approach of non-violence as a form of power. "Before this century," King observed, "virtually all revolutions had been based on hope and hate. The hope was expressed in the rising expectation of freedom and justice. What was new about Mahatma Gandhi's movement in India was that he mounted a revolution on hope and love, hope and non-violence."

He compared Gandhi's compassion for his oppressors with the notion of "Christian love" with which he had been brought up. King also found inspiration in Thoreau's essay *Civil Disobedience* (see commentary on p 286), which would inspire a range of protest strategies employed by the civil rights movement and later by the peace movement. The bravery to stand up to the status quo would arise from Thoreau, King said, and the tactics for how to do it would come from Gandhi.

The struggle

After he completed his doctoral studies at Boston University, King felt a moral obligation to return to the South, and became a pastor in Montgomery, Alabama. In 1955, after Montgomery resident Rosa Parks refused to move when she was asked to give up her bus seat to a white man, King found himself thrust into the role of leader of a movement for justice, and helped organize the Montgomery bus boycotts. He saw the bus company as simply the outward expression of a system that could no longer be justified, and argued for a program of civil disobedience: "We were simply saying to the white community, 'We can no longer lend our cooperation to an evil system.'" The boycotts aimed to demonstrate that "it is more honorable to walk in dignity than ride in humiliation." King chose to emphasize that black Americans were citizens, and were "determined to apply our citizenship to the fullness of its meaning."

Through his eloquent speeches in the various court cases to resolve the issue, King rose to national prominence, and Montgomery marked the start of the modern civil rights movement. In 1957 King formed the Southern Christian Leadership Conference (SCLC), which coordinated sit-ins, marches, boycotts, freedom rides, and efforts to ensure that black Americans could register to vote. The SCLC was a response to what he felt was the impotence of white Christian leaders before the race problem; they seemed more devoted to order than to justice, choosing to "stand on side-lines mouthing pious irrelevancies and sanctimonious trivialities." The protests made the headlines, and as the figurehead of the movement King was put on the cover of *Time* magazine. He drilled protesters not to retaliate to police violence; taking the moral high ground would shame the oppressors.

Another front was opened up in the legal system. King noted that since the Declaration of Independence, "America has manifest a schizophrenic personality on the question of race." Segregation and discrimination, he said, "are strange paradoxes in a nation founded on the principle that all men are created equal." The SCLC used the Constitution to great effect in the fight against "Jim Crow" racial segregation laws. In each court case, while the local police and government fought to protect the privileges afforded them by social superiority, eventually they would be overruled by higher courts. The Supreme Court ruling that Alabama's racial segregation laws for buses were unconstitutional gave the movement legal ammunition in its later struggles in Atlanta, Albany, Birmingham, St Augustine, and Selma. Each of these campaigns became more challenging and more dangerous, but with jails filling up, legal challenges, national coverage of church burnings and lynchings, and a march on Washington, civil rights issues would not go away.

King knew that liberal Americans would be alienated by riots, and so he relentlessly preached non-violent protest as a way of winning them over. He had to deal with criticism of his tactics from the more militant Malcolm X and the Black Panther movement, and all the time he was feeling great pressure and self-doubt. He had to endure bomb and arson attacks, intimidation by the Ku Klux Klan, assaults by police, arrest and imprisonment (in 1960, he received six months' hard labor for a traffic violation), and threats to his family, including wife Coretta.

The "inseparable twin": Racial and economic injustice

"A person participates in this society primarily as an economic entity. At rock bottom we are neither poets, athletes, not artists; our existence is centered on the fact that we are consumers, because we must eat and have shelter to live."

King believed that it was not enough for Christianity to deal only with questions of the soul while ignoring collective suffering such as unemployment, poor housing, and poverty. His radical approach to segregation applied equally to economic disadvantage. Employment opportunities were part of his early negotiations with white authorities, and the effects of segregation on jobs, housing, and education were an ever present theme in his speeches. Indeed, the March on Washington event was billed as being about black economic rights and opportunities rather than racial injustice per se.

In 1966 King took his family to live in the Chicago ghetto, where he found black people paying a third more than whites for similar accommodation, thus being subject to a "color tax." He exposed the vicious circle of welfare dependence that made property ownership impossible. Poor transport required people to make purchases in their neighborhood, so they were at the mercy of local white traders who jacked up prices. Such problems fueled riots in Chicago and Los Angeles. King and his allies took various steps: real estate agents who permitted unjust practices to continue were subjected to sit-ins, and landlords were confronted; shopkeepers were encouraged to stock goods produced by black-owned companies; banking with black-owned banks was promoted, which resulted in money being circulated back into the community; and the use of voting power to elect blacks to key positions was important in fostering a sense of power and responsibility.

Although King never formally endorsed a presidential candidate or indeed a sitting president, he admired the Kennedys, and lauded President Johnson for his understanding of the connection between discrimination and poverty, as well as his awareness that "if America does not use her vast resources of wealth to end poverty and make it possible for all God's children to have the basic necessities of life, she will go to hell." When, thanks to LBJ, the Civil Rights Act of 1964 and the Voting Rights Act of 1965 were finally passed, it was obviously a great victory for political equality, but, more importantly, it allowed for black America's economic emancipation.

Final comments

Despite politicians warning him to stick to civil rights, King campaigned against American involvement in Vietnam, which he thought unconscionable, particularly the disproportionate amount of poor people who had been sent to fight. "If America's soul becomes totally poisoned," he said, "part of the autopsy must read 'Vietnam.'" He wanted America to lead the world in a moral sense, pushing for justice, equality, and democracy, not as "self-appointed world policeman," and believed that America's meddling in Guatemala and other countries was simply about protecting economic interests and maintaining the military-industrial complex. King also campaigned for sanctions against the apartheid regime in South Africa, and visited Britain to provide encouragement to its black communities.

King was only really getting into his stride as a world statesman for justice at the time of his assassination in 1968, and it is natural to wonder what else he might have achieved. Would pressure on South Africa to free Nelson Mandela have come 20 years sooner? Would the war in Vietnam have ended earlier? Could he have done something to reduce the disproportionate amount of time that black men spend in prison, thus destroying their families and their economic chances?

Not long before his death, King was in a strangely reflective mood:

"Well, I don't know what will happen now; we've got some difficult days ahead. But it really doesn't matter with me now, because I've been to the mountaintop. And I don't mind. Like anybody, I would like to live a long life—longevity has its place. But I'm not concerned about that now. I just want to do God's will."

It is easy to overlook just how much King's faith illuminated his life and work. What made him rise above a figure like Malcolm X was his compassion for humanity, not only African Americans, and his ethic of Christian love was as powerful as any Gandhian concept. His greatness also flowed from his grounding in philosophy: Hegel's dialectics suggested to him that growth comes from struggle, and therefore political struggle was natural to humans if they wanted to move ahead. His life was also infused with a Kantian respect for the individual, whom, he said, "must never be treated as a means to the end of the state, but always as an end within himself." Beyond his actual achievements in politics, it is King's ability to convey the sacred potential and dignity of the individual that continues to inspire.

No Logo

"Four years ago, when I started writing this book, my hypothesis was mostly based on a hunch. I had been doing some research on university campuses and had begun to notice that many students I was meeting were preoccupied with the inroads private corporations were making into their public schools. They were angry that ads were creeping into cafeterias, common rooms, even washrooms; that their schools were diving into exclusive distribution deals with soft-drink companies and computer manufacturers, and that academic studies were starting to look more and more like market research."

"When we lack the ability to talk back to entities that are culturally and politically powerful, the very foundations of free speech and democratic society are called into question."

In a nutshell

Beware of private interests invading the public sphere. We are citizens, not consumers.

In a similar vein

Edward Bernays *Propaganda* (p 66)
Emma Goldman *Anarchism and Other Essays* (p 114)
Upton Sinclair *The Jungle* (p 260)
Richard Wilkinson & Kate Pickett *The Spirit Level* (p 298)

CHAPTER 24

Naomi Klein

K lein's parents disdained brands and packaged products—Barbie dolls were "a racket," they said, "first it's a doll, then a camper van, then the whole mansion"—and bought her only gender-free toys. Instead of spending weekends out shopping, they would take the family on trips into the Canadian wilderness. In reaction, Klein and her brother developed an attraction to the glossy promises of billboards, jingles, and products that their parents were not willing to buy. The glowing Shell and McDonald's signs past which they drove on the way home were more alluring than the majesty of forests and lakes. As a teenager, Klein was no different in her hypersensitivity about whether the jeans she was wearing were the right brand or not. So why, after she had been through university, did she come to share her parents' worries about consumerism? What was actually wrong with brands, and what did they have to do with politics?

Klein knew that strong marketing and advertising were simply part of North American capitalist culture; it was not this she was against. However, in *No Logo: Taking Aim at the Brand Bullies* she argues that by the mid-1990s something had changed. Many companies had shifted from seeing themselves as makers of products to developers and creators of brands (which was where all the money was). Yet the money lavished on these brands was so enormous that it led to cost pressures at the production end (for example, foreign workers being exploited and the rise of "McJobs" domestically), as well as to corruption of spheres normally considered public (for instance, advertising and sponsorship in schools and universities). With watered-down anti-trust laws added into the mix, corporations had begun to assert ever greater power and control over culture, and were providing less and less real choice.

A month or so after Klein had finished writing *No Logo* the first big "anti-globalization" protests occurred, at the Seattle meeting of the World Trade Organization, followed by others around the world. In a preface to the 10th anniversary edition of the book, Klein says that anti-globalization was always a misnomer; she and other activists were not against globalization per se, but against how "the rules of the game had been distorted to serve the narrow interest of corporations at every level of governance—from international free-trade agreements to local water privatization deals." The WTO and other bodies were part of a neoliberal consensus that lionized markets and sought to denigrate and reduce the state wherever possible.

The terrorist attacks of 9/11 pushed Klein's agenda back somewhat. "To engage in dissent in this climate was cast as unpatriotic," she says; attacking capitalism was like attacking America, and free trade became a patriotic duty, even helping in the War against Terror. Many of the government agencies that had during the 1990s been scaled back and underfunded—airports, hospitals, mass transit systems, water, and food inspection—returned to center stage and were found to be wanting in their ability to cope with terror threats. The heroism of the firefighters themselves demonstrated that "there is indeed a role for the public sector after all." And when news emerged of the practices of private firms such as Halliburton doing well out of the war in Iraq, it only confirmed suspicions that government now existed not for the many, but for the few.

All Klein's books, including the subsequent *The Shock Doctrine* (2007, on the effect of neoliberal economics on developing countries) and *This Changes Everything* (2014, on corporate resistance to climate change measures) challenge the assumptions sustaining the current world order. "We pay a high price when we put the short term demands of business (for lower taxes, less 'red tape,' more investment opportunities) ahead of the needs of people," she writes. "Clinging to laissez-faire free-market solutions, despite overwhelming evidence of their failings, looks a lot like blind faith, as irrational as any belief system clung to by religious fanatics fighting a suicidal jihad."

No Logo is divided into four parts: "No Space" looks at the swamping of culture and education by marketing; "No Choice" considers the squashing of cultural choice because it is inconvenient for corporations; "No Jobs" charts the rise of temporary, part-time, and outsourced labor; and "No Logo" gives examples of resistance and alternatives to "corporate rule." Although ostensibly about the new power of "brand bullies," the book's deeper question is: What are we now, consumers or citizens?

The book was a bestseller in 28 languages and it is often said to have helped politicize a generation, one that "baby boomers" had criticized for having little social conscience. In reality, Klein likes to point out, it was the older generation who had sold out.

A global village of lords and slaves

No Logo begins in the Spadina Avenue garment district of Toronto, where Klein notes that Emma Goldman (see commentary on p 114) spent time in the 1930s as a labor organizer. In the late 1990s the area was already undergoing a transformation, with the sweatshops where people had struggled being turned into deluxe "loft living" complexes, or rented out to artists, designers, and computer game creators. Yet there was still some of the old rag trade left, and the building that Klein lives in belongs to a man who made his money making and selling "London Fog" coats. Around this time, Klein visited a garment factory in Jakarta, where 2,000 women were earning around $2 a day. When she asked one woman what brand of clothing it was that the women were making on the day she visited, she was told: "London Fog."

In the mid-1990s, it was hard to go anywhere and not hear the word "globalization," and it was nearly always seen in positive terms. The internet, it was claimed, would empower people in poor countries to provide services and make money, while an increasingly interlinked world economy would give people everywhere better access to goods and services. The flattening of global economics and labor would mean that someone in Jakarta could enjoy going to McDonald's or having a Motorola phone as much as a Chicagoan or a Londoner. However, the "global village" idea, so keenly promoted by Western companies eager to find new markets for their products, soon began to look like a massive cover for exploitation. Rather than equalizing the world, it was entrenching and widening the differences. When Klein spoke to a 17-year-old girl making CD-Rom drives for IBM in a factory in Manila, she said how impressed she was that someone of her age could be making such high-tech equipment. But the girl replies, "We make computers, but we don't know how to operate computers."

The wealth and comfort of the rich world have long been supported by the "Third World," Klein admits, but historically poor countries tended to be exporters of raw materials, commodities, or unfinished goods. But in the 1990s workers in Indonesia, Vietnam, and elsewhere were putting together for a pittance branded products—from Nike shoes to Barbie dolls to Apple computers—that would then be sold at massive markups. The high prices were not justified by the raw materials needed to make these products, and certainly not the labor involved, but by huge marketing budgets.

Klein realizes that, in hindsight, the "political correctness wars" of the 1980s and 1990s to have every group in society properly represented and recognized in the media were something of a red herring in social justice terms. After all, not much progress was being made if women in North America were achieving equality and drawing attention to body image issues while those in South East Asia were sweating over machines making "Girls Rule" T-shirts for 10 hours a day. The political correctness agenda seemed self-indulgent next to the fact that the world appeared to be reverting to the dark days of capitalism.

Erosion of the public sphere

No Logo was not merely about sweatshops in developing nations; it was about Klein's feeling that Western countries were witnessing a creeping corporatization, a takeover of the public sphere by private interests. A key example was American universities signing sponsorship deals with sports shoe and soft drink companies. The problem was clauses in the contracts saying that the universities were not allowed to "disparage" Reebok or Coca-Cola or whoever they had signed with. An Amnesty group at Kent State University, which had a sponsorship deal with Coca-Cola, wanted to bring over a human rights speaker from the Free Nigeria movement to raise awareness of Coca-Cola's support of the then dictatorship. When the university authorities learned that the talk would be critical of the company, they denied funding for the event. Such deals, Klein argues, "re-engineer some of the fundamental values of public universities, including… the right to open debate and peaceful protest on campus."

She also refers to corporate sponsorship of labs and departments in universities. If the lab's research lessened the value of the sponsoring company, the university came under pressure not to publish it; and universities usually sided with the company, not the research team. In other cases, studies were designed to fit the interests of corporate-endowed research chairs (Taco Bell sponsored a hospitality school, Kmart a marketing department, Yahoo an IT studies centre, and so on), rather than the independent research efforts that one would expect of public universities.

When universities pretend they are corporations, what is lost, Klein says, is the idea that they are public spaces devoted to truth and objective debate. This cannot happen if half the university is sponsored by a corporation that, in getting its money's worth, forces the administration to muzzle free speech.

No real choice

In the late 1990s, the world was being bombarded with advertising such as Microsoft's "Where do you want to go today?" The question should have been, Klein says: "How best can I steer you into the synergized maze of where I want you to go today?" Colossal mergers, buyouts, and corporate "synergies" meant that an age of increased choice, interactivity, and freedom was an illusion. In reality, many of the brands and products were linked by single owners, enabled by the weakening of anti-trust laws that had begun under Reagan.

Corporate behemoths had mountains of cash to run smaller businesses into the ground, to exploit suppliers, and to engage in a "race to the bottom" to get products made at the least cost. This had led to a preponderance of chain stores, and to greater power for the corporations behind them. The strategy of Wal-Mart or Starbucks when it moved into a new state or region was to blanket it with stores to elbow out all competition; some of the outlets will not get enough custom, but overall the firm's revenue will increase. This "cannibalization" strategy is only possible in a company with very deep pockets. New superstores like Nike Town and Virgin Megastore aimed to purify the brands from having to compete with other brands in department stores. Canadian clothes retailer Roots even opened a summer camp to make sure its products were seen as part of an "ethos" and "heritage." Disney's branded town, Celebration, was complete with plenty of public spaces like town squares, minus the graffiti and loiterers, yet funding for real-world public spaces— schools, libraries, parks—was increasingly being scaled back.

Final comments

In many parts of the world, Klein argues, the previous colonial subjugation has been replaced by a corporate one called "globalization." Globalization is not only about capital's transcending of international borders, but must also come to mean a sense of global citizenship and global rights, with greater emphasis on the world "market" for democracy, human rights, labor, and environmental policy. In other words, the left needs to own globalization as much as the right.

Events such as the 14 suicides in 2012 at the Foxconn plant in China— which makes products for Apple, HP, Dell, Motorola, Nintendo, and Sony, and where workers are paid $1–2 an hour—should tell us that much of what Klein wrote about has changed little. Indeed, the themes of the book—corporate greed, the fragility of people power, government's capture by special interests—are as relevant 15 years later as they ever were. Even if her talk of a "neoliberal consensus" does not chime with your political views, it is worth listening to her warning about the takeover of public space by private interests. Being a consumer may be fun, but being a citizen is a privilege that carries a responsibility to protect and enhance the things that we hold in common.

Naomi Klein

Naomi Klein was born in 1970 in Montreal, to parents who had moved from the US to Canada in 1967 to escape the Vietnam War draft. Her father is a doctor and her mother a film maker who focuses on feminist issues. At the University of Toronto Klein became editor of the student newspaper, and left before finishing her degree to work at the Toronto Globe and Mail.

Klein has been an outspoken critic of US foreign policy, particularly its support of Israel, and has campaigned against the Keystone XL pipeline that would bring oil from Alberta's oil sands into America. She has been involved in Occupy protests and demonstrations at the G-20 summits, and is a contributor to The Nation, The Globe and Mail, *and* The Guardian.

The Gettysburg Address

"Four score and seven years ago our fathers brought forth on this continent a new nation, conceived in liberty, and dedicated to the proposition that all men are created equal."

"The world will little note, nor long remember what we say here, but it can never forget what they did here."

"We here highly resolve that these dead shall not have died in vain—that this nation, under God, shall have a new birth of freedom—and that government of the people, by the people, for the people, shall not perish from the earth."

In a nutshell

A nation founded in liberty and equality that sticks together through challenges and hardship will never fall.

In a similar vein

Alexander Hamilton, John Jay, & James Madison *The Federalist Papers* (p 120)
Thomas Paine *Common Sense* (p 238)

CHAPTER 25

Abraham Lincoln

Between July 1 and July 3, 1863, the forces of General Robert E. Lee's Confederate Army battled the Union General George Meade's Army of the Potomac at Gettysburg, Pennsylvania. Over 50,000 men were killed, injured, or missing between the two forces, and Lee retreated toward Virginia on the night of July 4. With the loss of a third of his army, it was a crushing defeat for the Confederacy.

On the afternoon of November 19, 1863, officials and crowds gathered at a dedication ceremony for the Soldiers' National Cemetery in Gettysburg. Following on from the feature oration by statesman Edward Everett, which would take took two hours, President Abraham Lincoln had been asked to give a few words to mark the occasion. Two minutes, 10 sentences and 272 words later, he was done. Soon after the event, Everett wrote to the President: "I should be glad, if I could flatter myself that I came as near to the central idea of the occasion, in two hours, as you did in two minutes."

Why is a speech that received little applause from the audience at the time now deemed to be one of the greats of American history and indeed world politics? The answer partly lies with the journey the listener is taken on, able to experience the founding of America at the beginning and at the end finding the nation at a crossroads. The American Civil War would take the nation down one of two paths. Men were losing their life in battle to decide whether the country stayed together or parts of it seceded. The listener is embroiled in this drama all the way through, as the President offers both a lament for the fallen and a way forward for the living.

Lincoln was not well at the time of the dedication, and his face was said to be sad, mournful, and almost haggard, with a ghastly color. He reported feeling weak and dizzy, and a protracted illness followed that proved to be a mild case of smallpox. It seems remarkable that he was able to speak in public at all. Some historians think that the speech was drafted on the train to Pennsylvania, but an analysis of the documents suggests that it could not have been written on a train table. It is more likely to have been composed half at the White House, with the rest completed in discussion with William H. Seward, the Secretary of State who was with Lincoln in Gettysburg.

What Lincoln said and why

Given the shortness of the speech, it is possible to examine the whole text here, both for meaning and for the use of rhetorical devices that affect the listener.

> *"Four score and seven years ago our fathers brought forth on this continent a new nation, conceived in liberty, and dedicated to the proposition that all men are created equal."*

We are taken back to a time 87 years earlier when great figures including George Washington, Thomas Jefferson, and Benjamin Franklin courageously declared freedom from British rule and a new republic was born. Some regard this opening passage as radical, as it asserts that the Declaration of Independence and not the Constitution, which came 13 years later, is the true expression of the Founding Fathers' intentions for the new nation. While slavery was not prohibited under the Constitution, the Declaration of Independence asserted that America was "dedicated to the prospect that all men are created equal." By choosing it as his benchmark, Lincoln redefines the war as a struggle for the principle of human equality, as well as saving the Union.

> *"Now we are engaged in a great civil war, testing whether that nation, or any nation so conceived and so dedicated, can long endure. We are met on a great battlefield of that war. We have come to dedicate a portion of that field, as a final resting place for those who here gave their lives that that nation might live. It is altogether fitting and proper that we should do this."*

The Civil War threatened to tear the nation apart and tested the more global principles under which it had been founded. Lincoln here uses an effective contrast of life and death in commemorating "those who gave their lives" so that the "nation might live." We take democracy for granted today, but it cannot be over-emphasized how important republican principles were to people at the time.

> *"But, in a larger sense, we can not dedicate, we can not consecrate, we can not hallow this ground."*

This line uses the rule of three, a powerful public speaking technique of repeating something in three slightly different ways to make what is said more powerful and memorable. Lincoln continues in solemn respect for the soldiers, understandably given that Gettysburg was one of the bloodiest and most decisive battles:

"The brave men, living and dead, who struggled here, have consecrated it, far above our poor power to add or detract. The world will little note, nor long remember what we say here, but it can never forget what they did here."

Ironically, Lincoln believed that this speech would not be remembered, and here uses a double contrast (remember/forget and say/did) to state that actions speak louder than words, and that those winning the battles were the ones acting memorably.

"It is for us the living, rather, to be dedicated here to the unfinished work which they who fought here have thus far so nobly advanced. It is rather for us to be here dedicated to the great task remaining before us — that from these honored dead we take increased devotion to that cause for which they gave the last full measure of devotion — that we here highly resolve that these dead shall not have died in vain — that this nation, under God, shall have a new birth of freedom — and that government of the people, by the people, for the people, shall not perish from the earth."

Words such as "dedicated," "devotion," "highly resolve," and "freedom" are used as a call to action. Where before Lincoln stated that the ground before them could not be dedicated, now he tells the audience that they should be dedicated to the "great task remaining before us," that of holding the nation together and making it prosper.

He concludes the address with one of the most memorable triplets in public speaking: "government of the people, by the people, for the people." This powerful ending echoes something that Lincoln had said in Congress in July 1861, that the United States was a "democracy—a government of the people, by the same people." In trying to rally the nation, the text of the address is highly inclusive; it is all about "we," a word repeated many times. "Here," referring to Gettysburg, is used eight times. These repetitions may not be consciously noticed, but deliver a powerful effect on the listener, providing a sense of hallowed ground and provoking a strong sense of kindred belonging.

Public response
The press response to the speech was divided along political lines. Republican journalists were full of praise, citing a heartfelt but compact piece of oratory. Democratic journalists generally panned it as silly, flat, and dishwatery. In the wake of Everett's oration, Lincoln's address would have seemed very short

to its audience, and the silence and delayed applause that followed may have been a desire to hear more than this brief taste.

In an audio recollection made a year before his death in 1939, William R. Rathvon described being present at the Gettysburg Address. He had been excused from school so that he could hear the President. Rathvon reports that Lincoln was mounted on a horse, which accentuated his unusual height. He was escorted by dignitaries, army officers, representatives of foreign countries, civil and military organizations, and a surging patriotic crowd. Rathvon and his friends were able to work their way through the crowd to within 15 feet of Lincoln, and he recalls the oration as coming out "in a serious manner, almost to sadness." Though Rathvon could not recall any of the exact words afterwards, he felt very patriotic about it, and would have fought anyone who cast aspersions on "Old Abe."

As a document

Commentators have pointed out similarities between Lincoln's address and Pericles' funeral oration, given during the Peloponnesian War to honor the war dead, which listed the virtues of democracy. Like Lincoln, Pericles began by acknowledging his esteemed predecessors. He stated: "I shall begin with our ancestors: it is just and proper that they should have the honor of the first mention on an occasion like the present." Both highlight that they are committed to a fair, democratic system for all their people. Pericles said: "If we look to the laws, they afford equal justice to all in their private differences." Both speeches honour the dead for their sacrifice, and they entreat the living to continue the struggle, Pericles stating: "You, their survivors, must determine to have as unfaltering a resolution in the field, though you may pray that it may have a happier issue." The Gettysburg Address similarly contains a word of warning as well as the promise of eternal blessings, in the form of political freedom.

There is debate about what constitutes the definitive version of the Gettysburg Address. There are five known copies of the speech, each called by the surname of the person who received it. Two copies were given to Lincoln's secretaries, John Nicolay and John Hay. These were prepared before the speech, and one was probably the reading copy, while the other was a draft version. Neither of these uses the phrase "under God," which was reported by eye-witnesses. Lincoln may have simply added the words during the delivery of his address. A signed version of the address that Lincoln gave to the Secretary of the Navy, George Bancroft, is the one inscribed on the Southern wall of the Lincoln Memorial in Washington, DC.

Final comments

Lincoln was assassinated in April 1865 by John Wilkes Booth, a Confederate spy. The Civil War had been a victory for the Union and the President had signed the Emancipation Proclamation, ordering that all slaves in the ten rebellion states be set free. Senator Charles Sumner of Massachusetts wrote at the time: "That speech, uttered at the field of Gettysburg... and now sanctified by the martyrdom of its author, is a monumental act. In the modesty of his nature, he said 'the world will little not, nor long remember what we say here, but it can never forget what they did here.' He was mistaken. The world at once noted what he said, and will never cease to remember it."

Martin Luther King, Jr. alluded to the Gettysburg Address in the opening of his "I have a dream" speech at the 1963 March on Washington, standing on the steps of the Lincoln Memorial. King likened the promises of equality the forefathers made to a "promissory note" to the black people of America. He argued that the hopes stemming from the Emancipation Proclamation and the Gettysburg Address had been unfulfilled for black Americans, and were now returned on account of "insufficient funds." With this reminder of the nation's founding principles, the civil rights movement pushed ahead to ensure that the promise of freedom and equality for all of its citizens was fulfilled.

Abraham Lincoln

Abraham Lincoln was born in a log cabin in Hodgenville, Kentucky in 1809. At one stage his family had to squat on public land in a crude shelter, hunting and farming until they could buy their own land. After the early death of his mother, his step-mother encouraged him to read and he became mostly self-educated. He did various odd jobs and later owned a shop, in which he acquired important social skills and became known as a great storyteller. During the Black Hawk War in 1832, he made important political connections and entered the Illinois state legislature as a member of the Whig party. He taught himself law, was admitted to the bar in 1837, and began to practice in Springfield, Illinois. After marrying Mary Todd, Lincoln served a term in the House of Representatives, where he spoke out against the Mexican-American War. His law career was successful, and he represented organizations such as the Illinois Central Railroad.

Lincoln helped form the Republican Party, and his "House divided" speech rallied his party against disunity on the slavery issue. His intellectual leadership saw him elected the 16th President of the United States, despite receiving few votes from Southern states, which soon seceded, bringing on the Civil War. Lincoln signed the Emancipation Proclamation and delivered the Gettysburg Address toward the end of the conflict, which ended in 1864, the same year he was re-elected.

Two Treatises of Government

"Men being ... by nature all free, equal, and independent, no one can be put out of this estate, and subjected to the political power of another, without his own consent."

"Every man is born with a double Right: First, A Right of Freedom *to his Person, which no other man has a power over, but the free Disposal of it lies in himself. Secondly,* a Right, *before any other man, to inherit, with his Brethren, his Father's Goods."*

In a nutshell

People have natural rights to their own life, labor, and property that no ruler should be allowed to take away.

In a similar vein

Edmund Burke *Reflections on the Revolution in France* (p 78)
Alexander Hamilton, John Jay, & James Madison *The Federalist Papers* (p 120)
Thomas Hobbes *Leviathan* (p 132)
Mencius *The Mencius* (p 192)

CHAPTER 26

John Locke

K nown as the "father of classical liberalism," John Locke has for centuries been an inspiration to people who prefer their politics to be based on reason rather than tradition. His emphasis on the rights of the people over the power of monarchs provided the perfect antidote to Thomas Hobbes' royal absolutism and patriarchal philosophy, and although his idea of government by popular consent may now be taken for granted (even by illiberal regimes that pay lip service to it), it was risky to voice such ideas in the seventeenth century.

At the time of writing the *Two Treatises*, Locke was an "exclusionist," arguing for James II not to become king because of his tyrannical ways and attempt to turn England Catholic. When James did ascend to the throne, Locke felt threatened and exiled himself to Holland. It was only after the king was overthrown by a combination of English politicians and Holland's William of Orange (who became William III of England) that Locke was safe to return. In this "Glorious Revolution" of 1688, the supremacy of parliament became reality and the age of arbitrary, dictatorial royal rule seemed over.

It was long thought that the *Two Treatises* were a justification for that revolution, but scholars now believe that Locke wrote most of the work between 1679 and 1681. So even if his hopes for political change were fulfilled, he was not the "philosopher of the revolution." Indeed, unlike Hobbes' *Leviathan* (see commentary on p. 132), which was a celebrated work in an England that had seen the restoration of the monarchy after the civil wars sparked by Cromwell, Locke's *Two Treatises* was largely ignored in his lifetime. The work only came into its own late in the eighteenth century among French Enlightenment thinkers such as Voltaire and Rousseau, and with the American Founding Fathers Jefferson and Madison. Lockean political philosophy was blamed for the French and American Revolutions and the secularization of Western society (he supported religious toleration and the separation of church and state), and his notion that "Every man has a Property in his own Person which no Body has any Right to but himself" influenced the anti-slavery movement.

For Locke, consent is the foundation of any polity, and he takes issue with any kind of government that forgets that it requires the overt or tacit consent of the people to govern. Given that he was calling the monarchs of his day, in effect, illegitimate dictators, it is no surprise that Locke published the first and second treatises anonymously, and that he does not name particular kings.

Kings are only men

Locke's First Treatise, the shorter of the two, is a systematic attack on Sir Robert Filmer's *Patriarcha*, a famed defense of absolutist monarchical government.

Filmer argues that just as no child is born free, but belongs fully to their parents, in the same way adults must always be in submission to their "parent," the monarch. He also asserts that God gave Adam lordship over the earth, and that this dominion extends to kings. Therefore, monarchs have a divine right to rule. The king is by necessity above the law.

Locke counters that the analogy between the father of a family and the father of a country (a king) does not work. The difference is that adults can think and act for themselves without being in a state of dependence. If one takes Filmer's concept to its logical conclusion, everyone (including princes and aristocrats) except the king would be slaves.

Regarding the divine right of kings, Locke says that this is plainly ridiculous. It has no scriptural basis, and even if it were true it would be impossible to trace the ancestry of any living king to the biblical Adam. Rather than the king having all the power and the populace none, Locke introduces the idea that people have natural rights at birth, including that of freedom. It is time for the "child" to assert its independence before the father.

All free in a state of nature

In the Second Treatise, Locke imagines a hypothetical state of nature in which all people are equal. This is not wanton anarchy, but the freedom to choose to live by a set of laws, not according to the arbitrary will of another.

Locke's state of nature is quite different from the brutal and lawless state of nature that Hobbes imagines. For Locke, even in humankind's early stages people's actions are shaped by (God-given) natural laws, which everyone recognizes at least in principle, including the law of the preservation of life: not harming others, not taking one's own life, and respecting what belongs to others. For "though this be a state of liberty," he says, "yet it is not a state of license." "Natural justice" exists whereby all have the right to punish an offender.

At a later stage, people do not mete out justice directly, since that must involve bias, and give over this right to a person charged with weighing up matters of crime and justice. Thus, an independent judiciary evolves to resolve any conflicts. In giving up a personal right in exchange for the provision of a service (justice), humanity enters into a "compact." This consent is the basis of civil society, and people freely enter into it to protect their lives and property.

People over monarchy

Locke's assumption that a person has "natural rights" at birth breaks away from the medieval idea that people are born to a certain station in life. "Politick Societies," he writes, "all began from a voluntary Union, and the mutual agreement of Men." Over time, monarchies arose, but they forgot that their elevated position was dependent on popular consent. The king is not the representative of God, but of the people, and "has no Will, no Power but that of the Law." If he goes against the will of society, expressed in its laws, then he no longer has the support of the people. If that happens, Locke famously says, then "it is lawful for the people... to *resist* their King."

Resisting or deposing the king is justified when he acts purely for his own advantage, rather than for the good of the people. When he rules well as a representative of the people, he has authority and legitimacy. When he departs from this, he becomes a mere tyrant.

The authority of parliament in Locke's time could be thwarted by the king, who had the power to call parliament to stand, or not – which happened in 1681–85. The monarch could also try to bring in new laws and bribe or intimidate people. In such situations, Locke says, a "state of war" ensues because the king's position is based on "Force without Authority." It is he, not the people, who is rebelling against the proper nature of things.

As part of his emphasis on natural law, Locke says that property rights precede specific forms of political organization, which means that no parliament or king should be able to take away from a person what is rightfully theirs; that is, what is established by precedent or law. Equally, a king has no right to raise taxes unless the majority of the people agree to it via their deputies or representatives in parliament. Taxation must only be for the public good. In making these points, Locke is thinking of the conduct of Charles II and James II.

Labor, property, and economics

Locke never claimed that property ownership should be the basis of political power; rather, all people were equal in a state of nature before they even made claims to property.

In his theory of labor value, people have absolute possession of their own body, and therefore their own labor. Whatever they extract from nature by the use of their own labor therefore becomes theirs too. By mixing their labor with a resource, they have made it their property. Given the extent of the world's natural resources, Locke points out, there will always be enough for others to develop, cultivate, and extract from nature. Humans have a basic right to subsistence, or to be free to live on nature's bounty. Yet as civil society comes into being, the subsistence society in which everyone has their own piece of land is replaced by an economy based on exchange, money, and trade. A person with some land exchanges a perishable harvest of wheat, for instance, for some imperishable silver. But in this more advanced economy the moral foundation of a person's right to their own body and labor does not disappear; rather, everyone benefits from the increasing complexity.

A constitutional form of government, Locke argues, is best suited to protecting human and property rights in a money exchange economy, since the power of commerce rests in the multitude of people engaged in it, not in some royal monopoly. Kingly power will be more arbitrary and prone to take away property or tramp over natural human rights.

Locke makes it clear that a free economy and property rights do not end moral responsibility. Writing in the First Treatise, he says that a person should be able to claim help from another's surplus when in need: "He that hath, and to spare, must… give away to the pressing and preferable Title of those, who are in danger to perish without it." The natural right to develop the land and gain property must be balanced by a natural law of redistribution that "gives every Man a Title to so much out of another's Plenty, as will keep him from extream want, where he has no means to subsist otherwise." Of course, freedom will lead in time to inequality, since people have different abilities, but this is all the more reason to be generous.

Final comments

In the *Two Treatises of Government* we can see the roots of several ideas that we take for granted today, including:

- "Human rights," which are presumed to exist through natural equality at birth, a situation that Locke depicts in his state of nature.
- Universal suffrage, which rests on political rights without the need for property (Locke has been an influence on movements for the right of women to vote and for other disenfranchised people).
- The welfare state, deriving from Locke's belief that those in honest need have a right to ask for help from those with a surplus.
- The wrongness of slavery, since "Every man has a Property in his own Person [which] no Body has any Right to but himself."

Against this legacy, critics of Locke have noted the following:

- His political philosophy rests on the assumption that there *are* natural human rights, but if you do not agree that there are, then his ideas seem overly optimistic. Hobbes' view of man may appear more realistic.

- He does not take full account of the fact that private property ownership leads to great inequalities, and his emphasis on property is a simple reflection of his being a member of England's better-off.
- He played a role in organizing the new British-American colony of Carolina, whose constitution (which he helped draft) set up a feudal aristocracy based on the slave trade.

These points may have merit, yet one other aspect of the *Two Treatises* makes Locke seem ahead of his time. He thought that foreign conquest was a mad idea, a simple case of "might over right." Conquest does not imply possession and has no moral foundation, even if few then questioned that it was the normal behavior of kings; indeed, he admits that his view "seems a strange doctrine, it being so quite contrary to the practice of the world." If he were transported to our day, Locke might be surprised to find that there are still plenty of tyrants whose regimes are founded on raw power. Yet he would be happy that they are in a minority, and that his philosophy of popular consent in politics is the norm.

John Locke

Born in 1632 in Somerset, England, John Locke was not high born (his father was a lawyer and minor official), but he attended the prestigious Westminster School in London. He won a studentship to Christ Church, Oxford (ironically the most royalist of the university's colleges) and after earning two degrees, stayed on to teach theology and politics before beginning his own research on medical and scientific matters. In 1667 he joined the household employ of Lord Ashley (later the Earl of Shaftesbury), and collaborated with the eminent physician Thomas Sydenham and natural philosopher Robert Boyle. The following year he supervised a life-saving operation on Shaftesbury's liver.

When Shaftesbury became Lord Chancellor, Locke worked with him as an adviser, and he later helped to organize the new colony of Carolina. After the Glorious Revolution he was made a salaried member of the Board of Trade, which charted the government's economic policy. He proposed adjustments to the Poor Laws so that everyone had the right to sufficient food and clothing.

Locke, who never married, spent his last years in Essex living with his old friend Lady Damaris Masham and her husband. He died in 1704.

While the Two Treatises of Government *and the* Letters Concerning Toleration *(1689–92) express Locke's political thinking, he is equally important for his trailblazing empiricist philosophy, best expressed in* An Essay Concerning Human Understanding *(see the commentary in* 50 Philosophy Classics*).*

Discourses on Livy

"Were any one, therefore, about to found a wholly new republic, he would have to consider whether he desired it to increase as Rome did in territory and dominion, or to continue within narrow limits."

"Those cities wherein the government is in the hands of the people, in a very short space of time, make marvelous progress, far exceeding that made by cities which have been always ruled by princes... and this we can ascribe to no other cause than that the rule of a people is better than the rule of a prince."

"For all countries and provinces which enjoy complete freedom, make... most rapid progress."

In a nutshell

States that allow a measure of freedom among their citizens tend to overshadow more controlled and homogeneous nations.

In a similar vein

Daron Acemoglu & James A. Robinson *Why Nations Fail* (p 26)
Aristotle *Politics* (p 54)
Alexander Hamilton, John Jay, & James Madison *The Federalist Papers* (p 120)
Paul Kennedy *The Rise and Fall of the Great Powers* (p 144)
John Locke *Two Treatises of Government* (p 168)

Niccolò Machiavelli

People go to considerable lengths to acquire a broken statue from ancient Rome or Greece, Machiavelli notes at the start of his *Discourses on Livy*, yet they pay little homage to the lawmakers, citizens, and kings whose efforts, ideas, and principles fashioned these great civilizations. For many centuries, Rome was a society that successfully balanced class interests, kept tyrannical rule at bay, and provided for the prosperity of its people in relative peace.

Renaissance humanists like Machiavelli received much of their inspiration from reading the classical histories, such as Titus Livius' account of the rise and dominance of republican Rome, *Ab Urbe Condita*. Livy's description of the order and sense of purpose of the republic in its heyday provided a contrast to the instability and weak leadership of the sixteenth-century Italian states.

Machiavelli was no idle theorist but played a significant role in the Florentine republic. However, in 1512, when the Medici family was swept back to power in Florence after 18 years in exile, his career as a high-ranking bureaucrat was over. He was arrested, tortured, then set free. At his farm at Sant'Andrea in Percussina, he hatched the idea of a book that might ingratiate himself with the family and allow for his comeback to politics. Though dedicated to Lorenzo de Medici, *The Prince* (see commentary in *50 Philosophy Classics*), Machiavelli's famous manual of power for rulers who have to put normal ethics aside in order to preserve the state, in fact failed to return him to the center of power. It is likely that he then settled down to his much longer work, *Discourses on Livy*.

The *Discourses* represent Machiavelli's preferred political model of a state that allows significant internal freedom and popular consent, but could still be strong in foreign policy terms. It is thus a defense of the republicanism in which he had believed all along, and he pointedly dedicates it not to a prince but to two of his friends. He did not expect the book to be published in his lifetime, which is just as well given some of the comments he makes on how Italian states were governed.

The *Discourses* are important in the history of political philosophy because they provide an antidote to Utopian schemes such as Plato's republic. Machiavelli believed that only a society in which conflict was allowed, indeed was part of the system, would be robust. Any system that tried to force an ideal order on people would in contrast be brittle or fragile, since it could not accommodate a plurality of views or dissent. Where Plato tried to arrest change, Machiavelli knew that institutions and public opinion constantly evolve, so it was wisest to accommodate change. In this he provides a model for the large, pluralist democracies that have been the most successful form of political organization in the modern era.

Rome got it right

Whatever form of government a state chooses, Machiavelli observes, it always seems to become corrupted given enough time. Monarchy inevitably turns into tyranny, aristocracy into oligarchy, and democracy into anarchy. Rome's great achievement in governance, the source of its stability, was to incorporate *elements* of monarchy, aristocracy, and democracy without letting any one of them dominate.

The Roman republic replaced kingly rule with two consuls (the equivalent of today's president or prime minister) and a senate drawn from the nobility, and in doing so incorporated monarchic and aristocratic elements into the state to good effect. However, these, in turn, were balanced by the tribunes, men whose job was to represent the concerns and demands of the general public. This role was created "to stand between the people and the senate, and to resist the insolence of the nobles."

With this augmentation, Rome (unlike Athens) had close to a perfect state, with all the elements of society recognized and with at least some access to power. It is in the tension between people and nobles, Machiavelli says, "that all laws favorable to freedom have their origin."

The right to accuse and impeach

"No more useful or necessary authority can be given than the power to accuse, either before the people, or before some council or tribunal, those citizens who in any way have offended against the liberty of their country."

Machiavelli argues that calumny, or slander, has been the downfall of many a state. One section of the population develops a grievance against some public figure, whom it seeks through underhand ways to destroy. This in turn provokes counter plots, which swirl around a city or state without the government having any control. Enmity and hatred grow stronger because they have no official or public expression, and they poison all of society. This is pretty much what Machiavelli observed in Florence, which became divided between the old nobility and those wanting reform. The flashpoint was the failure of Florentine commander Giovanni Guicciardini to defeat the city of Lucca. The rumor went around that he had been bribed by the Luccans to lose, but without a court to test the accusation Florence was inflamed by mistrust and ill-will.

In Rome, the facility to bring an accusation to a court or tribunal meant that it could be weighed according to the evidence and either proved to be groundless or exposed as truth. Since even a high official could be impeached if he were shown to have done wrong, the effect was that people in author-ity, for fear of being accused of something, were more likely to carry out their duties properly and incorruptibly. Machiavelli mentions the story of Coriolanus, who tried to starve the Roman people during a famine and so reduce their power. Members of the public were furious and ready to slay him. In the event, the tribunes made a formal accusation against Coriolanus and he was exiled, which was much healthier for the Roman state. In Rome the general populace and the senate were always at loggerheads, yet thanks to the impeachment facility the people's grievances with particular nobles could be fully expressed. At no time did either side call on a foreign power to help in wresting control, Machiavelli notes, "for having a remedy at home, there was no need to seek one abroad."

How to be powerful

For a state that wants to extend its power, Machiavelli says, it is best to imi-tate Rome. A state that simply wants to maintain itself should copy the city-states of Venice or Sparta.

Sparta was governed by a smaller cohort (king and nobility only) than Rome, and had a much smaller population. Its founder Lycurgus believed that its people should not be "diluted" by foreigners, so marriage with non-Spartans was not allowed, and citizenship was severely restricted. Such aspects helped it engineer tranquility within its borders, but meant that it did not grow. The Venetian state was divided into gentlemen and plebeians, and both had certain rights that were denied to any later immigrants to Venice; as the latter were not numerous, they could not upset the established order. Sparta and Venice did have periods of imperial domination, but these did not last, Machiavelli argues, because their forms of government were too based on the power of the higher classes, so the masses were less motivated to enlarge and protect the state, as in Rome.

Indeed, Machiavelli reckons that if the characteristics that ensured the unity and peace of Venice and Sparta were applied to Rome, it would never have become great. This is because Rome developed a constitutional state of affairs that made disorder *normal*. It allowed the arming of its lower classes and gave them a measure of political power through the tribunes. It also did not try to limit the size of its population, which gave it a big advantage in war but also meant that the plebeian classes were large compared to the nobility, and so were less easily controlled. Any new state, Machiavelli says, faces a choice of having a larger population that makes it possible to extend its dominion, at the cost of some unruliness, or lessening internal disorder but also being weak in military reach. Sparta was able to get dominion of all of Greece, but could not sustain it, and neither could Venice keep up its control over Italy. Machiavelli observes that in a case of life imitating nature, "it is neither natural nor possible that a puny stem should carry a great branch, so a small republic cannot assume control over cities or countries stronger than herself."

The better ruler: prince or people?

Machiavelli does not accept the view common among aristocrats that the people cannot be trusted. In fact, the people are no more changeable or inclined to poor decisions than are princes and individual rulers. Some of the public may be poor judges of character, but these are balanced out by those who can see through a person seeking office. Moreover, the Roman people were as patriotic and loyal as any of the nobility. For 400 years, they "never relaxed in their hatred of the regal name, and were constantly devoted to the glory and welfare of their country."

True, it is kings and nobles who tend to be the framers of legislation and the builders of institutions, but Machiavelli suggests he would place more trust in the people to respect laws and maintain institutions. Even if these may not always benefit a particular individual, that individual knows they exist for the greater benefit of all. In contrast, a ruler sees laws and institutions as a plaything to be changed to suit his or her interests. A people who have descended into anarchy can always be brought back to order and reason, Machiavelli says, but rulers easily become a law unto themselves, and can only be stopped by their death. Even a poorly run republic is likely to afford more opportunity and justice than a well-run kingdom.

Machiavelli does not agree with Livy that it was Fortune that made Rome great. Rather, it was its smartness in policy and government. Yes, the valor of Rome's armies allowed it to conquer many lands, but it was the state's unique institutions and talent for bureaucracy and managing people, allowing the best and brightest to rise, that enabled it to *keep* what it gained.

Final comments

Machiavelli's theory of power says that only states that are meritocratic, allow immigration, and have a desire to grow large will be able to command lasting influence. Add to this an emphasis on open government, a trustworthy judiciary, and an array of checks and balances that prevent any one person or party dominating, and you have a recipe for lasting success.

Rome's combination of republican ways and a large population allowed it to control the Mediterranean and beyond way longer than might have been expected. The US, another large and disorderly republic, has been able to dominate for similar reasons. In contrast, Japan—with virtually no immigration and a sense of the purity of the Japanese race—is more like Sparta. The Japanese were able to dominate their part of the world for a time, but their attachment to homogeneity prevented Japan from ever being a great power in the Roman or American sense.

Niccolò Machiavelli

Niccolò Machiavelli was born in Florence in 1469, the same year that Lorenzo de Medici became its ruler. His father was a lawyer, and Machiavelli received an education in Latin, rhetoric, and grammar. He lived through the reign of Savonarola and his Christian republic, and in the following years rose through the ranks of the new administration. In 1498 he was appointed Secretary of the Second Chancery of the Republic and of the Ten of Liberty and Peace. Two years later he went on his first diplomatic mission, meeting Louis XII of France, and in 1501 married Marietta Corsini, with whom he had six children. In 1502–03 he spent four months at the court of Cesare Borgia, a fearful ruler whom many consider to be the model for Machiavelli's prince. He was also part of missions to Pope Julius II and Emperor Maximilian. With the fall of the Florentine republic in 1512, Machiavelli was dismissed from his positions and, accused of conspiracy, was imprisoned, tortured, and then released.

Other writings include The Mandrake, *a satirical play about Florentine society;* The Art of War, *a treatise in the form of a Socratic dialogue; and a* History of Florence, *commissioned by Cardinal Giulio de' Medici. Machiavelli died in 1527, and is buried in Florence's Santa Croce Church.*

Long Walk to Freedom

*"I cannot pinpoint the moment when I became politicized, when
I knew that I would spend my life in the liberation struggle. To
be African in South Africa means that one is politicized from the
moment of one's birth, whether one acknowledges it or not."*

*"I had no epiphany, no singular revelation, no moment of truth, but
a steady accumulation of a thousand slights, a thousand indignities
and a thousand unremembered moments produced in me an anger, a
rebelliousness, a desire to fight the system that imprisoned my people."*

*"I have cherished the ideal of a democratic and free society
in which all persons live together in harmony and with equal
opportunities. It is an ideal which I hope to live for and to achieve.
But if needs be, it is an ideal for which I am prepared to die."*

In a nutshell

A people can be liberated through a persistent, dignified struggle.

In a similar vein

Saul Alinsky *Rules for Radicals* (p 32)
Mohandas K. Gandhi *An Autobiography* (p 110)
Martin Luther King *The Autobiography of Martin Luther King, Jr.* (p 150)

CHAPTER 28

Nelson Mandela

At the age of 16, Nelson Mandela had a coming-of-age ceremony that included a ritual circumcision. The occasion usually had an atmosphere of promise and power, but the speech that Chief Meligqili gave said otherwise. Manhood was now an empty, illusionary promise because his people were conquered, living as slaves and shack tenants. They had no strength, no power, and no control. The young Mandela, who thought of white people as benefactors rather than oppressors, was initially angered, but the words began to work on him.

A visit to his university (Fort Hare University College, run by missionaries and with black professors) by the great Xhosa poet Samuel Edward Krune Mqhayi made a similar impression. Dressed in a leopard-skin kaross and carrying a spear, Mqhayi spoke of the brutal clash between indigenous Africa and Europe, which did not care for African culture and therefore had no right to take over. He predicted a victory one day for Africans over the interlopers. Mandela could not believe the boldness of the speech.

When an arranged marriage loomed, Mandela ran away to Johannesburg. After trying to get work in the offices of a gold mine, he eventually found an articled clerkship in a liberal Jewish law firm. He also met a life-long ally in the struggle for freedom, Walter Sisulu, a real estate agent (when black people were still allowed to buy property) and local leader. At Sisulu's house Mandela met Anton Lembede, the leader of the Youth League, a militant pressure group within the African National Congress (ANC). Lembede articulated his ideas on Africa's liberation from paternalistic colonialism: The West and its culture were unnecessarily idolized, resulting in a black inferiority complex; Africans should recognize their own culture and achievements and dismiss the notion that whites were the chosen people and intrinsically superior. African nationalism was the battle cry, and a truly democratic form of government the goal.

This was heady stuff for Mandela. In the autobiographical *Long Walk to Freedom* he writes:

"At the university, teachers had shied away from topics like racial oppression, lack of opportunities for Africans and the nests of

laws and regulations that subjugate the black man. But in my life in Johannesburg, I confronted these things every day. No one had ever suggested to me how to go about removing the evils of racial prejudice, and I had to learn by trial and error."

He completed his articles for his law degree, married, bought a house, and had a child, then was elected to the Executive Committee of the Transvaal ANC.

What is the alternative?

South Africa's white-only elections in 1948 resulted in victory for the National Party, which had devised a new system for keeping Africans in their place called "apartheid." Literally meaning "the state of being apart," apartheid resulted in African-only schools, hospitals, transportation, townships, regulations, and passes. There were curbs on the trade union movement, mixed marriages were prohibited, and blacks were no longer able to buy property. Hundreds of oppressive laws entrenched a brutal hierarchy: Whites at the top, Blacks at the bottom, and Indians and Coloreds in the middle. Afrikaans, the language of the original Dutch farmer-settlers, took over from English as an official language. With race as the basis for South African society, elaborate tests were required that often broke up families. "Where one was allowed to live and work could rest on such absurd distinctions as the curl of one's hair or the size of one's lips," Mandela notes.

The codification of oppression led the ANC to mobilize in greater numbers, inspired by Gandhi's non-violent protests in India. It organized a Defiance Campaign of strikes and boycotts. Other groups held a Freedom Day, but the police fired at protesters and these sorts of public protests were banned. The 1950 Suppression of Communism Act was only partly related to curbing communism; its real purpose was to allow imprisonment of anyone on a trumped-up charge. The government attempted to silence the ANC, and began a policy of clearing out black townships such as Sophiatown to make way for white people.

Despite this harsher climate, in 1952 Mandela and Oliver Tambo established the first black law office in South Africa. It was inundated with cases from the first day and was highly successful. In those days, Mandela admits that he was a "hotheaded revolutionary" without a great deal of discipline. Furious about what was happening in Sophiatown, Mandela made a speech rejecting passive resistance and saying that non-violence was an ineffective strategy. With the police watching, he said that violence was the only weapon that would work against the agents of apartheid. He was censured for these comments by the ANC National Executive and he renounced his views in public, but privately kept to his belief that non-violence would never work. Mandela was banned from involvement with the ANC and his activities became more secret and illegal.

As an alternative to violence, the ANC produced a Freedom Charter, akin to the American Declaration of Independence, which outlined the demand for equal rights and the ability to vote, with a fair share of the country's wealth and land. It seemed a step in the right direction—until Mandela and the entire executive leadership of the ANC were arrested in December 1956. In the famous 1958–61 Treason Trial, Mandela and others were accused of trying to overthrow the state. While the trial dragged on in the absence of real evidence, Mandela's marriage to Evelyn Mase collapsed, and the time he was required to be away from the law practice saw that too fall apart.

Although the ANC members were acquitted, the authorities' embarrassment was so great that they were even more determined to quell insurrection. In 1960, 69 black demonstrators were killed at Sharpeville, a township south of Johannesburg, when they were peacefully surrounding a police station. Many were shot in the back trying to flee the gunfire. South Africa entered a State of Emergency in which the rights of blacks were further curtailed.

Trials of a freedom fighter

The debate about violence arose again within the now banned ANC, and Mandela was tasked with starting a separate military organization, the Spear of the Nation or MK. He read the works of Che Guevara, Chairman Mao, and Fidel Castro to learn the principles of revolution, and was influenced by nationalistic movements in northern Africa. After considering guerrilla warfare, terrorism, and open revolution, Mandela opted for sabotage. The subsequent bombing of a power station and offices took the government by surprise, and a new era in the freedom struggle had begun.

Mandela knew that he would soon be rearrested for something, so he decided to go underground. He grew his hair, wore a worker's blue overalls, and, since he had a car, pretended to be driving it for his *baas* (white master). During this outlaw existence, when a warrant had been issued for his arrest, the newspapers began calling Mandela "The Black Pimpernel." For several months he actually left South Africa to visit various African states, including Sudan, Haile Selassie's Ethiopia, and Egypt, to seek support for the ANC's cause and solicit donations. The trip was the first time Mandela had experienced freedom and had seen blacks either running their own states or being treated as equals, and it only inspired him further. However, back in South Africa he let his guard down, and in 1962 he was captured on the road to Cape Town.

At his trial, Mandela tried to put the onus of guilt on the government, and wore traditional clothing to symbolize that he did not recognize the white legal system and the charges it was making against him. Why was he not being tried by his own flesh and blood? Could he receive a fair trial in a white courtroom, with white prosecutors and a white judge? He used his statement to expose apartheid and explain why and how he had been led to this position. The sentence handed down for inciting a strike was five years without parole—but much worse was to come.

While locked up on Robben Island, Mandela was charged with sabotage, along with the entire ANC command. This was a more serious charge and carried a death sentence as the supreme penalty. The prosecution submitted an ANC plan of action as evidence for the use of guerrilla warfare, but it was a draft that Mandela had thought unrealistic. Once more, he used the trial as a platform to state his beliefs and strengthen the cause, saying that he was prepared to die for the sake of justice. The case attracted huge coverage from dozens of journalists and representatives of foreign governments. Perhaps because of the international pressure, the men "only" received life sentences. That seemed like a great victory.

Mandela returned to Robben Island with no prospect of ever leaving. There was a separate structure for political prisoners and they settled into a long routine of manual labor and harsh restrictions on diet, clothing, and communications with family. Mandela could receive one visitor and write and receive only one (heavily censored) letter every six months. Denied virtually all outside contact, obtaining a newspaper was prized almost above food. His second wife Winnie was being subjected to constant harassment from the police, which he learnt about via clippings from the warders. His mother and then his oldest son died, and he was refused the opportunity to attend their funerals.

Thaw and release

After two decades on Robben Island, Mandela and then Walter Sisulu and others were transferred to Pollsmoor Prison in Cape Town. They had communal arrangements and Mandela was able to hug his wife and daughter for the first time in 21 years. The ANC was enjoying new popularity and Desmond Tutu, then Bishop of Johannesburg, received a Nobel Peace Prize for his anti-apartheid work.

Civil unrest and international sanctions against South Africa began to take their toll on the government, and talks were held with the ANC. Mandela was moved to a halfway house so that he could attend higher-level meetings. The framework for negotiations focused on the demand for majority rule that at the same time would not result in domination of the white minority. South

African president Pik Botha had a stroke during this time and F.W. de Klerk became president. De Klerk began to dismantle apartheid and lifted the ban on the ANC. Amid great euphoria, Mandela was released in 1990, having spent 27 years in jail. In 1993 he and de Klerk were awarded the Nobel Peace Prize, and the following year, after the country's first non-racial elections, Mandela was elected President of South Africa. He would serve only one term; with Thabo Mbeki and de Klerk acting as his deputies, they worked together in a multiparty government.

Final comments

The unwinding of apartheid and the end of white rule in South Africa stand in contrast to other more violent revolutions in Africa, and *Long Walk to Freedom* shows why this was no fluke. After toning down his initial fiery talk, Mandela realized that a non-violent struggle would be more likely to gain worldwide support and shame the oppressors. He was right. Frantz Fanon's *The Wretched of the Earth*, which provided a rationale for militancy in overthrowing French colonial oppression in Algeria, exemplifies the path that Mandela chose not to take. The Algerian conflict involved far greater numbers of casualties and was fought with great venom, in contrast to the win–win spirit that characterized the last days of white rule in South Africa.

Having been militant as a young man, Mandela's time in prison provided the space to reflect and change his thinking toward reconciliation. Later, he would oversee the Truth and Reconciliation Commission to investigate crimes committed under apartheid, with Tutu as its chair. This helped people to move away from the past and focus on the future. Mandela was able to win over white and black South Africans, even if some felt that he was more interested in appeasing whites rather than helping blacks. Nevertheless, legislation such as the Land Restitution Act allowed people to regain what had been taken from them under apartheid. High levels of crime and the spread of AIDS could have been dealt with better, but in his 70s Mandela was becoming more of a figurehead than a policy implementer.

Mandela's political legacy was to provide a model of a democratic, prosperous state run by Africans. His legacy to humanity is the knowledge that change is possible, even with the longest odds. He writes:

"I am fundamentally an optimist. Whether that comes from nature or nurture, I cannot say. Part of being optimistic is keeping one's head pointed towards the sun, one's feet moving forward. There were many dark moments when my faith in humanity was sorely tested, but I would not and could not give myself up to despair."

1848

The Communist Manifesto

"The need of a constantly expanding market for its products chases the bourgeoisie over the whole surface of the globe. It must nestle everywhere, settle everywhere, establish connexions everywhere."

"You are horrified at our intending to do away with private property. But in your existing society, private property is already done away with for nine-tenths of the population; its existence for the few is solely due to its non-existence in the hands of those nine-tenths."

"What else does the history of ideas prove, than that intellectual production changes its character in proportion as material production is changed? The ruling ideas of each age have ever been the ideas of its ruling class."

In a nutshell

Worker exploitation and suffering will not end until the whole class structure is destroyed.

In a similar vein

Emma Goldman *Anarchism and Other Essays* (p 114)
George Orwell *Animal Farm* (p 232)
Upton Sinclair *The Jungle* (p 260)

CHAPTER 29

Karl Marx & Friedrich Engels

K arl Marx's grandfather and great-grandfather had been rabbis, serving the Jewish community in Trier, a city in the Prussian Rhineland. His father Heinrich was a lawyer and political liberal who had converted to Lutheranism to save the family from anti-Semitic laws; his mother Henrietta from a wealthy Dutch Jewish family who later started the Philips electronics company. Her brother, an industrialist and banker, would end up keeping Karl and his wife Jenny afloat with loans after they had settled in London. Marx also received frequent financial help from his intellectual partner Friedrich Engels, whose family owned a cotton mill in Manchester and had business interests in Germany. Thus, minus capital and the freedom it provides, it would have been hard for Marx to produce *Das Kapital*, his masterwork, or to keep up his activism in several countries. Yet for him, short-term financial difficulties paled next to his view of himself as the revealer of humankind's historical direction.

As a student he had been strongly influenced by Hegel. For a time he mixed with the "Young Hegelians," but broke away when he became dissatisfied with the Prussian philosopher's conception of the world as an idea. The world is decidedly physical, Marx thought, and it is within our power to shape society, economics, and politics. In his 1845 "Theses on Feuerbach" he wrote: "The philosophers have only interpreted the world in various ways; the point however is to change it."

Three years later, he and Engels produced *The Communist Manifesto*. It was written for the meeting in London of the Communist League, the first Marxist political party, but its stirring, even poetic language made it a vital document in the spread of socialist ideas, and indeed one of the most important political texts in history.

Time for revolution

Marx and Engels begin the *Manifesto* by providing an alternative history of Europe as one huge class struggle, noting that in their own time the dynamics of this struggle were quickly changing. Whereas in the past European society was characterized by many levels of rank from the lowliest peasant to the monarch, it was now coalescing into two monolithic masses: the bourgeoisie (the urban commercial class of burghers and traders) and the proletariat (the working classes).

The bourgeoisie had benefited massively from the opening up of new territories around the world, increasing world trade, and advances in technology, including navigation. This expansion had rendered obsolete the old feudal system, based on static class relations and inherited property. The guild system of closed trades and craftsmen had been pushed aside by the new dynamics of manufacturing; the division of labor between guilds was replaced by the division of tasks within each factory. All the new wealth generated meant that the bourgeoisie could afford to buy their freedom from the feudal nobility that had once held them under the thumb.

The success of the bourgeoisie helped build the character of the modern nation-state. More than that, Marx and Engels write, "The executive of the modern state" had become "but a committee for managing the common affairs of the whole bourgeoisie." Where once people's position in society was based on tradition, old ties and relationships were being swept away by a single common denominator. Money, they say, "has drowned the most heavenly ecstasies of religious fervour, of chivalrous enthusiasm, of philistine sentimentalism, in the icy water of egotistical calculation." Every person's worth now came down to their exchange value, and gradations in class according to birth, religion, and political allegiance were replaced by possession of the means to exploit others for commercial gain. In place of the old settled order, the epoch of the bourgeoisie was characterized by "everlasting uncertainty and agitation," because the desire for profit was constantly seeking increases in productivity, and looking out for new markets to which to sell. All of this necessarily involved a big shaking up of social relations. "All that is solid melts into air," Marx and Engels famously claim, "all that is holy is profaned."

They were in awe of the explosion of technology and production, from the railways to canals to mass agriculture. However, the new system brought an unforeseen problem: overproduction. Manufacturing capability had become so advanced that things could be produced at a rate greater than what was demanded, so leading to a boom-and-bust business cycle. Although the worker has no say over how capital is deployed, his life and livelihood are now "exposed to all the vicissitudes of competition, to all the fluctuations of the market." Moreover, the individual worker becomes a mere "appendage of the machine"; he no longer has the individual craftsman's pride in his work, but is a mere element in a monotonous factory process. Since anyone can do his job, his wages go down. He is a commodity. The factory owner is in stiff competition with other capitalists, so his concern must be driving down prices (and thus wages). Meanwhile, all the lower rungs of the middle class (the small manufacturer, artisans, shopkeepers) are absorbed into an amorphous proletariat, since their tiny resources cannot compete with the capital and organization of the industrialists, and their skills are made obsolete by new methods of production.

Over time, the proletariat combines to stabilize and raise wages and improve conditions, creating trade unions. Most of these efforts fail, but the increasing class consciousness results in the creation of political parties and calls for legislative change, such as limits on working hours. In a world in which all social relations are based on capital, it becomes obvious to the proletariat that morality, culture, religion, and law are not "universal" but rather bourgeois conspiracies to keep them in their place.

What Communism can do for you

Marx and Engels make a point of saying that Communism is not in competition with any other workers' movements, but rather seeks to unite them in an international movement. They stress also that the *Manifesto* is not the ideas of a single "would-be reformer" (that is, Marx), but is an expression of the broader process of class struggle and its inevitable end point in the transformation of property relations. Central to the Communist way is abolition of private property. But how can you strip away the hard-earned gains of an artisan or shopkeeper? Marx and Engels maintain that they are not interested in this kind of property, they mean property "based on the antagonism of capital and wage labor." When the whole of society is based on it, capital ceases to be something personal; it is part of the power structure.

Communists would not do away with the right of a person to work in exchange for money to support himself. What they would change is the fact that this labor is used to enrich someone else. In a Communist system, the laborer's output would go to improve the *life* of that laborer. The bourgeoisie protests that such a system would be the end of the freedom to buy, sell, and trade, and of the right to individuality. Yet as it stands, the bourgeois economy results in the dependence of the working class, and the factory system eliminates individuality. Was not the extreme concentration of wealth, based on the exploitation of the many by the few, the biggest injustice?

To the bourgeoisie, Communism's most shocking idea was the abolition of the family. What Marx and Engels actually meant was the abolition of the bourgeois family, with its togetherness, possessions, and stability, while the laborer hardly sees his own offspring thanks to long hours of toil, and his children may be forced to work in a factory or become prostitutes. Marx and

Engels also counter the claim that Communism would bring a disruptive level of community and equality among women. In reality, they write, the bourgeois woman is a "mere instrument of production," just another thing to be exploited by the bourgeois male.

Communists were also accused of wanting to abolish nations and states, but Marx and Engels answer that the proletariat *had* no nation. If workers did have any political rights, these were made hollow because they were kept poor and exploited. Much more important than the nation-state was the similarity and unity of the working classes across all countries, and the *Manifesto* predicts that once this solidarity is further developed, the basis for wars would disappear. Government would simply be technocratic, only for solving problems in relation to redistribution and organization of the means of production.

Marx, economics, and human nature

Even the true believers in Communist revolution like Lenin admitted that there was hardly anything in Marx's writings about the economics of socialism—how it would work in practice. It was left to Lenin to come up with lame slogans such as: "Socialism is the dictatorship of the proletariat, plus the widest introduction of the most modern electrical machinery."

Given that Marx and his followers distrusted economics (at least mainstream economists such as Ricardo and Adam Smith, whom they dismissed as bourgeois), it should come as no surprise that the political economies they spawned were so deeply flawed. As Hayek puts it: "If socialists knew anything about economics, they would not be socialists." Once the aristocrats were gone and farms were operating with the new machines, what then? Humans need higher aims in order to live meaningful lives; having enough to eat is not enough. In contrast, liberal or open societies allow for the pursuit of billions of different personal aspirations.

Greed and the profit motive were not the drivers of societies, Marx believed, but rather symptoms of a corrupt social system with the wrong priorities. Individuals were simply instruments of the system, and only by overturning the system itself would people actually be free. All the problems of society were down to institutions that had been created for the selfish interests of certain classes. Though at first glance the institutional view seems to make sense, Marx failed to see Adam Smith's basic logic that a society that allows everyone to pursue their selfish interests leads to the best allocation of resources. Perhaps against logic, such a society (rather than a planned one focused on equality) will quickly become richer. The old adage that capitalism succeeds because it has a low view of human nature, and communism fails because it conceives of man too highly, is hard to refute.

Final comments

French economist Thomas Piketty argues in *Capital in the Twenty-First Century* that advanced economies have shifted in emphasis from wage earning to capital owning, with the result that wealth has become increasingly concentrated, social mobility has decreased, and a highly educated, cosmopolitan bourgeoisie has become removed from the traditional wage-earning working and middle classes. When the pie is growing bigger for all, Marx seems irrelevant. If it grows bigger for one group only, suddenly his ideas about class and exploitation again mean something. Communism as a form of government may have manifestly failed, but this does not mean that those who believe in capitalism should ridicule Marx. If any system fails to give people a chance to improve their lives, revolution will always be a real prospect.

Karl Marx & Friedrich Engels

Karl Marx was born in 1818 in the Prussian Rhineland. After attending the Universities of Bonn and Berlin, he gained a doctorate from the University of Jena, but was considered too radical to be given an academic post. He married Jenny von Westphalen, of a Prussian aristocratic family, in 1843. Following a stint as editor of a radical newspaper in Cologne, Marx moved to Paris, mixing with Pierre Joseph Proudhon (famous for the saying "property is theft") and anarchist Mikhail Bakunin, and becoming friends with Engels. He was forced to leave Paris in 1845 after pressure from the Prussian state, but continued agitating from Brussels, writing German Ideology *and* The Communist Manifesto. *After being thrown out of Belgium and refused entry to Prussia, Marx moved to London in 1849. He was never granted citizenship, but lived there until his death in 1884.*

Friedrich Engels was born in 1820 in Barmen (now Wuppertal in Germany) into a Pietist family. His father hoped a period working in the family's cotton mill in Manchester would moderate his radical views, but in 1845 he published The Condition of the Working Class in England, *an exposé of factory conditions and child labor. Engels' partner of 20 years was the working-class Mary Burns. When she died in 1863, he took up with her younger sister Lizzie, and married her just before her death in 1878. After Marx died, Engels spent years editing the unfinished volumes of* Das Kapital. *He died in 1895, his estate going to Marx's children. His books include* The Peasant War in Germany *(1850),* The Origin of the Family, Private Property and the State *(1884), and* Socialism: Utopian and Scientific *(1880).*

The Mencius

"The people are of supreme importance; the altars of the gods of earth and grain come next; last comes the ruler."

"Human nature is good just as water seeks low ground. There is no man who is not good; there is no water that does not flow downwards."

"The Three Dynasties won the Empire through benevolence and lost it through cruelty. This is true of the rise and fall, survival and collapse, of states as well."

In a nutshell

The strength and longevity of empires rest on benevolence and good relations between people and state, not on conquest or expansion.

In a similar vein

John Locke *Two Treatises of Government* (p 168)
Sun Yat-sen *Three Principles of the People* (p 272)

CHAPTER 30

Mencius

n China's turbulent Warring States period (403–221 BCE), people sought refuge in philosophy and religion to make sense of events. The ideas of Confucius (551–479 BCE; see commentary in *50 Philosophy Classics*) seemed to provide answers, but as with all great thinkers his teachings needed to be adapted and reinterpreted to remain relevant. Born around a century after Confucius died, Mencius (the Latinized name of Mengzi or "Master Meng") took Confucian teachings and applied them to the challenges of his own times.

Like Confucius, Mencius was a traveling wise man who attempted to advise governments, but because they were concerned mostly with trying to defend or expand their territories, his more subtle and virtuous approach to attaining peace, power, and prosperity was little heeded. After he retired he wrote the seven books of *The Mencius*, combining wisdom from the ancient odes with Confucian philosophy. Scholars now surmise that the book was written or put together by others, using the notes left by Mencius' disciples, but either way his voice and wisdom shine through.

Along with *Great Learning, Doctrine of the Mean*, and Confucius' *Analects*, *The Mencius* is one of the "Four Books" that are the basis of Confucian philosophy. Mencius trod a middle path, speaking for the ancient customs and traditions of Chinese life while at the same time seeking a more enlightened government. Today, the Confucian canon helps provide a moral backbone for a quickly changing Chinese society, although not everything Mencius says is in tune with the thinking of the current powers that be.

Moral authority

In fourth-century China, a feudal system was being replaced by centralized government divided into administrative districts. The growing power of governments was also leading to more wars. Ruling states, like the Yin, had claimed a "mandate of heaven" for their dominance, but Mencius tried to show that such mandates could only last as long as the ruling power acted in an upright and moral way. If it did not, another one would replace it whose power was more justified. Under the new "legalist" philosophy, the same laws applied to everyone in the land. However, legalism was not a moral philosophy, and rested on a conception of man as acting only in his selfish interests. In Mencius' view the legalist "power for power's sake" was no longer enough.

A large part of the ruler's role, Mencius says, is to regulate society such that resources are sustainable. A ruler does not let people cut down all the trees or drain all the ponds for fish, and he requires each farm to have its own mulberry tree for silk production and its own animals to feed the extended family. If people aged 70 and over can have meat and wear silk, Mencius says, the kingdom has been a success.

"Is there any difference between killing a man with a knife," Mencius asks King Hui of Liang, "and killing him with misrule?" No, replies the king. If that is so, Mencius says, make sure the royal household does not have feasts and fat horses while people are dying from starvation. When a ruler looks out for his people more than himself, they will know it and their loyalty will make the kingdom strong.

Empires that last

In Mencius's era, it was assumed that the nature of a ruler is to want to extend his territory, avenge earlier losses, and rule over the many. Yet "seeking the fulfillment of such an ambition by such means as you employ," Mencius says in a famous line, "is like looking for fish by climbing a tree." Not only will it not deliver what the ruler wants, it will bring other bad consequences.

In foreign policy, going to war is always a last resort. It must be done without any thought of gain, and only to remove terrible rulers whose power cannot be lessened in any other way. Furthermore, the state must be morally superior, otherwise it has no authority to prosecute this war.

A general rule, Mencius says, is that empires are won through benevolence and lost through greed and cruelty. Moral authority always wins out over coercion and brute force: "One who puts benevolence into effect through the transforming influence of morality will become a true king, and his success will not depend on the size of his state."

Human nature

How we see human nature shapes our politics, and this was particularly true of Mencius. The Confucian principle of *jen* means benevolence, goodness, and humanity. *Yi* means doing what is right in a particular situation. Both are important in Mencius' thinking, but he went beyond Confucius in his emphasis on the basic goodness of human nature. There was a view that humans were simply driven by desires (food, sex, etc.), but Mencius said that only simple or small men lived like this. Greater types subordinated their instincts to their "heart" or reasoning faculties; this is what separates us from the animals.

"Reason and rightness please my heart," he said, "in the same way as meat pleases my palate."

Mencius' view of human nature naturally led to his conception of the benevolent (and successful) ruler, well expressed here: "No man is devoid of a heart sensitive to the suffering of others... With such a sensitive heart behind compassionate government, it was as easy to rule the Empire as rolling it on your palm."

Final comments

Like Confucius, Mencius values societal harmony above all else, and talks at length of the "appropriate relations" between people. There is a reason things are ordered as they are; everyone has a role in life and by trying to go beyond it, this order is upset. If a ruler is benevolent he should command allegiance and respect in the same way as we are loyal to a parent. If people see fit to criticize their princes and rulers and constantly chatter and complain, this may be the end of the state. In Mencius' moral universe looking after one's parents is a sacred duty, but of almost equal importance is to watch our character. He shows disdain for people who pursue a life of profit-seeking, which is worthless if one has not improved one's self.

Such messages are not without relevance in a China that, 2,400 years on, is increasingly market oriented. The challenge of the Chinese government is to balance rapid growth and the achievement of material aims with retaining social cohesion, but that is unlikely to be achieved if the aims are only material. In the way he put community bonds and the development of personal character first, Mencius still has some lessons for modern China.

Mencius

Mencius was born in 372 BCE in the state of Tsou, now Shandong Province, only 20 miles from Confucius' birthplace. Little is known of his early life except that his father died when he was young and his mother Zhǎng made sure he received a good education. When she died he observed the traditional three years of mourning, and in today's China Zhǎng is still held up as the model of a good mother. Mencius is also said to have studied under Confucius' grandson Zisi.

On a mission to persuade rulers to adopt his outlook, Mencius took a job in the court of King Hsuan in the state of Ch'i, followed by a period with King Hui of Liang. When his advice was mainly ignored, he decided to retire. Mencius was nevertheless influential while he was alive and had feudal lords among his disciples. He lived well into his 80s.

The quotes in this commentary are from the translation of The Mencius *by DC Lau.*

The Fourth Revolution

"Countries that can establish 'good government' will stand a fair chance of providing their citizens with a decent standard of life. Countries that cannot will be condemned to decline and dysfunction."

"The West has to change because it is going broke. The emerging world needs to reform to keep forging ahead."

"Bit by bit a new model is emerging. We are living through changes just as dramatic as the ones associated with Hobbes and Mill and the Webbs, though nobody has yet succeeded in putting this Fourth Revolution into memorable words and clothing it in a distinctive philosophy."

In a nutshell

Liberal democracy has lost some allure, but by slimming the welfare state and re-emphasizing personal freedoms, it can again be a model for the world.

In a similar vein

Francis Fukuyama *The End of History and the Last Man* (p 104)
Thomas Hobbes *Leviathan* (p 132)
Mancur Olson *The Rise and Decline of Nations* (p 226)
Margaret Thatcher *The Autobiography* (p 278)

CHAPTER 31

John Micklethwait & Adrian Wooldridge

I n the twentieth century, democracy triumphed. In 1900 there were no countries that held elections in which every adult could vote, but by the year 2000
there were 120 countries that did, covering 63 percent of the world's population. Since then, however, democracy has made no further gains and has even
been eroded. In Iraq following the war, and in Egypt following the revolution,
hopes of democracy have been replaced by chaos. Established democracies
such as South Africa have seen growing corruption, and Russia, Turkey,
and Hungary have become increasingly illiberal. Why should the leaders of
such countries be attached to democratic principles when the world's most
dynamic economy, China, is undemocratic, and when Western democracies
are poorly run?

Micklethwait and Wooldridge begin *The Fourth Revolution: The Global
Race to Reinvent the State* with a vignette about CELAP, the training school for
China's elite bureaucrats. "Just as China deliberately set out to remaster the art
of capitalism a couple of decades ago," they note, "it is now trying to remaster
the art of government." Yet the students are only taught about Western capitalism, not Western government, which is seen as wasteful, sclerotic, and mired in
debt. The Chinese instructors are more likely to hold up Singapore as a model,
with its successful combination of authoritarianism and free markets.

Whether it is China, America, Europe, or Africa, the authors suggest that
the biggest challenge facing the world over the next couple of decades is fixing
government. In the rich West, most people only know one model of government: the expanded welfare state that has been dominant since the Second
World War. Unsustainable in its current form, its reform will be the biggest
test yet of the liberal-democratic model. Will it be possible to combine social
provision, economic growth, and personal freedoms?

Though the book will be a little journalistic for some tastes, *The Fourth
Revolution* is a great snapshot of government in the second decade of the
twenty-first century. What it lacks in timeless gravitas it makes up for in the

sweep of its view and its audacity in proposing how government will look in the decades to come.

Revolutions 1, 2, 3, and 3½

Micklethwait and Wooldridge argue that the West's economic and political dominance in the last couple of centuries, particularly that of America and Britain, was down to its openness to new ideas in government and willingness to implement them, from the liberalism of John Stuart Mill's "nightwatchman state" to the Founding Fathers' technocratic checks and balances on the Constitution.

The first revolution in government was when seventeenth-century European nations transformed themselves from principalities and kingdoms into centralized states. Because they were in stiff military and economic competition with each other, this increased their effectiveness. They were "powerful enough to provide order but light enough to allow innovation." The need to be better saw them surge ahead of states in other parts of the world. The intellectual force behind this revolution was Thomas Hobbes, who believed that the only answer to chaos and brutality was a super strong state, or monarch as he imagined it then, whose power was unquestioned.

Then in the second revolution of the eighteenth and nineteenth centuries, revolutionary ferment in France and America brought new forms of accountable and meritocratic government. In Britain, a new emphasis on efficiency and freedom saw a civil service based on merit rather than patronage. Cronyism was reduced, markets made free, and personal liberties enshrined.

By the twentieth century, the minimal liberal state no longer seemed enough and we saw the emergence of the modern welfare state. This third revolution was a response to inequality, and was hard fought. Today, Britain's National Health Service is considered a national treasure, America's social security programs are here to stay, and no advanced society can be seen to lack a safety net. The problem is that this net became a cushion of entitlement, and the welfare state became a bloated Leviathan. "Government used to be an occasional partner in life…," Micklethwait and Wooldridge note. "Today it is an omnipresent nanny."

In the 1980s, Milton Friedman, Margaret Thatcher, and Ronald Reagan seemed to win the argument about the need for smaller government, but in reality, Britain's public spending only went from 22.9 percent of GDP to 22.2 percent, and Reagan could not get the House of Representatives to match his tax cuts with spending cuts. In the 1990s and 2000s, both left (calling for more measures to improve diversity and health and safety) and right (War on Terror, war on drugs, surveillance) contributed to government expansion. The Friedman–Thatcher–Reagan model had only been half a revolution.

What went wrong?

"The West has lost confidence in the way it is governed," Micklethwait and Wooldridge argue, providing California as an example. Big, broke, and inefficient, it has 37 million people but one Senate seat. It has overlapping layers of government, and spends the same amount on its prisons as it does on education. Determined lobby groups seem able to hijack the system, just as Mancur Olson predicted (see commentary on p 226).

Over in Italy, the state owns 574,000 official limousines for 180,000 highly paid elected representatives it can ill afford. Europe as a whole is experiencing a demographic crunch. Its population is expected to decline from 308 million to 265 million by 2060, and the number of people over 65 will rise from 28 percent to 58 percent. Spending will increasingly go on welfare and defense, leaving less to spend on education, investment, or anything else. As in California, public-sector unions will defend their privileges, while the average voter will pay more in tax.

What to do

Scandinavian countries have shown that it is usually more efficient for the state to be chief funder rather than itself the provider of services. In every other aspect of life organizations compete for our custom, and it makes them more efficient and better. Why would the same thing not happen for organizations that are competing for schoolchildren, patients, and jobseekers? Indeed, many private companies now focus on providing public services, such as Serco, which runs bus services in Australia, prisons in Britain, and driver licensing in Canada. Naturally, the interaction between state and private companies does not always go well. British Rail is divided into hundreds of pieces and is arguably a mess, but this is not an argument for taking services back into public management, rather for improving contracts and accountability, and giving citizens more information about how private providers are performing.

In Canada in the mid-2000s, a budgetary crisis forced the country to ask the basic question: What is the state for? To its surprise, it found that simply "turning the tap off" did not plunge the nation into ruin, but created an efficiency revolution. Something similar is happening in Britain, which since 2010 has cut £35 billion from government departments, with more to come. Yet such huge cuts have not plunged the country into the dark ages. Rather, efficiencies have been produced that would be the norm in the private sector, such as local councils sharing facilities. Meanwhile, Britain is partly following the Swedish model in education. Instead of thousands of standard high schools, it is seeing big growth in state-funded "academies" that have significant autonomy, similar to America's charter schools. Teacher unions and left-wing politicians are wary, but parents love the choice and children are benefiting.

Micklethwait and Wooldridge set out some specific aspects that need reform. First, governments should sell assets that they have no business running. In 2012, the members of the OECD collectively owned 2,000 companies with a value of $2 trillion, employing 6 million people. Many of these businesses relate to transport networks, energy networks, and telecoms, on the grounds that if they were sold to private companies the public would be ripped off. Yet Micklethwait and Wooldridge argue that the key is not ownership, but simply regulating the networks properly. Socialistic France is well known for its large stakes in companies such as France Telecom and Renault, but why does the US government own Amtrak, which is perennially in trouble, along with prisons, post offices, and airports? Its property portfolio is worth hundreds of billions of dollars, including 900,000 buildings. Despite the reforms and privatizations of the 1980s, governments still have vast assets, the sale of which could reduce crushing debt—and ensure that the enterprises were better run.

Secondly, governments must reduce subsidies that favor the rich or well connected. The left has focused on redistribution of national wealth, but it would be far more efficient and better to "dismantle the welfare state for plutocrats." The lobbying clout of the financial industry means that banks are effectively subsidized, and America's tax loopholes are exploited by the well-off. American farmers are still getting between $10 billion and $30 billion a year from Congress; in comparison, New Zealand ended all farm subsidies in 1984, even though it is four times as agriculture dependent as the US, and the result has been big rises in productivity and the development of niche export markets.

Thirdly, the entitlement systems of rich countries must be reformed so that they benefit only people who genuinely need them, instead of "promising entitlements that future generations will have to pay for." All welfare states need to increase responsibility: doctors' visits should cost at least a token amount, and people on the dole should do some work or be trained for work. This is already happening, but it is really only the start. And just as the creation of central banks free of political control has been a success, so the policy on entitlements should be handed to independent commissions.

James Madison wrote in *The Federalist Papers* (see commentary on p 120) that the chief purpose of the Union was to create effective centralized government, but this government would only keep legitimacy in the long term if it were self-limiting. Today, Micklethwait and Wooldridge argue, governments should start by not making promises they cannot keep, such as eliminating terrorism or poverty, which tend only to decrease the freedoms of everyone else. "It is time to put the 'liberal' back into 'liberal democracy,'" they say. The fourth revolution is about returning the emphasis to individual rights over social rights. This is both right in terms of values, and necessary in terms of the survival of democracy itself. It can only be achieved in the face of entrenched private and public interests, from gerrymandered electorates to crony capitalism, but a revolution of this type promises to revivify politics and give a boost to economies. Without such a revolution, money will increasingly go to vested interests and less often to those who really need it, only increasing cynicism about democracy.

Final comments

At the time *The Fourth Revolution* was written, both authors were with *The Economist*, a magazine in the classic liberal mold of John Stuart Mill that generally favors a smaller state. Yet Micklethwait and Wooldridge are not anti-state or libertarian, and quote Alfred Marshall: "The State is the most precious of human possessions." It is more than a "necessary evil" and they recognize that "you would be crazy to prefer to live in a failed state like the Congo, where the absence of Leviathan makes life truly 'nasty, brutish, and short', than in a well-run big state like Denmark." Yet neither does this mean that the state can keep going as it is now. The way through is a new emphasis on liberty. When the welfare state overtook the liberal state, personal freedoms were no longer central, yet these were the engine of nineteenth-century prosperity and progress. It will be possible for the rich West to retain a fair chunk of its social provision at the same time as growing economically, but only if it unleashes the power of the individual. By creating a smaller but still strong state with greater personal liberties, countries can depend on the most powerful force known to produce wealth and well-being: their people. Both Europe and America moved ahead of other places in the world because of this emphasis on liberty and the rights of the individual. They can do so again.

John Micklethwait & Adrian Wooldridge

Born in London in 1962, John Micklethwait studied history at Oxford. After a two-year stint with Chase Manhattan Bank, he joined The Economist *in 1987, rising to become its editor-in-chief in 2006. In 2015 he became editor-in-chief for Bloomberg News. Adrian Wooldridge is the management editor at* The Economist *and writes the "Schumpeter" column. The pair have co-written several books, including* The Witch Doctors: Making Sense of the Management Gurus *(1996),* A Future Perfect: The Challenge and Hidden Promise of Globalization *(2000),* The Company: A Short History of a Revolutionary Idea *(2005),* The Right Nation: Why America Is Different *(2005), and* God Is Back: How the Global Rise of Faith Is Changing the World *(2010).*

The Subjection of Women

"The principle which regulates the existing social relations between the two sexes—the legal subordination of one sex to the other—is wrong in itself, and now one of the chief hindrances to human improvement."

"Men do not want solely the obedience of women, they want their sentiments… They have therefore put everything in practice to enslave their minds."

"The second benefit to be expected from giving to women the free use of their faculties, by leaving them the free choice of their employments, and opening to them the same field of occupation and the same prizes and encouragements as to other human beings, would be that of doubling the mass of mental faculties available for the higher service of humanity."

In a nutshell

No civilization worth the name can justify the subjection of women, nor can it afford to do so if it wishes to remain strong.

In a similar vein

Margaret Thatcher *The Autobiography* (p 278)
Mary Wollstonecraft *A Vindication of the Rights of Woman* (p 304)

CHAPTER 32

John Stuart Mill

I n nineteenth-century Britain, the status of women was an item on the progressive agenda that had not been properly addressed, and John Stuart Mill wondered why this was so. Britain could really not call itself an advanced civilization, he reasoned, when 50 percent of its population could not vote or even choose to work if they wanted to. As a good Utilitarian, he knew that everyone in society benefits when the intellectual power of women is unleashed through education. Beyond this rational benefit is the sheer upsurge in happiness and well-being that would come from female emancipation, the movement between "a life of subjection to the will of others, and a life of rational freedom."

Consistent with his authorship of the manifesto of liberalism, *On Liberty*, Mill reminds us that "after the primary necessities of food and raiment, freedom is the first and strongest want of human nature." Attempts by men through the ages to restrict women's freedom have been self-defeating, he argues in *The Subjection of Women*, as any measure to reduce another person's freedom (unless that person is a real threat to society) has the effect of lessening the happiness of the coercer. All despots, whether in the home or on the throne, discover this moral law.

He anticipates the argument that Britain and other advanced countries had got where they were through existing customs and laws in relation to women. Civilization was not exactly dependent on women's emancipation. Perhaps, Mill says, but then we do not know how much sooner wealth and civilization might have come about if women had been given more choice and power. Britain had become great despite, not because of, its willingness to keep the lights of women under a bushel.

It was one thing to call for a change to the legal status of women, but a pretty strong statement in 1869 to demand "perfect equality, admitting no power or privilege on the one side, nor disability on the other." So as not to scare people off, Mill notes: "No enslaved class ever asked for complete liberty at once." When originally constituted, the Commons made few claims for power beyond freedom from arbitrary taxation and monarchical oppression. Similarly, the women of his time were after no more than the right to vote and to have the chance to enter the professions, then closed to them.

Scholars now debate whether Mill's wife Harriet Hardy Taylor wrote some or any of *The Subjection of Women*, but either way as one of the first women in Britain to call for women's rights and suffrage, she was a strong influence. Her *The Enfranchisement of Women* was written in 1851.

Might, right, and modernity

Mill admits that it is a large task to call for female equality, because views on women are so strongly rooted in sentiment and feeling, which is hard to overturn even with the best arguments. Those wanting to preserve the status quo have the weight of tradition and custom behind them; after all, things must be as they are for good reason. Yet in the modern era, he asks, what is the basis for the subjection of women to men? If women lost their power due to men's monopoly on force, did it follow that "might" should forever win out over "right"?

If it were the case that past societies had tried every form of government—men ruling over women, women ruling over men, each having perfect equality—then we should accept that the first of these is simply "what works." In fact no such experiments had been carried out, Mill notes. Men, from the earliest times, had brought together two facts—the importance of women to them and their weaker muscular strength—and set out to keep women in bondage. Later, men would convert "what was a mere physical fact into a legal right, [and] give it the sanction of society." This was a kind of slavery that became regularized in the form of an informal social compact: Women would be protected if they gave up the rights they would have had if they were not living with men. Women in Mill's time were more dependants than slaves, he admits, yet their position still carried the taint of their original brutal enslavement. It was part of a continuum.

Given that more and more labor was mental, Mill notes, the "law of the strongest" in physical terms was an anachronism. Yet this law seemed to be part of our psychological fabric, and those who possessed power never wished to relinquish any of it. This fact explained why, in a society such as Britain that was ostensibly meant to run on principles of equal justice, women's subservient position had barely changed; indeed, it had gone backward since the early Middle Ages, when women had greater rights to property. Yet somehow, women's status had been framed in such a way that it did not jar with civilization, "any more than domestic slavery among the Greeks jarred with their notion of themselves as a free people."

Most British people were against the slave trade, apart from those directly profiting from it, and most considered themselves lucky that they did not live under an absolute monarch or military despot. Yet British men were not willing to consider the subjugation of women as on a par with these other forms of domination. Everyone who desires power, Mill notes, desires it over those closest to him, and women were in no position to bargain for more power or rights. Because of this, the family, Mill observes, will likely be the last bastion of inequality.

It is only natural

Part of the difficulty of change was the popular concept of the "nature" of women. Girls were said not to be interested in abstract ideas and therefore to need less education. When reaching maturity they only wanted to find a good husband; their domain was the home, and naturally so.

Mill asks: "Was there ever any domination which did not appear natural to those who possessed it?" He points out that "instinct" and "nature" are simply what we observe in ourselves that we cannot explain by rational means. Even one as great as Aristotle believed that humans could be divided into those with "free" natures and "slave" natures. In the Middle Ages, the domination of the peasantry by the nobility seemed supremely natural; each person had their station in life. Yet "unnatural" is nearly always to be translated as "uncustomary," Mill notes. Because women's subjection had become a custom, any new female rights seemed to be unnatural. Foreigners were often astonished to learn that England's monarch was a woman, but to the English it was taken for granted, because it was customary. Moreover, Mill observes, "what is now called the *nature* of women is an eminently artificial thing—the result of forced repression in some directions, unnatural stimulation in others."

Just give them the chance

Women are not slaves in the usual sense, Mill says, in that men do not simply seek their obedience, but want their sentiments too. However, to achieve this they go overboard, arranging culture and society so that women will not even consider the possibility of an alternative life to that set out before them. Women become psychological slaves. They are educated from an early age that they must be submissive, live completely for others, and have no ambitions of their own. Their power comes from being attractive to men.

This cozy paradigm, however, was coming up against changing times. After all, this was the enlightened second half of the nineteenth century, when being born black or white, aristocrat or commoner, no longer absolutely determined one's possibilities. If that were so, being born female or male should not solely shape one's chances either. In advanced countries women were, with royalty, the only people whose lives were so marked out for them at birth, while all men, at least in theory, were able to become anything they wanted; the new industrial wealth that was being created did indeed see some incredible rags-to-prominence stories.

Mill brings into the argument his doctrine of liberty and economic philosophy. No one thinks of writing a law to make strong men blacksmiths, he says, because they will gravitate to the job anyway, while weaker men will go into other fields. Freedom and competition lead people to the careers best suited to their talents, and this is how it should be. To order, at the outset, that only certain people can do certain jobs is morally wrong; if that is so for men, what rationale is there for setting in stone what women can or cannot do? True to his utilitarian outlook, Mill says that employment should be left up to the "market" of talents and dispositions to sort out who can do a task well, whether male or female. Moreover, as any job involving difficulty and importance always seems to have fewer people available for it than needed, why not deepen the pool of people to draw from? This can only benefit everyone.

Reactionaries of Mill's time noted that hardly any great things had been produced by women. To this he replies:

"If no woman has hitherto been a great historian, what woman has had the necessary erudition? If no woman is a great philologist, what woman has studied Sanscrit and Slavonic, the Gothic of Ulphila and the Persic of the Zendavesta? Even in practical matters we all know what is the value of the originality of untaught geniuses... When women have had the preparation which all men now require to be eminently original, it will be time enough to begin judging by experience of their capacity for originality."

The marriage market

According to English custom, a father decided who married his daughter, and on signing the register she became "the actual bond-servant of her husband: no less so, as far as legal obligation goes, than slaves commonly so called. She vows a lifelong obedience to him at the altar, and is held to it all through her life by law." The wife gave up her right to her own property, including any inherited. Changing this one element, Mill says, would end the all too common situation of a man trapping a woman into marriage just to get her money.

He is not saying that there are no good husbands, more that the law needs to take account of bad ones, who beat their wives and leave no way out for a wife except being socially outcast. Mill's passages on domestic violence had their intended shock value with Victorian readers, who were used to having such matters swept under the carpet. He further antagonized by suggesting that the model for family government is not the despot, but a democratic division of powers.

"We have had the morality of submission," he says, "and the morality of chivalry and generosity; the time is now come for the morality of justice."

Final comments

Britain saw some major changes around the time Mill published *The Subjection of Women*: the Reform Bill of 1867 gave working men in towns the right to vote; Forster's Education Act of 1870 provided primary education for all; in 1870 Civil Service examinations began in order to choose people for jobs based on merit rather than payment for office; in 1871 Oxford and Cambridge Universities allowed people of all religions to be admitted; women's colleges were founded at Oxford and Cambridge, and secondary education for women was improved; and trade unions gained a charter of rights to reflect their new power. Last but not least, the Married Women's Property Act of 1870 allowed women to be financially independent from their husbands and to keep inherited property. This was just what Mill had called for, but the longer struggle for women's right to vote did not succeed for almost 50 more years.

John Stuart Mill

Born in 1806 in London, John Stuart Mill had a famously intensive education thanks to his father James, a philosopher and economist. Largely excluded from playing with other children, Mill learned Greek at the age of 3 and Latin at 8; by 12 he was well versed in logic, and at 16 he was writing on economic matters. After further studies in France in history, law, and philosophy, while still in his teens Mill began a career at the East India Company, where his father had a senior position. He served in the Company until the Mutiny of 1857, when he retired as a Chief Examiner. Concurrently to his bureaucratic career he started the Utilitarian Society alongside Jeremy Bentham, and helped established University College, London. He was an editor and contributor of the Westminster Review *and other magazines. His activism in social reform led to an arrest for handing out birth control information to London's poor. Mill met Harriet Hardy Taylor in 1830, and they had a chaste friendship for 20 years before finally marrying after Harriet's husband died.*

Mill was elected to parliament in 1865, and campaigned for women's right to vote and other liberal issues. He was also president of the National Society for Women's Suffrage. His large body of writings covering logic, economics, religion, metaphysics, epistemology, current affairs, and philosophy includes A System of Logic *(1843),* Principles of Political Economy *(1848),* Three Essays on Religion *(1874), and his* Autobiography *(1873). Mill's* Utilitarianism *(1863) refined the Benthamite philosophy and kept it influential for a new generation. In 1872 Mill became godfather to Bertrand Russell. He died the following year in Avignon, France.*

Politics Among Nations

"Whatever the ultimate aims of international politics, power is always the immediate aim. Statesmen and peoples may ultimately seek freedom, security, prosperity… may define their goals in terms of a religious, philosophic, economic, or social ideal… But whenever they strive to realize their goal by means of international politics, they do so by striving for power."

"The first lesson the student of international politics must learn and never forget is that the complexities of international affairs make simple solutions and trustworthy prophecies impossible."

In a nutshell

The currency of international politics has always been raw power, both to influence and to dominate physically.

In a similar vein

Carl von Clausewitz *On War* (p 98)
Thomas Hobbes *Leviathan* (p 132)
Paul Kennedy *The Rise and Fall of the Great Powers* (p 144)
Joseph S. Nye *The Future of Power* (p 220)

CHAPTER 33

Hans Morgenthau

Every generation, Hans Morgenthau observes in *Politics Among Nations: The Struggle for Power and Peace*, throws up new ideas and philosophies that seek to replace the battle for power with something more rational. Nineteenth-century liberals believed that constitutional democracy would in time replace absolutism and autocracy, so eliminating the causes of war. For pacifists and utopians, statecraft could be replaced by greater scientific knowledge about the real source of problems; setting up the League of Nations, for instance, was preceded by much talk of the "science of peace" and the "natural frontiers" of geography to decide state borders.

These magic pills of international affairs have continually come up against a reality that is "complicated, irrational, incalculable," Morgenthau writes. In truth, "the struggle for power is universal in time and space and is an undeniable fact of experience"; politics always comes back to human nature, or the "bio-psychological drives" to live, propagate, and dominate. Whether domestic or international, the motive for political action is of three basic types: to keep power, to increase power, or to demonstrate power. It is disingenuous to talk about world affairs in terms of scientific or rational "international relations," because in reality, "international politics is of necessity power politics." It is always ultimately about interests, rather than abstract ideas of equality or justice. Given this, Morgenthau says, the best the world can hope for through international politics is "the realization of the lesser evil rather than of the absolute good."

Morgenthau's German Jewish family was forced to flee the Nazis in the early 1930s. After emigrating to America in 1937, he enjoyed a remarkable career as a top academic and public intellectual, and as an adviser to two presidents. One of the great works of the "realist" school of politics, *Politics Among Nations* has gone through seven editions since its first publication in 1948, and remains a staple of university international relations reading lists. Since Morgenthau's death it has been updated with fresh examples by his colleague Kenneth W. Thompson.

Politics and morality

Many nations clothe themselves in moral defenses and align their purpose with God or with destiny. Realist politics takes a wide view of such claims, seeing that only interest in terms of power is a reliable way of understanding foreign policy. Realism does not discount or disregard the moral dimension of politics, Morgenthau says, and morality is an important part of international power, but it must be filtered "through the concrete circumstances of time and place."

National survival is more important than taking an unequivocal moral stand, for what is the point if a statesman is "right" but his nation loses standing, power, or legitimacy? In the realist view, prudence is the key virtue in political morality. The West faced a moral dilemma over whether to recognize the Communist government in China when it came to power in 1949. On a moral basis, the West was justified in ceasing contact. However, the political dimension required that there still be dealings with communist China, at the very least to keep open the channels of trade and diplomacy.

A person whose nature was purely political would be a beast, Morgenthau says, while one whose nature was purely moral would be a fool, never acting realistically or prudently. Just as you would not apply the standards of politics to a priest or a monk, so you cannot apply purely moral standards to a politician. The way to judge him is by political standards; that is, whether he maintains the power of the state. People routinely deceive themselves about the true nature of politics, but politicians and statesmen have no such luxury, and may sometimes need to do things that would make the average person squeamish. Though Morgenthau does not mention him, this is exactly what Machiavelli said four centuries earlier in *The Prince*.

The balance of power

Morgenthau emphasizes the principle of the "balance of power" as the key stabilizing factor in political history. It works because it follows the universal rule of equilibrium. A great power usually becomes arrogant or overstretches, thus creating resistance or vulnerability, which allows another power to rise up.

Just because the balance of power theory goes back to ancient Rome, Greece, and India does not mean that it is outdated, he stresses. Experience only lends it credence. In the century following the Napoleonic Wars, both Britain and America had to judge which European power posed the greatest threat to the balance of power. Churchill noted that several times in its history, Britain could have simply joined up with the most aggressive or strongest power and won some of the spoils, but instead it always took the more difficult course.

Prestige and power

An important part of the struggle for power, Morgenthau says, is seeking prestige. It is as basic to relations between nations as it is between individuals, because "what others think about us is as important as what we actually are."

Nations try to make a good impression through diplomatic, ceremonial, or symbolic efforts, and through the display of military force. At the Potsdam Conference in 1945, Churchill, Stalin, and Truman could not agree who should enter the room first, so they all walked in at once from three different doors. Peace negotiations between the United States, the North and South Vietnamese governments, and the Vietcong were delayed for 10 weeks because of a conflict over the shape of the conference table. Absurd disputes such as these reveal what is actually at stake in negotiations.

The goal of prestige is to project such a reputation for power that a country can save on its actual deployment. The Roman and British empires are good examples of this, as was the United States while it prosecuted its Good Neighbor policy. The perception that a nation has unrivaled power, combined with restraint in using it, only increases the respect and awe of other countries. In each case, these nations made "the burden of superiority as easy as possible to bear." It was just not worth it to usurp them; better to join them and enjoy being part of their prosperity and power.

The role of prestige was telling in the Second World War, when both Germany and Japan had very low estimations of the willingness and ability of America to enter the war. The actual power of the US was greater than its prestige, so the German and Japanese assumptions proved to be fatal mistakes. Equally, Britain's naval prestige at the start of the war was greater than its actual strength, which delayed Hitler's attempt to invade. The awe in which the British Navy was held was as powerful a deterrent as its actual fleet and firepower. "To demonstrate to the rest of the world the power one's own nation possesses, revealing neither too much nor too little, is the task of a wisely conceived policy of prestige," Morgenthau writes.

Ideology and power

Because the immediate goal of politics is power, and this is not always acceptable, ideology provides a useful and acceptable mask in foreign policy. A leader can defend his own actions as just, while maintaining that those of others are wicked. A nation will defend its own expansion as necessary for security, while another country's expansion into foreign countries is termed "imperialism."

Every nation needs to justify its actions morally, or it will become a pariah. Hitler invaded Czechoslovakia on the pretext of allowing its German-speaking people to return to the Fatherland; it could not be sold as "the first step in Nazi domination of Europe." More recently, Vladimir Putin's invasion of Crimea and Eastern Ukraine was carried out on the basis of "the security of Russian-speaking Ukrainians"; it could not be promoted as a power grab to assert Russian influence in Eastern Europe over the West. "Ideologies, like all ideas," Morgenthau says, "are weapons that may raise the national morale and, with it, the power of one nation and, in the very act of doing so, may lower the morale of the opponent."

Inequality between rich and poor countries, Morgenthau notes, offers boundless space for ideological posturing. Poor countries can blame their problems on colonialism, imperialism, and capitalism, and the wealthy nations will feel a moral obligation to heal the divide, even if many of the actual problems relate to poor governance, corruption, and irrational economic policies.

The problem with ideology is that its cost is political effectiveness. The Wars of Religion produced a century of bloodshed, which eventually led to each side realizing that one's survival did not depend on the other's annihilation. In Morgenthau's time, the equivalent was the Cold War. When he died neither side had "won" it, although the creeds of communism and capitalism both seemed to their believers to be universally applicable. To keep their power, he says, "nations must be willing to compromise on all issues that are not vital to them." In fact, a nation only becomes aware of its true national interests when it has dispensed with "the crusading spirit of a political creed."

The failure of militarism...

Militarism is the belief that the largest army, or most powerful air force, or the greatest number of nuclear weapons, is what determines national power. The essence of power, Teddy Roosevelt said, is "to speak loudly and carry a big stick." The problem with militarism is that it has little appreciation of the intangibles of power. "The failures of Spartan, German and Japanese militarism," Morgenthau observes, "compared with the Roman and British policies of empire-building, show the disastrous practical results of that intellectual error which we call militarism."

The more national power is actually used, the more resistance it finds. Since the rise of the modern system of states in the fifteenth century, Morgenthau writes, no state has been able to impose its will on the world for any length of time by force alone. Britain was only able to maintain its influence even after its empire began to crumble thanks to the goodwill that it created by not using force. As in life, moderation and restraint tend to increase longevity.

...and the rewards of diplomacy

Wealth, military muscle, a large landmass, and a big population may be the raw materials of national power, but diplomacy combines them all into a coherent whole. Diplomacy is the "brains of national power," Morgenthau says. It is how a nation makes the most of what it has and projects it onto the world, helping it to influence situations where its interests are at stake. If a nation's judgment is poor or if it lacks vision, all its natural or industrial advantages will be wasted. Diplomacy has often failed, but much of the time it has succeeded. For much of the nineteenth century Britain and Russia were at loggerheads over the Balkans, Dardanelles, and eastern Mediterranean, but in the 50 years after the Crimean War, actual conflict was prevented. In the Cold War, patient diplomacy was assisted by a balance of power and roughly agreed spheres of influence. Even if international politics is a power game, diplomacy is still a super-important tool in nations achieving their goals and preventing costly wars that might risk the collapse of their power.

Final comments

Morgenthau reminds readers that "no attempt to solve the problem of international peace by limiting the national aspirations for power has succeeded." No League of Nations or United Nations has the power to settle or solve conflicts of the magnitude of the Cold War. Still, what little the UN has achieved is better than nothing, and its weakness should not be an excuse to leave international politics up to nations themselves.

If a "world state" ever came into being, Morgenthau says, it would only happen via the consent of sovereign states who could admit that their own power, and that of other nations, should be voluntarily checked. Such a body would not transcend human nature; on the contrary, it would work only after accepting the reality of the human drives for power and gain. Ignoring them and only appealing to what is noblest in human beings is, ironically, a sure recipe for conflict and war.

Hans Morgenthau

Born 1904 in Coburg, Bavaria, Hans Morgenthau attended universities in Frankfurt, Berlin, and Geneva before practicing as a lawyer in Germany. From 1932–35 he taught law in Geneva, and after settling in the United States he became a professor of politics and history, becoming director of the Center for the Study of American Foreign Policy at the University of Chicago. He was an adviser in the Kennedy and Johnson administrations, but was dismissed in 1965 because of his strident opposition to the Vietnam War. He supported international control of disarmament and nuclear weapons, and was critical of the CIA's support of repressive regimes such as Pinochet's Chile. His friends included Hannah Arendt and Reinhold Niebuhr, and he was noted for his lectures on Aristotle's politics.

Morgenthau survived the crash of a Swissair plane at Athens airport in 1979, but died the following year after a brief illness. For more, read Christopher Frei's Hans J. Morgenthau: An Intellectual Biography *(2001).*

Anarchy, State, and Utopia

"Individuals have rights, and there are things no person or group may do to them (without violating their rights). So strong and far-reaching are these rights that they raise the question of what, if anything, the state and its officials may do. How much room do individual rights leave for the state?"

"A minimal state, limited to the narrow functions of protection against force, theft, fraud, enforcement of contracts, and so on, is justified... any more extensive state will violate persons' rights not to be forced to do things, and is unjustified."

In a nutshell

Social justice that is achieved through redistribution is not just at all, but is more like theft.

In a similar vein

Lord Acton *Essays on Freedom and Power* (p 20)
F.A. Hayek *The Road to Serfdom* (p 126)
John Locke *Two Treatises of Government* (p 168)
Karl Popper *The Open Society and Its Enemies* (p 248)

CHAPTER 34

Robert Nozick

Although today it is fashionable to call oneself a libertarian, railing against the excesses of the Big State, in the mid-1970s anyone calling for severely limited government was firmly on the political fringe. Robert Nozick, a philosophy professor, started out thinking that this view of the state and society was callous; he believed that it is the state's duty to help people. Yet Nozick could not escape the logic of an outlook that he believed allowed for genuine personal freedom yet prevented the violence and disorder of anarchy. He recognizes at the outset of *Anarchy, State, and Utopia* that a minimal state may suffer from not being as exciting as one that promises to do a lot for people, but he hopes to convince readers that "the minimal state is inspiring as well as right." The book had such an impact because it was an uncompromising, almost shocking answer to the ideological paradigm of the mid to late twentieth century, redistributive justice, which undergirded the welfare state and was best expressed in a theoretical sense in John Rawls' *A Theory of Justice*.

In the Preface, Nozick even admits that he did not enjoy the fact that most of America's East Coast intelligentsia did not agree with his uncompromising views, not least because his position on the limited role of the state put him with some "bad company," as he puts it. He distances his well-reasoned outlook from that of ultra-libertarian Ayn Rand, for instance. *Anarchy, State, and Utopia* is not a strident political tract, but a philosophical work that admits its own weak points and pays due respect to opposing arguments.

Another reason for its enduring success is its relative accessibility. Even Peter Singer, a pillar of leftist philosophy, saluted the book's simple language and said that, even if he believed that Nozick's arguments were wrong, their power meant that promoters of the big state would now have to go to some intellectual lengths to justify their stance.

The point of states

The fundamental question of political philosophy, Nozick suggests, is: Why have a state at all? Why not simply have anarchy?

He begins by noting Locke's "state of nature" theory, that each person pursues their own ends in freedom as long as they do not harm another person or try to take their property or freedom. Within a given geographic area there may be competing protective bodies who claim to be the dispensers of justice. They may go to war with each other for dominance. All power then goes to the body or group that wins the "market" for authority, and in return for this it demands submission and obedience. This compact involving consent to a monopoly of force in return for protection and clear justice is the beginning of the state as we know it.

Nozick rejects the contract theory of how a state arises. Instead, he sees it arising through the "invisible hand"; that is, everyone pursuing their own interest results in the development of institutions to protect all. Either way, he argues, only a "nightwatchman" state, which protects citizens from violence, theft, and fraud, and enforces contracts, can be justified. To give the state any further function, to turn it into an arbiter not only of who owns what, but of *why* they should or should not own it, will necessarily require a reduction of liberty.

Distributive injustice

Nozick considers the reasons for justifying a more extensive state, which often falls under the term "distributive justice." This is not a neutral term, he notes, but involves someone having to decide what is distributed, or redistributed, and how much. Therefore, one must go to the core: the fact that some*one* owns what is to be distributed. Things do not come into the world from nowhere; someone must have organized, bought, or developed resources to create it. If one forms a society based on the philosophy "For each according to his needs," then *who* has created something matters little. The only question is how it should be fairly distributed. Yet what is fair about not recognizing the creator of the value in the first place? If anything in a society is to be justly transferred, it must only be through the choice of its owner, who can choose to whom they give, exchange, or sell it. This is the essence of Nozick's "entitlement theory."

Nozick discusses the "injustice" of a football or baseball player earning hundreds of thousands of dollars a week. If millions of people are prepared to watch a game because he is playing, is the star attraction not justified in receiving so much money? In a free society, people decide freely what is of value to them; resources shift around according to value, not need. If one thinks this is wrong and wishes to base the same society on need, one must begin restricting people's freedom of action. One has to make those who pay money to see the baseball star give it to more "worthwhile" ends. Furthermore, if it is deemed that the benefits of a product or service must be distributed to society at large, entrepreneurs will no longer have an incentive to create or build anything.

Nozick rebuts the ideas of philosopher John Rawls' landmark *A Theory of Justice* (see commentary in *50 Philosophy Classics*). Rawls' "difference principle" requires that more resources go toward members of society who come into the world with a natural disadvantage. A society cannot simply be for the protection of property or life, it must strive to be fair. Nozick argues that the difference principle does not work, even within a family. Should a family devote most of its resources toward the least talented child, and require that any resources spent on the other children be paid back by trying to improve the situation of their less fortunate sibling? If this makes no sense at the family level, Nozick wonders, why should it apply to society at large? Moreover, Rawls' theories are all about the rights of those in need; nothing is said about the rights of the giver.

Rawls' problem with Nozick's entitlement principle is that it allows for the distribution of resources in a way that is "arbitrary in a moral sense." That is, inequality of resources is simply not justified when it arises simply from natural endowment, good fortune, social circumstances, or accidents of birth. In return, Nozick is amazed that Rawls fails to mention that someone might have worked to develop the resources they own; everything noteworthy about a person is down to "external factors." On one hand, Rawls says that his theory is about the dignity and self-respect of human beings; on the other, he discounts human autonomy and the quality of a person's choices.

At the heart of Rawls' principle of justice, Nozick says, is envy. He offers an alternative equation. First, people are entitled to their natural assets. Second, if they are entitled to something, they are entitled to whatever flows from it, including the things they own. In short: "Whether or not people's assets are arbitrary from a moral point of view, they are entitled to them, and to what flows from them."

Nozick also address taxation, which he describes as "forced labor," since it involves forcing someone to work extra hours in order to pay for another person's need. People would object if they were asked to work five extra hours a week to pay for the needs of the ill or unemployed, but that is what taxation is. "Whether it is done through taxation or wages or on wages over a certain amount, or through seizure of profits, or through there being a *social* pot so that it's not clear what's coming from where and what's going where," Nozick writes, "principles of distributive justice involve appropriating the actions of other persons." Those who receive something from this social pot become *part owners of you* through ownership of your labor. This goes against all liberal ideas (notably those voiced by Locke) that a person is the owner of themselves, their labor, and the produce of their labor. Nozick concludes by suggesting that a bigger, redistributing state would only be justified if citizens were *willing* to sell themselves into slavery via onerous taxation.

A utopia that preserves freedom

While asserting that "no state more extensive than the minimal state can be justified," Nozick admits that this kind of state is hardly one that can "thrill or inspire the heart." It seems pale or insubstantial compared to the bigger states of which utopian theorists or nationalists dream. He introduces an alternative model in which a minimal state presides over an unlimited number of smaller "utopias" or polities that set their own rules about how to live. All that the state will do is to protect the individual against violence and allow freedom of movement. Its role would not be to inspire, only to preserve the ability of anyone to set up, join, or leave a community.

This framework is better than a standard libertarian vision, Nozick asserts, because it allows for communities to exist that would not normally be tolerated on libertarian grounds. Indeed, some communities may be quite strict, with curbs on what people can read or their sexual behavior, and some may be communistic or very paternalistic. Yet people would have freely chosen to live in such communities. There could also be micro-communities, such as a worker-controlled factory, which could exist within a wider free, capitalist society.

Nozick admits that there are questions about the "meta-utopia" framework: Who would set it up? What would be its powers? Its major role, he says, would be enforcement: stopping one community from invading another, taking it over, and enslaving its people; and providing a means of conflict resolution between communities. It would also enforce the right of individuals to leave a community if they wish. Yet the framework would not have the usual "universal" moral principles of most national constitutions. Indeed, he says, there are "some things individuals may choose for themselves, no one may choose for another." Instead, his framework offers "the best of all possible worlds," combining individual freedom to choose with the fact of human nature that people wish to live with others according to certain values, and *voluntarily* to restrict their own choices and possibilities. It combines the age-old desire for people to improve their lives, following deeply held dreams, values, and visions, with the underlying liberty not to be forced to live in a particular regime or community.

"Is not the minimal state, the framework for utopia," he asks in his conclusion, "an inspiring vision?" While forgoing so many of the self-appointed tasks that we have come to expect of government, in its place is absolute clarity on the inviolate rights and freedoms of the individual, "who may not be used in certain ways by others as means or tools or instruments or resources."

Final comments

The basis of Nozick's entitlement theory is that "economic goods arise already encumbered with rightful claims to their ownership." One cannot say that a farm or a factory or an automobile is in any way a public good ripe for redistribution. The fundamental question should not be (as was the twentieth-century zeitgeist) how we can achieve equality, but rather: Who owns this, and how is their ownership protected? Ignore or cover over this last question, and the whole edifice of the state becomes, morally, a house of cards. For Nozick the only "rights" people truly have are those to property properly gained. "Social justice" is something to be pursued by civil associations or private bodies and individuals according to their philosophy or whim, and is *not* something that concerns the state. When the state has made itself into the bringer of social justice, it means a correspondingly higher level of compulsory taxation. Running through the book is a sense of effrontery that the redistributionists can take the moral high ground, when in practice their ideals result in the erosion of a person's right to keep the wages or profit gained from their labor, instead having to give up a chunk of the income "for the greater good."

Nozick admits that his idea of allowing a multitude of communities and utopias to try themselves out would result in plenty of failures, and that this would in turn bring calls for the state to return to a role as "promoter of the good," as Plato imagined it. But Nozick stands with de Tocqueville, who said that only by living in freedom will people come to recognize and exercise virtues, and take responsibility *ourselves* for developing that goodness. This focus on personal responsibility is surely better than giving all the moral power to the state.

Robert Nozick

Born in Brooklyn, New York in 1938 to Russian immigrant parents, Robert Nozick discovered the work of Plato in his teens and majored in philosophy at Columbia University. He received a PhD in philosophy from Princeton University in 1963, and taught there for two years before taking up positions at Harvard and Rockefeller University. At 30 he became a full professor at Harvard, where he stayed for the rest of his career.

Anarchy, State, and Utopia won Nozick a National Book Award and was included in "The Hundred Most Influential Books since the War" by The Times Literary Supplement. It was his only really political book. His other four, Philosophical Explanations (1981), The Examined Life (1989), The Nature of Rationality (1993), and Invariances (2001), are more purely philosophical and cover, among other areas, decision theory, consciousness, free will, and the nature of love and happiness. Nozick died in 2002.

The Future of Power

"States are no longer the only important actors in global affairs; security is not the only major outcome they seek, and force is not the only or always the best instrument available to achieve those outcomes."

"Soft power may appear less risky than military or economic power, but it is often hard to use, easy to lose, and costly to establish."

"A smart power narrative for the twenty-first century is not about maximizing power or preserving hegemony. It is about finding ways to combine resources into successful strategies in the new context of power diffusion and the 'rise of the rest.'"

In a nutshell

Power in today's world is diffuse and no longer flows from military might alone; the nations with the best narratives and ideas win.

In a similar vein

Edward Bernays *Propaganda* (p 66)
Paul Kennedy *The Rise and Fall of the Great Powers* (p 144)
Hans Morgenthau *Politics Among Nations* (p 208)
Fareed Zakaria *The Post-American World* (p 310)

CHAPTER 35

Joseph S. Nye

J oseph Nye, a leading foreign policy scholar, is well known for coining the term "soft power," but he would be the first to admit that soft power alone is not enough. States obviously need military power along with diplomatic, cultural, and moral clout, and the combination of these elements constitutes what he calls "smart power."

Nye begins *The Future of Power* by mentioning the 2008 Russian invasion of Georgia. Russia's choice to use "hard power," he says, "undercut its claims to legitimacy and sowed fear and mistrust in much of the world." China, meanwhile, had a soft power victory in the same year with the successful staging of the Olympics in Beijing. Indeed, Premier Hu Jintao explicitly said that the Olympics were part of a concerted effort to exert soft power. Given that many states were suspicious of China's military and political intentions, such an investment seemed a smart move in conveying the idea of a "peaceful rise." Meanwhile, a Pew Research Center poll showed that the majority of people in 25 countries thought that China would eclipse the US as the world's superpower, and even the US government's National Intelligence Council thought that by 2025 America's dominance would be "much diminished."

Yet for Nye, the more interesting issue is not which country is rising and which declining, but rather how power itself is changing. Is "power" today the same as it was 50 or even 20 years ago, and if not, what is it that makes a country powerful? And could non-state actors even become more important than nations in the twenty-first century?

Dimensions of power

Instead of assuming that power is invested in states, Nye suggests, we should consider what *resources* create power. For example, sixteenth-century Spain rose on the back of colonies and gold bullion, while the power of nineteenth-century Britain derived from the industrial revolution and sea power. What are the resources that determine power in our time? Is it any longer sufficient to use military dominance or gross domestic product as an indicator? And how do we measure the "balance of power" in an information age?

He asks us to understand power in today's world as a three-layered chessboard: on the top board of military power, the US remains the only superpower;

on the middle board of economic power, we now live in a multipolar world with many countries having economic heft; and the lower chessboard relates to the realm of diffused power that goes beyond nations, from global capital flows to computer viruses, from terrorist networks to the effects of climate change and pandemics. Instead of the assumption that states with the most powerful military will be dominant, there is an appreciation that the most successful states create "smart" power, defined as "the combination of the hard power of coercion and payment with the soft power of persuasion and attraction."

"Two great power shifts are occurring this century," Nye writes, "a power transition among states and a power diffusion away from all states to nonstate actors." In the world of states themselves, the big story will continue to be "the return of Asia." In 1750, Asia had half the world's population and output. This shrank to a fifth with the rise of Europe and America in the industrial revolution. By 2050, Asia will be on the way to returning to its historical share. Yet in the age of global information, nation-states no longer have the power they once did, because money, ideas, and diseases flow easily across national borders, and issues like climate change and terrorism are by nature transnational. "It is not enough to think in terms of power *over* others," Nye writes. "We must also think in terms of power to accomplish goals that involves power *with* others."

Because power is now more complicated and more defuse, a country like America will have to depend more on other nations to get things done. It will "require a more sophisticated narrative than the classical stories of the rise and fall of great powers." That is, instead of their usual sport of wondering whether they are still number one, Americans should be thinking more in terms of whether the way the world is ordered is or is not a good reflection of their interests and what they believe are universal values. Indeed, suggests Nye, success may depend not simply on who has the most military hardware, or even who is the richest, but who has the "best story." America will still promote itself as a beacon of freedom and democracy, while China's story will be the return and peaceful rise of a great civilization.

The hard and the soft

States may no longer go to war as much as they did in the nineteenth and twentieth centuries, but military power will still be an intrinsic part of world politics, Nye says, a form of very expensive insurance that nations feel they need to take out. However, the actual threats are more likely to be from non-state actors and domestic insurgents. America can do precision unmanned bombing raids of targets, but its much poorer enemies can create havoc with car bombs and suicide bombers. "Shock and awe" is no longer enough.

American forces have had to put new emphasis on counterinsurgency, or protecting civilian populations. After they have made an area safe by some judicious and perhaps minimal use of hard power, they then go in and do the soft power work of building roads, schools, and clinics.

There is no contradiction between hard power and soft power, Nye says, it is just another way of achieving outcomes, and may be at least as fiercely fought over as hard power resources. The competition for perceived legitimacy, for instance, which is an attempt to deny another entity (whether a state, company, or NGO) its soft power, is going on all the time. Just prior to the Beijing Olympics, filmmaker Steven Spielberg sent an open letter to Chinese premier Hu Jintao to get China to help with the peacekeeping force in Darfur. China promptly sent an emissary there. At a point when it was vulnerable, not wanting to be embarrassed in front of the world, it acted.

A problem for politicians is that soft power often evolves over a long time-frame and is embedded in a nation's culture, so it cannot be quickly or easily deployed. It may seem an easy way to gain power compared to military or economic might, but "it is often hard to use, easy to lose, and costly to establish." If a country is seen as manipulative, soft power simply becomes propaganda, Nye notes, and the nation deploying it loses all credibility. In addition, "Soft power is a dance that requires partners." It has no influence, it seems, in getting North Korea to abandon nuclear weapons, for that is a regime that only responds to hard power, if at all. Soft power is not a zero-sum game, Nye points out. China can gain greater esteem at the same time as America or any other country. Indeed, if China increases its soft power to the point where it feels secure in not having to resort to military power to achieve its aims, then everybody wins.

Nye admits that if he were the leader of a country that had to choose between hard and soft power, he would take hard power any day, as it can be a matter of survival. Yet if one wants one's nation to advance and hold its own over the long term, it is best to have both. Rome stayed an empire for so long because it was open to immigrants who could rise up through the ranks. Its openness and ideals gave it pulling power. Today, authoritarian regimes should recognize that the greatest source of soft power is openness. If a state muzzles its people, it instantly has a credibility problem. The BBC's World Service has credibility because the organization has a charter that protects it from government interference. Other forms of soft power, such as cultural and academic exchanges, can also have a powerful effect over time. Anwar Sadat, Helmut Schmidt, and Margaret Thatcher were among future world leaders who enjoyed sponsored educational exchanges in America, and around half of Iran's present governing body have US degrees.

Cyberpower

Though the death knell of the nation-state has often been sounded, people increasingly feel that they are part of communities that are not limited by state borders. Worldwide communities, say of environmentalists, do not necessarily wish to challenge state power directly; they are simply adding a layer of power that was not there before. Of course, international movements like socialism, the peace movement, and feminism have been around for a long time, as have international organizations like the Red Cross and the Catholic Church. Yet there are many more now, they involve greater numbers of people, and all have access to technology—including terrorists who hark back to a seventh-century ideal of Islam. Nye contrasts the "cyberpower" of today with the sea power and land power of yesterday. Unlike sea power, which required massive investments in shipbuilding and armory, the cost barriers to entry to cyberspace are virtually nil; and as the internet was designed for ease of use and accessibility, not security, governments are on the back foot.

Although this revolution would seem to help non-state actors and small states, and reduce the power of large states, many of the dynamics of international politics still apply. A big state can fund huge intelligence agencies and employ thousands of people to disrupt or hack into computer networks. Russian hackers attacked Estonia in 2007 and Georgia in 2008, and in 2010 the Stuxnet worm (probably sent by Israel) shut down some processes in Iranian nuclear facilities. What would be the effect, Nye wonders, if hackers shut down the electricity systems in a northern city like Chicago or Moscow? In wintertime, this could be more devastating than dropping bombs. As with regular warfare, each country has to weigh up the costs of attack. For instance, if state-funded hackers in China launched an attack on American companies that damaged the US economy, the downturn would harm China too, given that the countries are so economically linked.

Diffusion of power is not the same as equality of power, Nye says. States will still have a big role in cyberspace, in national filtering and defense technology, regulation of service providers, and new cyberwar defense divisions alongside traditional land, air, and sea power. The stakes are too high for governments to leave the cyber domain to the private realm.

Smart power

The "smart power" approach is about clarity of goals and awareness of how to achieve them. It involves making or keeping important economic, military, and political alliances, and cooperating with global institutions, even for a hegemonic state. Bodies that transcend national borders will increasingly matter, if only because so many of today's issues, from climate change to terrorism to infectious diseases like Ebola, are pan-national. The best word to describe America's position today is not "empire" or "hegemon," Nye suggests, but *preponderance*. It may be dominant militarily and economically, but its weight and heft should not deny the power and wealth of other actors. Using soft power, part of its remit must be to maintain public goods such as an open international economy and a commons of seas, space, and the internet, and be a mediator of international disputes before they escalate.

Final comments

Many of Nye's points were prescient. For example, cyberattacks, such as North Korea's alleged assault on Sony Pictures in 2014, have only increased. The concepts of hard and soft power continue to be useful ways of understanding the moves of actors in global politics, while the more nuanced smart power provides a recipe for state effectiveness.

A 2014 speech by Chinese premier Xi Jinping described China as like the "big guy in the room." Despite his size, he was not trying to dominate the others. The analogy could easily have come from Nye, but relating to the US as well. Power today is not simply about the assertion of power or achieving hegemony, or asking whether it will be the "American century" or "China's century." Power grows if it is used in a way that tends to benefit everyone, but as soon as people think it is being used only for selfish purposes, it lays itself open to attack and diminishment. The future belongs to those countries that can wage war in a positive sense, on the battlefield of ideas and images.

Joseph S. Nye

Joseph Nye, Jr. was born in 1937 and gained his first degree from Princeton University. He was also a Rhodes Scholar to Oxford, studying philosophy, politics, and economics, and obtained his PhD in political science from Harvard in 1964. At Harvard his positions have included Director of the Center for Science and International Affairs and Dean of the John F. Kennedy School of Government. Nye has been an adviser on security and foreign policy issues in several US administrations, including Assistant Secretary of Defense for International Security Affairs under President Clinton. He sits on the Foreign Policy Board advising the Secretary of State and on the Council on Foreign Relations, is co-chair of the Center for a New American Security Cyber Security Project, and is on the editorial board of Foreign Policy. *Books include* The Paradox of American Power *(2002),* Soft Power: The Means to Success in World Politics *(2004), and* Understanding International Conflicts *(2009, 7th edn).*

The Rise and Decline of Nations

"On balance, special-interest organizations and collusions reduce efficiency and aggregate income in the societies in which they operate and make political life more divisive."

"[Of] two societies that were in other respects equal, the one with the longer history of stability, security, and freedom of association would have more institutions that limit entry and innovation [and] encourage more social interaction and homogeneity among their members."

In a nutshell

Over time, stable societies generate interest groups that will do anything to protect their members, at the cost of society at large.

In a similar vein

Daron Acemoglu & James A. Robinson *Why Nations Fail* (p 26)
John Micklethwait & Adrian Wooldridge *The Fourth Revolution* (p 196)
Richard Wilkinson & Kate Pickett *The Spirit Level* (p 298)

CHAPTER 36

Mancur Olson

When economist Mancur Olson began writing *The Rise and Decline of Nations: Economic Growth, Stagflation, and Social Rigidities*, it became obvious to him that this is a subject that we know very little about. A frequent explanation for differences among nations is "culture." For example, medieval Protestants had a certain work ethic that pushed them ahead of their Catholic peers; Germans had always done well due to their industriousness compared to their southern European counterparts; and the Japanese prospered thanks to their ethnic homogeneity and singularity of purpose. But when Olson looked at the evidence, he found that cultural explanations may work for certain periods or in particular places, but do not hold true as a general rule.

Perhaps a better explanation for long-term prosperity is political stability. The two, after all, always seem to go hand in hand (Acemoglu and Robinson's *Why Nations Fail* is a recent supporter of this view; see p 26). Yet Olson's rejection of this thesis is even more forthright. He notes that the longer a society is around, the more likely it is that its policy and laws will become driven by special interest coalitions (industry organizations, cartels, unions, farmers' lobbies, and the like) that seek to benefit their members at the expense of society as a whole. Stability has a cost, and perhaps only revolution or war can "reset" a society to its former social mobility and economic dynamism.

At the time the book was written it was widely accepted that pressure groups were a healthy part of democracies, but Olson showed that not all groups are equal. Those with an advantage (in funding, organization, or influence) tend to see that advantage increase over time. Indeed, Olson's book has never been more relevant in his own country. His model foresaw the polarization of American politics, the power of lavishly funded Washington lobby groups, the legislative and budgetary sclerosis of the past few years, and the widening gap in incomes as a small portion of society manages to win tax relief and gains most of the benefits of growth.

Collective action: Costs and benefits

In 1965, Olson's *The Logic of Collective Action* revealed the way in which, over time, human nature tends to distort and undermine democratic and egalitarian principles. On a rational basis, one might assume that if a group or organization benefits from the economic growth of a society, it is in its interests to support and encourage overall growth. After all, if the economy is growing then people will be buying more goods or services. In reality, special interest groups rarely take this outlook; they believe that it is more productive to gain a larger slice of the economic pie for themselves, rather than pushing for a bigger pie. A better image, Olson says, is of wrestlers going at each other in a china shop. They do not care about the damage, they just want to win.

The "rent-seeking" behavior of special interest groups, coalitions, cartels, and lobbies naturally tends to reduce the efficiency of the economy overall. Barriers to entry in an industry, for instance, come with substantial costs. A certain profession will seek legislation that admits only people with particular qualifications, on public safety grounds. The protection given to this profession means the public have to pay more, so their money is not being productively spent elsewhere. In short, "the great majority of special-interest organizations redistribute income rather than create it, and in ways that reduce social efficiency and output."

Carving up society's wealth in this way also diminishes the importance of common political interests. During a war, a society may pull together to defeat the enemy. There is a perceived common benefit that outweighs all others. But in struggles for society's goods and wealth, no one can win without another party losing, which breeds resentment. When the power of special interest groups and coalitions grows, politics becomes more divisive and unstable, as prior electoral choices and policies are undone or reversed due to the lobbying power of affected groups. A country no longer represents a forward progression of prosperity, freedom, and justice over time that benefits all, but an arena in which the most powerful slug it out for their own gain.

Special interest economics

There are clear economic effects when special interest groups gain undue power. Most importantly, it leads to a reduction in the ability to adapt to change. For example, a union might campaign against the introduction of a technological innovation that will lessen demand for its workers, even if it means significant benefits to the productivity of an industry and the prosperity of society. Industry cartels, too, are often resistant to innovation, because one company's development of a new technology can threaten others' prosperity. When an industry is not cartelized, in contrast, there will be vigorous competition from each player to outdo the others by making technological or productivity gains.

A society driven by special interests will develop ever more complex regulation that reflects a non-level playing field. Special considerations built into laws to favor a certain group are then challenged by other groups, and government grows larger trying to deal with it all. Furthermore, Olson notes that "the articulate and educated have a comparative advantage in regulation, politics, and complex understandings." That is, they may thrive in an environment that does not reward innovation and creativity as much as it does understanding how the levers of power work in a compromised economy. The unfortunate effect of this is that society's brain power goes toward preserving the status quo instead of making it more dynamic.

That societies strongly influenced by special interests grow more slowly than those where this is not the case can be understood by looking at totalitarian regimes that have wiped out all competing interests other than the state, or where war and regime change destroyed all previous interest coalitions. Germany and Japan grew so quickly after the Second World War, Olson says, because there were no established interests standing in the way of rapid growth. Hitler had made unions illegal, and in Japan left-wing labor organizations had been repressed. Add to this the anti-monopoly provisions established by the Allies in both countries after the war, and you have a recipe for robust growth. In contrast Britain, a country of long-standing stability and institutions, had anemic growth rates in the postwar period. It seemed ungovernable, with frequent industrial action thanks to overly powerful unions. Olson also mentions Hong Kong, Taiwan, Korea, and Singapore, who zoomed ahead in the postwar period. Because all had been previously owned or administered by other countries, they had not had the freedom to develop distributional coalitions and strong special interests to hamper growth.

Olson found that his thesis could be applied to differences within countries too. The western and southern states of the United States had grown more quickly in recent decades because they lacked the longstanding political institutions of the northeastern and midwest regions, where special interest groups and business organizations had had longer to develop and influence policy. People soon get a sense of when a region or country has been captured by a few, leaving less opportunity for the average person to thrive.

Finally, freer trade grows economies and companies, Olson says, because it allows them to get around or undercut vested interests and coalitions, either on their home turf or in other places: "If there is free international trade, there are international markets out of the control of any lobbies." If the barriers come down, Ricardo's famous principle of "comparative advantage" comes into full swing, and countries start producing what they are better at or are able to do cheaply, instead of adopting "me too" industry policies that protect inefficient industries and businesses. When foreign firms are allowed to come in and compete with local ones, they make the local market competitive, helping to eliminate cartels and cozy arrangements, and bringing in new ideas in production and innovation that a tariff wall might have kept away.

Government is not the problem

Olson argues that there is only a weak connection between the *size* of government and economic growth. Both France and Sweden, he notes, grew steadily in the postwar period despite their large government sectors. Size of government is less important than whether sectional interests have a paralyzing effect on the economy. Indeed, why did Sweden and Norway, which had strong special interest groups as in Britain, grow at good levels after the war when Britain did not? The chief reason is that the labor organizations in both Scandinavian countries were "encompassing"; that is, they had very large unions covering most of the workers in the economy. It was therefore in their interests to see the economy grow overall. Britain's unions were narrower and more extractive. Neither did Sweden and Norway's unions seek tariffs on imported goods as unions had elsewhere; this rendered them relatively open to market forces, which in turn made their industries more efficient.

Classical liberal economic theory says that government is the cause of slower growth, and only if it is made smaller and gets out of the way will freer markets create prosperity. Yet Olson notes that the "government is by no means the only source of coercion or social pressure in society." Cartels, for instance, tend to develop regardless of government (including laissez-faire government). His point is that nations decline not because they are overtaken by the interests of the left or right, or because the state grows too large, but because a process that is meant to deliver benefits for all is corrupted by a few. We should bear this truth in mind when we see business or trade groups attacking the size of government as inimical to the prosperity of the nation; they should first look to see the extent to which their lobbying for particular consideration or legislation limits the dynamism of the economy. Indeed, we assume that redistribution of wealth in a society is always with the motive of taking from the rich to alleviate the position of the poor, but much redistribution is from the poor to the rich, Olson says. Medical care systems tend to be built on the advice of practitioners, who are already well off, rather than the general public, who are the users. Tax loopholes help the rich get even richer, and "corporate welfare" tends to shore up failing companies that really should be left to go under.

The insidious nature of special interests skewing law and institutions runs across the board. Minimum wage laws and union wage scales, Olson argues, stop companies and workers from making new agreements that would benefit both, and the result is higher than necessary unemployment. It cannot simply be said that a nation declines because it is captured by the interests of billionaires and private corporations, because the effects of too-powerful unions can be just as bad on economic dynamism. It is not the specific groups that Olson was so worried about as much as the generic phenomenon of special interest capture.

Final comments

It is clear that some countries are able to reinvent themselves without going through the violent upheaval that Olson claims may be necessary to break the hold of special interests. When *The Rise and Decline of Nations* was published, Britain was undergoing a kind of revolution under Margaret Thatcher. The marketization of its economy through privatization, liberalization of the financial markets, and dismantling of union power ended the sclerosis of the 1970s and created a fast-growing economy.

One of Olson's interesting contentions is that class relations work in the same way as industry or labor interests. That is, social classes or castes limit intermarriage with other classes not simply out of social snobbery, but to manage economic exclusivity. The smaller a class is, the more focused it can be on asserting and maintaining its power to the exclusion of others. An aristocracy is simply a more extreme version of special interest dynamics in which great stability goes hand in hand with economic stagnation. Whenever we see stability we should ask: Is it borne of all people and groups in society having a say in how it is run, and a share in its benefits? Or is it the result of some groups having skewed laws and institutions in a way that suits them? A successful society puts in place multiple checks, balances, and provisions to counter the reality pointed out by eighteenth-century economist Josiah Tucker: "All men would be monopolists if they could."

Mancur Olson

Mancur Lloyd Olson, Jr. was born into a farming family in 1932 in Grand Forks, North Dakota. After graduating from North Dakota Agricultural College in 1954, he won a Rhodes Scholarship to Oxford, studying philosophy, politics, and economics, and in 1963 gained a PhD in economics from Harvard.

Olson was a lecturer at Princeton University from 1960–61, an assistant professor there from 1963–67, and from 1967–69 worked for the US Department of Health, Education, and Welfare. In 1970 he became a professor at the University of Maryland, remaining there for the next three decades. He died suddenly in 1998, and his Power and Prosperity, *looking at the problem of governance in emerging economies, was published in 2000.*

Animal Farm

"...nearly the whole of the produce of our labour is stolen from us by human beings. There, comrades, is the answer to all our problems. It is summed up in a single word—Man. Man is the only real enemy we have. Remove Man from the scene, and the root cause of hunger and overwork is abolished for ever."

"A few days later, when the terror caused by the executions had died down, some of the animals remembered—or thought they remembered—that the Sixth Commandment decreed 'No animal shall kill any other animal'. And though no one cared to mention it in the hearing of the pigs or the dogs, it was felt that the killings which had taken place did not square with this."

In a nutshell

Despite the best of intentions, most revolutions simply substitute one ruling class for another.

In a similar vein

Hannah Arendt *The Origins of Totalitarianism* (p 48)
Karl Marx & Friedrich Engels *The Communist Manifesto* (p 186)
Alexandr Solzhenitsyn *The Gulag Archipelago* (p 266)

CHAPTER 37

George Orwell

Prevented from joining the British forces due to a lung condition, when the Second World War began George Orwell joined the Home Guard, grew vegetables, and wrote freelance for journals and newspapers. From 1941–43 he worked for the BBC's Eastern Service in London, overseeing broadcasts to India. Though he and most of his friends were on the left, he had long been suspicious of communism, at least in its totalitarian form. In July 1941 he wrote in his diary:

> *"One could not have a better example of the moral and emotional shallowness of our time, than the fact that we are now all more or less pro Stalin. This disgusting murderer is temporarily on our side, and so the purges, etc., are suddenly forgotten."*

While literary editor of the magazine *Tribune*, he began writing *Animal Farm*. The novel was rejected by T.S. Eliot at Faber & Faber and by Victor Gollancz, who thought it a needless attack on the Soviet regime, which was after all in alliance with Britain and America and had just helped defeat the Nazis. After a deal with Jonathan Cape foundered, Secker & Warburg published the book in 1945.

Orwell's allegory of the Bolshevik Revolution and the early years of Stalinism masterfully and entertainingly uncovers the moral failure of communism, showing up the naïvety of those who still thought that Stalinist Russia was a worthy experiment. The fact that Orwell considered himself a democratic socialist gave his judgment on the regime extra force. He was never against socialism itself, he said, but against fascism and totalitarianism.

If Orwell had expressed his views in a factual way, as he did with *Down and Out in Paris and London* or *The Road to Wigan Pier*, he would still have made an impact, but the timeless storyline of *Animal Farm* meant that it appealed to millions.

A revolution stirs

Manor Farm is owned by Mr Jones. He gives his animals only what they need to survive and keeps the rest. None of the hens' eggs are allowed to hatch into chickens, and all the foals are taken away from their mother at a year old. As soon as the productiveness of any of the farm animals wanes, they are taken off to the abattoir without sentiment.

Old Major, a pig, wants to wake up the other animals to their condition. Man is the enemy, he tells them, who can only be overthrown by banding together. In one of his speeches Old Major says: "Weak or strong, clever or simple, we are all brothers. No animal must ever kill any other animal. All animals are equal."

After Old Major dies, the animals' initial excitement at his ideas turns to patient expectation that one day their time will come. The smarter ones begin programs of secret education in "Animalism," their philosophy of rebellion, and deal with questions from the doubters. One points out that they only survive because Mr Jones feeds them. What happens if they get rid of him? Mollie the mare asks: "Will there be sugar after the Rebellion?" Snowball, one of the smart pigs, replies that there is no way to make sugar on the farm, and besides, sugar is not necessary as there will be plenty of oats.

When farmer Jones begins to neglect his farm and spend more time at the pub, the underfed animals see their opportunity. They overcome his men and take over Manor Farm, burning the reins, whips, and nosebags that had degraded them, and flinging the farmer's castration knives down the well. They turn his house into a museum so they can remember the regime that had almost crushed them, and change the property's name to Animal Farm.

Making it work

The animals make a tremendous effort to get the harvest in, and delight in the fact that they have produced every morsel they eat. Each Sunday they raise their flag (a hoof and a horn on a green background), sing their anthem "Beasts of England," and have a communal meeting.

The first of the Seven Commandments of Animal Farm is "Whatever goes upon two legs is an enemy," and the second, "Whatever goes upon four legs, or has wings, is a friend." The animals who can learn to read have a certain power, while it becomes clear that others will never grasp letters and words. For them, the commandments have to be boiled down to one simple statement: "FOUR LEGS GOOD, TWO LEGS BAD."

With this simple belief drummed into them, the animals do not protest when it is revealed that all the cows' milk, and all the apples from the orchard, are being appropriated by the pigs. Thanks to their superior intelligence, they are now managing Animal Farm on behalf of everyone, and they need these things to function properly. The alternative is Mr Jones' return.

Animals on other farms across the country are now singing "Beasts of England" and other farmers are getting worried that the same might happen to them. Jones is anxious to get back his property, and along with two neighboring farmers leads an attack. Animal Farm is viciously defended, and the Battle of the Cowshed is set down as an important milestone in its history.

However, there is soon division among the animals. Napoleon, the farm's new leader, has raised some puppies to be fiercely loyal to him, and has them intimidate Snowball to such an extent that he flees from the farm. Napoleon now decrees that the Sunday meetings are unnecessary, and instead puts in place a committee of senior pigs who can manage the farm. Some of the animals do not like this, but are too afraid to say so. Boxer the horse decides that if Napoleon has decreed it, it must be right. The skull of Old Major is dug up and placed on a pedestal, and each week the animals file past to pay their respects.

Much of the farm's resources are directed toward the great project of providing a windmill for the farm. Napoleon announces that they will engage in limited trade with other farms, not for commercial gain, of course, but to get crucial supplies. A grudging respect grows among humans for the animal enterprise. Although they hate what has happened, they cannot deny that the animals seem to be running things on their own.

History is not set in stone

One autumn night there is a huge storm, and the animals wake to find the windmill destroyed. They blame the disaster on Snowball, and unite around Napoleon's call for the windmill to be rebuilt. A tough winter brings food supplies low, and humans begin to suspect that the farm is running aground. Yet in their pride, the animals go to some lengths to portray themselves as living in abundance, even if it means some sleight of hand. Mr Whymper, the human they reluctantly engage to help with finances and trading, is shown a storehouse filled with bins of apples and wheat. Only the top of each bin contains the produce; just below the top layer they are filled with sand.

Everything wrong on the farm is increasingly blamed on Snowball, who is said to come at night and wreak vengeance. He had clearly been in league with Mr Jones from the start, and had fled the scene at the Battle of the Cowshed. This jarred with the animals' memories, but if Napoleon is adamant that Snowball is a traitor, then he is. So there can be no "wrong" views or insurgency, Napoleon oversees forced confessions and executions of "traitors" shown to be in league with the enemy Snowball.

For the greater good

A cult now develops around Napoleon. He eats off Mr Jones' Crown Derby dinner service, and songs are sung in his praise. All negative feeling is focused on the neighboring human farmers Pilkington and Frederick, who are said to treat their animals horribly.

Each Sunday the pig Squealer reads out the farm production figures, showing that the amount of particular commodities has doubled, or tripled; the animals do not question this. Rations are always "readjusted," never "reduced." Meanwhile, the hens have to keep producing more eggs on less rations, while all the pigs seem fat enough, and there are more rules about how pigs must be accorded special respect. All barley is to be reserved for them, and they receive a ration of a pint of beer a day. Napoleon enjoys lamp oil, candles, and even sugar in the house, while these are forbidden to the others. He promises to build a school house, and the animals are constantly reminded of their freedom and dignity through rousing speeches, songs, and processions.

When Boxer, one of the farm's greatest workers, falls ill, it is announced that he will be sent to the vet in a nearby town and get the best treatment. So when he is taken away, the animals are shocked to see written on the side of the van "Alfred Simmonds, Horse Slaughterer, Dealer in Hides and Bone meal." They try to stop the van leaving, but to no avail. Boxer is not seen again.

The ruling classes

As the years wear on, most of the generation who remembered the original Rebellion are no longer around. Even those who do remember all that had been promised, and not delivered, do not complain. After all, Napoleon says that the greatest happiness is in hard work and living frugally. Meanwhile, the pigs and dogs keep tight control over the farm, doing important work and receiving commensurate benefits. The pigs teach themselves to walk on two legs, and begin wearing clothes and carrying whips. The house now has a telephone and a radio, and receives newspapers. One morning the commandment painted on the side of the barn about the equality of all animals now reads: "ALL ANIMALS ARE EQUAL, BUT SOME ANIMALS ARE MORE EQUAL THAN OTHERS."

A delegation of humans comes to the farm and is entertained in the house. The farmer Pilkington is heard to say: "If you have your lower animals to contend with, we have our lower classes!" Pilkington congratulates Napoleon on the farm's low rations, long working hours, and lack of pampering. In reply, Napoleon notes that the animals are not actually revolutionaries, but just want to live in peace and prosperity. The term "comrade" will soon be abolished. As the animals gaze through the glass, what strikes them is that the faces of the pigs and those of the men do not seem very different.

Final comments

Who does each farm character represent? It has been surmised that Old Major is Karl Marx, Napoleon Stalin, and Snowball the exiled Trotsky. Mr Jones represents the old imperial Russian regime before the Revolution, and

Pilkington and Frederick the Allied powers of America and Britain. The pigs resemble Stalin's bureaucracy, the dogs his secret police. The efforts to build the windmill evoke the Five Year Plans, and the confessions and executions recall Stalin's show trials. The farm's battles mirror events such as the Battle of Stalingrad, and "animalism" is of course communism.

However, such is *Animal Farm*'s allegorical power that it transcends its direct Russian inspiration to be a message about all forms of totalitarianism, then, now, and in the future. Orwell's warnings cover the increasing aggrandizement and decadence of the ruling cadre; domination of the community by a single, ruthless leader, and the development of a cult around him; the desperate covering up of the regime's inadequacies by creating vivid (often imaginary) internal and external enemies; rewriting history to suit ideological correctness; keeping the masses in willful ignorance through propaganda; and treating people as units of production to meet targets that only ever go up, never down.

Today, "Orwellian" describes any kind of oppressive regime or unwarranted electronic surveillance. Orwell's other dystopian masterpiece, *Nineteen Eighty-Four* (1949), in which he coined the phrases "Big Brother," "newspeak," "doublethink," and "thought police," took the ideas of *Animal Farm* to their logical and sinister conclusion. Orwell's pessimism about human nature told him that in any society, power tends to get the upper hand over freedom.

George Orwell

Eric Arthur Blair was born in Motihari, India, in 1903, and his father Richard worked in the Indian Civil Service. While he was still a baby, his mother took him to England and settled him and his sisters near Henley. He attended school in Eastbourne, Sussex, then won a scholarship to Eton. After the English Civil Service examinations he was posted with the Indian Imperial Police in Burma. This was followed by time in London and a stint in Paris as a journalist, which provided material for his first book under the pen name George Orwell, Down and Out in Paris and London *(1933). In 1936 he went to Spain to join the anti-Franco forces, and after being shot through the neck returned to England.*

For most of his life Orwell survived on income from paid book reviews, columns, and political commentary, and for a time worked in a North London bookshop. In the 1930s he wrote six books: Burmese Days *(1934),* A Clergyman's Daughter *(1935),* Keep the Aspidistra Flying *(1936),* The Road to Wigan Pier *(1937),* Homage to Catalonia *(1938), and* Coming Up for Air *(1939).*

Orwell was diagnosed with tuberculosis in 1947, but managed to complete Nineteen Eighty-Four *at a remote farm on the Scottish island of Jura. He died in a London hospital in early 1950. Eileen O'Shaughnessy, his wife, had died in 1945 while he was a war correspondent in Europe.*

Common Sense

"The cause of America is in a great measure the cause of all mankind."

"Until an independence is declared, the Continent will feel itself like a man who continues putting off some unpleasant business from day to day, yet knows it must be done, hates to set about it, wishes it over, and is continually haunted with the thoughts of its necessity."

In a nutshell

Self-determination is the right of every people and nation, but it still requires courage to turn it into reality.

In a similar vein

Edmund Burke *Reflections on the Revolution in France* (p 78)
Alexander Hamilton, John Jay, & James Madison *The Federalist Papers* (p 120)
Abraham Lincoln *The Gettysburg Address* (p 162)
John Locke *Two Treatises of Government* (p 168)
Alexis de Tocqueville *Democracy in America* (p 292)

CHAPTER 38

Thomas Paine

When Englishman Thomas Paine, a former corset maker and customs officer, published *Common Sense* anonymously in January 1776, he had been living in America for less than 15 months. Paine had fallen on his feet thanks to a letter of introduction from Benjamin Franklin, whom he had met in London. He landed a job as editor of *Pennsylvania Magazine*, increasing its circulation with coverage of controversial issues, and his own essays in favor of the abolition of slavery and the rights of women raised his profile.

Common Sense caused a sensation, and was copied and reprinted across the American colonies. In July the same year, the Continental Congress printed its Declaration of Independence. While the latter was formal and statesman-like, Paine's pamphlet was indignant and passionate, and aimed to spark the fire of American independence. It largely succeeded.

Although it is hard to appreciate now, when the year 1776 began revolutionary sentiment, while on the rise, was hardly shared by all. The idea of overthrowing British rule was radical, even if the colonial master was largely despised, and even if it won a war America would have to go through the upheaval of changing laws and institutions. Understanding this ambivalence, Paine created a straw man in the form of the English monarch George III, exaggerating his powers a little in order to show him up as the enemy of true democracy. Paine also attacked Britain's vaunted constitution, portraying it as the handiwork of a privileged upper class who legislated to protect its interests. Only with the enemy painted in such vivid colors, he felt, would he be able to get the average American to feel indignant and stir desire for change. It helped significantly that Paine wrote in the simplest terms possible, avoiding long words and scholarly references in favor of biblical analogies. A further ingredient in the success of the 25,000-word *Common Sense* was its author's ability to create a sense of historical inevitability. America's cause, he said, was simply the latest version in humankind's long quest for greater liberty and equality. It was on the right side of history.

Perhaps even Paine did not see how far and how quickly matters would move. Only a decade after *Common Sense*, Madison, Jay, and Hamilton's *The Federalist Papers* would provide a nuanced, policy-focused, detailed defense of the new Constitution, helping Americans to come to terms with the new system of government, and finally razing to the ground the institutions of British colonial rule. Nevertheless, every revolution needs to be powered initially by emotion, and this was the role of *Common Sense*.

What is wrong

In Part I ("On the Origin and Design of Government in General, with Concise Remarks on the Constitution"), Paine notes that government of any kind is a necessary evil, a "badge of lost innocence." Security is the fundamental purpose of government, and we will support whatever provides the most protection and benefit to us at the least cost.

Paine considers the English constitution under which America was administered. He admits that, compared to the rest of the world, the English system seems like a beacon of liberty, but with a closer glance anyone could see that it was anachronistic. While parading under the name "democracy," in fact England was still a monarchy and still had the House of Lords, both of which were hereditary. The monarch is held to be sovereign, separate from the people, and stripped of real power. But if that is the case, Paine asks, why have the monarchy at all? In reality, the king remains the "overbearing power" in the triumvirate of monarch, Lords, and Commons. "Though we have been wise enough to shut and lock a door against absolute monarchy," he says, "we at the same time have been foolish enough to put the crown in possession of the key." Monarchy is a form of idolatry and goes against the natural equality of human beings; it is "the Popery of government." Nature makes a mockery of the principle of hereditary succession, because although an original monarch may be a person of substance, later generations are likely not to measure up. Society may be stuck with an infant king, or one who is too ill or old to govern properly. "Of more worth is one honest man to society and in the sight of God," Paine writes, "than all the crowned ruffians that ever lived."

To the argument that America had done well under British governance, he says: "We may as well assert that because a child has thrived upon milk that it is never to have meat, or that the first twenty years of our lives is to become a precedent for the next twenty." He attacks the idea that Britain is the "Mother" or "parent" to America. In fact, its parent is Europe, since many of its settlers came from countries other than Britain, and Americans feel a brotherhood with "every European Christian." Moreover, America had to support Britain in the wars against Spain and France, who were not America's enemies.

Paine correctly notes that America's genius is not for war but for commerce, and it is through becoming an independent trading nation with free ports that it will foster friendship with European countries. In terms of both defense and commerce, America has no benefit in being part of Britain; in fact, it will prosper more on its own. It was Paine who first used the words "United States of America" when defending American revolutionary action against the British naval high command. Only a full union of the states would bring, he famously said, "importance abroad, and union at home."

What needs to be done

In Part II ("Thoughts on the Present State of American Affairs"), Paine complains that Americans do not feel confident enough to rule themselves, doffing their hat to superior English culture and institutions. He uses the words "coward" and "sycophant" to describe any American who still looks passively for reconciliation with England. Those whose parent or brother died fighting, or who have lost property, he notes, see the situation differently. He quotes Milton: "never can true reconcilement grow, where wounds of deadly hate have pierced so deep." After April 19, 1775, when British soldiers killed eight Americans at Lexington Green, the point had passed for trying to make peace. It was clear that the English were not going to budge. At any rate, Paine says, America is too far away from Britain to be managed well, and its affairs will only grow more complex. Moreover, the idea of huge America being a satellite of much smaller island-nation Britain "reverses the common order of nature."

At the time Paine was writing there were 13 American colonies, and he proposes forms of representation to a "Continental Conference" made up of politicians and people:

> *"The conferring members being met, let their business be to frame a CONTINENTAL CHARTER, or Charter of the United Colonies; (answering to what is called the Magna Carta of England) fixing the number and manner of choosing members of Congress, members of Assembly, with their date of sitting, and drawing the line of business and jurisdiction between them: (Always remembering, that our strength is continental, not provincial:) Securing freedom and property to all men, and above all things, the free exercise of religion, according to the dictates of conscience; with such other matter as is necessary for a charter to contain."*

A decade before it was actually produced, this was a good summary of what was needed in the Constitution, and what it eventually contained.

The strength to go it alone

Mere "reconciliation" with Britain, Paine says, will lead to much greater rebellion in the future, costing more American lives. It is better to separate totally *now*: "It is not in the power of Britain or of Europe to conquer America, if she do not conquer herself by DELAY and TIMIDITY," he writes. In Part IV ("Of the Present Ability of America"), Paine argues that if the situation is left longer, the colonies will grow stronger and more jealous of each other. Form a union while the American nation is still young, and there will be goodwill among members.

Paine also makes a case for America needing to establish its own navy. Most of the British navy is at any time thousands of miles away, he points out, so cannot properly defend American shores. Moreover, unlike many European nations that have to trade in order to gain the materials needed to build a navy, America is largely self-sufficient, possessing everything required to build and maintain ships and ports.

In an Appendix, Paine notes that although America is but a child in economic terms, its future as a rich nation can be assured, but only if it is able to chart its own course with its own legislative powers. Prophetically, he writes:

"The birthday of a new world is at hand, and a race of men, perhaps as numerous as all Europe contains, are to receive their portion of freedom from the event of a few months."

Final comments

Paine's criticism of the English constitution was overdone, but he needed to paint things in black and white, to create a real enemy so that the benefits of American independence could be clearly demonstrated. Though it is hard to believe now, figures including George Washington, Thomas Jefferson, and Benjamin Franklin had all supported the retention of ties with Britain into the mid-1770s, and it took someone of the force of Tom Paine to show that such hedging of bets was only harming America; the revolution had to proceed, even if it meant taking up arms.

Washington hailed the "unanswerable reason" in Paine's writings, and would use his simple, powerful words to motivate his troops. English author William Cobbett wrote: "Whoever had actually written the Declaration of Independence, Thomas Paine was its real author." But Paine was not able to persuade his friend Thomas Jefferson to include in the Declaration a clause abolishing slavery, so sowing the seeds for the American Civil War.

Thomas Paine

Born in 1737 in Norfolk, England into a Quaker family, Thomas Paine was an only child. He followed in his father's footsteps as a corset maker before becoming a customs officer, and campaigned (until he was sacked) for higher wages for excise men. In 1774 he came to the attention of Benjamin Franklin, who urged him to emigrate to America. In the same year as Paine published Common Sense, *he fought with the Continental Army and saw action in New Jersey as aide-de-camp to General Nathaniel Greene. He also published the first of his 13 "American Crisis" pamphlets, which contained the famous lines: "These are the times that try men's souls. The summer soldier and the sunshine patriot will, in this crisis, shrink from the service of their country; but he that stands it now, deserves the thanks of man and woman." This was read to revolutionary troops before the successful battle of Trenton, New Jersey on Christmas Day 1776.*

In 1777 Paine was appointed Secretary to the Committee on Foreign Affairs, and in 1781 traveled to Paris at his own expense to obtain French financial assistance and moral support for the continuing war of independence. In 1788 he returned to England to visit his parents, and met Mary Wollstonecraft and Edmund Burke. From 1791 he spent a decade in France, where he was elected member for Calais in the National Convention and helped draft the new constitution for the French Republic. He unsuccessfully called for King Louis XVI to be banished from France rather than executed. In 1793 Paine was imprisoned for 11 months in Paris for his moderate views, but was released after pressure from the new American ambassador, James Monroe. Paine's time in France produced The Rights of Man *(1791), a rejoinder to Edmund Burke's denunciation of the French Revolution,* The Age of Reason *(1794/1795), and* Agrarian Justice *(1797).*

In 1802 Paine returned to America and divided his time between New York City and his farm at New Rochelle, which the state of New York gave him in 1784 in thanks for his services to the Revolution. He died in 1809.

Crito

"Then will they not say: 'You, Socrates, are breaking the covenants and agreements which you made with us at your leisure, not in any haste or under any compulsion or deception, but having had seventy years to think of them, during which time you were at liberty to leave the city, if we were not to your mind, or if our covenants appeared to you to be unfair. You had your choice, and might have gone either to Lacedaemon or Crete, which you often praise for their good government, or to some other Hellenic or foreign State. Whereas you, above all other Athenians, seemed to be so fond of the State, or, in other words, of us her laws (for who would like a State that has no laws?), that you never stirred out of her: the halt, the blind, the maimed, were not more stationary in her than you were. And now you run away and forsake your agreements. Not so, Socrates, if you will take our advice; do not make yourself ridiculous by escaping out of the city."

In a nutshell

Citizenship makes us party to a contract with the state; unless we emigrate, we have no right to refute its laws.

In a similar vein

Aristotle *Politics* (p 54)
Thomas Hobbes *Leviathan* (p 132)
Robert Nozick *Anarchy, State, and Utopia* (p 214)

CHAPTER 39

Plato

Plato was a young aristocrat whose family had long played its part in the Athenian state. He would have a couple of unsuccessful attempts at politics himself, but was more interested in poetry and, after falling under the sway of his teacher Socrates, philosophy. The seismic event of his life was the death in 399 BCE of Socrates, who had been charged with subverting Athens' youth. Plato's *Euthyphro*, *Apology*, *Crito*, and *Phaedo* are accounts of the great man's trial, last days in a prison cell, and actual death. They are a rendering of the philosophy of Socrates, who never wrote anything himself, including his famous "Socratic dialogue" style of questions and answers that aimed to arrive at the essence of things.

Crito is the record of a conversation between Socrates, while on death row, and his rich friend Crito. It is one of the first expositions of the idea of the social contract, or the relationship between citizen and state, which has been reprised many times over by the likes of Hobbes (*Leviathan*) and Rousseau (*The Social Contract*). The thrust of Socrates' argument to his friend is that the rule of law, however flawed, is something to be treasured.

You'd be mad not to leave

Just before dawn in Athens state prison, Socrates awakes to find himself in his cell with Crito, a kindly, older man of some means. Socrates wonders why Crito did not wake him, and Crito replies that he wanted to give his friend a few more minutes of peaceful oblivion before he had to face up to his horrible situation once again.

Ironically, it is Crito who is more depressed and anxious than Socrates; he wonders how Socrates can be so calm in the circumstances. Socrates, in reply, says it would hardly be right for a man of his age to be fearful of death, and asks Crito specifically why he has come. Crito informs him a ship will soon be arriving at Sunium, about 30 miles from Athens, part of the sea mission commemorating Theseus' defeat of the Minoan civilization. Since tradition dictates that no prisoner can be executed while that is taking place, Crito suggests that Socrates has perhaps one more day to live. Socrates disagrees, saying he has had a dream in which a beautiful woman told him he would not go "home" for another couple of days.

Crito pleads with Socrates to consider escaping from prison, not just because he does not want to lose his friend, but because people will never believe that Crito could not have facilitated the escape. They will think he did not try because he did not want to pay bribes to the authorities. Socrates replies that he does not care what people think, the truth will come out in the end. The power of public opinion is overestimated, and moreover will never be able to change individuals' character and ethics. Crito in turn wonders if Socrates is unwilling to escape only to protect his friends, who after all could lose their properties if they were found to be involved. He tries to assure Socrates that the money involved to pay people off is not huge, and that after he had escaped he would be welcome in many places, particularly Thessaly. Trying another tack, he says it would be wrong for Socrates to allow his life to be ended now, when he has more years and wisdom to give. He suggests that Socrates is taking the easy way out, and should face up to his responsibilities, which is surely the way of virtue that Socrates has long preached.

Doing the right thing

Socrates says he cannot be swayed by friends, and makes his decisions based on reason alone. He asks Crito: Is it correct that some opinions are worth more than others? Crito replies in the affirmative. When one is in training for something, Socrates says, it matters who is giving praise or criticism. One listens to a revered teacher, and discounts the opinion of others who know less. If we follow the advice of those who know about health and well-being, for instance, we will prosper; if we follow the habits and attitudes of the mob, our health will soon deteriorate. By the same token, Socrates says, a person whose mind and morals have been severely compromised will find that life is hardly worth living. To avoid this, we must live according to a universal moral standard, not the outlook of the masses, although it is these people who have the power of life and death over us. Crito agrees, hoping his friend is now becoming realistic about his situation. Socrates disappoints him by saying that, regardless of this power, it is not life itself but a *good* life that is important—an existence based on the pursuit of honor and justice. If that is so, the question must be whether it is right and just for Socrates to evade the law and escape. For surely the biggest risk is not death, but doing what is wrong, even if we have been wronged ourselves.

If we obey any laws, Socrates says, we should obey them all, even if we think they are wrong. This is not to say that we are equal to the law; indeed, the status of the citizen before the law is similar to that of the son to the father, or the worker to his employer. As long as he considers himself part of the family, or the firm, then it is the father's or boss's law that he must obey. Just as there may be occasion for the son to placate the father, in awareness of his superiority, so it becomes right for the citizen to allow the state to mete out justice as it sees fit, and equally to go to war on behalf of the country if it requires it.

Listen to the Laws

Socrates imagines the Laws of the Athenian state as a single entity who is talking to him. The Laws make the point that Socrates has barely ever left Athens. Must he not have been happy living there? At his trial he had not even proposed being banished from Athens as an alternative to death. Even if Socrates now decided to escape from prison and live in another state, he would instantly become its enemy, since if he could not obey Athens' laws, why would he feel compelled to obey the new state's? Additionally, by fleeing Socrates would only confirm the jury's verdict that he was a corrupter of the state and its youth, since he thought so little of law and order. Therefore, the Laws finally tell him, "Do not take Crito's advice, but follow ours."

By this point, it is clear to Crito that Socrates will indeed follow the advice of his imagined Laws. Socrates' final words are: "Let me follow the course obviously set out for me by God."

Final comments

To Socrates, laws may have been manmade, but they were part of a divine plan to see eternal truths become manifest. The Greek goddess Themis was the personification of divine order, law, and custom, and today is often represented as Lady Justice, blindfolded in her objectivity, and holding a set of scales. Though the jury who sentenced Socrates was far from objective, he still felt that when one disobeys a law, one is spitting in the face of the idea of Justice itself.

Plato

Plato was born circa 428 BCE, but not much is known of his early life. After Socrates' death he traveled widely across Greece, Italy, and Egypt, spending time with philosopher Eucleides and Pythagorean thinkers. In his 40s, he returned to Athens and founded his famous Academy, which became the center of intellectual life in the city. One of his students was Aristotle.

Plato made a couple of attempts to enter politics, first after Athens' defeat in the Peloponnesian War, and a year later when democracy was restored. But the experience disillusioned him, and he concluded that change could only come through a totally new approach to government. The Republic (see commentary in 50 Philosophy Classics) is his outline of an ideal state, but also carries his theory of justice, his explanation of the three parts of the soul, and his famous allegory of the cave. Plato died in 348 BCE.

The Open Society and Its Enemies

"I see now more clearly than ever before that even our greatest troubles spring from something that is as admirable and sound as it is dangerous—from our impatience to better the lot of our fellows."

"The enemies of freedom have always charged its defenders with subversion. And nearly always they have succeeded in persuading the guileless and well-meaning."

In a nutshell

Look to modest solutions for social problems, which still allow for liberty and do not push all responsibility onto the state.

In a similar vein

CHAPTER 40

Karl Popper

Karl Popper defines civilization as the transition from small, closed, tribal society to the larger, open society that enables real human freedom. History has consistently thrown up reactionary movements and states that oppose the concept of the open society and wish to return humanity to a society of control. Indeed, Hitler's invasion of Austria in 1938 was Popper's spur to sit down and begin writing *The Open Society and Its Enemies*. Like his friend Hayek, he was concerned that social science and philosophy were not able to see that "national socialist" societies required unseemly methods in order to hold together.

The first volume of the book is devoted to dethroning Plato and revealing him as the greatest exponent of the closed society. The second mainly looks at Marx, showing how his belief in the "inevitability" of a new society based on a small set of ideas created the foundation for horribly illiberal regimes. Popper has no doubt that both Plato and Marx were well-intentioned, even fine people; but that is exactly his point. Such regimes spring from "our impatience to better the lot of our fellows." In contrast, an open society does not seek to create a Utopia, a City of God, a great Republic, or a Worker's Paradise. Its more modest desire is to find piecemeal solutions to specific problems, and otherwise to preserve individual freedom and responsibility. It is better to be reasonable, Popper says, than to be clever.

Plato's "spell"

Plato lived in a time of wars and upheavals. In response, Popper says, he developed the belief that "all social change is corruption or decay or degeneration." The only meaningful forces are those that operate hidden from view on the absolute level; these Plato called "Ideas." Truth, Beauty, Justice, and so on are perfect and unchanging. An "arrested state" built around such Ideas would be less likely to be corrupted.

Plato saw that the state could be easily corrupted by class war and material and economic self-interest. First one has Timocracy (rule by aristocrats seeking fame and honor); then Oligarchy (rule by rich families); then Democracy (rule according the majority, but in effect lawlessness); and finally Tyranny ("the fourth and final sickness of the city").

The only way society can work in a semi-perfect way is via control and putting the "right" people in place, while preserving individual and class distinctions in a way that benefits the whole. Plato's solution for avoiding class war is "giving the ruling class a superiority which cannot be challenged." His Republic would only educate this class, and only have this class in charge of arms. The rest of the populace would be like sheep or cattle, treated "not too cruelly, but with the proper contempt," as Popper puts it. But this ruling class must stay unified, and Plato would make this happen by having all its property and its women and children held in common, since family splits and economic self-interest cause disloyalty. There would be no real intermingling of classes, and indeed a system of human breeding would ensure that the higher class continues to produce the best-quality offspring.

Given Plato's hatred of Athenian politics, Popper argues that his ideal state was a return to the closed, tribal societies that came before the city-state, in which the wise ruled over the ignorant many. Because this was based on the natural inequality between men, it was therefore stable. It was urban society that introduced the idea of social mobility and selfish economic interests, which created inherent instability and made change and turmoil the order of the day.

Who matters more, the state or the individual?

Though Plato's republic never came into being, Popper argues that it provides the template for every kind of state based on a collectivist mindset and social engineering "for the greater good." Time and again, we have seen how Platonic good intentions destroy freedom and strip people of their potential and creativity, since their personal aspirations no longer matter next to the good of society.

Plato famously drew an analogy between the state and the individual. Today we tend to think of the quality of the state as related to the combined contributions of its citizens, but Plato took the opposite view: The quality of the individual is only brought out in respect to the strength and justice of the state. Its laws exist "to create men of the right frame of mind; not for the purpose of letting them loose, so that everybody can go his own way, but in order to utilize them all for welding the city together." The most brutal collectivist and totalitarian regimes can trace their lineage back to such sentiments, with the One always being greater than the Many. Popper also quotes from Plato's *Laws*: "Every artist… executes the part for the sake of the whole, and not the whole for the sake of the part." Indeed, despite the noble intentions of the happiness of its citizens, Plato's state can in no way be considered superior in design to the modern totalitarian state, which after all also had stated goals of justice, happiness, and prosperity.

In Popper's time the conventional view of Plato was still that he was a great humanitarian nobly offering a City of God to the world, and the reactionary elements of the republic and its laws were glossed over. This perception of Plato as a liberal was reinforced by the mistranslation of the title *The Republic*, which should really be "The City-State" or "The State." A republic suggests a state run by the people, when Plato's actual design was for a super elite in control and a lobotomized worker class.

No more utopias

The problem with Plato's "utopian engineering," as Popper describes it, is that it is convincing and attractive, and seems so rational. Yet how many wise people are there who can conceive of and implement a successful high-minded society from scratch? It is so much less exciting to aim to create a single new institution to heal some societal ill, or fix an existing one, yet such efforts are in fact more likely to work because more people are involved who want them to succeed. Compromise is often pictured as an evil, but its results can have more stability than things created by diktat or decree. Meanwhile, all utopian visions involve sacrifices from those who must give up what they possess now in the name of the new, greater good. Any dissenters need to be quieted, or it will lower the morale of everyone else. As Lenin menacingly said, "You can't make an omelette without breaking eggs."

Popper sees Plato as having the mind of an artist who has seen a perfect vision and is now attempting to produce a faithful likeness in the real world. Politics itself is the highest art, and what artist worth the title is open to compromise? Even when the canvas is cleaned, it is done with vigor. Yet "the view that society should be beautiful like a work of art leads only too easily to violent measures," he says.

For Popper, people are not means to an end, but have the right to carve out their own lives according to their own plans, as long they do not hurt others. Trying to make a heaven on earth invariably leads to a hell, so it is much better to follow an incremental approach that rationally fixes individual social problems based on the evidence of what works.

Hegel, Marx, and the poverty of historicism

Social philosophies that see a direction in history, in which surface events are "controlled by specific historical or evolutionary laws whose discovery would enable us to prophesy the destiny of man," Popper calls "historicism." An old example, he says, is the idea of the "chosen people," who are an instrument of God's will on earth. Others include Marxism, which sees a certain class as inheriting the earth, and racism, which is seen as a "natural law" by which one race will naturally prevail over the rest. In all historicist ideas, the individual is nothing before the wider forces and movement of history.

Popper attacks Hegel as a deeply flawed philosopher who worshipped the state (indeed, he was the first official philosopher of the Prussian state) in the same way as Plato did. The individual is nothing next to the moral authority of the state, to whom he owes everything. "Nearly all the more important ideas of modern totalitarianism are directly inherited from Hegel," Popper argues. All moral authority is invested in the state, and so propaganda and lying are permissible. War is ethical if it brings glory to the nation. Hegel counterpoised the idea of the heroic man with the debased bourgeois person living only for material ends. Such ideas helped foment the warrior attitude in Germany as a rising power prior to the First World War. Popper notes that to philosopher Arthur Schopenhauer, an arch anti-nationalist, Hegel's ideas had a devastating effect on Germany.

Marx came to reject everything about Hegel's philosophy save the idea of historical inevitability. He did not believe that social engineering or tinkering with the existing system is possible, because those in the social system cannot be objective about it—they cannot really see what is going on and are mere expressions of larger forces. It is only when the proletariat becomes "class conscious" and understands that it is being exploited that change will come. One of Marx's ideas is that, against these larger impersonal historical forces, day-to-day politics and policy-making do not really matter.

Historicists may claim that only an idea or a certain leader will allow a nation to fulfill its potential, but this view is the opposite of trust in reason and science as the means of betterment. Indeed, historicism gets in the way of a scientific approach to solving social problems, for when we pose as prophets, we give up our responsibility for the present. Popper suggests that the key to understanding why people support grand historicist ideas is that it absolves them of personal responsibility. After all, if the composition of society is due to impersonal forces, the development of the individual is unnecessary.

Marx thought of himself as a rationalist, but in Popper's eyes a rationalist is someone who supports "not only intellectual activity but also observation and experiment"; that is, someone who puts empirical facts first. This is an approach of reasonableness, admitting that I may be wrong and you may be right, but the facts will lead us the right way. This is not what either Plato or Marx was about. Both had agendas that led them into false assumptions that floored their whole theories. Reasonableness is more important than cleverness, and is actually social, involving give and take. We do not put our thinking above that of others.

Final comments

For Plato, "justice" simply meant "that which is in the best interests of the state"—whether it was strong, united, stable. The freedom of the individual was nothing next to this. Plato's enemy was equality and egalitarianism, values that had run through the veins of the Athenian state since Pericles. At their heart was a new emphasis on the individual that had allowed the transition from tribal states to Athenian democracy. Shockingly, Plato's real enemy was the individual, Popper says, which would throw a spanner in the works of his caste state.

Today, there is an echo of the closed society in people who expect the state to do everything, or blame every problem on the government. They have not grasped the central feature of the open society: that along with freedom from tribal taboo and fixed social relations, there is an expectation of personal responsibility. That we are left up to our own devices is a strain, Popper admits, but it is the price that we pay for living in freedom.

Karl Popper

Karl Popper was born in Vienna in 1902. His father was a lawyer who took a keen interest in the classics, philosophy, and social and political issues. His mother inculcated in Popper a passion for music, and he almost followed it as a career. At the University of Vienna he became heavily involved in left-wing politics and Marxism, but after a student riot abandoned it entirely. At this time he also discovered the psychoanalytic theories of Freud and Adler, and heard Einstein lecture on relativity theory; the latter's critical spirit, and its total absence in Marx, Freud, and Adler's work, impressed Popper. He got a primary school teaching diploma in 1925, took a PhD in philosophy in 1928, and qualified to teach mathematics and physics in secondary school the following year.

Popper is best known as a philosopher of science, and his book The Logic of Scientific Discovery *(1934; see commentary in* 50 Philosophy Classics*) brought him renown. It was followed by* The Poverty of Historicism *(1936). After the growth of Nazism compelled Popper to leave Austria, in 1937 he took up a position at the University of Canterbury in New Zealand, where he remained for the duration of the Second World War. In 1946 he moved to England, where he became professor of logic and scientific method at the London School of Economics. He was knighted in 1965 and retired in 1969, although he remained active as a writer, broadcaster, and lecturer until his death in 1994.*

Discourse on the Origins and Basis of Inequality Among Men

"Inequality, being almost non-existent in the state of nature, derives its force and its growth from the development of our faculties and the progress of the human mind."

"The first man who, having enclosed a piece of land, thought of saying 'This is mine' and found people simple enough to believe him, was the true founder of civil society. How… much misery and horror the human race would have been spared if someone had… cried out to his fellow men: '…You are lost if you forget that the fruits of the earth belong to everyone and that the earth itself belongs to no one!'"

In a nutshell

Society corrupts man's natural inclination to live in peace, and government only tends to increase and entrench differences in power and wealth.

In a similar vein

CHAPTER 41

Jean-Jacques Rousseau

I n the 1740s, Jean-Jacques Rousseau was a man very much on the rise. The Geneva-born intellectual had moved to Paris and become friends with Voltaire and Diderot, and these *philosophes* breathed new life into Parisian salon society. Until this time admittance to fashionable circles was only by social pedigree, but suddenly wit and original insight mattered. Rousseau was already known for his contributions to Diderot's famous *Encyclopedia*, a manual of Enlightenment thinking, and then in 1750 he caused a sensation with a prize-winning essay ("Discourse on the Arts and Sciences"), which argued that man in his natural state was good, and it was civilization that had corrupted him; the exact opposite of the thinking of the day. The following year, Rousseau entered another essay competition. The Academy of Dijon's question "What is the origin of inequality among men, and is it authorized by Natural Law?" allowed him to continue the theme of his earlier essay, but with a different angle. This time he did not win, but again his work was influential.

Contemporary debates about inequality and social justice have their roots in Rousseau's concept that it is not natural inequality between humans that is to be despised—physical and intellectual differences between people are a fact, whether we like it or not—or even meritocracy, but the fact that society tends to entrench and magnify initial variations in ability and success, creating an inherited elite. Rousseau never said that we should try to turn back the clock and revert to hunter-gathering. Rather, each generation should have a reset button so that people are distinguished because of what they have done rather than their parents' achievements.

Some of Rousseau's anthropological assertions about early humans seem airy opinions now; most of his knowledge came from what he had read in travelers' accounts of native peoples in Africa and South America. He did not know (as anthropologists do now) that inequality also crept in to hunter-gather societies; in native America there were wealthy traders of seashells, and Alaskan fishing societies were divided into masters and slaves. Yet he was broadly correct in noting that pre-modern societies considered inequality to be the key social problem; they were only too aware of the effects of pride, greed, and envy on social cohesion. Rousseau remains relevant today because he is a reminder of two things: that inequality has costs; and that it is perfectly justified for society to do something about it.

The real nature of man

Giving a nod to the "Natural Law" part of the essay question, Rousseau begins by arguing that there are certain natural laws that existed before man became a reasoning being. One is the instinct for self-preservation, the other is dislike of seeing another person or animal in pain. That a human being will not hurt another unless his own life is at stake Rousseau takes to be a natural principle that precedes the development of knowledge and reason. He says this in direct opposition to the view of Hobbes (see commentary on p 132), who saw human beings as naturally rapacious and competitive. "All these philosophers talking ceaselessly of need, greed, oppression, desire and pride," Rousseau writes, "have transported into the state of nature concepts formed in society. They speak of savage man and they depict civilized man."

Rousseau provides an alternative view of early man as self-sufficient and living peacefully, turning to aggression only occasionally out of defense. What Hobbes missed in his estimation, Rousseau says, is the extent of man's compassion, generosity, mercy, pity, friendship, and benevolence. This should not surprise us, for even animals possess a degree of compassion, such as the way a horse will try not to step on another beast, or an animal is affected by a dead member of its own species. In summary, man in his primal state was instinctively compassionate, not instinctively mean as Hobbes thought.

Corrupted by society

Rousseau contrasts the healthy lives of early man with the myriad health problems of civilized man. In modern societies the poor toil non-stop and often eat badly or not at all, while the rich live idly and eat food that is too rich, leading to all sorts of maladies. He rejects the interventions of medicine, noting how good Nature is at healing if a body is left undisturbed. Modern man is consumed by worries and thinks too much, in contrast to early humans who, like all animals, simply reacted to their environment. The simple man of nature does not calculate, he just acts, and accordingly has more real nobility:

"It is reason which breeds pride and reflection which fortifies it; reason which turns man inward into himself; reason which separates him from everything which troubles or affects him. It is philosophy

which isolates a man, and prompts him to say in secret at the sight of another suffering: 'Perish if you will; I am safe.'"

Most of our ills are self-created, and would not exist if we had stuck to "the simple, unchanging and solitary way of life that nature ordained for us." It could just be that in his simplicity early man was superior to us. Rousseau asks, with some justification, whether "anyone has ever heard of a savage in a condition of freedom even dreaming of complaining about his life and killing himself?"

How inequality emerges

Society is not built on any natural inequality between people, Rousseau ventures, but rather has evolved into a system by which those who happen to have gained power lord it over the rest. He divides inequality into two kinds. The first relates to physical or mental qualities—it is a simple fact of life that some people are born stronger or smarter than others. The second kind of inequality concerns how some people become esteemed by others—they are richer, more honored, or more powerful than others, commanding obeisance.

Man in a state of nature lives in a small group in which all individuals do the same thing and have the same knowledge; it is impossible for there not to be equality. In contrast, the wide variety of upbringings, situations, and styles of life in civilization leads to "instituted inequality." Some people live in luxury, never having to work, while others toil every day without respite, depending on the circumstances into which they were born.

While Hobbes pictured man in his basic state as violent and seeking to dominate, in fact the life of early man centered around sharing, claims Rousseau. If someone was under attack from another person or tribe, he would just go somewhere else. There was no scope for domination. It is in society that servitude and domination become entrenched in institutions. As man's "reason" has grown, he has also become more wicked. Compared to the independence of early man, modern humans are a mere reflection of society. They are educated, but in all the culture's errors as well as its knowledge.

Rousseau contrasts the natural and healthy *amour de soi-même* or self-esteem that man had in his communal pre-civilization state with the *amour-propre* that succeeded it: love of self fueled by pride in relation to others. This

"universal desire for reputation, honours and promotion... devours us all... excites and multiplies passions, and in turning all men into competitors, rivals or rather enemies... causes every day failures and successes and catastrophes of every sort by making so many contenders run the same course."

The evil of property

To Rousseau, property is the original sin of inequality. The best time in human history, he says, was the epoch between primitive man and civilization, a time when man became organized but was not subject to a division of things. As long as humans lived in small groups, sharing everything and providing only for themselves, they were happy. As soon as one person thought it was okay to own more than his fair share, the pride of property began, men became workers in someone else's field, or someone's mind, and oppression began. The quest for more property also led to jealousy, greed, and generations of war.

Though Marx only references Rousseau a few times in his writings, Rousseau's vehement attitude to property presaged Marxism. Voltaire was not willing to let this extreme view go unchallenged, and wrote in the margins of his copy of the *Essay*: "What! He who has planted, sown, and enclosed some land has no right to the fruit of his efforts! Is this unjust man, this thief to be the benefactor of the human race? Behold the philosophy of a beggar who would like the rich to be robbed by the poor!"

Seeds for revolution

Rousseau notes that people originally came under the umbrella of a ruler in order to be protected from violence and to protect what property they had, but in reality the state became the means for the rich to get richer and to lord it over everyone else. The new laws "transformed adroit usurpation into irrevocable right, and for the benefit of a few ambitious men subjected the human race thenceforth to labour, servitude and misery."

Early forms of power and government often had some legitimacy. A man was made king by common assent, or likewise an aristocracy was recognized or a democracy evolved. However, very quickly what power did was to entrench extremes of poverty and wealth, mastery and servitude. When a ruler gave a certain family privileges of nobility or rank, it glued that family to the prevailing system of power and its maintenance. Its original service to society was forgotten over time; it existed to perpetuate its own power and wealth. Indeed, "the more idlers who could be counted in a family, the more illustrious it became." Rousseau is referring to the aristocratic families of France, a country whose social stratification and inequality were more rigid than England. He ends the essay with words that would be taken as an incitement to the French Revolution:

"for it is manifestly contrary to the law of nature, however defined, that a child should govern an old man, that an imbecile should lead a wise man, and that a handful of people should gorge themselves with superfluities while the hungry multitude goes in want of necessities."

Final comments

Although Rousseau never used the phrase, "equality of opportunity" was the kind of principle he felt that any good society should have. Otherwise, the longer a society existed, the prizes and benefits would increasingly fall to those who had simply inherited them, rather than those who had earned them. But naturally, given the self-interested nature of human beings, such rights to equality must be spelled out beforehand and held as universal. John Rawls' famous "veil of ignorance" concept requires that no one in society knows in advance whether they will be king or pauper, merchant or servant. In this state of unknowing, how should laws be made so that all benefit while preserving individual freedom? This understanding of society's purpose as "fairness" was exactly what Rousseau was aiming at, and his spirit continues to inhabit social revolutionary movements today. A society should not exist simply to keep order or protect property, but must have some moral purpose.

Jean-Jacques Rousseau

Jean-Jacques Rousseau was born in Geneva in 1712. His mother died only a few days after his birth. His father Isaac, a watchmaker, instilled in him a love of reading, particularly classical literature, and educated him at home. At 16 Jean-Jacques became an apprentice engraver. Over the border in Catholic Savoy, he befriended a Catholic noblewoman, Françoise-Louise de Warens. He enjoyed her great library, received music lessons, and became a music teacher. When he was 20 he became her lover. In his mid-20s Rousseau remained focused on music, creating a new system of musical notation, and at 31 worked for the French Ambassador to the Venetian Republic, but it was not a proper diplomatic role and he felt like a servant. Back in Paris he began a relationship with his laundrymaid, the barely literate Marie-Thérèse Levasseur. They would have five children, but all were given up to orphanages.

Rousseau was a successful composer of ballets and operas, and in 1752 had a work performed for Louis XV, who offered to be his patron. He was keenly interested in education, and his famous Émile (1762) tried to show how children could be brought up so that they would not seek to dominate, but to have an equal feeling with others. Because he criticized existing education practices and dogma, Rousseau was severely attacked by the Church. He was forced to flee Paris and the attacks made him paranoid. After an invitation from his friend David Hume, he sought refuge in Britain, but later had a famous falling out with Hume. In England he began writing The Confessions, one of the first autobiographies. After returning to France in 1767, he completed this work along with The Reveries of the Solitary Walker. Rousseau died insane in 1778; his remains were placed alongside Voltaire's in Paris's Panthéon.

The Jungle

"A very few days of practical experience in this land of high wages had been sufficient to make clear to them the cruel fact that it was also a land of high prices, and that in it the poor man was almost as poor as in any other corner of the earth."

"Things that were quite unspeakable went on there in the packing houses all the time, and were taken for granted by everybody; only they did not show, as in the old slavery times, because there was no difference in color between master and slave."

"You would begin talking to some poor devil who had worked in one shop for the last thirty years, and had never been able to save a penny; ... had never traveled, never had an adventure, never learned anything, never hoped anything; and when you start to tell him about Socialism he would sniff and say, 'I'm not interested in that—I'm an individualist!'"

In a nutshell

When people become mere replaceable machines of production, the whole of a society is dehumanized.

In a similar vein

Rachel Carson *Silent Spring* (p 84)
Emma Goldman *Anarchism and Other Essays* (p 114)
Karl Marx & Friedrich Engels *The Communist Manifesto* (p 186)

CHAPTER 42

Upton Sinclair

n 1904, young muckraking journalist Upton Sinclair spent several weeks undercover in a Chicago meatpacking plant. The socialist newspaper for which he was working, *Appeal to Reason*, published his fictionalized account in parts the following year. In 1906 Doubleday agreed to publish *The Jungle* as a book, and it caused a sensation.

Sinclair's goal had been to expose the terrible lot of America's turn-of-the-century working classes, and to make a case for socialism; the novel's protagonist, Jurgis Rudkus, is only saved from destruction when he discovers the socialist cause. The actual effect of the book, though, was to change meat industry practices. The public were horrified that they may have been sold tubercular beef and contaminated sausages, and President Theodore Roosevelt, who had previously believed that Sinclair was a socialist crackpot, was galvanized into action. In 1906 he helped bring in two pioneering pieces of legislation: the Meat Industry Act and the Pure Food and Drug Act, the latter establishing the body that would become the Food and Drug Administration.

Although Sinclair later reflected "I aimed at the public's heart, and by accident hit it in the stomach," history has shown that *The Jungle* served its intended purpose. In attempting to show the real social cost of everyday consumer goods on the people who labor to make them, his book is a clear antecedent to modern titles such as Naomi Klein's *No Logo* (see commentary on p 156), which politicized a generation by exposing the conditions in which poor-country workers labor to produce designer goods sold in the rich world.

Sinclair was a master storyteller who had earned a living from fiction since his college days. Although harrowing, *The Jungle* provides a perfect window into the brute days of American capitalism, giving a sense of the awesomeness of the new mass production methods and their dehumanizing nature, as well as the unlikelihood of the small man ever making headway against the great industrial trusts and firms. Although Sinclair is considered one of the great propaganda novelists, this is a work of literature that will stay with you.

Great expectations

The book begins with a wedding feast for petite 16-year-old Ona and burly Jurgis Rudkus, newly arrived immigrants from Lithuania. Listening to the fiddle player, the guests' minds drift back to the rivers, forests, and farms of the old country, helping them forget the slums and saloons of Chicago. They will not earn in a year the $300 that the wedding costs, but a traditional wedding is the last thing these people will give up; it makes them feel like a king or a queen for day, and they can live on that memory.

Ona and Jurgis come to Chicago in a party of 12, and along the way are cheated out of most of their money by agents and officials. On arrival, not speaking any English, a policeman sends them on a tram past mile after mile of dreary, cheaply made row houses on what had once been prairies. As they get closer to their destination, they notice a strange odor. They are in the Stockyards district of Chicago, also known as the "Back of the Yards," and join other Lithuanians, Poles, and Slovaks in tenement flats of up to a dozen people to a room.

A contact from Lithuania gives the group a tour of Packingtown, where 20,000 cattle and hogs, and 5,000 sheep, are brought on trains every day to be slaughtered and processed. The only piece of green in the whole of Packingtown is a patch of grass in front of the offices of the packing firm, which makes mountains of bacon, sausages, canned beef, deviled chicken, lard, and fertilizer. They witness hogs being strung up on their hind legs before having their throats cut, then processed by a stream of men, each with their own specific task. The Packingtown plants of Brown's and Durham's employ 30,000 men and women. Before the time of the mass-produced automobile, it is the greatest concentration of labor and capital ever found in one place. The plants are supported by a local population of 250,000, their meat is eaten by 30 million Americans, and their products are sent around the world. The guileless Jurgis feels elated that he will be part of this great operation.

The group pour all their savings into buying a "new" house, which later turns out to be 15 years old and made of the cheapest materials. The houses are part of a scam by which, if the occupiers miss even one monthly payment, the property is immediately repossessed and sold on to some other unlucky family. The house that Jurgis, Ona, and the others bought had been turned over no fewer than four times over the last few years.

Grandmother Majauskiene, a neighbor, tells them that Packingtown has seen waves of European immigrants—Germans, Irish, Poles, Slovaks, and now Lithuanians—all used as factory fodder. The packing companies extract every bit of labor value from them, before replacing them with cheaper immigrants. Nevertheless, the group are hopeful about their future.

Work until death

Jadvyga and Mikolas also want to get married, but Mikolas is in the dangerous trade of beef-boning, in which the workers receive regular gashes, and not all of them heal. In the subzero Chicago winters, the men carving up the carcasses are not allowed to wear gloves, so their hands freeze, causing accidents. In the last three years Mikolas has had to stay at home for months with blood poisoning, and as he is paid piece-rate this destroys his income. When he returns to work he has to wait around packing houses at six in the morning just in case he is offered a job.

Jurgis and Ona's group includes several children, but even they are not spared Packingtown. Federal laws say that children cannot work until they are 16, but the packing companies do not check. After all, a child who receives one third the full adult wage saves the company a lot of money. Stanislav, 14 years old, gets work in part of the factory producing canned lard, and works for 10 hours a day putting cans under a machine that squirts out the fat. The factory has no windows, so for half the year he barely sees the sun.

Diseases abound among the workers: rheumatism among the ice-store men, acid burns among the wool pluckers. The fertilizer men stink to high heaven and can never rid themselves of the smell. The men working on the "killing beds" freeze in winter and some die of sunstroke in summer. Those toiling in the boiling meat tanks occasionally fall into them. If a worker manages to stay uninjured and alive, he is subject to "speeding up," an inhuman quickening of pace in order to meet profit targets. Wages and piece rates are continually going down, not up; unbelievably, as the speeding up makes labor more productive, in the eyes of the packing houses this means they can pay workers less. If any worker has had enough, there are plenty more to take his or her place.

Sinclair paints a scene in which workers have such a fear of losing their jobs that they do not allow themselves to look up even for an instant when a factory tour group of well-dressed men and women stare at them "as at some wild beast in a menagerie." The packing houses are like a great machine that takes in people and spits them out when they are injured or diseased or simply all used up. A man seldom lasts more than 10 years, and if he does may limp along only with the crutch of alcohol, provided by overpriced saloons.

Not fit for consumption

Sinclair reports on the sickening contempt for health and safety in the packing plants. One plant takes only old or diseased cattle, including those that have been fed on "whisky-malt," brewery refuse, which produces large boils on the animals' skin. This kind of meat is used in the "embalmed beef" given to American soldiers, and is later shown to have killed more soldiers than had died in action.

Jurgis learns that Durham's makes something called "potted chicken," which is actually a mixture of tripe, pork fat, and beef hearts. "Deviled ham" has not an ounce of ham but plenty of chemicals. Gone-off hams are pumped with a chemical that eliminates the tell-tale odor, and sausages that have gone moldy and white are dressed with borax and glycerine and thrown back into the churning sausage mix to be recased. Hundreds of rats run about the meat storage houses, and sometimes dead ones end up in the sausage mixture. No one bats an eye. There are 360 meat inspectors at Packingtown, but all they are required to do is make sure that diseased meat is kept in Illinois. This means that the carcasses of steers with tuberculosis are quietly taken away to Chicago to be sold.

Slowly sinking

Jurgis' father Antanas is too old to be offered work, so in desperation he bribes someone to give him a job, for which in return he will have to give up one third of his wages. Such graft is normal. His job is to scrape bits of meat off the floor so they can be added to the canned meat. In a freezing, damp cellar, he develops a cough that will not go away and sores all over his body, and he soon dies.

As *The Jungle* progresses, the group are just about able to pay their mortgage, but then one of the canneries closes. In the downturn Jurgis' wages are cut in half, and when a steer runs amuck in the yards, he breaks his ankle. Unable to work, the family are thrown into panic. How will they pay for the rent, the coal, the insurance, the food?

Sinclair piles tragedy on tragedy. Jurgis discovers that Ona has only been able to keep her job because of sexual favors to her boss, Mr. Connor; after beating Connor up, Jurgis is put in prison. On release he finds that the group have been evicted from their house, and Ona is about to give birth to their second child. He is unable to afford a doctor, and she dies.

Trying to support the extended family, Jurgis goes back to work, and one evening returns to find his son has drowned in a puddle in the unpaved street. Jurgis becomes a hobo chasing farm work, but in the winter finds himself back in the city with a job at the meat plant. As a single man without dependants his condition improves and he even becomes a manager, but again all is lost in the great strikes that almost cripple the packing industry.

Only toward the end of the book, when Jurgis is befriended by middle-class socialists campaigning against working conditions, is there a glimmer of hope. He becomes a true believer, and his struggles now have meaning instead of random misery.

Final comments

The Jungle can be seen as an unreasonable attack on the American Dream, given that most immigrants survived and eventually prospered, and working conditions did improve thanks to corporate paternalism or union agitation. Yet many did not make it, and they must be remembered too.

Sinclair might be shocked to learn that today sweatshops abound in several countries where there is little concern for health and safety, the wages are a pittance, and the managers act like overlords. We can console ourselves that such conditions are a natural "passing stage" through which any industrializing country goes, but it is still in our power not to buy products that give no idea of origin, and seem suspiciously cheap. It is not merely technology or capital that has produced the things we use and consume every day; a *person*, somewhere, has produced them, and *The Jungle* is a timeless reminder of this.

In *The Human Condition*, Hannah Arendt made a distinction between labor (the activity we need to do to stay alive) and work (the meaningful production of something that may outlast us). Rarely has the distinction been better expressed, or Marx's emphasis on the dehumanizing nature of much labor under capitalism rung truer, than in Sinclair's book.

Upton Sinclair

Upton Sinclair, Jr. was born in Baltimore, Maryland in 1878. His father was a liquor salesman who came from a respected Southern family, and his mother a strict Episcopalian. In Sinclair's teens the family moved to Queens, New York, and he later studied law at Columbia University. He supported himself by writing dime stories and pulp fiction, and after graduating published four novels. They did not sell well, but publication of The Jungle *gave him fame and the money to start Helicon Home Colony, a socialist utopia in Englewood, New Jersey.*

Sinclair stayed in the public eye with books and pamphlets exposing corruption in American life, including The Brass Check *(1919), which led to a code of ethics in journalism. In the 1920s he moved to California, and twice ran unsuccessfully for Congress as a socialist. He continued to campaign for civil liberties and the free speech of workers in Los Angeles, and his popularity saw him win the Democratic candidature in the 1934 Californian election for governor. He did not win, but on a platform of "End Poverty in California" in a state still clawing itself out of the Great Depression, he received over 800,000 votes.*

In his long life Sinclair wrote over 100 works of fiction and non-fiction, including The Fasting Cure *(1911),* Goslings: A Study of the American Schools *(1924),* Oil! *(1927), and* I, Candidate for Governor: And How I Got Licked *(1935). Between 1940 and 1953 he produced 11 bestselling novels in the Lanny Budd series, one of which won him the 1943 Pulitzer Prize for Fiction. Sinclair married three times, and died in New Jersey in 1968.*

1974

The Gulag Archipelago, 1918–56

"Ideology – that is what gives evildoing its long-sought justification and gives the evildoer the necessary steadfastness and determination… Thanks to ideology, the twentieth century was fated to experience evildoing on a scale calculated in the millions."

"They took those who were too independent, too influential, along with those who were well-to-do, too intelligent, too noteworthy… Thus the population was shaken up, forced into silence, and left without any possible leaders of resistance. Thus it was that wisdom was instilled, that former ties and former friendships were cut off."

"Once it was established that charges had to be brought at any cost and despite everything, threats, violence, tortures became inevitable."

In a nutshell

Cruelty and injustice are inevitable when ideology
is combined with total state power.

In a similar vein

Hannah Arendt *The Origins of Totalitarianism* (p 48)
George Orwell *Animal Farm* (p 232)
Karl Popper *The Open Society and Its Enemies* (p 248)

CHAPTER 43

Aleksandr
Solzhenitsyn

n the blaze of publicity that came with the Nuremberg Trials after the Second
World War, the full horror of Nazi atrocities was revealed. Stalinist Russia,
in contrast, seemed like a much more forgiving regime, and many on the
left in the West still thought that communism was the future. Yet behind the
showreels of happy peasants on collective farms and joyous factory workers
was the reality of mass displacement, starvation, and injustice on a scale that
not even Hitler could have engineered.

The Gulag Archipelago is Solzhenitsyn's monument to the millions tortured and murdered in Soviet Russia between the Bolshevik Revolution and
the 1950s. He began writing it in 1958, three years after finishing an eight-
year sentence in the Gulag, an acronym for *Glavnoye Upravleniye ispravitel-
no-trudovyh Lagerey,* or "Chief Administration of Corrective Labor Camps."
The manuscript was smuggled out of the Soviet Union on mimeograph, then
published in France in 1973 and the US and UK in 1974. Solzhenitsyn had
been expelled from the Soviet Union and was living in the United States; to
Americans he was living proof of the brutality of the Soviet regime.

Isaiah Berlin commented: "Until *Gulag*, Communists and their allies had
persuaded their followers that denunciations of the Soviet regime were largely
bourgeois propaganda." A book that changed minds and changed the world,
its existence made it impossible for the USSR to claim moral superiority over
capitalism and democracy. As Doris Lessing said: "Its importance can hardly
be exaggerated. It helped bring down an empire."

The Gulag Archipelago is based on Solzhenitsyn's recollections and notes
along with reports, letters, and reminiscences from 227 anonymous witnesses.
He did not think his account would be published in his lifetime, even less that
his book would become a bestseller, he would appear on the cover of *Time*
magazine, and he would win the Nobel Prize for Literature. Yet he was never
complacent, for unless each generation learned about the horrors of regimes
like Stalin's, he believed, history was doomed to repeat itself.

Land of the zeks

The title comes from Solzhenitsyn's perception of the hundreds of Soviet labor camps as islands, ruthlessly cut off from the rest of Russia. Although often thousands of miles apart, they were joined in a psychological sense and so formed a Gulag nation of the oppressed, its citizens (inmates) known as "zeks."

In the first months after the October Revolution, Lenin demanded strong institutions including the Red Army, police, and courts to ensure discipline and order, and called for forced labor for those who disobeyed. As early as 1918 Lenin was laying the groundwork for the Gulag, noting in a telegram to "lock up all the doubtful ones" and "secure the Soviet Republic from its class enemies by isolating them in concentration camps." By the end of 1920 there were 84 camps across 43 provinces, and the Gulag only expanded. In 1923 Solovki camp had around 1,000 inmates; by 1930 there were 50,000.

Whereas the camps had once been a means to cleanse society of "doubtful" people, now it became a system of slave labor for building large infrastructure projects including railroads and canals, and for logging, mining, and opening up remote territory. The White Sea–Baltic Canal was constructed without any advanced machinery at all, just zeks wielding picks and axes. It was completed "on time" in 1933, but Solzhenitsyn's estimate of the death toll is 250,000.

"Work norms" required men to work for ridiculous hours, often in freezing conditions. The philosophy was "correction through labor," but in some of the more severe camps it was understood to mean "destruction through labor." The aim was to get as much out of a prisoner before sheer exhaustion, hunger, or illness took their toll. With much of the official food allocations taken by guards or camp criminals, prisoners would eat dead, rotting horses, lubricating grease, and tree moss simply to have something in their stomachs.

A climate of fear

Solzhenitsyn was arrested while serving as a captain in the Soviet army in Prussia in 1945. He had written a letter to a friend that included veiled criticism of Stalin, and for this he was given eight years in the Gulag for "anti-Soviet propaganda." There was no trial and no chance of appeal.

The waves of arrests and brutal punishment were claimed to be happening according to the rule of law, yet the legal system had become a wafer-thin membrane covering the crimes of the state. The Criminal Code of 1926 allowed for any kind of thought or action to be interpreted as an effort to overthrow the Soviet state, and unlike most other statutes there was no maximum penalty. Many students were arrested on charges of "Praise of American Technology," "Praise of American Democracy," or "Toadyism Toward the West." Most people sent to the camps were ordinary Russians who faced draconian punishment for the mildest of "crimes": 10 years for taking a handful of potatoes or a spool of thread. As the means of production was now in popular hands, such incidents automatically made one an enemy of the people.

Solzhenitsyn refers to a party conference in Moscow province that ended in a toast to Comrade Stalin. Everyone leaped to their feet to applaud and stayed clapping vigorously for the next 10 minutes, no one willing to be the first to sit down. Eventually the director of a paper factory sat down, and everyone else followed suit. It was precisely in such small actions, Solzhenitsyn notes, that the authorities "discovered who the independent people were." The factory director was arrested the same night and given a 10-year sentence on some invented pretext. After he had signed the final document of the interrogation admitting his "guilt," the interrogator said to him: "Don't ever be the first to stop applauding!"

Solzhenitsyn asks: Would Chekhov have believed that Russia could descend into such barbarism in modern times? The characters in his plays, if they had had to go through the Gulag, would have ended up in insane asylums.

Evils of interrogation

After an arrest, the aim of interrogation was not to find out what a person may or may not have done, but "in ninety-five cases out of a hundred, to exhaust, wear down, weaken, and render helpless the defendant, so that they would want it to end at any cost." Most interrogations took place at night, the accused yanked from their bed in front of their family and carted off to Moscow's notorious Lubyanka prison. Solzhenitsyn describes some of the methods used to make sure that "confessions" were signed and sentences agreed to, including: forced sleeplessness for up to a week in a vertical punishment cell in which it was impossible to lie down; hunger and thirst, and being made to drink salt water; filling the cell with ice cold or stinking hot air; and straitjackets, hot rods forced up one's rear, beatings, and isolation. Before 1938, formal documentation was required for torture, but after the waves of thousands of arrests became normal there were no longer the resources for such niceties, and interrogators were given unlimited powers of interrogation to reach their "quotas."

As confession was the basis for the whole system, it was to be obtained at any cost, and the methods of the "most successful" interrogators were copied. Bluecaps, as the interrogators were called, knew that nearly all the charges were made up ("Just give us a person—and we'll create the case!" was their slogan), but they received multiple benefits in return for maintaining the system: power, regular pay, and promotions. Why would an interrogator feel any mercy toward a prisoner who was standing in the way of meeting targets and advancing?

Yet the prison guards and authorities "needed ideological arguments in order to hold on to a sense of their own rightness—otherwise insanity was not far off." Just as the Spanish Inquisitors could justify all their actions in the name of God, everything Soviet security did could be attributed to Stalin's wishes and the glory of the proletariat. "Thanks to ideology," Solzhenitsyn writes, "the twentieth century was fated to experience evildoing on a scale calculated in the millions." And thanks to ideology this could be done with eyes that remained "dry and clear."

Much, much worse
In trying to demonstrate the barbarity of Stalinist Russia, Solzhenitsyn often compares it to the era under the Tsars. Instead of communism bringing a new glorious era for the worker, it simply replaced one system of serfdom with another that was much worse. After all, serfs never worked more than sunrise to sunset and they always had Sundays off, plus holidays throughout the year. Starvation never occurred in Old Russia.

In Tsarist Russia hundreds of crimes could meet with capital punishment, but the number of people executed only averaged 17 per year. After the Bolshevik Revolution capital punishment made a triumphant return. In only 16 months, from June 1918 to October 1919, over 16,000 people were shot. In the wave of 1937–38 it is estimated that 500,000 "political prisoners" were shot, and another half million "habitual thieves." Solzhenitsyn provides testimony that at Cheka headquarters in Moscow 200 people a night were shot over these two years, but the truth was even worse. Declassified Soviet archives now show that in 1937–38 over 1.5 million people were detained, and of these 680,000 were shot.

Solzhenitsyn suggests creating a book of photographs of every person who perished under Stalinism. He includes in *The Gulag Archipelago* six photos of such people, with their names underneath and where and when they were shot. It is hard not to be affected by these portraits.

Final comments
Solzhenitsyn refers to the risk that readers will be so taken aback by the book's contents that they will think: "Yes, it was bad, but it could not happen here." If only that were true, he says. In reality, "all the evil of the twentieth century is possible everywhere on earth." The combination of average people and unlimited power has terrible consequences, and it often happens in regimes with a universal standard or ideology that precludes free thinking. This is why educators, intellectuals, journalists, and clergy became targets under Stalin: They were thought to be too attached to values that were independent of the system.

After Stalin died in 1952, and chief of intelligence Beria was executed the same year, a whiff of greater liberality swept across Russia, and that included the Gulag. Yet the camps remained, and indeed the USSR was still throwing people into prison for political reasons (and keeping them in solitary, for example the dissident Natan Sharansky) until Gorbachev's time.

The Gulag Archipelago covers three volumes and 1,800 pages, but Edward Ericson's excellent abridgment (470 pages) still gives plenty of details and all the vital insights. There is much Russian history in the book and you may find yourself looking up events and historical figures to understand fully what Solzhenitsyn is saying. It is a history lesson as well as a literary tour de force and Solzhenitsyn was too modest in describing it as a work of journalism. His distinctive voice runs through it.

Alexandr Solzhenitsyn

Alexandr Isayevich Solzhenitsyn was born in Kislovodsk in 1918, six months after his father, an artilleryman in the Russian army, was killed in an accident. He was raised in Rostov, north of Moscow, by his mother, who worked as a shorthand typist. Although he wanted to be a writer from an early age, he enrolled to study mathematics and physics at Rostov University, graduating in 1941. He would later say that his mathematical training saved his life, as it provided him with easier jobs in the Gulag. The first part of his prison sentence was spent in various correctional work camps, followed by time in a scientific institute and in special camps for political prisoners, including Ekibastuz in Kazakhstan, where he worked as a miner, bricklayer, and in a foundry.

Shortly after finishing his sentence, Solzhenitsyn was pronounced "Exile for Life" and sent to Kok-Terek in southern Kazakhstan for three years, where he taught in a primary school and was able to write secretly. It was only in 1961, after Khrushchev's speech denouncing Stalin had circulated in Russia, that Solzhenitsyn dared seek publication of his novel One Day in the Life of Ivan Denisovich *(1962), a fictional rendering of his time in Ekibastuz. It brought him acclaim, but as he became more outspoken about censorship his novels* Cancer Ward *and* The First Circle *(both 1968) were banned. While expelled from the Soviet Writers' Union, in 1970 he was awarded the Nobel Prize for Literature; he did not attend the ceremony for fear of not being allowed back into the USSR.*

In 1974 Solzhenitsyn was arrested, interrogated by the KGB, and charged with treason. He was deported to Germany and spent time in Zurich before settling in Cavendish, Vermont. He returned to live in Russia in 1995, and died in Troitse-Lykovo, Moscow in 2008.

Three Principles of the People

"Our people are by nature peace-lovers! In ordinary etiquette we emphasize modesty. In our political philosophy we uphold the principle that 'only he who loves not killing is able to unite the Empire.' Thus there is a fundamental difference between the political thinking of the foreigners and that of the Chinese."

"We must know that the power of democracy is like the power of the great waters such as the Yangtze and Hwang Ho. There are sections of these rivers which actually run toward the north or toward the south, but in the end, they all go toward the east; and nothing is powerful enough to prevent them from running eastward. The political tendency of the world ran from theocracy to monocracy, then from monocracy to democracy; and its power is irresistible."

In a nutshell

Modern China's achievements stem from the revival of a nationalist spirit that preceded communism.

In a similar vein

Edward Bernays *Propaganda* (p 66)
Mohandas K. Gandhi *An Autobiography* (p 110)
Nelson Mandela *Long Walk to Freedom* (p 180)
Mencius *The Mencius* (p 192)

CHAPTER 44

Sun Yat-sen

Now revered in China as the leader of the first popular revolution, Sun Yat-sen was strikingly international. He spent his high school years in Hawaii, studied medicine in Hong Kong, where to his family's dismay he converted to Christianity under the influence of English missionaries, and after his first failed attempt at overthrowing the Qing dynasty in 1895, spent years living in Japan, the United States, and Britain. His forced exile allowed him to study Western politics, and he constantly worked to get the support of the Chinese diaspora for the nationalist cause. Sun was raising funds in America when, after numerous attempted uprisings orchestrated from abroad, China had its 1911 revolution. The following year the first Chinese republic was formed with Sun as its president.

Sun's revolutionary organization, the Tongmenghui, was transformed into a political party, the Kuomintang or Nationalist Party, but when Sun found himself usurped by the rapacious general Yuan Shikai, he was again exiled, this time from a country divided into south and north. In 1923 Sun returned to head the Southern Republic; after Sun's death, Chiang Kai-shek would unify China again along the lines set out in *Three Principles of the People*. Of course, the nationalist republic would be swept aside by Chairman Mao's communists in 1948, when Chiang Kai-shek's forces retreated to Formosa (Taiwan) to continue what it believed was the legitimate Chinese republic. Assisted by the US, Taiwan would become firmly capitalist.

Despite not being a communist, Sun is that rare figure who is highly esteemed in both the People's Republic of China and Taiwan. He is mentioned specifically in the preamble to China's constitution and thousands visit his huge mausoleum in Nanjing. His portrait is hoisted in Tiananmen Square each May Day and National Day, and two universities are named after him. In Taiwan, Sun's image appears on the walls of schools and on banknotes. He is also fondly recalled in Chinese diaspora communities, with Sun Yat-sen statues in San Francisco, Toronto, and Melbourne.

Sun's three principles of nationalism, democracy, and livelihood are also known as the San Min doctrine. He espoused it in countless lectures, which were later put into book form in *The Three Principles of the People*, in Chinese the "San Min Chu I." In Chinese, "Min" means the people, and "Ch'uan" power or rights. In the Preface Sun describes the three principles as the "salvation of the nation," because they will ensure that China is recognized as the equal of other nations, and bring it political stability and economic justice.

Nationalism (mínzú)

In the past, Sun notes, the Chinese people had been focused on pride in the family or in the clan. There was less awareness of China as a nation. In other countries the word "nation" can have two meanings: It can be both an ethnic group with a common background, and an administrative entity that rules over certain territories. In China, Sun argues, this cannot be so; China the legal entity and China the race of people are one and the same. He admits that there were around 10 million non-Chinese in the country including Mongols, Manchus, Tibetans, and Tartars, yet says that they are insignificant next to the 400 million ethnic Chinese who have a common heredity, religion, and customs. As the largest national group in the world, resting on 4,000 years of civilization, it is time for China to regain its recognition and place among other nations.

Under the heading "political force," Sun catalogues everything that had belonged to China but had been taken by other states. Britain now had Hong Kong and Burma, and Korea and Formosa (Taiwan) had gone to Japan after the Sino-Japanese War. The western powers had tried to divide up China among themselves to exploit it for trade, but China had resisted. Sun's Kuomintang started reassuring smaller Sino states like Mongolia that their enemy was not a united China, but the Western states who would seek to invade and dominate the Chinese landmass.

He calls for protective tariffs against imported Western goods, particularly fabrics, which were having a severe influence on the mills and weavers in the Chinese countryside. Chinese exports were not keeping up with what was coming in, creating a kind of bondage for the Chinese people. China now had many foreign banks, which squeezed the people of money through low interest rates, charges, and poor rates of foreign exchange. Shipping was also dominated by foreigners, particularly the Japanese, and taxes paid by Chinese people to foreign powers in the Concessions of Tianjin, Dairen, Hankou, Hong Kong, and Formosa amounted to hundreds of millions of dollars a year. Foreign companies had special treaty privileges, giving them virtual monopolies on many areas of business. At the least, Sun thinks, China could begin developing its own industries and creating its own banks.

He claims that China has become attached to "cosmopolitanism"—what today would be called globalization—but in the process has forgotten nationalism. Yet the attractions of cosmopolitanism are an illusion. It will only put

China in hock to one power or another. Only nationalism will make China for the Chinese, Sun says.

Nations tend to prosper when they have a sense of crisis, when they feel under threat. This is exactly what was lacking in modern China, Sun feels. In military terms, he warns that Japan could overrun China in ten days. America could sail to China, invade, and take it over in a month. With a strategic base in Hong Kong, plus its navy and backup forces sailing from Australia and India, Britain could do the same in a couple of months. The only reason no power had taken over China is that they were all jealous of each other's sphere of influence.

Democracy (minquán)

Sun sees Chinese history as progress toward democracy from theocracy and monocracy. He recognizes that some think China is not suited to being a republic, like America. Yet Sun claims that both Confucius and Mencius were exponents of democracy, or at least of the idea that kings and emperors required public consent to rule. Mencius said: "The people are the most important element of the state, the territory comes next, and the king last." If the king treated people poorly he was no longer the sovereign, but a "single fellow," and as such deserved to be overthrown.

Sun refers to Rousseau being on the right track in wanting greater freedom and power for the peoples of the world. He notes that the German Kaiser, Russian Tsar, and Austrian emperor had all been overthrown, and that imperial and monarchical government was on its way out everywhere, with the exception of Britain's constitutional monarchy. Of course, Sun was more focused on the creation of a republic than the realities of one person, one vote, so his understanding of democracy may be different to ours now. What he meant was the sovereignty of the people, a concept that was in line with the thinking of Confucius and Mencius, and that allows today's Communist party in China to claim that it is democratic.

Another reason to get rid of the imperial system, Sun says, is that it encourages civil war, because ambitious men will always seek to wrest control. It is harder to do this in a republic. When there is sovereignty of the people, every person in the land is themselves an "emperor," "no-one can quarrel for the throne," and the chance of civil war is greatly diminished.

Sun also lays out plans for a five-branch system of Chinese government, incorporating the European branches of executive, parliament, and judiciary, but adding two derived from Chinese history: a Control Yuan, the administration for supervising and making accountable all offices of government; and an Examination Yuan, to administer civil service qualifications.

People's livelihood (minshēng)

Sun recalls a Chinese saying: "Heaven creates a worm, And the earth creates a leaf/ Heaven creates a bird, And the earth creates a worm." This is meant to show that every living thing is provided for, but in fact things are not so straightforward for human beings living in modernity.

Although Sun is clearly influenced by Marx in his thinking on the "Social Question" of labor, he asserts that the Kuomintang's Doctrine of Livelihood is significantly different to socialism or communism. He does not agree with Marx that history is simply a matter of the oppressors and the oppressed, observing that in America and Europe the working classes had enjoyed major improvements in social conditions and living standards. Class struggle is not the cause of social progress, but was best seen as a social disease that spreads only when people are not seeing their lives improve. Moreover, labor is only one element of the production of goods and the creation of surplus value, and should not be the basis of a whole social theory. In relation to modern industry, Marx was simply wrong, Sun says. He uses the example of the Ford factory, which had decreased working hours, increased wages, and reduced prices. Everybody was a winner—there was no exploitation.

Sun's idea was to make capitalism and socialism work together to build a modern Chinese civilization, blending state controls of land and the distribution of resources to ensure minimum levels of prosperity, with the dynamism of capital (even foreign capital) and technology. His economics were never really followed through in Taiwan, but his vision of a nationalist China that blended a market system with socialist principles ("Socialism with Chinese characteristics") is what actually came into being on the mainland. Contemporary China has largely fulfilled Sun's aims.

Final comments

Reading Sun Yat-sen makes you appreciate why contemporary China is so paranoid about giving up even a centimeter of territory that it believes belongs to it historically, and why it clamps down hard on any separatist movements. Because in the past national consciousness has sometimes been lacking, it now goes quite the other way. No diminution of nationhood can be tolerated.

Will China keep to its historical pattern of being non-imperial, happy to be dominant merely in its sphere of influence? Or will it seek to be a power that puts its stamp on the world in every way? In Sun's ideas we find a probable answer that reaches deep into history. Under the subheading of "The peace-loving quality of the Chinese," he notes China's strong anti-imperial strain. He is proud of the fact that it has often resisted invading other countries, and instead, because of its power as a great civilization, has attracted "tributary states" that admiringly volunteered their allegiance. This "soft power," as we would call it now, attracted rather than compelled neighbors, and was in contrast to the West's militarist and imperialist approach.

China's resurgence does not mean that it wants conflict with America, Japan, or other nations, or even to become the world's top power. It may be generations before it matches America's military might; in the meantime, the government's focus will be on maintaining centralized power within its borders and increasing national wealth and living standards. The Communist Party knows that its primary role is not geopolitical, but keeping the population happy and prosperous—which is entirely consistent with Sun's vision.

Sun Yat-sen

Born into a peasant family in 1866 in a village in Guangdong province, at the age of 13 Sun Yat-sen joined his older brother in Honolulu. He quickly picked up English and went to high school there. At 17 he returned briefly to China before going to Hong Kong to complete his schooling, and in 1892 obtained a medical degree from the Hong Kong Medical College. After China was defeated in the Sino-Japanese War of 1894–95, he gave up his medical career in favor of bringing revolution to China. After a failed revolt (his childhood friend Lu Hao-tung would become the first "revolutionary martyr," executed by the Qing regime in 1895), he began a life of exile. While in London he was kidnapped and brought to the Chinese legation, but escaped thanks to the help of his friend James Cantlie and the British Foreign Office. Sun toured Europe, studying its political institutions, and it was during this time that he developed his three principles.

Following the Boxer Rebellion in 1900, revolutionary fervor spread in China. A meeting in Japan of representatives of revolutionaries across China and expat Chinese merchants resolved that the country be rid of dynastic rule. In 1911 the city of Wuchang fell to the revolutionaries, other cities followed, and the Manchu regime collapsed. In 1916 Sun married his former secretary, Song Qingling, who after his death became a key figure in the Kuomintang. Because she sided with the communists in China's Civil War, she would be important in the Chinese Communist Republic after 1950, and served as acting head of state from 1976–78. Sun died in 1925 in Peking.

The Autobiography

"Once the state plays fast and loose with economic freedom, political freedom risks being the next casualty."

"Strong defence was a necessary, but not sufficient, means of overcoming the communist threat. Instead of seeking merely to contain communism, we wished to put freedom on the offensive."

"I always believed that our western system would ultimately triumph, if we did not throw our advantages away, because it rested on the unique, almost limitless, creativity and vitality of individuals."

"My political philosophy... is founded on a deep skepticism about the ability of politicians to change the fundamentals of the economy or society: the best they can do is to create a framework in which people's talents and virtues are mobilized not crushed."

In a nutshell

Successful societies depend on the flourishing of individuals.
This does not happen if personal freedoms are curtailed
or when the state is seen as the solution to all ills.

In a similar vein

Lord Acton *Essays on Freedom and Power* (p 20)
Isaiah Berlin *Two Concepts of Liberty* (p 60)
F.A. Hayek *The Road to Serfdom* (p 126)
John Micklethwait & Adrian Wooldridge *The Fourth Revolution* (p 196)
Karl Popper *The Open Society and Its Enemies* (p 248)

CHAPTER 45

Margaret Thatcher

I n 1975, *The Wall Street Journal* described Britain as "the sick country of Europe," its undoing not brought about by natural disasters but by "the calculated policies of its Government and by their resigned acceptance by the people." In a speech in New York the same year, Margaret Thatcher, the new leader of Britain's Conservative Party, agreed, pointing the finger at the "progressive consensus, the doctrine that the state should be active on many fronts in promoting equality: in the provision of social welfare and in the redistribution of wealth and incomes." The effect was overtaxation, a stifling of enterprise, a war on profits, inflation that ate away people's savings, and constant growth of spending and the state. Back in Britain Thatcher was attacked by the governing Labour party for "running down Britain," when in fact her message was hope: that Britain could still regroup and prosper despite the ravages of socialism.

Thatcher's forthrightness increased her standing with the British public, the press, and her own party, and she began to be taken more seriously, beyond the novelty of being the country's first female party leader. In London early the next year she gave a foreign policy speech that shot an arrow into the soft bed of complacency on Russia, highlighting the imbalance in NATO and Warsaw Pact forces and the fact that the USSR was arming much faster than the US. Covering the speech, a writer for the Soviet *Red Star* newspaper described the unyielding Thatcher as "The Iron Lady."

The Autobiography is an abridged version of Thatcher's two volumes of memoirs, *The Downing Street Years* (1993) and *The Path to Power* (1995). Still full of detail and running to 738 pages, this edition leaves out some of the footnotes, appendices, and lengthy policy discussions, but retains all the key events and issues; unless you have weeks to spare reading the original volumes, this is the best book for discovering Thatcher's mind and philosophy.

Although Thatcher did not have the literary flourish of her hero Churchill, she writes extremely well. There are surprisingly few personal asides and reflections; family holidays in Brittany or Cornwall are mentioned only in passing, before pages and pages are devoted to the intricacies of missile treaties or trade union law. She admits that her appetite for talking policy and politics was unlimited, and she took the weight of office seriously (there is little of the informal "what it is like to be prime minister" approach of Tony Blair's autobiography, for instance). What also comes across is Thatcher's sheer mastery of detail. Famously existing on four or five hours of sleep a night, she constantly flummoxed opposition politicians, her own ministers, and foreign leaders by being better briefed. Her early career as a chemist, plus her legal training, gave her a "forensic" (a word of which she is fond) approach to policy matters, and she is dismissive of the generalist politicians and bureaucrats who did not fully grasp the science of nuclear systems or the basis of monetary policy. Because after decades of creeping socialism in the UK she was launching a new philosophy on the country, she was all the more concerned that her positions were fully worked out and watertight.

Early clarity

Thatcher's father Alfred Roberts was a grocer in Grantham, near Nottingham, and she recalls "wonderful aromas of spices, coffee and smoked hams" wafting up to the rooms in which the family lived above the shop. Although Margaret and her sister never lacked anything, and indeed the family prospered in the 1930s and 1940s, they were keenly aware that there was not much of a safety net. Grantham's success depended on its civil and religious institutions and on the industry of its families, and people did not naturally look to government to be helped. The Roberts' lives revolved around work and the Methodist church, and she believes that her father's statement "Never do things just because other people do them" set her up well. In a time when most Methodists and Nonconformists were left-leaning, the family stood out by their conservative politics, going against the strong pacifist feeling of the interwar years. In Margaret Roberts the conviction grew that "personal virtue is no substitute for political hard-headedness." She shared with her father, who would become mayor of Grantham, the then unfashionable view that fascism and communism were simply two sides of the same coin. They were deeply suspicious of Hitler's motives at Munich, and when war broke out the family sponsored a Jewish girl who was fleeing Vienna.

At Somerville College, Oxford, Roberts threw herself into her chemistry degree, for a time studying under Nobel Prize winner Dorothy Hodgkin, and was part of the Conservative students group. She was still at Oxford when the Conservative Party lost the 1945 general election, and found it inexplicable that the British public had removed Churchill from power. Only in hindsight did she see that wars have a way of centralizing government power and instilling a collectivist spirit; in fact, it was not such a great transition from wartime government to socialism under Labour. While the Conservative party was seen as stuffy or peopled by rich dandies, Labour was very much the party of "smart" people who felt that socialism was the future.

Around this time Roberts read Hayek's newly published *The Road to Serfdom* (see commentary on p 126). She already had a fundamental dislike of collectivism, and the book gave her the philosophical basis for resisting social planning models. Hayek showed how these could begin innocently, yet the curtailment of some economic freedoms "for the good of all" inevitably led to the erosion of political liberties.

Rising power

After graduating, Roberts took a job at a plastics firm in Colchester, but the pull of politics was too great. Seeking endorsement to stand for election as a Conservative MP, she met Denis Thatcher, managing director of a paint and chemicals company and a died-in-the-wool Tory who was 10 years older. At 24 she was the youngest person running in the 1950 election, and she did not win. After marrying, the couple enjoyed life in London and took holidays in Rome and Paris. No longer needing to work, Margaret Thatcher took up legal studies (interrupted by the birth of her twins Carol and Mark in 1953) and successfully completed her Bar exams. With the assistance of a good nanny, she began as an assistant lawyer and specialized in tax law. Then, overcoming the doubts of party officials that she could combine motherhood with politics, she became a candidate for a winnable seat, Finchley in North London. After the Conservatives lost the 1966 election, she had time to spend a few weeks in America; she found the contrast with an overregulated and overtaxed Britain deeply inspiring.

After Conservative Ted Heath's victory in 1970, Thatcher got her first post, as Education Secretary. The education system, she felt, "largely existed for the benefit of those who ran it, rather than those who received it." The Education Department was left-leaning and was all for large comprehensive high schools, whereas her idea was "to encourage variety and choice rather than 'plan' the system"; she succeeded in saving some selective grammar schools from closure. However, in her efforts to modernize primary schools some areas of funding had to be cut, including free milk. She was termed "Thatcher, the milk snatcher," and the *Sun* called her the "Most Unpopular Woman in Britain." In the face of such personal attacks many politicians do not last, she reflects, but she chose to march on.

She was increasingly disillusioned by the Heath government's many policy U-turns and poor economic performance. In his favor, Heath had brought Britain into the European Economic Community, but he was unable to stem the power of the unions, and kept to the postwar consensus that wages and prices needed to be controlled as part of an agreement with industry and unions. With British industry inefficient and overmanned thanks to union power, Thatcher felt in her bones that the Conservative party had to provide a radical alternative to the managed economy. In opposition (Heath lost power in 1974) she worked on housing policy, strengthening her belief in homeownership as the basis of democracy; this at a time when council homes constituted a quarter of all housing stock in Britain.

Thatcher's thinking was increasingly influenced by Keith Joseph, who ran the Conservatives' policy and research department and furnished arguments to show how government intervention invariably had unintended costs. The big problem at the time was inflation, and Thatcher came to the view that monetary policy (or controlling how much money was flowing into the economy) was the means to beat it. At this stage she supported Joseph to take over from Heath as Conservative leader, but support grew for Thatcher herself to run for the post, thanks in large part to her excellent performances in the House of Commons. Though history makes her rise to power seem inevitable, she recalls being genuinely shocked when, in 1975, she was made party leader.

Theory into practice

In 1978, the Conservatives ran a "Labour Isn't Working" advertising campaign with an image of a dole queue. Unemployment had hit 1.5 million. The 1978/79 "Winter of Discontent" of industrial and power strikes saw heaps of garbage left uncollected; lorry drivers, train drivers, nurses, and even gravediggers on strike; and winter snows and floods—but it did the Conservatives a favor by exposing the logical outcome of socialist policies. It was also a chance to appeal to people who had never traditionally voted Conservative, but who had had enough of Labour prime minister Jim Callaghan. Thatcher's resolve against union power stiffened, and she began developing policies for private postal ballots before strikes, restricting strikes among essential services, and eliminating closed shops (workplaces where union membership was compulsory). She felt that the public was behind her, but in the 1979 election campaign she assumed nothing: "I never had any illusion that if we lost or even if we failed to win an overall majority I would be given another chance."

In fact the victory was larger than she or anyone else imagined (a 43-seat majority), giving her a mandate for change in British politics. Among those who had voted her in were skilled workers and their families. Thatcher had drawn them away from their usual socialist allegiances, and she felt a strong responsibility to keep their trust. She began the union reforms, brought in a council house purchase scheme, reduced income taxes (but raised value added tax), eliminated controls on pay, prices, and dividends, and removed a number of planning controls. Also to go were controls on foreign exchange, to encourage investment in the UK and British investment abroad. The government started to reduce the size of the public sector, which represented almost 30 percent of the British workforce in 1979; in the following decade, thanks to privatization and natural attrition, this was brought back to 24 percent.

Yet the government's spending was not reduced enough to prevent high inflation of around 17 percent. When a government spends and borrows too much, the nation is punished by the markets with higher borrowing costs, which push up interest rates across the board and harm business. Thus, Thatcher knew, government was directly responsible for a lagging economy if it did not get the country's finances right; and as recession deepened, there would be more demand on the public purse. Her head of policy John Hoskyns noted at the time that the government's position, trying to introduce major reforms amid a high unemployment rate and high inflation, was "like trying to pitch a tent in the middle of a landslide." Thatcher was determined to hold course, and famously told parliament: "To those waiting with baited breath for that favorite media catchphrase, the 'U-turn', I have only one thing to say. 'You turn if you want to. The lady's not for turning.'"

There were still plenty of "wets" in her cabinet, left-leaning Conservatives who adhered to the postwar economic orthodoxy of tax and spend. Over successive reshuffles she gradually made her team resemble her own thinking, but initially her free market approach made her a stranger to her cabinet. The government's Medium Term Financial Strategy aimed to keep inflation lower by restricting the money supply and reducing government borrowing, while in industrial policy Thatcher was determined to get the British government out of what should be the private sector. Her privatization program (British Telecom, British Airways, British Steel, British Leyland, and British Gas, among others) was revolutionary.

Waterloo 1: The Falklands

Thatcher was lucky that the Falklands crisis came along when it did. Only a couple of years into her government, her economic policies were still taking time to have an effect, but Argentina's invasion of the islands provided her with a perfect chance to display her unyielding character. Less remembered now are her government's efforts to achieve a diplomatic resolution, but when this failed she did not hesitate to take back the islands, whose population was overwhelmingly British. The success of the operation won her respect abroad for standing up to an aggressor, but, more importantly, gave her a dramatic boost with the British public, so used to being told to accept their country's military and economic decline. The US at first prevaricated by proposing an "interim administration" in which Argentina and Britain would share power over the islands, but such ideas were nauseating to Thatcher, and her friend Ronald Reagan came round to her view that there was no alternative to military force.

"That a common or garden dictator should rule over the Queen's subjects and prevail by fraud and violence? Not while I was Prime Minister," she writes.

Waterloo 2: The miners' strike

Since 1974, £2.5 billion of British taxpayers' money had been put into the coal industry, which actually had a good future so long as uneconomic coal pits were closed. But the unions resisted, and there was massive political pressure to give in to them in order to preserve energy supplies and save jobs.

So hardline Marxist and so imbued with a hatred of the Tories was Arthur Scargill that as soon as he was elected leader of the National Union of Miners, Thatcher says, she knew she would have to deal with a major strike. Her government had quietly begun to build up stocks of coal to outlast any industrial action. Despite Scargill's efforts to create a total nationwide strike, in fact many pits kept operating; those men who wished to continue working were harassed and abused. Evidence emerged that the miners' union had received money from Libyan Colonel Gaddafi and had also received assistance from Soviet miners. If Scargill was turning the strike into an anti-capitalist crusade, Thatcher would fight it on the principle of a person's right to work unmolested, and ending union militancy. The year-long strike finally ended when ordinary trade unionists rejected Scargill's use of it as a political weapon, and his attempt to defy the laws of economics by keeping pits open that had no future.

Freedom fighter

Thatcher's time in office included the end of the Cold War, British colony Rhodesia becoming Zimbabwe, negotiations for the handover of Hong Kong to China, the Iran–Iraq war, the invasion of Grenada, the bombing of the US marine HQ in Beirut, and the Soviet invasion of Afghanistan. Although she liked Jimmy Carter on a personal level, she felt that his weakness in the face of communism was unpardonable, and that his philosophy of the limits to growth and austerity went against everything America stood for. When Reagan was marked out as a serious contender for the presidency she was delighted to find a kindred spirit; like her, he was not content merely to contain or balance the Soviet Union, but believed that it should be actively thwarted because it kept a large section of the world population under coercion. While it is hard to appreciate now, and despite the evidence of dissidents and refuseniks about the moral bankruptcy of the Soviet regime, this view was a minority one, with large numbers of politicians and pundits in the West thinking that the best policy was peaceful accommodation.

The chapter on Thatcher's early "grooming" of Mikhail Gorbachev is fascinating. She had gone out of her way to identify a rising star of Soviet politics who could usher in a period of change, and invited Gorbachev and his wife Raisa to Chequers, the country residence of British prime ministers. They developed a warm relationship, but in private talks and public speeches Thatcher did not hold back in confronting Gorbachev, noting in particular the lack of freedom of speech and movement within the USSR's borders, and the fact that it had not changed its policy of turning the world to communism or funding conflict, from Ethiopia to Nicaragua. She noted the difference between the Western and communist systems as "a distinction between societies in which power was dispersed and societies based on central control and coercion."

Neither Reagan or Thatcher then knew the extent of the USSR's economic malaise, and therefore its political fragility, and they would be as surprised as anyone at how quickly the empire fell to its knees.

Final comments

The British public did not realize how radical Thatcher would be when they elected her. The monetarist, free market ideas she brought to government had been little tried in practice; Friedman and Hayek were not mainstream economists, but their stars rose as she showed that their thinking worked. Thatcher's program of privatization, which turned many Britons into shareholders, was also something new and was imitated around the world. Her "Big Bang" reforms to the City of London made it a financial powerhouse, pulling in capital from around the world and employing thousands. The number of days lost to strikes was 29 million when she came to office, yet dropped to 2 million. Inflation more than halved during her government, and she reduced the top rate of tax from 83 percent to 40 percent. In foreign policy, her condemnation of communism and promotion of freedom predated Reagan's, and her view that Europe should be an economic grouping to increase trade, with nation-states retaining full power over their own destinies, proved prescient.

When Thatcher died in 2013, her legacy was hotly debated. During her time in office the Conservatives lost all support in the North of England and Scotland, becoming a party of the rich South. On the other hand, her economic policies were warmly embraced under Blair's Labour government ("we are all Thatcherites now," Blairite Peter Mandelson famously said). Yet Thatcher knew that her "revolution" was not fully implemented, and that the battle to preserve individual freedoms and limit the size of government was a perennial one. As *The Economist* wrote, "for countries to flourish, people need to push back against the advances of the state. What the world needs now is more Thatcherism, not less." Thatcher became one of the great twentieth-century leaders because, at a time when greater economic and political liberty was seen as "impractical," she made it the center of her program.

Civil Disobedience

*"All men recognize the right of revolution; that is, the right
to refuse allegiance to and to resist the government, when its
tyranny or its inefficiency are great and unendurable."*

*"Any man more right than his neighbours,
constitutes a majority of one already."*

*"There will never be a really free and independent state, until the State
comes to recognize the individual as a higher and independent power."*

*"The mass of men serve the State thus, not as men
mainly, but as machines, with their bodies."*

In a nutshell

People should act according to their conscience first,
above any law imposed by government.

In a similar vein

Mohandas K. Gandhi *An Autobiography* (p 110)
Martin Luther King *The Autobiography of Martin Luther King, Jr.* (p 150)
Nelson Mandela *Long Walk to Freedom* (p 180)
Plato *Crito* (p 244)

CHAPTER 46

Henry David Thoreau

The Transcendentalists, a group of New England intellectuals including Thoreau, Ralph Waldo Emerson, Walt Whitman, and Margaret Fuller, believed that knowledge comes through intuition and imagination rather than logic and the senses alone. Individuals are at their best when independent and self-reliant, and should trust themselves to be their own authority on what is right and wrong. The intrusions of society and institutions, especially organized religion and political parties, were liable to corrupt the individual, especially if the conscience was overlooked. Thoreau put transcendentalist ideas into practice in a famous life experiment. At the start of *Walden* (see the commentary in *50 Self-Help Classics*), he wrote:

> *"I went to the woods because I wished to live deliberately, to front only the essential facts of life, and see if I could not learn what it had to teach, and not, when I came to die, discover that I had not lived."*

The 1840s were turbulent times in America, with a crisis emerging between the anti-slavery North and the pro-slavery South. Thoreau spent a night in jail in July 1846 for refusing to pay his poll tax, in protest at government policies relating to slavery and the Mexican-American War. He was prepared for a longer stay, but his time in prison was cut short by an anonymous donor— some say his aunt—who paid the tax for him. In January 1848 he used the experience as the basis of a lecture at the Concord Lyceum, "The Rights and Duties of the Individual in Relation to Government," which was published in Elizabeth Peabody's *Aesthetic Papers* and became known as *On the Duty of Civil Disobedience*, or simply *Civil Disobedience*.

Rooted in both scholarship and literature, *Civil Disobedience* contains references to Confucius, the Bible, Shakespeare's *Hamlet* and *King John*, English dramatists Cyril Tourneur and George Peele, as well as Renaissance astronomer Nicolaus Copernicus and religious reformer Martin Luther. Some references are obscure to the modern reader, but the thrust of the essay—that citizens have a right to withhold support from a government if its actions are perceived as immoral—is timeless, and transcended the original reasons that prompted Thoreau to put pen to paper.

Legislation and higher law

The Mexican-American War followed the US government's 1845 annexation of Texas, which would lead to its gaining much of present-day Arizona, New Mexico, Utah, and California. The war seemed to proceed with little debate in Congress, and was viewed as part of the nation's "Manifest Destiny" to expand westward to the Pacific. It generally had popular support. However, many people felt that the invasion of a sovereign country and murdering Mexicans on their own soil were travesties of America's founding ideals. The war was not only aggressive and expansionist, but seemed likely to extend slavery to the new Southern states; as a lifelong abolitionist, this was something that Thoreau could not accept.

His position in *Civil Disobedience* is that while it is not the duty of any person to eradicate the wrongs of society, at the least they should not knowingly be a part of it. People are supposed to obey the law, but an individual should not blindly follow these laws or do so in a way that goes against their conscience. Morality and ethics are the "higher law," even above statutes agreed by a popular majority.

Thoreau took issue with English philosopher William Paley, who argued that government should always be obeyed because expediency required it. Thoreau could not countenance expediency as the basis for a just society. If the state could unjustly imprison fugitive slaves or Mexican prisoners, then it followed that "the true place for a just man is also a prison." Civil disobedience and revolution are in fact the only choice when one is made to decide between right and wrong, and Thoreau points to the American Revolution itself as an example. Yet he finds Americans' refusal to accept ever-increasing taxation from the British government a less compelling reason for rebellion compared to the tyranny of war and slavery. It is not enough to express opposition through the mechanism of government; our individual actions are all important when making our objections. "We should be men first," Thoreau tells us, "and subjects afterwards."

Person and government

Thoreau believed in the adage: "That government is best which governs least." Government "never of itself furthered any enterprise," but usually gets in the way. The purpose of government is to allow individuals to be free to go about their business; people needed to be like Indian rubber, to "bounce over the obstacles which legislators are continually putting in their way," Thoreau says. He would have liked no government at all, but in the meantime he would just like *better* government, one that did not treat people as machines or animals, sending them off to war whether they supported the fight or not.

The most obvious counter to Thoreau's idea of civil disobedience is Socrates (see commentary on Plato's *Crito* on p 244), who reasoned that if one lives within a state then it is wrong not to obey its laws, even if one disagrees with them. However, Thoreau could not get past the fact that, within a democratic system based on majority rule, weight of numbers crushes individual conscience. Matters are settled not on the basis of wrong or right, but according to expediency. Politicians can be "bought off" or may make deals to support somebody else's legislation in order to gain votes for their own. Voting is little more than a game that has only a tinge of morality about it; it does not settle or define questions of right and wrong, and therefore an individual should not simply leave big moral issues to be decided by the majority.

Why do governments always persecute the minority, or individuals who make themselves inconvenient? Should they not be listening to every dissenting voice to make sure that their policies are not flawed or wrong? The fact that governments do not do this suggests that their interests are with might rather than right, but at the same time it frees the citizen to withdraw their consent and act according to conscience:

"If the injustice is part of the necessary friction of the machine of government, let it go, let it go; perchance it will wear smooth, certainly the machine will wear out... but if it is of such a nature that it requires you to be the agent of injustice to another, then, I say, break the law. Let your life be a counter friction to stop the machine."

Thoreau was familiar with the writings of anarchists such as Lysander Spooner and Josiah Warren, both also from Massachusetts, but his thinking is more akin to today's small-staters or mild libertarians who accept the existence of some form of political organization, however minimal. He never minded paying highway taxes, for instance, because he used roads, and he was glad his taxes went to pay for schools. Moreover, he had reverence for the American Constitution; it was individual governments he had a problem with.

Thoreau's political views should be understood in the wider metaphysical context in which he was writing: They flowed from a deeper idealism about humanity in which people evolve their moral consciousness and self-reliance and act accordingly. A strong democratic state was fine for the mass of people who did not habitually question the motives of politicians, but for those with a strong conscience it seemed a very compromised way to run things. He uses a biological analogy: "If a plant cannot live according to its nature, it dies; and so a man."

Final comments

The idea of civil disobedience, although not the term itself (it was first applied to Thoreau's essay after his death), did of course have a long tradition in America. The Boston Tea Party at the start of the American Revolution was a response to perceived injustices from a faraway government, and the right to exercise civil disobedience when circumstances warranted it became very much a part of what it meant to be an American. Thoreau's ideas should also be seen within the context of nineteenth-century liberalism. When he writes "the progress from an absolute to a limited monarchy, from a limited monarchy to a democracy, is a progress towards true respect for the individual... There will never be a really free and independent state, until the State comes to recognize the individual as a higher and independent power," he could have been channeling John Stuart Mill, and indeed Mill's *On Liberty* would be published 10 years later.

The Transcendentalists were in part influenced by Indian religion, including the Bhagavad Gita. This may have sparked Gandhi's interest in Thoreau; Gandhi credited *Civil Disobedience* with being a "chief cause of the abolition of slavery in America" and it influenced his campaigns of non-violent resistance in South Africa and later in India. Martin Luther King, Jr. read the essay as a student and cited it as his first contact with the theory of non-violent resistance and the idea of choosing jail rather than supporting the policies of the government. King wrote in his autobiography that he "became convinced that non-cooperation with evil is as much a moral obligation as is cooperation with good." Civil disobedience was central to the anti-war protests of the 1960s, and more recently the Occupy movement against social and economic inequality, as well as Hong Kong's peaceful protests in favor of democracy, are Thoreauvian examples of political action.

Henry David Thoreau

Henry David Thoreau was born in Concord, Massachusetts in 1817. After grad-uating from Harvard in 1837, he took a position as a schoolteacher, but, after objecting to the required use of corporal punishment, went to work in his father's lead pencil-making business. He began paying serious attention to the natural world in 1839 with a voyage down the Concord and Merrimack rivers, a journey related in a book published 10 years later.

Thoreau spent 1841–43 as part of the household of Ralph Waldo Emerson, on whose land was Walden Pond. He worked as a land surveyor, whitewasher, and gardener, as well as lecturing and writing for magazines, including the Transcendentalist journal The Dial. The essay "Slavery in Massachusetts" was published in 1854, the same year as Walden. Cape Cod (1865) and A Yankee in Canada (1866) were published after his death in 1862. Emerson's essay "Thoreau" marvels at his friend's phenomenal knowledge of nature and practical skills.

Thoreau's participation in the abolitionist movement included support for the Underground Railroad to free slaves. He met ex-slave Frederick Douglass, author of the famous Narrative, and supported John Brown, who was hanged for trying to arm slaves.

Democracy in America

"The people reign in the American political world as the Deity does in the universe. They are the cause and the aim of all things; everything comes from them, and everything is absorbed in them."

"In Europe, we are wont to look upon a restless disposition, an unbounded desire of riches, and an excessive love of independence, as propensities very dangerous to society. Yet these are the very elements which insure a long and peaceful future to the republics of America."

In a nutshell

What democracies lack in aristocratic sophistication
they make up for in freedom and justice.

In a similar vein

Daron Acemoglu & James A. Robinson *Why Nations Fail* (p 26)
Edmund Burke *Reflections on the Revolution in France* (p 78)
Alexander Hamilton, John Jay, & James Madison *The Federalist Papers* (p 120)
Thomas Paine *Common Sense* (p 238)
Jean-Jacques Rousseau *Discourse on Inequality* (p 254)

Alexis de Tocqueville

The official reason for Alexis de Tocqueville's 1831 trip to America was to make a study of its prisons, but this was a pretext for a much more ambitious venture: a full analysis of American social and political life as it was in the 1830s. The result was one of the best pieces of writing then and now into the character, customs, and institutions of the American people.

A French aristocrat with generations of privilege and wealth behind him, de Tocqueville was the perfect contrast to the nation he wished to study. His natural skepticism toward democracy and revolution is what makes *Democracy in America* so fascinating—it is no gushy travelogue, but is filled with remarks on what this new world lacks along with its strengths. It became a meditation on the nature of free societies everywhere and their prospects. De Tocqueville compares the "tranquility" of authoritarian or aristocratic government to the tumult of democracy. This tranquility was largely an illusion, he concludes, for the longer a people are oppressed by the rule of a few who do not govern in their interests, the more fragile a regime becomes, and the more ripe for revolution.

Egalitarian from the start

"Among the novel objects that attracted my attention during my stay in the United States, nothing struck me more forcibly than the general equality of condition among the people."

From its early days, de Tocqueville notes, "the soil of America was opposed to a territorial aristocracy." He meant this literally as well as metaphorically. The land was not rich enough to sustain both tenants and owners, and with limited availability of labor large farms did not make sense. Instead, holdings were broken up into smaller portions for a farmer to own and farm for himself. Thus the principles of serfdom were broken and the ethic of self-reliant individualism took hold. This was just as the new settlers wanted it.

A big difference between North and South was there from the start. Settlers in the South were "adventurers without resources and without character," who, after finding there was no gold, soon brought in slaves as a way to make money from the land. In contrast, New England's early settlers were better educated than in the South, neither rich nor poor, and from the beginning there was an ethos of equality. Crucially, these Puritans were coming to America not out of economic desperation, but to seek political and religious freedom that had been withheld from them at home. They were on the one hand deeply obedient and submissive when it came to faith and religion, and on the other deeply distrustful of all political authority. Thus the success of New England was down to an unusual combination: a consuming love of religious freedom, and openness to all new ideas of political organization that would preserve such freedom. These two elements would form the bedrock of American politics.

Inheritance had been a driving force in social conditions in Europe, forming the layers of privilege and "affecting, as it were, generations yet unborn," de Tocqueville writes. Yet in America after the Revolution English inheritance law was abolished. It was no longer assumed that wealth would pass to the first son, so property and wealth began to circulate more freely. Within a generation, any families who would have been considered aristocratic in England became part of the mass. In this way, America "escaped the influence of great names and great wealth." Americans love money more than anyone, he notes, but it tends not to last beyond one generation. Each new life represents a blank slate in a way that Old Europe could not comprehend.

Americans and government

The principle of the "sovereignty of the people" became part of American culture from the start, even if it was mostly informal, local, and small scale, through town assemblies and the like. The American colonies were of course "owned" by England in their early days, but Britain was more concerned with centralized power, which left the often remote towns and municipalities to get on with developing political life at the grassroots level. Everyone was expected to take part in political life, so Americans grew used to charting their own destiny. Their practice of government at the local level helped them appreciate its limits, and, combined with the love of freedom, there arose a preference for minimal, decentralized governance. While prosperity meant that there was "no public misery to serve as a means of agitation," even material inequality did not create grounds for instability, because everyone accepted that there was a level playing field and that they were left to their own devices.

Yet the writers of the Constitution realized that if the nation was to stay in one piece there would need to be a fair degree of centralized power, and moreover that there were some things only a central government could do, such as organizing an army, creating a monetary system, running a postal service, building main roads to connect the country, and levying taxes. The government would be big enough to get things done, but not so big that it would attract men seeking fame or power. De Tocqueville contrasts this with republics in South America, which lacked a true federal structure so that power was always *imposed*, rather than shared. Each individual American, de Tocqueville says, by his willingness to defend the Union, is also defending his own patch of land or town.

In a chapter on America's political parties, he points out that although they compete vigorously, in contrast to most countries none wishes to overturn the basic form of government or the constitution. Instead, politics is about details and specific policies. Today, visitors to the US are often surprised by the huge controversies that swirl around the media, often about no great issues of state, or the obsession with celebrity lives. De Tocqueville observed this early on, noting that the visitor "is at a loss whether to pity a people who take such arrant trifles in good earnest, or to envy that happiness which enables a community to discuss them."

This focus on small things was not merely the sign of a prosperous nation, but the hallmark of a people who did not expect government to solve their problems. Indeed, when an American dreams up some new enterprise that will be for the good of the people, he does not go to the government to seek support or funding for it, but rounds up the resources himself or forms an association. The result is that "the sum of these private undertakings far exceeds all that the government could have done." Here we are not just talking about power to the people in one glorious moment (as some French revolutionaries saw it), but an inherent feeling of the power of the people that extends and develops over time. The American constitution did not promise happiness via the government, but was only a framework for the fair pursuit of happiness, leaving the details up to you and your neighbor—or you and your neighbor together. Indeed, for de Tocqueville civil associations are a key element in resisting "the tyranny of the majority."

Freedom of the press

De Tocqueville notes the difference between American newspapers and those in his home country. In France the papers have a preponderance of news on great events, and a few advertisements. In America, three-quarters of the pages are filled with ads, with the remainder for political news and fluffy anecdotes. Missing almost entirely are the sort of deep and passionate discussions found in the European press. The other big difference is press concentration. In France all the news-making is centered in Paris, and is in the hands of a few. Since in America in the nineteenth century there was no true metropolis, news was more local and decentralized. Anyone could set up a newspaper and there were already hundreds of them, reinforcing the press's plurality of power. People could say what they liked, but there was such a wide diversity of opinions that it had no revolutionary effect. De Tocqueville makes his position clear:

"The more I consider the independence of the press… the more am I convinced that, in the modern world, it is the chief, and, so to speak, the constitutive element of liberty. A nation which is determined to remain free is therefore right in demanding, at any price, the exercise of this independence."

Democracy's risks and benefits

Examining the electoral process, de Tocqueville notices that in America national elections are only the tip of the iceberg. He notes that women go to political speeches "as a recreation from their household labors," and "debating clubs are a substitute for theatrical entertainments." This habit of being free to speak one's mind was basic to being an American citizen.

Throughout the book de Tocqueville expresses wariness of what he calls the "tyranny of the majority." Americans respect the voice of the majority in the same way that the French in the Ancien Régime did not question the wisdom of the king. A majority may misuse its power in the same way that an individual might. Yet to balance this, he finds that the ability of American courts to judge that a particular law is unconstitutional "forms one of the most powerful barriers which has ever been devised against the tyranny of political assemblies."

Equality, freedom, and innovation

In an aristocratic society, De Tocqueville notes, only a few people are able to engage in advanced learning and science. One's station in life determines what one will know. In America most people see it as their right to engage in discussion, self-study, and general self-improvement. De Tocqueville feels that the standard of scientific inquiry, arts, and learning was much inferior to Europe, yet he salutes the ardent desire of Americans to know more, and to gain this knowledge "after their own fashion."

He also observes that in a democratic country, the working population constantly strives to increase productivity and innovate so as either to lessen the workload, or to get more work done in less time. There are incentives that do not exist in regimes where workers do not earn more if they are more productive. In a democratic country like America, where the patronage of kings and nobility is lacking, the aim becomes to produce a good, average product that can be useful (and sold) to the greatest number. De Tocqueville would have thought it no accident that the Model T Ford, which made motoring available to the masses, came out of America and not France or Russia.

Final comments

Because of its great inequality of wealth and education, France had produced sublime art, architecture, and literature, raising some individuals to dizzy heights. Democratic societies, de Tocqueville notes, level everything out, such that singular quality is replaced by the quest for abundance, and nobility of character by the desire for self-enrichment. Yet who is he, he wonders in the last part of *Democracy in America*, to prevent such a large movement of humankind? He reminds himself that although his eyes are firmly fixed only on what is great or fine, God's eyes see all people equally, and "what appears to me to be man's decline is, to His eye, advancement." In a reference to Napoleon and others like him, Tocqueville says: "It would seem as if the rulers of our time sought only to use men in order to make things great; I wish that they would try a little more to make great men... no form or combination of social polity has yet been devised to make an energetic people out of a community of pusillanimous and enfeebled citizens." What democratic societies lack in refinement, they make up for in being more just.

Alexis de Tocqueville

Alexis de Tocqueville was born in 1805. His aristocratic great-grandfather was executed in the French Revolution, and his father was a royalist prefect who had supported Charles x, the last Bourbon king of France. After the July Revolution of 1830, de Tocqueville, Sr. lost his peerage and had to resign his prefect's position at Versailles. With the family's position now precarious, de Tocqueville, Jr.'s commission to visit America was welcomed. He was accompanied by lawyer and prison reformer Gustave de Beaumont. Democracy in America was published in two volumes, the second in 1840. Its success turned the shy de Tocqueville into a public figure, lauded by people such as John Stuart Mill.

Though de Tocqueville studied law and held some legal positions, he spent most of his working life in politics. Between 1839 and 1848 he was a member of the French Chamber of Deputies, advocating decentralization and an independent judiciary. He opposed Napoleon III's coup in the Revolution of 1848, but still helped to write the Second Republic's constitution. He was briefly vice president of the National Assembly and foreign minister, but retired from politics in 1851 to write The Old Regime and the Revolution. *The book he wrote with de Beaumont on the US penitentiary system was influential in prison reform.*

De Tocqueville died in 1859 in Cannes, from tuberculosis. He was survived by his wife Mary Mottley, whom he had met during a period in England. His mother had tried to prevent the match because Mary was Protestant and poor, but it was said to be a happy marriage.

The Spirit Level

"In societies with greater inequality, where the social distances between people are greater, where attitudes of 'us and them' are more entrenched and where lack of trust and fear of crime are rife, public and policy makers alike are more willing to imprison people and adopt punitive attitudes towards the 'criminal elements' of society. More unequal societies are harsher, tougher places."

"Greater inequality actually increases the need for big government— for more police, more prisons, more health and social services of every kind. Most of these services are expensive and only very partially effective, but we shall need them forever if we continue to have the high levels of inequality that create the problems they are designed to deal with. Several states of the USA now spend more on prisons than on higher education. In fact, one of the best and most human ways of achieving small government is by reducing inequality."

In a nutshell

Inequality is not a problem only for the have-nots—the evidence suggests that it drags everyone's well-being down.

In a similar vein

CHAPTER 48

Richard Wilkinson & Kate Pickett

B ritish epidemiologists Richard Wilkinson and Kate Pickett wrote *The Spirit Level: Why Equality Is Better for Everyone* following years of research into health inequalities, or why health is related to personal wealth. Epidemiology, or the study of the control, distribution, and prevention of diseases, is almost by definition political. In the past government's role in health was mostly a fight against infectious diseases; today it is more likely to be a war against lifestyle ailments such as heart disease, obesity, and diabetes. While some afflictions such as breast cancer visit all levels of society equally, a larger number of physical and mental illnesses are strongly related to income and class.

The belief of early socialists that inequality tends to promote prejudice and reduces societal harmony is now being proved correct by the data, Wilkinson and Pickett say, and this tells us that "inequality is divisive, and even small differences seem to make an important difference."

In the same way that evidence-based medicine is driven by what works and what does not, they call for a new "evidence-based politics"; that is, policies shaped by research in the social sciences that clearly show the route to greater social well-being. This route, in their minds, is signposted "Equality."

The psychology of inequality

Wealth on its own does not lead to any reduction in health and social problems. What matters is the *distribution* of wealth within a particular country; their analysis is restricted to developed economies for which there is data, Wilkinson and Pickett explain. Among people living below the official poverty line in the United States, not many actually do not have enough to eat; poverty in richer countries more often means having to make choices between having basic requirements such as food or heating, and keeping up appearances, for example by spending a whole month's income to buy a new mobile phone. "What matters," the authors say, "is where we stand in relation to others in our own society."

The relationship between inequality and class is defined in epidemiology as the "social gradient" or "social distance." Overall, there is a clear link between health and social problems and the steepness of a society's social gradient. Income differences generate ways of living and being that tend to entrench social and health problems over time. If a country wants to improve levels of achievement in schools, it will do so not by fiddling with classroom techniques or class sizes, but by addressing the wealth inequalities creating the social conditions that make education seem unimportant to parents and students.

People feel a sense of inferiority when encountering others of a higher class, and obviously the chances of such encounters increase the more unequal a society is. French sociologist Pierre Bourdieu talks of class in terms of "symbolic violence," Wilkinson and Pickett note. In very hierarchical and unequal societies, people take out their frustrations not on those above them, but on those below: "The captain kicks the cabin boy, and the cabin boy kicks the cat." It makes sense that in more unequal societies, people's focus is on dominance. In more equal ones, there is a greater concern for inclusiveness and empathy.

The experience of inequality, social class, and status differences is a form of "social pain." This tells us why unequal societies are more socially dysfunctional, but it also suggests that striving for a more equal form of society is not utopian, but practical. After all, the greater the class differences, the more costly it will be to support and pay for all the problems stemming from social deprivation, and this is one of the reasons why the health and social problems of the poorest have a deleterious effect on the rest of society.

There has been a significant rise in mental illness in the last few decades. World Health Organization studies show that Japan, Germany, and Spain have at any one time 10 percent of the population with a mental illness, whereas the less equal UK, Australia, and New Zealand have rates of between 20 and 25 percent, and the US, the most unequal country in terms of income, over 25 percent. In a more unequal society, people spend more time chasing higher income, social status, material wealth, and possessions, at the expense of relationships and family life, with concomitant effects on their mental well-being.

Health and social costs

Wilkinson and Pickett's primary observation that the greater the inequality, the greater the extent of health and social problems turns out to be true not only across countries, but within them too. Louisiana, Missouri, and Alabama have the most unequal distribution of incomes in America, and also have the worst health and social problems. New Hampshire, Vermont, and Utah have relatively low income inequality, but also rank among the lowest in health and social problems. There is an astonishing 28-year difference in life expectancy between poor blacks and rich whites living in the same geographic areas of the US.

Low status at work is strongly linked to poorer health in a range of countries. Every country has low-status jobs, but the psychological effect of the work is balanced if there is a decent minimum wage. Obesity is also lower in countries where there are smaller differences in income. For instance, 30 percent of adults in the US are obese, compared to only 2.4 percent of adults in Japan. Obesity is closely linked to a person's sense of their social status, more than income or education level. Stress makes people eat for comfort, particularly food high in sugar and fat, and drink more alcohol.

The more unequal the country, the worse its educational attainment. The Programme for International Student Assessment (PISA), which tests 15-year-olds around the world, found that in math and literacy, more unequal societies generally had worse overall scores. The low average literacy scores in the US are because scores for children from lower socioeconomic backgrounds drag down the overall result. Countries where there is a history of welfare provision and lower inequality have smaller social differences in reading ability.

Teenage pregnancies are more common in more unequal countries, and more common in the US states with the greatest income inequality. Teenage motherhood tends to exclude young women from normal career paths and the rest of society, so reinforcing the lower socioeconomic status that they are likely to have had in the first place.

There is a further clear relationship between greater inequality and higher homicide rates. The US murder rate, at 64 per million, is over four times higher than the UK's, and twelve times higher than Japan's. Within the US, Louisiana's murder rate, at 107 per million, is seven times higher than New Hampshire's. States and countries with great inequality also have higher rates of imprisonment.

There is only data for eight countries, but we know that (contrary to the myth of the American Dream) social mobility is lowest in America, the UK comes next, Germany is in the middle, and Canada and the Scandinavian countries give people the highest chance of moving up the social scale.

It affects all of us

"The truth is that the vast majority of the population is harmed by greater inequality," Wilkinson and Pickett say. In more unequal societies, people—all people, not only the poor—are "five times as likely to be imprisoned, six times as likely to be clinically obese, and murder rates may be many times higher." In these countries, even if one could remove the poorest from the equation, the rest of society is still more susceptible to these factors than the total populations of more equal societies.

Critics of *The Spirit Level*, such as Peter Saunders (author of *The Rise of the Equalities Industry*), suggest that most of the apparent link between inequality and social problems in America is a politically correct way of disguising the real driver of crime: race. Saunders says that the presence of large black populations in American states is the best predictor of problems, not inequality itself. Yet Wilkinson and Pickett note that the death rates of white Americans alone are worse than those of many other societies as a whole. Across all educational levels, American white men are significantly more likely to have diabetes, hypertension, lung disease, and heart disease than English white men with similar incomes. This suggests that there is something about the nature of societies themselves, not race, that predicts social and health problems.

The politics of equality

One might argue that rising inequality is simply a natural outcome of changing technology and demography, but Wilkinson and Pickett disagree, claiming that it is the result of changes in the political landscape: weakening trade unions, changes in incentives via taxes and benefits, and a lurch to the right. Wage differentials rise, taxes are made less progressive, minimum wages go out the door, benefits are cut, and so on. Inequality is entirely a political result, and it can be changed through politics too.

In 2007, the CEOs of America's 365 largest companies received over 500 times the pay of the average worker in those firms, and in many the CEO will earn more in a day than some of his workers will earn in a year. The pay gap in 2007, Wilkinson and Pickett note, was around 10 times what it was in 1980. Yet the argument for greater equality is not necessarily one for a bigger state, they contend. Both Sweden and Japan have low levels of social and health problems and low death rates, but they differ in how their equality is achieved: Sweden's is via redistribution and a large welfare state, while Japan's is via greater equality of incomes *before* taxes. Moreover, the authors say that the degree of public social expenditure as a proportion of GDP is "entirely unrelated" to indices of social and health problems. Government may spend a large amount to try to prevent social and health problems, or have to spend significantly to deal with the consequences, but in both cases the *underlying* problem is inequality.

Wilkinson and Pickett refer to surveys by Duke University and Harvard University asking participants to look at three unlabeled pie charts. The first showed each fifth of a population having the same amount of wealth as the others; the second illustrated the very unequal distribution of wealth in the US;

and the third demonstrated the distribution of wealth in Sweden. No matter whether they were rich or poor, Republican or Democrat, around 90 percent of participants said they would prefer to live in a country with the Swedish distribution. It is one thing to have a strong belief in free markets, small government, and individual responsibility, but another to have to live in a society where many people are left behind and to bear the cost that this ideology entails.

Final comments

Wilkinson and Pickett see history as one long move toward greater equality, a "river of human progress" that takes in the limitation of royal rule and the slow rise of democracy, the principle of equality before the law and the end of slavery, the extension of suffrage to women and non-property owners, the provision of free healthcare and education, greater labor rights and unemployment insurance, and efforts to eliminate poverty. It is hard to argue against this trajectory, and difficult to rebut the hundreds of peer-reviewed studies they refer to pointing to the ill effects of inequality. Yet it seems somewhat of a stretch to say, as they do, that "economic growth, for so long the great engine of progress, has, in the rich countries, largely finished its work." Surely it is only growth that can transform the poor into the middle classes, and only growth that can create the wealth that governments are so keen to redistribute?

Per Albin Hansson, Swedish prime minister from 1932 to 1946, had a vision of his country as a classless society, and largely saw it come true. The Swedes do not pine for the more free-wheeling economics and social atomization that tend to characterize the Anglo-Saxon countries, and seem fine with the degree of civil liberties they possess. The Swedish example should tell us that, if it is able to distinguish itself from the stigma of being against civil liberties or communist, the equality agenda is likely to feature strongly in twenty-first-century politics as an alternative to Milton Friedman-style economic liberalism.

Richard Wilkinson & Kate Pickett

Born in 1943, Richard Wilkinson is Professor Emeritus of Social Epidemiology at Nottingham University, and Honorary Professor of Epidemiology at University College London. His books include Mind the Gap: Hierarchies, Health and Human Evolution *(2002) and* The Impact of Inequality: How to Make Sick Societies Healthier *(2005).*

Kate Pickett is Professor of Epidemiology at the University of York, and was UK National Institute for Health Research Career Scientist from 2007 to 2012. The Equality Trust, a think tank, was established by the authors in 2009.

A Vindication of the Rights of Woman

"Still there are some loop-holes out of which a man may creep, and dare to think and act for himself; but for a woman it is an herculean task, because she has difficulties peculiar to her sex to overcome, which require almost super-human powers."

"What, in unenlightened societies, colour, race, religion, or in the case of a conquered country, nationality, are to some men, sex is to all women; a peremptory exclusion from almost all honourable occupations."

"Is one half of the human species, like the poor African slaves, to be subject to prejudices that brutalize them?"

In a nutshell

Without education, women will always be second-class citizens.

In a similar vein

Edmund Burke *Reflections on the Revolution in France* (p 78)
John Stuart Mill *The Subjection of Women* (p 202)
Thomas Paine *Common Sense* (p 238)
Jean-Jacques Rousseau *Discourse on Inequality* (p 254)

CHAPTER 49

Mary Wollstonecraft

The small fortune that Mary Wollstonecraft's father Edward had been left by his own father, a London weaver and property owner, should have kept him, his wife, and seven children in pleasant prosperity. However, in eighteenth-century England involvement in business and trade was a barrier to entering society, so instead of expanding the business the feckless Edward threw everything into climbing up the social scale, moving out of London to buy a country estate. As a teenage girl, Mary watched as his pretensions to being a gentleman led the family into straitened circumstances; nor did she enjoy his drinking and despotic rule over the family. Thanks to England's law of primogeniture, even what money remained was destined to go to her slightly older brother, Ned. Women could not own land in their own right, and once married they lost all independence. A woman had no legal protection against being beaten by her husband, no recourse to divorce, and no right to the couple's property or earnings. She was simply the property of her husband.

Having witnessed her mother's life of misery, the headstrong Mary resolved never to marry, but that meant she would have to find a way to support herself. After a time as a companion to a society lady in Bath, she spent part of her 20s starting up and running a school in Newington Green, a hub for dissenters in north London (although she herself was Anglican). The venture was not a success and put her into debt, but did lead her to develop her own philosophy of education.

In 1787 Wollstonecraft began working as a reviewer for the new *Analytical Review*, through which she met many reformist writers and thinkers, including Thomas Paine. In the same year she published her first book, *Thoughts on the Education of Daughters*, quickly followed by a novel, *Mary: A Fiction*. She was one of the first women to set herself up as a writer—"I am going to be the first of a new genus... I tremble at the attempt," she wrote to her sister Everina—and actually make a living from it. The pioneering publisher Joseph Johnson helped her greatly, giving her translation work and printing everything she wrote, and Samuel Johnson was a mentor and friend.

Apart from her family situation, the big shaper of Wollstonecraft's mind was the French and American revolutions. While a teacher she befriended

Rev. Dr. Richard Price, a preacher whose support of the French revolutionaries was stirring up the idea that perhaps England itself would need to undergo radical change. Price's views provoked Edmund Burke to pen his defense of royalty, property, and tradition, *Reflections on the Revolution in France* (1789), to which Thomas Paine responded with *The Rights of Man*. Wollstonecraft's 1790 pamphlet *A Vindication of the Rights of Men* was a sort of open letter to Burke and was widely discussed and reviewed. At the time the rights of women still seemed a preposterous idea to many, but with egalitarian fervor the order of the day, Wollstonecraft felt that the time was right for her ideas. A little over a year later, *A Vindication of the Rights of Woman* was published. It would sell 3,000 copies, not many compared to Paine's bestseller, but it brought her lasting fame and notoriety. The book was among the first to raise the issue of women's rights, and was read in America as well as Britain. We know that Abigail Adams, wife of American Vice President John Adams, read it and pressed her husband to "remember the Laidies" in his work to frame the new constitution.

The *Vindication* was direct for its time, a flavor of which is given by the final, biting line of her Introduction: "some women govern their husbands without degrading themselves, because intellect will always govern." In its attack on the perception of women as no more than pretty objects, it is the ancestor of Simone de Beauvoir's *The Second Sex*, Germaine Greer's *The Female Eunuch*, Betty Friedan's *The Feminine Mystique*, and Naomi Wolf's *The Beauty Myth*.

Wollstonecraft begins by imploring French statesman Talleyrand to take account of girls in drawing up his plans for France's new national system of education. She proceeds to respond to various published ideas on the role and education of women, notably those of Jean-Jacques Rousseau.

How different are women?

Wollstonecraft wonders: Is it nature or civilization that has made women so different to men? Women, she says, are like flowers planted in too rich a soil, in whom "strength and usefulness are sacrificed to beauty." The flower blooms for a time, but its leaves soon fade and the plant never reaches maturity. She puts much of the blame on education, specifically male educators of women, who are "more anxious to make them alluring mistresses than rational wives." The result is that women spend their time looking for love, instead of gaining the respect that their abilities should award them.

Yet women are ultimately answerable to God, not men—who after all are fallible beings—and although women and men were made different so that the species can continue, surely God gave both sexes the same capacity for virtue and at least a similar capacity for reason. Wollstonecraft admits that men have physical superiority, but observes that, not content with this, they seek to make women even lower. Women, in turn, live only for the attentions and flattery of men, and "do not seek to obtain a durable interest in their hearts." This is tragic, since women as well as men "are placed on this earth to unfold their faculties," not to spend their time in "perpetual childhood." If virtue is something timeless and universal, what prevents women from developing the same amount of it as men? Weak women, however superficially attractive, invariably become the object of contempt. The ambition of either sex must be to become a person of character, developing the mind and the body.

Education for growth, not dominance

Rousseau's thinking on education, expressed in his novel *Émile* (1762), did not extend to the education of girls, and for this Wollstonecraft holds him to account. If even this supposedly enlightened exemplar of his age could only see women as the pleasure and helpmate of men, then it would take much to right the wrong.

In marriage, the woman's graceful ivy was seen as ornamenting the man's sturdy oak. Alas, Wollstonecraft says, if only husbands were so stable and reliable, rather than more like "overgrown children." Yet thanks to upbringing and lack of education, their wives are similarly weak. They lack order in their activities, because they were never taught method or reasoning. They learn only "in snatches," by observations picked up through daily life and society, and have no body of abstract knowledge against which to test what they discover. Women's mental understanding has always been sacrificed to the need to look good or seem charming, and even their body is only half-developed through lack of exercise or physical training.

Men are prepared for a profession, but women are trained only to expect marriage as "the great feature of their lives," the resulting mental vacuum meaning that they are given to many small vexations and passions. "And will moralists pretend to assert, that this is the condition in which one half of the human race should be encouraged to remain with listless inactivity and stupid acquiescence?" Wollstonecraft asks. The purpose of female education was not women's power over men, she underlines, but simply power over themselves.

At the end of the *Vindication* she proposes a system of national, mixed-sex education. Boarding schools are hotbeds of brutality and libertinism, she says, which corrupt minds early. At the other extreme is home education, which tends to give children an inflated sense of self; they are, after all, superior to their own tutors and governesses. To Wollstonecraft, England's system of education is set up to create a sprinkling of great men and geniuses, but this at the expense of the majority who receive no education or an ill-suited one.

She imagines day schools with classes of boys and girls together, dressed in uniform to lessen the sense of class consciousness. Students would run free on expansive grounds, and not be allowed to remain sedentary for more than an hour at a time. Less intelligent girls and boys would be separated to learn practical work or trades, or prepare for domestic employment, while the brighter or richer ones would go on to learn languages and more advanced subjects. If schools are made more equal, Wollstonecraft reasons, society will hopefully become more egalitarian too. Children "should be sent to school to mix with a number of equals," she writes, "for only by the jostlings of equality can we form a just opinion of ourselves."

Women's equality in the context of history

Wollstonecraft writes that "it cannot be demonstrated that woman is essentially inferior to man, because she has always been subjugated." Like soldiers and slaves, because they are uneducated women must be blindly subservient to authority. Yet their position does not reflect any natural state of affairs, but has come about through the diktats of "civilization."

Her complaint is not simply about women's position in society, but the society itself, which allows idiot sons of the rich to coast through life without doing anything productive, while women are nothing more than property. A society that should be based on merit and the development of ability and virtue is instead organized relentlessly according to sex, class, and wealth. She longs for a time when men and women can give each other respect and fellow feeling, with neither the "libidinous mockery of gallantry, nor the insolent condescension of protectorship." She decries the lack of electoral representation, at a time when less than 1 percent of the population—property-owning men—could vote. She even hints that women should be directly represented in the future.

Final comments

Virginia Woolf, in a famous 1929 essay, likened Wollstonecraft's life to an experiment. An important aspect of the experiment was her romantic relationships. She was close to painter Henry Fuseli, but alarmed his wife when she suggested that the three of them live together. After moving to Paris at the start of the French Revolution, Wollstonecraft fell in love with an American trader and adventurer, Gilbert Imlay. She bore his child, Fanny, but the pair never actually married and she returned to England brokenhearted. Finally there was her marriage to William Godwin, famous for his radical *Political Justice* (1793), which among other things attacked the institution of matrimony. Although she forced Godwin's hand when she became pregnant and the pair maintained separate homes, it was a happy relationship as long as it lasted.

Wollstonecraft died straight after the birth of their daughter Mary (later the author of *Frankenstein* and wife of poet Percy Bysshe Shelley), and it would be Godwin's candid biography of his wife that would, unfortunately, stir the false legend of Wollstonecraft as a loose woman. It was only when Victorian suffragists like Millicent Garrett Fawcett began writing about her that Wollstonecraft's reputation was restored. George Eliot, Jane Austen, Henry James, Charlotte Brontë, Elizabeth Barrett Browning, and early social- ist Robert Owen are among those who noted their debt to Wollstonecraft, along with John Stuart Mill and his wife Harriet, whose 1869 essay *The Subjection of Women* came 75 years after the *Vindication*. Anarchist Emma Goldman claimed Wollstonecraft as an influence, and her current admirers include Ayaan Hirsi Ali, a Somali writer and critic of the status of women in Islamic societies.

If Wollstonecraft's holy grail was equal relations between the sexes, the more concrete legacy she sought was women's right to be properly educated. It would take another century before English women were admitted to univer- sity, and even today there are places where men think it wrong for girls to go to school. The spirit of Mary Wollstonecraft is with them.

Mary Wollstonecraft

Born in 1759 in London's Spitalfields, Mary Wollstonecraft grew up around London and in the north of England. Her job as a lady's companion in Bath was followed by a governess position with a wealthy Anglo-Irish family, the Kingsboroughs. Back in London she was one of a group of reformers and writers known as the English Jacobins, who hailed the French Revolution as the future of humankind. Her enthusiasm was balanced by what she witnessed of The Terror. In Paris she began her rocky relationship with Gilbert Imlay, and in 1795 tried to commit suicide using laudanum, but he saved her. In the hope of keeping the rela- tionship going, she undertook a journey through Scandinavia to represent him in some business affairs. Her account of the trip, Letters Written during a Short Residence in Sweden, Norway and Denmark, *was published the following year and sold well. After her final break with Imlay, Wollstonecraft threw herself off a bridge into the Thames, but was fished out alive. She married Godwin in March 1797, and died in September the same year. Other works include the novel* Mary: A Fiction *(1788) and a children's book,* Original Stories from Real Life *(1791), illustrated by William Blake.*

The Post-American World

"This is a book not about the decline of America but rather about the rise of everyone else."

"Openness is America's greatest strength… America has succeeded not because of the ingenuity of its government programs but because of the vigor of its society. It has thrived because it has kept itself open to the world—to goods and services, to ideas and inventions, and, above all, to people and cultures."

In a nutshell

Even in a world of fast-rising nations, America will remain politically dominant because its power is backed by economic might.

In a similar vein

Samuel P. Huntington *The Clash of Civilizations* (p 136)
Paul Kennedy *The Rise and Fall of the Great Powers* (p 144)
Joseph S. Nye *The Future of Power* (p 220)

CHAPTER 50

Fareed Zakaria

When he stepped off the plane from India in 1982, 18-year-old student Fareed Zakaria was not sure what to expect of the United States. Relations between the two countries were testy to say the least, but he was struck by the friendliness and optimism of Americans, personified by Ronald Reagan. Despite the upheavals of the recent past—Nixon's resignation, the energy crisis, the Iranian hostage crisis, plus a resurgent USSR, and high unemployment and inflation—America still considered itself unique and exceptional and looked to the future.

A decade later, after studies at Yale and Harvard, Zakaria was editor of *Foreign Affairs* and a rising star in the American foreign policy world. Then while at the helm of *Newsweek* he wrote a cover article post-9/11, "Why They Hate Us," which brought him national recognition. As an immigrant with a Muslim background, he was perfectly placed to give America an outsider's view of itself. His punditry continues with a weekly slot on CNN covering world affairs.

Zakaria wrote *The Post-American World* while America was riding high economically, in 2006 and 2007, but it was published in 2008 as the global financial crisis got under way. Though he did not see it coming, in the preface to a revised 2011 edition he argues that because "the Great Recession" originated in the US, it only accelerated the transition to a world where American dominance was no longer assumed. Many emerging nations did not follow the US into recession, and indeed seemed to have a new resilience and independence.

It's not you, it's them

It is not that the US is doing badly, Zakaria says; in fact, it has many great strengths that will help it retain its historical share of world output. It is rather that the rest of the world has copied many of these strengths. His book, therefore, is not about America's decline, but about "the rise of everyone else."

Taking a historical view, Zakaria says that the US is the most globally dominant power since Imperial Rome, stronger even than a combination of other nations. Yet we forget that only 100 years ago the world was multipolar, with various European governments vying for power, only to be replaced by a Cold War duopoly of the US and Russia. It is only since 1991, after the Cold War ended, that there has been a single superpower. This unipolar world may be a historical aberration, and does not sit well with economic reality. In the coming world order, Zakaria says, "economics trumps politics." Three of the four biggest economies of the future (China, India, and Japan) will be non-Western. There are now many nations that are growing fast, at least 4 percent a year, while the rich industrialized nations struggle with debt, sluggish growth, and unemployment. Between 2000 and 2007 income per person across the world grew at the fastest pace in history (an average of 3.2 percent)—which happened despite 9/11, wars in Iraq and Afghanistan, Russia's new belligerence, North Korean nuclear build-up, and Iran aiming at nuclear capability.

Zakaria was writing before India and China's growth rates slowed substantially—India's to 4.5 percent in 2014 and China's to 7.4 percent. Nevertheless, the massive populations of both countries mean that even with more modest rates of growth, they will remain central to the unfolding economic and political drama of the twenty-first century.

Don't need you any more

Zakaria recalls the period of Indian independence negotiations when Louis Mountbatten, Britain's last viceroy to India, said to Gandhi: "If we just leave, there will be chaos." Gandhi replied: "Yes, but it will be our chaos." Today, much of the world is dissecting and rejecting standard Western narratives and assumptions. Chinese officials, for instance, are perplexed that the West can look down on China's support of Sudan to get access to its oil, while at the same time America has long propped up the medieval monarchy of Saudi Arabia for the same reason. There is a rising bank of nations who are no longer so eager to fit in to Western international institutions; these countries can simply form alliances with each other (for instance, India does not see Iran to be as much of a threat as America does, so links are strong between the two nations). This shift is often nothing to do with antagonizing America or the West, but rather because "the world is moving from anger to indifference, from anti-Americanism to post-Americanism," Zakaria maintains.

While America seems insular and inward looking to most outsiders, it continues to give report cards on other countries. It promotes free trade, yet its trade is a much lower percentage of GDP than in countries such as Germany, and it has high barriers to trade and levels of protectionism. The things America has promoted to the world over the last 50 years—free markets, trade, immigration, technological and business innovation—have been adopted to the extent that other countries are often better at them than the US. America globalized the world, Zakaria says, but in the end forgot to globalize itself.

A peaceful rise?

China's economy has doubled every eight years for the last three decades. It now exports in 24 hours the same amount of goods as for the whole of 1978. The world's 20 quickest-growing cities are all in China. The country's foreign reserves are double those of Japan and three times those of the European Union.

The world is astounded by the numbers involved in China's economic rise, but Zakaria asks what it will mean for global politics. History shows that as living standards rise, people want political freedom. Marx was the first to note that market economies tend toward democracy, and China's economy is increasingly liberal. A young Chinese journalist told Zakaria: "The brightest people in the party are not studying economic reform. They are studying political reform." Could China become more and more like Singapore, relatively open and liberal but with single-party rule? To survive, the Chinese Communist Party will need to find greater legitimacy. Real democracies are messy, Zacharia notes, but on the other hand there is little risk of revolution.

Ultimately, China's intentions may be irrelevant; its sheer size and rate of growth will bring its own consequences. However, there is an alternative path of power open to China, Zakaria suggests. It knows that it is unlikely ever to match US military supremacy, so can instead focus on maintaining and growing its sovereignty and commercial power. This more patient path to influence, offering an alternative to "hectoring and arrogant" America, is one of growing Chinese "soft power." It may well outfox the US.

The Indian difference

There is no longer any kind of race between China and India, Zakaria notes. China's economy is four times bigger than India's (China's GDP per person is around $6700, while India's is only $1250) and is growing faster. India still has 300 million people living on only a dollar a day. Yet a greater number of Indians were lifted out of poverty between 1997 and 2007 than in the 50 years before that, and demography is in its favor. India will enjoy a "youth bulge" in the years ahead compared to China's youth gap, thanks to the latter's one-child policy. Other strengths are English (Indians "speak globalization fluently," as Zakaria puts it) and democracy. Visitors to India complain about its crumbling roads and poor airports, and indeed India will never look like China in terms of infrastructure because the government cannot simply order projects into existence. "Democracy makes for populism, pandering, and delays. But it also makes for long-term stability," Zakaria notes. India has independent courts, a central bank, an honest Electoral Commission, and good relations with the West. Finally, it has many top-quality private international firms, compared to China's, which are mostly state run.

Zakaria argues that India's progress is being held up by its ruling class and creaking bureaucracy. It is very difficult for central governments to impose economic or foreign policy reform, often giving in to regional and local interests and pressure groups. Yet Zakaria compares India today to the US in the late nineteenth century. Domestic issues slowed America's rise to power. By 1890 its economy was bigger than the world power of Britain, but politically and militarily America was still very much in the shadow of the European powers. It took decades for its diplomatic influence to grow to match its economy, because the US state was weak and its political structures decentralized—just like India today.

Why America will not fade

As a naturalized American whose livelihood depends on US media companies, it would have been counterproductive for Zakaria to be an out-and-out promoter of the idea of American decline. In the last chapter, "American Purpose," he goes to some lengths to show why in fact he is very optimistic about his country's future. Some have compared the US to imperial Britain, but the analogy does not apply, Zakaria argues, primarily because the US is economically strong. It has been the largest economy for over 130 years, and its quarter share of world economic output has been roughly steady for a century. And while Britain's navy drained its treasury, US defense spending is an affordable 5 percent of its annual output. Its military spending is greater than the next 14 countries after it, and it accounts for half of global military R&D. As US GDP grows year on year, it will only maintain its dominance. Nor is it losing its technological or entrepreneurial edge. Nanotechnology and biotechnology are dominated by US firms, and it has most of the world's best universities, a fact that is not likely to change for a long time.

On the minus side, Zakaria discusses America's mediocre school system, low savings rate, increased regulation and red tape, high corporate tax, government gridlock, costs of the healthcare system, and loss of middle-class and manufacturing jobs overseas. The problem, he says, is that "a 'can-do' country is saddled with a 'do-nothing' political process," taken over by "money, special interests, a sensationalist media, and ideological attack groups."

If at least some of these problems can be solved, the future looks bright. The US population is likely to grow by 65 million by 2030, while Europe's population is quickly aging and the continent is less and less willing to take in the migrants who would keep its economic growth higher. In the meantime the US continues to accept millions of highly skilled and ambitious migrants. Immigration, Zakaria says, is the key to it not becoming a declining world power. It will be the first truly "universal nation" in terms of people of every ethnicity and background, giving it different perspectives, ideas, and dynamism. All these assertions have been borne out in the years since the book was published.

Final comments

Zakaria's favorite sport of tennis provides an analogy for his main argument. In the 1980s, over half of the players who made the cut for the US Open were American, while in 2007, only 20 Americans succeeded. It is not that US players got worse, rather that many more countries (Russia, South Korea, Spain, Serbia) began developing top players in addition to the old troika of great tennis nations of America, Britain, and Australia. "In other words, it's not that the United States has been doing badly over the last two decades. It's that, all of a sudden, everyone is playing the game." America has long been the great capitalist country, but now others are copying its financial strengths.

The US has a history of worrying that it is losing its edge, Zakaria notes, only for these fears to be unfounded. It is hard to believe now how anxious Americans were in the 1980s that Japan could overtake the US in technology and wealth. In fact, Japan has endured years of stagnation while the US created a large number of world-beating technology companies and saw big increases in GDP and population. America has the openness to new ideas, diversity of people, and entrepreneurial dynamism that other countries can only try to copy. However, it will only preserve its hegemonic status if it is seen as existing for the benefit of all, upholding the liberal values and ideas that it believes are universal. Great nations stand for something other than their own power, Zakaria argues.

Fareed Zakaria

Fareed Zakaria was born in 1964 in Mumbai. His father Rafiq was an Islamic scholar, author, and politician who pushed for Indian independence. His mother Fatima is a journalist and editor. While at Yale, Zakaria was president of its Political Union, a debating society, and editor of the Yale Political Monthly. *One of his teachers was Paul Kennedy (see commentary on p 144).*

While earning his PhD at Harvard, Zakaria studied under Samuel P. Huntington (see commentary on p 136) and Robert Keohane. In 1992 he became managing editor of Foreign Affairs, *and began teaching international relations at Columbia University. From 2000 to 2010 he was editor of* Newsweek, *and now has a column in* The Washington Post. *His CNN program* Fareed Zakaria GPS *(Global Public Square) has been running since 2008. Other books include* From Wealth to Power: The Unusual Origins of America's World Role *(1998) and* The Future of Freedom: Illiberal Democracy at Home and Abroad *(2003).*

50 More Politics Classics

1. Jane Addams *Democracy and Social Ethics* (1902)
Social reformer Addams believed that democracy was not merely a set of laws but a moral obligation of all citizens. It is not enough to believe passively in the innate dignity of all human beings. Rather, one must work daily to root out racial, gender, class, and other prejudices from personal relationships.

2. Mikhail Bakunin *God and the State* (1871)
The best-known work of this Russian anarchist or "libertarian revolutionary socialist," in his time almost as famous an ideologue as Karl Marx.

3. Frederic Bastiat *The Law* (1850)
Written just after the French Revolution, a warning that the new "democratic" order in reality meant the hijacking of the state by special interests that could plunder the nation via taxes, tariffs, transfer payments, etc. The law was becoming a creative entity used by the state instead of the upholder of personal liberty and law for all. This anti-socialist classic was written over a century before Hayek's *The Road to Serfdom.*

4. Jeremy Bentham *An Introduction to the Principles of Morals and Legislation* (1789)
The great utilitarian's argument that a just society is most likely to be achieved by using an objective calculus of maximizing pleasure and minimizing pain.

5. William Beveridge *Report of the Inter-Departmental Committee on Social Insurance and Allied Services* (1942)
Better known as "The Beveridge Report," this British economist's recommendations were a blueprint for the modern welfare state. Targeting the five "giant evils" of squalor, ignorance, want, idleness, and disease, the report proposed for the first time a National Insurance scheme and called for a National Health Service to be established.

6. Robert Caro *The Passage of Power: The Years of Lyndon Johnson IV* (2012)

The fourth volume of Caro's magisterial series covering Johnson's life, including the Kennedy assassination and the new president's deft use of power to ensure that the Democratic legislative program, including civil rights, became law.

7. **Edward Hallett Carr** *The Twenty Years' Crisis 1919–1939* (1939)
Published on the eve of the Second World War, this was quickly recognized as a defining work in the fledgling discipline of international relations. Carr criticized the liberal trust in treaties and the League of Nations, maintaining that national power was still the key force in politics.

8. **Noam Chomsky** *Profit Over People: Neoliberalism and Global Order* (2011)
Chomsky defines neo-liberalism as the public abdicating power to corporations, with the result that populations suffer declines in education and health, and increased inequality between the richest and the poorest.

9. **Robert Dahl** *Polyarchy: Participation and Opposition* (1972)
Dahl, sometimes called the "dean of American political scientists," argues that democracies are best examined in terms of two variables: the degree of competition between competing actors or parties; and the level of electoral participation. "Polyarchy," the system toward which we should move, is high competition and high participation.

10. **Frederick Douglass** *Narrative of the Life of Frederick Douglass, an American Slave* (1845)
One of the first accounts of slavery by a fugitive slave, the *Narrative* combines a harrowing story with an exposé of slavery's effects including ruination of family life, extreme poverty, and dearth of education. A key work in the abolitionist movement.

11. **Jacques Ellul** *Propaganda: The Formation of Men's Attitudes* (1973)
Still acutely relevant today, French Christian anarchist Ellul explains how propaganda goes beyond politics to be about making the individual serve and conform. One of his insights is that those people who consume the most media are the most propagandized.

12. **Frantz Fanon** *The Wretched of the Earth* (1961)
Fanon's passionate call for Algeria to be rid of its French rulers was taken up as a liberation bible by the colonized everywhere, although its advocacy of violence has troubled many readers.

13. **Betty Friedan** *The Feminine Mystique* (1963)
Friedan's bestseller brought on the "second wave" of feminism by highlighting the abandonment of female potential thanks to gender stereotyping; the book raised awareness of educational inequality for girls and increased expectations for meaningful careers and work among women.

14. Doris Kearns Goodwin *Team of Rivals: The Political Genius of Abraham Lincoln* **(2005)**

Lincoln asked his bitter rivals from the Republican presidential nomination to become his closest advisers, building a cabinet strong enough to endure the trials of the Civil War. This is one of the most popular works of American history in recent times and a favorite of President Obama's.

15. Antonio Gramsci *The Prison Notebooks* **(1929–35)**

The key insight of Gramsci, one of the leading twentieth-century Marxist thinkers, concerns "hegemony," or how capitalist states maintain themselves. One does not take, but *becomes* the state, he said.

16. Germaine Greer *The Female Eunuch* **(1970)**

Though many of its references are now dated, Greer's book was central to the politics of sexuality in the 1970s. The picture she draws of servile suburban woman out of touch with her sexuality aimed to spark societal reorganization, particularly in the family and the economy.

17. Ernesto Che Guevara *Guerrilla Warfare* **(1960)**

This outlines Guevara's doctrine for guerrilla fighters against Caribbean-style dictatorships, but has been used as a universal manual for revolution.

18. Jürgen Habermas *The Structural Transformation of the Public Sphere* **(1962)**

During the eighteenth century a new "public sphere" emerged from civil society's need for information; it led to the flourishing of reason and provided a balance to state power, but was later corrupted by commercialism and consumerism.

19. Jonathan Haidt *The Righteous Mind: Why Good People Are Divided by Politics and Religion* **(2013)**

A social psychologist's bestselling explanation of why liberals, conservatives, and libertarians have such different intuitions about right and wrong. Based on fascinating research.

20. David Halberstam *The Best and the Brightest* **(1969)**

An absorbing account of how US elites sank into the quagmire of Vietnam, providing lessons for foreign policy development and decision making.

21. G.W.F. Hegel *Philosophy of Right* **(1820)**

Hegel's attempt to systematize ethical theory, natural rights, the philosophy of law, political theory, and the sociology of the modern state into the framework of a "philosophy of history."

22. Immanuel Kant *Perpetual Peace: A Philosophical Sketch* **(1795)**

Kant wrote this essay in 1795 during a lull in the French Revolutionary Wars. He believed that the Treaty of Basel was an example of how civilized nations might limit the destructiveness of war in the future.

23. Kautilya *The Arthashastra* **(4th century BCE)**
An ancient Indian book of statecraft, economic policy, and military strategy that has been compared to Machiavelli in its brutal-realist view of politics.

24. Robert Keohane *After Hegemony* **(1984)**
Can the world prosper and remain at peace without the weight of a hegemon? Keohane's rebuttal of realpolitik analysis argued that international frameworks had come of age; cooperation between states did not require the threat of force from a single great power.

25. Ibn Khaldun *Muqaddimah* **(1377)**
The Arab scholar's great unfinished work of history presents his idea of the best kinds of government, which he defines as "an institution which prevents injustice other than such as it commits itself." He favored an Islamic state, but was also influenced by Aristotle's rationality. Ibn Khaldun observed that all civilizations eventually fall because luxuries distract them, the government begins to overtax citizens, and property rights are eroded.

26. Henry Kissinger *Diplomacy* **(1994)**
A sweeping history of international politics beginning with the Treaty of Westphalia. Statesman Kissinger argues that America transformed the states system by putting ideals like democracy above the ambitions of individual nations. Should be read alongside his 2014 *World Order*. ✓

27. Lee Kuan Yew *From Third World to First* **(2000)**
The Singaporean statesman is considered a sage by other world leaders, and his story of the creation of a rich nation-state in a few decades is gripping.

28. Walter Lippmann *Public Opinion* **(1922)**
A classic critique of the American media and public opinion focused on newspapers, but many of his criticisms are applicable to television and the internet. Lippman's concern about the "manufacture of consent" inspired Noam Chomsky's scathing critique of the free market media industry.

29. Malcolm X *The Autobiography of Malcolm X* **(1965)**
A compelling account of a political and spiritual awakening, tracing Malcolm X's conversion to Islam and how it turned him from petty criminal to voice for black power. Before his assassination in 1965, he had begun to see American racism as a battle in a larger universal war against bigotry and close-mindedness.

30. John Mearsheimer *The Tragedy of Great Power Politics* **(2001)**
A University of Chicago professor's controversial idea of "offensive realism," according to which states do not simply accept balance of power

arrangements (defensive realism), but actively seek hegemony over other states. By intervening and acting first, nations believe that they will survive and thrive amid uncertainty.

31. Ralph Miliband *The State in Capitalist Society* **(1969)**
The key work of Britain's leading postwar Marxist thinker (and father of British Labour politician Ed Miliband), which deconstructs the capitalist state, showing that it is not a neutral set of institutions but rather reflects the interests of the dominant capitalist class. Surprisingly relevant to today's politics.

32. Montesquieu *The Spirit of Laws* **(1748)**
Montesquieu's ideas about the separation of powers and checks on the power of the executive had a profound impact on the architects of the American constitution.

33. Barrington Moore, Jr. *Social Origins of Dictatorship and Democracy* **(1966)**
A classic of comparative political analysis, arguing that it is the relationship between peasants and landowners in a given country, more than any other factor, that determines whether that country will eventually become democratic, communist, or fascist.

34. Thomas More *Utopia* **(1516)**
More was a real-world politician who advised and then was executed by Henry VIII. Scholars are still debating whether his imaginary society was tongue in cheek or a genuine alternative to the world in which he lived, but the term utopia remains central to political discourse.

35. Reinhold Niebuhr *Moral Man and Immoral Society* **(1932)**
The US theologian and thinker argues that individual morality is intrinsically incompatible with communal political life. We cannot reconcile how we would like to act as individuals with the brutal realities of the collective.

36. Richard Neustadt *Presidential Power: The Politics of Leadership* **(1960)**
A Harvard political scientist's landmark study of US presidents and their styles, arguing that presidential power is the weak link alongside the judiciary and the legislature.

37. Pierre-Joseph Proudhon *What Is Property? An Inquiry into the Principle of Right and of Government* **(1840)**
Proudhon was the first person to proclaim himself an anarchist, and is famous for the statement "Property is theft." He drew a distinction between "good" property, which is used and owned by a person or group as a result of their labor, and "bad," which is owned at a remove to exploit others, including the payment of rents and interest. This is the essence of the anarchist critique of capitalism.

38. Ayn Rand *Atlas Shrugged* (1957)

Rand believed that her objectivist philosophy of rational egoism would have the most impact in the form of a novel. Although hardly high literature, the book retains its power as a warning against collectivism and a paean to laissez-faire capitalism and ultra-liberalism.

39. Murray Rothbard *For a New Liberty: The Libertarian Manifesto* (1973)

A seminal work in the libertarian movement by an American economist and political theorist, arguing that the free market and voluntary human action can do a more efficient and fair job of supplying society's needs and wants than government. Libertarian solutions are given for pollution, poverty, war, threats to civil liberties, and education.

40. Carl Schmitt *The Concept of the Political* (1932)

A German legal theorist's influential essay positing that political life is best understood in terms of the distinction between friend and enemy, much as morality can be understood in terms of the distinction between good and evil, or economics in terms of the profitable and the unprofitable. To ensure national security, states must categorize other states in this way.

41. Herbert Spencer *The Man versus the State* (1884)

This great Victorian's political philosophy is less celebrated than his evolutionary theory, but it has been influential. Warning of the power grabbing and waste of centralized government, he writes: "there is in society… that beautiful self-adjusting principle which will keep all its elements in equilibrium… The attempt to regulate all the actions of a community by legislation will entail little else but misery."

42. Leo Strauss *Natural Right and History* (1953)

Strauss was a scholar of classical political philosophy and in this book he upholds the distinction between right and wrong in ethics and politics, in the process rebutting the relativism and nihilism of modern political thought. He believed that philosophy and political philosophy were inextricable, and at the University of Chicago he built an intellectual foundation for modern political conservatism, tutoring "neocon" Paul Wolfowitz and critic Allan Bloom, among others.

43. Thucydides *The History of the Peloponnesian War* (5th century BCE)

A Greek general's famous account of the war that ended the Athenian empire. The first fact-based historical view of war, which influenced generations of historians and political scientists.

44. Eric Voegelin *The New Science of Politics* (1987)

An influential political philosopher's essays on the modern political religions, including Marxism, National Socialism, Hegelianism, Nietzschianism, and Heideggerianism. To Voegelin, these thinkers are all best described as "gnostics" in their effort to create God's kingdom on earth. He instead advocates a return to Aristotelian politics.

45. Kenneth Waltz *Theory of International Politics* (1979)

A major text in international relations, presenting the "realist" view that national security is the primary aim of states, and that leaders rise or fall on their ability to make their countries more powerful or richer.

46. Michael Walzer *Just and Unjust Wars: A Moral Argument with Historical Illustrations* (1976)

From the Athenian attack on Melos to the My Lai Massacre, from the wars in the Balkans through the first war in Iraq, Walzer examines the moral issues surrounding military theory, war crimes, and the spoils of conflict.

47. Sidney Webb & Beatrice Webb *Methods of Social Study* (1932)

With their socialist Fabian Society, the Webbs had a huge impact on British public policy in the Edwardian era, providing the rationale for a welfare state and founding the London School of Economics to improve research into the causes of poverty and inequality.

48. Max Weber *Politics as a Vocation* (1918)

Known for his theory of bureaucracy, this great sociologist also provided a template for ethical political leadership. The ideal politician must have passion for issues and be willing to take a stand at the possible expense of popularity.

49. Huang Zongxi *Waiting for the Dawn: A Plan for the Prince* (1662)

The Ming dynasty political theorist has long been an inspiration for democratic reformers in China, with his emphasis on bottom-up government by laws and consensus rather than autocratic fiat.

50. Yevgeny Zamyatin *We* (1921)

A dystopian novel set in the twenty-sixth century CE describing life under the regimented totalitarian society of OneState, ruled over by the all-powerful "Benefactor." A key inspiration for Orwell's *1984* and Ayn Rand's *Anthem*.

Credits

Many of the great works of politics have had multiple translations and/or publishers. Quite a few are now in the public domain, but you should check their copyright status for the country in which you live. The list below is a guide to editions used in researching this book.

Acemoglu, D., & Robinson, J. (2013) *Why Nations Fail: The Origins of Power, Prosperity and Poverty*, London: Profile.

Acton, J.E. (1956) *Essays on Freedom and Power*, London: Thames & Hudson.

Alinsky, S. (1989) *Rules for Radicals: A Practical Primer for Realistic Radicals*, New York: Vintage.

Allison, G., and Zelikow, P. (1999) *Essence of Decision: Explaining the Cuban Missile Crisis* (2nd edn), New York: Longman.

Angell, N. (1913) *The Great Illusion: A Study of the Relation of Military Power in Nations to Their Economic and Social Advantage*, London: William Heinemann.

Arendt, H. (1967) *The Origins of Totalitarianism* (3rd edn), London: Allen & Unwin.

Aristotle, *Politics*, trans. B. Jowett, The Internet Classics Archive, http://classics.mit.edu//Aristotle/politics.html

Berlin, I. (1969) *Four Essays on Liberty*, Oxford: Oxford University Press.

Bernays, E. (2005) *Propaganda*, New York: Ig Publishing.

Burke, E. (1968) *Reflections on the Revolution in France*, ed. and intro. C.C. O'Brien, London: Penguin.

Carson, R. (1968) *Silent Spring*, London: Penguin.

Churchill, W. (2005) *The Second World War: Volume 1, The Gathering Storm*, London: Penguin.

Clausewitz, C. (1976) *On War*, ed. and trans. M. Howard and P. Paret, Princeton, NJ: Princeton University Press.

Fukuyama, F. (2012) *The End of History and the Last Man* (20th anniversary edition), London: Penguin.

Gandhi, M. (1957) *An Autobiography: The Story of My Experiments with Truth*, Boston, MA: Beacon Press.

Goldman, E. (1910) *Anarchism and Other Essays*, New York: Mother Earth Publishing.

Hamilton, A., Madison, J., and Jay, J. (2003) *The Federalist Papers*, ed. C. Rossiter and notes by C.R. Kesler, New York: Signet.

✓ Hayek, F.A. (1994) *The Road to Serfdom*, Chicago, IL: University of Chicago Press.

Hobbes, T. (2002) *Leviathan*, Gutenberg.org, http://www.gutenberg.org/ebooks/3207

Huntington, S. (1997) *The Clash of Civilizations and the Remaking of World Order*, London: Simon & Schuster.

Kennedy, P. (1989) *The Rise and Fall of the Great Powers: Economic Change and Military Conflict from 1500–2000*, London: Fontana Press.

King, M.L. (2000) *The Autobiography of Martin Luther King, Jnr.*, ed. C. Carson, London: Abacus.

Klein, N. (2010) *No Logo*, 10th anniversary edition, London: Fourth Estate.

Locke, J. (2003) *Two Treatises of Government and A Letter Concerning Toleration*, New Haven, CT: Yale University Press.

Machiavelli, N. (2004) *Discourses on the First Decade of Titus Livius*, trans. N. Hill Thomson. Gutenberg.org, http://www.gutenberg.org/files/10827

Mandela, N. (1994) *Long Walk to Freedom*, London: Abacus.

Marx, K. and Engels, F. (1998) *The Communist Manifesto*, London: Electric Book Company.

Mencius (2003) *The Mencius*, trans. and intro. D.C. Lau, London: Penguin.

Micklethwait, J., & Wooldridge, A. (2014) *The Fourth Revolution: The Global Race to Reinvent the State*, London: Allen Lane.

Mill, J.S. (2008) *The Subjection of Women*, Gutenberg.org, http://www.gutenberg.org/files/27083

Morgenthau, H. (1993) *Politics Among Nations: The Struggle for Power and Peace*, rev. Kenneth W. Thompson, New York: McGraw-Hill.

Nozick, R. (1974) *Anarchy, State, and Utopia*, Oxford: Basil Blackwell.

Nye, J. (2011) *The Future of Power*, New York: Public Affairs.

Olson, M. (1982) *The Rise and Decline of Nations: Economic Growth, Stagflation, and Social Rigidities*, New Haven, CT: Yale University Press.

Orwell, G. (1989) *Animal Farm*, London: Penguin.

Paine, T. (2013) *Common Sense*, London: Waxkeep Publishing.

Plato (1969) *The Last Days of Socrates: Ethyphro, The Apology, Crito, Phaedo*, trans. H. Tredennick, London, Penguin.

Plato, *Crito*, trans. B. Jowett, Internet Classics Archive, http://classics.mit.edu/Plato/crito.html

Popper, K. (1966) *The Open Society and Its Enemies, Vols I & II*, London: Routledge.

Rousseau, J.-J. (1984) *A Discourse on Inequality*, trans. and intro. M. Cranston, London: Penguin.

Sinclair, U. (1965) *The Jungle*, London: Penguin.

Solzhenitsyn, A. (1986) *The Gulag Archipelago*, London: Harvill Press.

Sun Yat-sen (1963) *The Three Principles of the People: San Min Chu I*, trans. F.W. Price, Taipei: China Publishing Company.

Thatcher, M. (2013) *Margaret Thatcher: The Autobiography 1925–2013*, London: Harper Press.

Thoreau, H.D. (2004) *On the Duty of Civil Disobedience*, Gutenberg.org, http://www.gutenberg.org/files/71/71.txt

Tocqueville, A. de (1964) *Democracy in America*, New York: Washington Square Press.

Wilkinson, R., & Pickett, K. (2010) *The Spirit Level: Why Equality Is Better for Everyone*, London: Penguin.

Wollstonecraft, M. (2001) *Vindication of the Rights of Woman*, Kindle public domain edition.

Woodward, B., & Bernstein, C. (1998) *All the President's Men*, London: Bloomsbury.

Zakaria, F. (2011) *The Post-American World: Release 2.0*, London: Penguin.

Acknowledgments

Most of my books have been about personal development, psychology, and philosophy, but until I became a writer my interest lay in politics and government. I studied these subjects at university before starting a career in public policy. It was therefore a joy to come full circle and write this book, revisiting some of the great texts I had read years ago and discovering new ones.

I am grateful to the following people who helped with *50 Politics Classics*.

The list of 50 titles and the Introduction were evolved and refined in discussion with publisher Nicholas Brealey.

Sally Lansdell edited the manuscript and got it ready for publication. There is always so much amazing information and insights that compete for inclusion in the 50 Classics books that it is not an easy task to bring the word count down and express the essentials.

Ruth Killick handled publicity for the book and got it noticed early on.

Ben Slight helped with sales in the UK office, and Chuck Dresner handled sales and marketing in North America. Nicholas Brealey continues to get the series published in other languages.

Stephen Repacholi provided substantial editorial and research help with several of the commentaries, and was a great sounding board as the book took shape.

A health scare two months before the book was due for delivery made me grateful for everything, including the chance to write these books. I recovered reasonably quickly thanks to the help and support of my sisters Caroline and Teresa who came out from Australia, other family and friends, and Tamara and Beatrice Lucas who had to change their schedules to look after my daughter.

I dedicate the book to Sarah Ravenscroft (b. 1945), who passed away as it was being finalized. Sarah personified freedom, equality, and power.

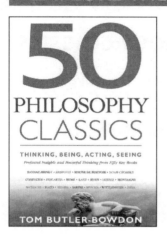

50 PHILOSOPHY CLASSICS

Thinking, Doing, Acting, Seeing

Tom Butler-Bowdon

978-1-85788-596-5

£12.99 UK / $19.95 US

For over 2000 years, philosophy has been our best guide to the experience of being human and the true nature of reality. From Aristotle, Plato, Epicurus, Confucius, Cicero and Heraclitus in ancient times to 17th-century rationalists Descartes, Leibniz and Spinoza, from 20th-century greats Jean-Paul Sartre, Jean Baudrillard and Simone de Beauvoir to contemporary thinkers Michael Sandel, Peter Singer and Slavoj Zizek, *50 Philosophy Classics* explores key writings that have shaped the discipline and had an impact on the real world.

From Aristotle to Wittgenstein, *50 Philosophy Classics* provides a lively entry point to the "king of disciplines". It seeks to enlighten and explain rather than merely instruct, helping readers comprehend some of the key questions – and possible answers – at the centre of human existence. Insightful commentaries on famous texts, biographies of each author, "In a nutshell" summaries and representative quotes give a taste of the writings that have changed the course of intellectual history – and keep changing minds today.

"Explains with remarkable lucidity ideas of fifty philosophical thinkers from ancient times to the present day. Complex views on a range of important and enduring issues are made accessible to the general reader. … Enjoyable and instructive."

C.L. Ten, Professor of Philosophy, National University of Singapore

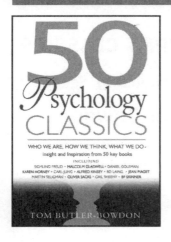

50 PSYCHOLOGY CLASSICS

Who We Are, How We Think, What We Do

Tom Butler-Bowdon

978-1-85788-386-2

£12.99 UK / $19.95 US

What is more fascinating than the human mind? With *50 Psychology Classics: Who We Are, How We Think, What We Do – Insight and Inspiration from 50 Key Books*, Tom Butler-Bowdon introduces readers to the great works that explore the very essence of what makes us who we are.

Spanning fifty books and hundreds of ideas, *50 Psychology Classics* examines some of the most intriguing questions regarding cognitive development and behavioral motivations, summarizing the myriad theories that psychologists have put forth to make sense of the human experience. Butler-Bowdon covers everything from humanism to psychoanalysis to the fundamental principles where theorists disagree, like nature versus nurture and the existence of free will.

In this single book, you will find Carl Jung, Sigmund Freud, Alfred Kinsey and the most significant contributors to modern psychological thought. *50 Psychology Classics* will enrich your understanding of the human condition.

"This delightful book provides thoughtful and entertaining summaries of 50 of the most influential books in psychology. It is a 'must read' for students contemplating a career in psychology."

V.S. Ramachandran MD PhD, Professor and Director, Center for Brain and Cognition, University of California, San Diego